The World, the Flesh and the Devil

By the same author
A Dark and Distant Shore

THE WORLD,
THE FLESH
AND THE DEVIL

Reay Tannahill

C

CENTURY PUBLISHING

LONDON

For my uncle
JAMES C. WYLIE
with love

First published in Great Britain in 1985 by
Century Hutchinson Ltd
Brookmount House, 62–65 Chandos Place
London WC2N 4NW

ISBN 0 7126 1049 9

Photoset by Rowland Phototypesetting Ltd
Bury St Edmunds, Suffolk

Printed in Great Britain by
Richard Clay (The Chaucer Press), Bungay, Suffolk.

CONTENTS

Author's Note

Many of the characters in this book did exist, and their public actions – like the events in which they were involved – are a matter of historical record. However, very little indeed is known about the personalities and private lives of even the most distinguished of them, and nothing at all about the two main protagonists, Bishop Cameron of Glasgow, and Archdeacon Crozier of Teviotdale.

Of the major characters below, listed roughly in order of first appearance, those who are purely fictional are identified by an asterisk.

[Gavin] John Cameron
Gabriel Condulmer, or
   Condulmero, later Pope
   Eugenius IV
Pope Martin V
Thomas Myrton
William [Columba] Crozier, or
   Croyser
* Ninian Drummond
* Sévèrine de Verne
* Sir Harry Graham

Malise Graham, Earl of
   Strathearn
* Blane de Verne
* Lady Elinor Stewart
* Adam de Verne
* Vittoria d'Aragona
Walter Stewart, Earl of Atholl
Master Laurence of Lindores
Sir Robert Graham
Patrick Graham
Queen Joan of Scotland

King James I of Scotland
Sir John Forrester
* Lady Moragh Macleod
Poggio Bracciolini
Alexander Macdonald, 3rd
   Lord of the Isles

Archibald, 5th Earl of Douglas
Paul Crawar
Sir Robert Stewart
Anthony Altani, Bishop of
   Urbino

Some of the ecclesiastical material in *The World, the Flesh and the Devil* may surprise or shock the modern reader, but the years of the Great Schism and after were not happy ones for the Church, and the morality of the Church was, in any case, the morality of the times. It should also be remembered that the Church in the medieval period was as much a political as a religious force, with inevitable results. I have taken no liberties with the material here, because fiction could scarcely be more remarkable than the facts.

I would like, finally, to give my warmest thanks to Michael Walsh, historian of the Catholic Church and former member of the Society of Jesus, who was kind enough to read the typescript for accuracy in ecclesiastical history, terminology, and theology.

PROLOGUE

1411

GAVIN JOHN CAMERON, who was eleven years old and going to be a bishop one day, eased his dagger out from between the man's ribs, wiped it on a clump of bracken, dried it with some moss, and then slid it carefully back into the special loop on his belt.

He was proud to see that, though his hands might be red, they weren't shaking. And no one would have known that his heart was jigging around inside him like a hen on a hot griddle as he forced himself to look again at the body sprawled before him on the heather.

Abruptly, he released his pent-up breath. Dear God, but it wasn't what he had expected when he had set out that morning to reform the world!

HE HAD spent most of the previous night awake at the window of his room, torn between apprehension and exhilaration, knowing that it would be years before he saw his home again and yet itching to be gone.

It had been a beautiful night, with stars in their thousands strewn across the moonless sky and the dog-star shining on the horizon like some bright, white, Beltane fire. Father Duncan said the stars were a kind of holy book, like the Gospels; it was just that, instead of telling you what had already happened, they told you (if you knew how to read them) what God had destined for the future. Father Duncan himself had no idea how to read them; for a priest, there were some shocking gaps in his education. Gavin couldn't understand why he hadn't made the effort to learn something whose potential usefulness should have been obvious even to a child of six.

One result was that now, even while Gavin's instincts told him that the brightness of the sky must be a good augury for what lay ahead, his brain was by no means convinced.

It was uncanny how the stars lit up only the heavens and left the earth in shadow. If there had been a moon, the mountains round the loch would have stood out bold and clear, their outcrops, corries and ridges as familiar in the grey-black livery of night as in the purples, greens and smoky blues of day. The sand would have glittered like a salty ribbon round the shores of Loch an Vele, and the loch itself would have had a gleam on it like the back of a wet seal. And, fifty feet below where Gavin was perched, there would have lain, like a soft and silvered ghost upon the water, the reflection of Kinveil, the gaunt old island watchtower that was his home.

But under the stars tonight there was nothing but a great, wide vault of blackness.

His heart gave a sudden lurch. Holy Church said the Last Judgement was due any day now. What if it had come, and no one had told him? What if God had had enough of the world and the whole sinful human race, and had opened a huge abyss to swallow everything up? What if he could see nothing under the stars *because there was nothing there to see?*

It would be grossly unfair, he thought, just when he was ready to set out on his great adventure.

Holding his breath, he prised a fragment of stone out of the crumbling masonry round the window, tossed it down into the murk, and then, by way of insurance, began saying a *Miserere*. But he had scarcely got beyond the *Deus* when he heard the rattle of the pebble hitting the rocks, and then the small, reassuring splash as it bounced into the water.

'Holy Virgin!' he grumbled at himself. He was always letting his imagination run away with him, even though Father Duncan said that speculating about things one didn't understand showed up the imperfections in one's faith. Human beings weren't supposed to understand the workings of the divine. Gavin couldn't see why not.

He couldn't see, either, why he was sitting here dreaming about Kinveil under the moon, when Kinveil's moon was usually invisible behind a blanket of sea mist, or sheets of rain whose big fat drops splattered through the rotting timbers on to his sleeping head and woke him as urgently as the tocsin, or downpours so weighty that it seemed as if all the nine choirs of angels must be simultaneously engaged on baling out the vaults of heaven.

As a sensible, rational human being, he told himself sternly, he ought to have his mind on more important things. There was so much he was going to have to learn from teachers wiser than Father Duncan, who was an old man, and slow of thought, and set in his Highland ways.

Sliding down off the sill, he stretched himself, flexing the muscles in his thin, adolescent body. He was still at the all-elbows-and-knees stage of growth, and his feet had the sinewy look common among Highlanders who went barefoot all their lives, but his features were already beginning to hint at the man he would become. In later years, he was to find strangers assuming from his black hair, tawny complexion, and aquiline nose that he was a Genoese, or a Basque, or even an Egyptian. But these, like his imaginative streak, were a heritage from his Celtic forbears. Also in him was another and very different strain that, in maturity, would show in his unusual height and slenderness, in his sometimes brutal effectiveness, and in eyes that were clear and darkly grey as a winter sea – the eyes of the Vikings who had raided and ruled all round the north and west coasts of Scotland six hundred years before.

Gavin, as it happened, had no great opinion of the Vikings, partly because he thought them barbarians, but also, and rather more pertinently, because recent generations of Camerons had inherited all their restlessness without any of their talent for making a profit out of it. Which was one of several good reasons why he was setting out tomorrow on the two-hundred-mile walk to St Andrews, where rumour had it that Bishop Wardlaw was trying to set up Scotland's first university.

Gavin was ambitious, but it was a fact of fifteenth-century life that only the rich and the nobly born were considered fit to govern, and he was neither. There was, however, one route to advancement that even

13

someone quite poor could take if he had the benefit of a good education and was willing to become a priest. The two things went together, because all education was in the hands of Holy Church, which valued it as much as it valued sanctity. Some said more. And since kings needed clever men as their administrators, they usually chose them from among the highest ranks of the clergy. In most countries, the king's right-hand man was the chancellor, and the chancellor was almost always a bishop.

Admittedly, Scotland didn't have a chancellor at the moment. It didn't have a king either, only a regent, because seventeen-year-old King James had been a prisoner of the English for the last five years. But he would be freed some day; with luck, just about when Gavin was ready for him.

Gavin had it all planned out. What he was going to do, as a first step, was work his way up through the university and the priesthood until he reached the positions he had set his heart on, Bishop of (preferably) Glasgow and Chancellor (undoubtedly) of the Realm. He hoped it wouldn't take too long, because after that he had to start setting this restless, lawless, divided native land of his to rights. He felt quite strongly that it was something that needed to be done, and nobody else seemed to be doing it.

Though becoming a priest meant forswearing body for soul, heart for mind, substance for spirit, to eleven-year-old Gavin it seemed a small price to pay for the chance to fulfil his dreams.

Dreams. Dreams? He tried to laugh at them sometimes, and was embarrassed that he couldn't, or not with any sincerity; he hadn't recognized, yet, that to laugh off one's dreams was to die a little. So he told himself firmly that he, Gavin John Cameron, *could* turn them into reality, *could* achieve what he had set his heart on. It was only a matter of application, and determination, and careful tending of the fires that burned, hidden but persistent, within him.

Suddenly, the excitement surged up inside him again until he felt that his chest would burst under the pressure. Only a few hours now, and life would begin. A year or two's proper tutoring, then university, and then – and then! – he would show the world what a Cameron of Kinveil could do!

He fell asleep, inevitably, at the back end of the night, and when he was roused by his mother's screech of 'Gavin!' – effortlessly audible above the early-morning din of the courtyard – the sky was already clear and luminous, ready for the dawn.

He had intended to set out on his great adventure by striding off, mature and dignified, into the rising sun. Instead, he tumbled blearily from his pallet, muttering adolescent imprecations as he shook out the saffron linen shirt, belted it round his thin haunches, and tried, all thumbs, to pop open the loop that took his father's old iron dagger. Inscribed on its pommel were the high-sounding words *Potius mori*, which was the Kinveil motto and meant 'Rather die'. Rather than what, Gavin had never discovered.

Slithering out of the window of his eyrie, he shinned down the dangling heather-root ladder that was all Kinveil possessed in the way of a staircase. His father had said, once or twice, that they must build some proper steps, but nothing had come of it. Nothing had ever come of his father's ideas, except misfortune.

He cast a glance about him just as his bare feet touched the ground, and even while he looked, the first rays of the sun ran with a hop, a skip, and a jump round all the mountain peaks and set the quartz in them glittering, quartz that was clearer by far – or so his father had said – than the glass that rich Lowland folk used in their windows in place of shutters. Kinveil didn't have any glass, of course; it didn't have any shutters, either.

And then there was a salmon-coloured girdle round the whole margin of mountains and sky, and the shadow of Kinveil's tower materialized on the water, long and black and sharp as the finger of Satan, pointing to the western islands and the unknown seas beyond. For a moment, Gavin's eyes followed its direction. To sail west, and west, and west, until one reached the very spot where the sun went down . . .

He shrugged. Although it would be quite exciting to be the first man ever to reach the edge of the world, it wouldn't do much to improve the troubled state of Scotland. Absently, he wondered whether there might be anything in this strange idea that the earth wasn't flat, but round.

Sniffing the air, he decided it was going to be another beautiful day. A pity. Gavin didn't like being too hot any more than he liked being forever wet. By choice, he would have set out on his adventures on a bracing morning in April, with fresh blue skies and a bright sun, and big, buxom white clouds surging along with the wind behind them. On a morning when birdsong and the cries of new lambs served to emphasize the curious silence that, to Gavin, always seemed to hover round trees and plants when they were heavy with bud, as if they were holding their breaths for one last moment before they took the decision to hazard their leaves in the uncertain sun.

But it wasn't April. It was August, and it was going to be sweltering.

3

HE TURNED at the sound of his mother's brusque, almost unfriendly voice. With her hair raggedly knotted, her skirts kilted up for the milking, and her complexion lifeless as it always was in the mornings, she had scarcely changed in all her son's memory of her. He had thought wistfully, sometimes, that it would have been comforting if she had found it possible to love him, just a little.

Because she was a woman of unrelenting will, he knew very little of her. He could not tell that it was willpower alone, now, that dragged her through the days and the weeks and the months. It would not do so for much longer, she knew, but she had told no one, least of all her son. She didn't want him to abandon all his high hopes and stay at Kinveil, or not out of duty. And she could not expect him to stay out of love. His father had always told her that she was a most unlovable woman, and because, despite his failings, he had been a cultivated man, she had believed him. So she had taken care to show Gavin only the most arbitrary affection, terrified that anything more would force him into trying, and failing, to love her in return. Life would place enough burdens on the boy's shoulders without that.

'Haff you said your prayers?' she scolded. 'Do you haff your dirk? I haff aal the things here for your journey.'

Her son was petulant. 'Must I take all that? *Pater de coelis deus* . . . *Spiritus sancte* . . . Och, see the weight of this sack of oatmeal! And the griddle plate, too! *Sancta mana ora pro nobis* . . . *Sancta dei genetrix ora pro nobis* . . . And why should I be needing a shirt of mail that is big enough for three of me? *Sancta virgo virginum ora pro nobis* . . . It is the university I am going to, not the wars!'

'You know ferry well that you will be needing it. There hass been fighting over by Aberdeen. They are saying that the Earl of Mar hass made collops of His Lordship of the Isles, but that iss only what they are saying. For aal I know, they may be fighting still. See now, and stay out of their way! And the shirt wass your father's. You will be growing into it.'

Gavin hitched the skin bag of oatmeal over his shoulder and spoke his parting words. 'They have no sense,' he said austerely to his mother, who would not live to see her child again. 'How will Scotland ever be a country if the mountains and the plains cannot agree?'

4

'GOING to the *school* in his *da*'s old *shirt*!'

Half a dozen of the glen children had elected to see Gavin on his way, and were prancing along the loch side behind him, chanting. He found it hard to ignore them. They had been his friends when they were small, but as they grew up and began to hear some of the tales of Cameron infamy that were enshrined in the mythology of the glen, everything had changed.

Gavin could understand it, and it made him deeply uncomfortable to have to pretend that he didn't. Privately, he blushed not only for his father, but for his grandfather, and his great-grandfather as well. He also had the feeling that when he saw all the other ranks of his forbears lined up before the throne of justice on Judgement Day, the ones he didn't know about would turn out to be every bit as bad as the ones he did.

Great-grandfather had been the first Cameron of Kinveil, a man who couldn't bear to see a good opportunity going to waste. He had fought for Robert the Bruce at the battle of Bannockburn almost a hundred years ago, and when the victorious Bruce had despatched companies of troops to annex the possessions of those lords who had been rash enough to turn out for the wrong side – gambling that England would win, as usual – great-grandfather had found himself in charge of the company bound for Kinveil.

The sight of the sturdy old watchtower, a relic of times when this part of the coast had been the favourite target of Norse raiders, had been enough to give great-grandfather ideas. He was beginning to tire of his rootless life, to think of settling down, and good stone buildings were as hard for a poor soldier to come by as the keys of St Peter.

He moved in. When the local people disputed possession, he held it by superior force of arms (which, as far as Gavin could discover, meant that, though his aim wasn't as good, he had more bows and arrows than they had). Then he took the prettiest of the widows to wife, gave the others to his men, and that was that.

Not for another forty years did Kinveil have any further contact with the outside world, and by that time the watchtower had passed to Gavin's grandfather, and the throne of Scotland to Robert the Bruce's son. Grandfather, confronted by a reproachful representative of the crown with the better part of an army at his back, had been all injured innocence. What had he, and his father before him, been doing but acting as guardians of the king's peace in these troubled times, holding Kinveil in the king's name?

The royal envoy hadn't been impressed by grandfather's arguments, but he hadn't been much impressed by Kinveil, either. So he'd agreed to a bargain involving blind eyes all round, security of tenure, and a number of unenforceable feudal dues. Afterwards, as an earnest of goodwill, grandfather had executed a round dozen of the local malcontents and exhibited their heads on Kinveil's crumbling ramparts. It was a beautiful and virtually foolproof way of settling old scores, and grandfather had used it again, several times, before he fell into a gully and broke his neck.

And then there was father, who had left his younger brother to look after Kinveil and gone off to make his fortune as a merchant in Aberdeen. Failing in that, but reluctant to return to the spartan life of the glens, he had allowed himself to become entangled in a blood feud between some Cameron cousins and the Mackintoshes, Macphersons, Macbeans, and a wide variety of Mac-others whose names Gavin couldn't remember. The end of it all had been a tournament to the death involving thirty champions from each side, supervised by the new King Robert III. Gavin's father had been the sole Cameron survivor, not because of his prowess with lance and sword, but because he could swim like a fish. Disliking the way things were going, he hadn't hesitated to remove himself from the scene by diving into the Tay and striking out briskly for the other shore.

As if it had all been too much for him, in the dozen years that remained of his life Gavin's father had indulged in only three positive gestures. He had married, begotten his solitary offspring, and died. Gavin was firmly of the opinion that his mother had had a great deal more to do with all three events than his father had.

SWITCHING the sack of meal to his other shoulder, Gavin responded to the children's jeers in the way best calculated to annoy them. Adopting the pretentious Lowland accent he had learned from his father, he said disdainfully, 'Not school, university. *You* may be content to do without a proper education, but *I* am not!' Devoutly, he hoped Father Duncan's teaching had been good enough to qualify him for admission. At least he could read and write, and there probably weren't more than a dozen people in the whole of the western Highlands who could say as much.

The smallest girl, Moragh, asked timidly, 'What iss you going to do after that, Gaffin?' Privately, she thought Gavin was wonderful, but as far as the other children were concerned, she was in a minority of one.

'I'm going to be a great churchman.'

'Like Father Duncan?'

'*Dia!* No!' He was annoyed with Father Duncan, who had bestowed a cursory blessing on him the afternoon before, saying he would be too busy with the milking to do it this morning. 'And see you,' the old man had added, 'you must be making your confession effery time you haff the chance. Confession once a year iss only for folk who iss good and meek and mild. No, you may *not* be explaining things to God personally if you cannot find a priest! It iss ferry wrong. Indeed, there wass someone saying to me chust the other day . . . What wass it, now? Och, yess, Lollardy, that iss the word they wass calling it. Lollardy. It iss a kind of heresy. The Lord does not like chust anyone talking to Him, do you see? You haff to be a priest before He will be listening.'

Gavin hadn't questioned it, though he did wish that God would make a few allowances occasionally.

To Moragh, he said, 'No, I'm going to be a bishop.'

'Why not an *arch*bishop?' Donny Mackenzie sneered.

'Because we don't *have* archbishops in Scotland, that's why!'

Moragh's eyes filled with tears. 'But a bishop iss chust another kind of a priest! If you iss a bishop, God will not be letting you come back and marry me!' She was six years old, a neat little thing even in the long, swaddling folds of her drab-coloured smock, and Gavin thought that, with her slanting brown eyes, amber and rose complexion, and straight, heavy black hair, she would develop into a real Highland beauty one of these days.

Touched, he stopped and turned. 'Yes, well. I'm sorry, Moragh. But you just *have* to be a priest if you want to make your mark on the world, even in things that don't have anything to do with God.' Belatedly tactful, he added, 'And at least, though I can't marry you, I can't marry anyone else either, can I?'

She didn't say anything, but her eyes took on the faraway look that always meant she was having an attack of the second sight – or pretending she was. Gavin had never been quite sure which.

Donny, who was thickset, red-haired, two years older than Gavin, and anything but a fool, lighted not on what Gavin had said, but what he had implied. 'Make your mark *on the world*? You mean on the Lowlanders, and the Sassenachs, and the French, and all those other folk that iss nothing to do with us. The Highlands iss not grand enough for you, iss that what you are saying? You are a traitor, Gavin Cameron, that iss what you are! A traitor!'

He had a catapult, and as he stood there flexing its gut between his fingers, the sun glanced off the surface of the loch and lightened his eyes to the colour of peaty water. There was a glint in them, not only of his customary belligerence, but also of envy. More than anything, Donny, too, wanted to go adventuring.

'Nonsense!' Gavin said, holding himself erect before the inimical little band and scarcely flinching when Donny's pebble struck with paralysing accuracy on his unprotected ankle bone. He went on standing there for a few moments longer, with challenge (he hoped) in his gaze, until it seemed that his foot and calf muscles might be sufficiently recovered to obey him, and then he turned and stalked off on his way, head held high.

A small hail of stones from the other children followed him, but none of them hurt, except the last one, and it wasn't a physical hurt. Just before he felt it, he heard Moragh's high little voice crying, '*Wicked* Gaffin!' He knew the child was copying the others, that she was siding with them because she was very small and didn't know what else to do, but that didn't make it any better. She was an appealing little thing.

For the first time in his life, he was aware of a sudden, independent stirring of his body under the chainmail and the saffron shirt and the scrip that hung down from the front of his belt like an over-sized codpiece. The hot, melting, unfamiliarity of it made him gasp, and he stumbled a little in his stride, but the others were still there, staring after him, and by the time he was out of their sight it was all over.

In a way, though, it was another kind of beginning. A sense of freedom began to tingle in his veins, and his spirits rose with every step he took. He twirled round once, twice, three times, and then went dancing on his way, grinning to himself like a mooncalf, until he tripped over his feet and was abruptly restored to sobriety.

6

WHEN he reached the first of the high passes, the sun was at its zenith and he decided to stop for his bannocks and cheese.

There wasn't a cloud in the sky, and the whole landscape smelled of warm heather. The Five Sisters and The Saddle, which on dull days seemed to loom over the pass, today stood back from it on either side, their peaks clear and pale and remote. There were two buzzards, one old and one young, planing and soaring high up in the blue, while far below them the martins dashed about in droves, hunting their dinner – the only birds Gavin knew that were as fussy as humans about having their meals on time.

Dropping his burdens in the shade of some rocks, he shook himself to try and unstick the shirt from his back. He was wearing the chainmail habergeon over it, and it rattled and jangled like a whole troop of armoured horse, sending up a curlew that had been standing nearby, stiff-legged and long-beaked, among the green pithy reeds that always spelled bog. Gavin decided he would have a drink first and then take the habergeon off. He was tired of the weight on his shoulders, of the way the metal rings soaked up the heat, of the feel of the cuffs flopping over his knuckles and the skirts clanking round his bare knees as he walked.

He had been walking for the best part of five hours now, uphill all the way, alongside the track made by generations of Highland sheep and shepherds on their migration to and from the summer pastures. He was annoyed with himself for not having foreseen the state the track would be in. There had been a deluge before and during the migrants' recent return from the hills, and then the sun had come out and stayed out, as if it were never going to go in again. As a result, the track was baked as hard as furrowed whinstone, and so pitted by feet and hooves that it looked as if it had been ravaged by the pox. Gavin had expected to keep up a swinging pace for the first few miles, but instead he had been forced off the track altogether and on to the rough ground that flanked it.

He knelt gratefully by the stream and cupped his hands to drink. It was lovely water, clear and cold and pure, better by far than the sickly-sweet, cloudy, oat ale that everyone drank in the glens. Then, refreshed, he removed his belt, and was trying to get a grip on his mailed shoulders so as to tug the habergeon over his head when he raised his eyes and saw the man picking his way towards him from about fifty yards upstream.

He was a complete stranger, youngish, with long, greasy fair hair and a patchy beard that hung in elf locks round his chin. The eyes in the sun-browned face were astonishingly pale, as if the sky were showing through empty sockets. He was wearing nothing but a loose, ragged smock and a shifty smile, and he carried no weapon that Gavin could see.

Abandoning his struggle with the habergeon, Gavin waited for the man to say something and, when he didn't, himself raised his voice and spoke the polite 'Aye-aye' that did duty in Scotland for good morning, how are you, fine day, and most other salutations of the kind. The man still said nothing, but his eyes flickered over to where Gavin's belongings lay in the shade by the stream.

Gavin couldn't believe what happened next. In the violent, self-seeking climate of the times, he should at least have been suspicious, but he had been disarmed by the sun, and the warmth, and the calm quiet of the landscape. It wasn't the kind of day for trouble to happen. So he stood there, and went on standing there, vaguely puzzled, even when the stranger stopped, bent down, reached out, and then straightened up with a large and businesslike rock in his hand and a look on his face that reminded Gavin of the wolves that roamed the glens. His breath smelled like a wolf's, too, even from several yards away. Fastidiously, Gavin wrinkled his nose.

If one of the martins hadn't swooped down to within inches of his head and jolted him out of his trance, his great adventure might have ended there and then.

But his brain suddenly took in what was happening and, with a yelp of alarm, he skipped out of reach faster than he had ever skipped in his life before, exclaiming idiotically as he went, 'What in the name of . . . ?' It came out as a high-pitched squeak, and terminated abruptly as the rock went hurtling past his head and he ducked, leapt to one side, and almost lost his footing.

In the flailing moment it took for him to recover, he discovered that his dominant emotion wasn't fear but indignation – indignation at the sheer absurdity of being thought rich enough to rob, when what lay there by the stream was all he possessed in the world. A sack of meal that might last a year if he rationed himself; an iron griddle for cooking his oatcakes on; a scrip containing bannocks, cheese, and a handful of silver pennies.

And a belt, with a knife in it.

Then he *was* frightened. The stranger hadn't seen it yet, but he would if Gavin made any move towards it. And he might get there first.

So, when the man lunged at him, Gavin swerved away from the stream and the rocks and the knife, backing hurriedly downhill to his right and praying that there would be no outcrops or heather roots to trip him up. But he couldn't back away fast enough and soon he had no choice but to turn and run. If he had any idea in mind, it was to lead the man round in a circle, relying on his own lightness and agility to stay ahead until he could reach the knife. But the chainmail handicapped him terribly, bundling itself between his legs so that he found himself slipping and floundering down the hillside with the man's outstretched hands only a few inches from his back.

And then the man took a flying leap, and Gavin went crashing to earth with one of his ankles held in a grip so tight that it felt as if the bones were being crushed to powder. It was the same ankle that Donny Mackenzie had hit with his pebble that morning.

Gavin let out a howl of anguish, even as he began kicking and struggling with every ounce of his strength. He might have saved himself the trouble. The man simply ignored him, lying there solid and immovable as a fallen mountain, making strange grumbling noises under his breath. Gavin knew he was only waiting for the first hint of an opportunity to extend his grip and pin Gavin firmly to the ground. Firmly – and finally.

He did the only thing he could think of. Twisting round and back, he succeeded in lacing his fingers in his enemy's long hair and bouncing his head up and down with all his might. At first it hurt him more than it hurt the man, because he was bouncing the man's head off his own tormented calf muscles. But then, somehow, he managed to move his leg just a little, and the next time the man's face came down it was on to a fold of chainmail with solid rock underneath. There was a choking

23

shriek, and for a moment Gavin was free. But he was scarcely halfway to the knife, moving at a desperate, one-legged scuttle, when the man was after him, and then past him, and then standing before him, snarling, with the knife in his hand and the pale sky shining through the sockets of his eyes.

If there had been any uncertainty in Gavin's mind before, there was none now. He recognized, without the remotest shadow of a doubt, that the man intended not only to rob him but to kill him, and the chainmail wasn't going to stop him. His expression was ferocious behind the blood that masked his nose and dripped down his beard, and he was holding the knife on a level with Gavin's throat. Every tiny hair on Gavin's body rose independently and shivered.

The man was saying something now, over and over, in a dialect that Gavin didn't recognize. Perhaps he was an islander, a refugee from the battle near Aberdeen trying to find his way home. It didn't matter very much. A quiver of overwrought laughter rose unexpectedly in Gavin's chest. Whatever the man was saying – and it was nothing friendly – at least he was saying *something*. And that was an improvement on the grunting silence that had ruled until now.

In the Gaelic of the glens, Gavin exclaimed, 'Stop it, will you stop it! What is it you are after? I will be giving you some oatmeal, if that is what you want! There is no need to kill me for it!'

There was concentration on the man's face, as if he were trying to work out what Gavin had said. Gavin had the feeling it wouldn't make any difference even if he succeeded, but, swiftly, he repeated, 'What is it you are after? I will be giving you some meal if you want it!' Sensation was beginning to come back into his leg, but he needed to gain time, and the man looked as if he might be one of those people who couldn't think and act simultaneously. Urgently Gavin spoke again. 'Are you hungry? Are you needing some of the oatmeal I have in that bag there?'

But almost at once he had to back away as the man, abandoning the attempt to understand, stabbed viciously at the empty air and then began feinting with the knife, to right and then to left, high and then low, sure of himself, sure of his prey, a wildcat playing with a vole. One thrust came much too close, and there was a faint jangle as the knife caught in one of the links of Gavin's mail.

He had a craven desire to turn and run, to run anywhere out of sight and out of reach of this God-forgotten maniac, but he couldn't. It wasn't a question of bravery, nothing to do with upholding the honour of the Camerons; the family motto, 'Rather die', had never seemed sillier. He didn't run because he didn't dare. The man had longer legs than he, and nothing wrong with his ankles. Gavin had no doubt that, before he had taken more than a few steps, he would feel the first stinging bite of the knife as it sank into the back of his neck.

He couldn't risk taking his eyes off the man, not even long enough to pick up a stone. He thought yearningly of the griddle. A crack over the skull with that would do the trick, but he couldn't think how to get his hands on it.

And then it happened. Reacting to a direct lunge, Gavin hopped back three paces and felt the ground give under his feet, wetly, glutinously, receptively. The bog.

His face, he knew, must show his panic, but he didn't move or struggle. He simply stood, swaying slightly, as he tried to keep his balance, in mud up to his ankles, his eyes fixed on his enemy, who had stopped just in time and was standing grinning on the dry ground scarcely a yard away.

Gavin swallowed and said quietly, 'Help me! Please help me!' It was something the man *had* to understand.

He understood all right. Safe on the bank, he threw back his greasy head and laughed.

Gavin moved his toes slightly and there was a sucking noise from the bog. Clamping his lower lip between his teeth, he drew in a shaking breath and said again, 'Help me!' and then, his voice rising, 'For the love of God, help me!'

It was still the same world, still the same sunny, untroubled noon, with no sound other than the sweet, gossipy chittering of the martins swooping after the bog-insects nearby, and the mewing of the buzzards high above. The mountain tops were still clear, and there was still the smell of warm heather, overlaid with a scent of bog myrtle and a new, pungent tang of mud.

He wriggled his toes again, but this time the bog made no sound.

After a moment he released his breath very slowly and, watching the man's eyes, burst out, 'I daren't move! You know I daren't move, or the bog will suck me under! Dear God, help me, *help me*!' The hysteria in his voice sounded pretty convincing, he thought.

There were people in the glen he had never liked very much, people who were self-satisfied, uncaring, humourless, even just thoughtless. But none of them would have stood by, laughing, and watched a human being die by inches. That was something they did in the cities, not in the Highlands. For the first time in his life Gavin discovered what it was to hate someone.

When he spoke again, his voice was uncharacteristically rough. 'God rot you!' he exclaimed. 'God rot your miserable soul! Help me, you son of the fiend! *Help me!*' He clasped his hands before his mouth, and they were shaking.

Safe on his hummock, the stranger gave way to a paroxysm of mirth. It was clear that he was enjoying himself hugely. Much more, and he'd be settling down on a nice mossy rock for the afternoon, cheering and applauding as if Gavin were one of the more uproarious bits in a morality play.

Sourly, Gavin let him get on with it. Then, taking a deep, sustaining gulp of air, he embarked on a highly artistic crescendo of wails and moans and pleas for mercy, extending his arms in supplication while taking good care not to move any of the muscles in the lower part of his body, just in case the firm ground under his feet wasn't as firm as he thought it was.

It was now or never. The man was rocking back and forward, his whole body quaking, his eyes half closed and streaming with tears of merriment, fists pressed to his aching sides. The dagger was pointing away from Gavin.

Gavin relaxed his legs, bunched the muscles of his waist and shoulders, let out a screech his mother would have been proud of, and launched himself at his enemy with all the force of eleven purposeful years.

His head and the man's stomach connected with a gratifying thud, and the pair of them went flying on to the heather, the man underneath and Gavin on top, hanging on like grim death to the hand that held the knife. Briefly, very briefly, the advantage was his. Somehow, he succeeded in forcing the man's arm up, and then slamming the point of his elbow down on the ground with a violence that owed nothing to strength and everything to desperation.

The man's hand jerked open, and the knife flew free into the air.

It landed on the heather half a dozen yards away, and Gavin was after it like lightning, but the relief was so great that his fingers fumbled and he dropped it, and then dropped it again. And when he had a grip on it at last, and was trying, with scrambling haste, to rise, he missed his footing and fell sideways on his hip and elbow, the knife projecting from his fist like a groundspike.

It was then that the sky above him was blotted out, as the stranger threw the whole weight of his spreadeagled body, like some vast winged monster, on top of him.

For the rest of his life, Gavin was to remember that moment in nightmares. Not often, but always when there was some great decision that had to be taken, and when he alone had to take it. At the time, he believed it was chance and chance alone that had impaled the plunging body on his dagger.

7

AFTERWARDS, when he had cleaned the dagger and washed the blood from his hands, he discovered that, inside him, there was no exultation, no relief, not even revulsion. Only a small, empty cloud of astonishment. It was very peculiar.

He couldn't think what he ought to do about the body. It seemed vaguely improper just to walk off and leave it lying there on the purple, green and copper patchwork of the August hill, but there was no way of burying it, and it would take more time and strength than he possessed to gather enough loose rocks to build a cairn over it. He supposed it would just have to stay where it was, meat for the hoodie crows who had materialized, as they always did, out of the empty air, and were perched waiting on the bleached and long-dead trees beside the stream.

They always went for the eyes first.

It was then, quite without warning, that the reaction hit him.

He had to fight against it for a long time, crouched on the ground, his head between his knees and his fists balled tight against his lips. But he won in the end; he wasn't sick, and he didn't cry.

8

HOURS later, when the sun was just beginning to slide into the western sea and Gavin had put another dozen miles between himself and his childhood, he suddenly realized that the reason why he was so hungry was that the bannocks and cheese he had meant to eat at noon were still reposing in the scrip that hung from his belt.

It was an understandable omission, considering the kind of day it had been. Exhausting, disturbing, but – in retrospect – tremendously stimulating. It wasn't given to many boys, he thought resiliently, to overcome three such challenges in so short a time.

He had set out on his life's adventure. He had jousted with death, and won. And he had carried out his first grown-up pastoral duty when he had knelt over the body on the hill and commended its murdering soul to God's eternal mercy. A pedant might have found something to criticize, there, because Gavin hadn't known the words of the office for the dead and had had to make do with the prayer against the plague (*Pater de coelis deus miserere nobis, Fili redemptor mundi deus miserere nobis . . .*) But he had felt much better for it afterwards, and thought that the soul of the departed probably had, too.

One problem had nagged, briefly, at his mind. Looking down at the body, he had said aloud, 'Well, it *was* your own fault! You shouldn't have gone around trying to kill people.' It was only then that it had occurred to him that God might not approve of bishops-to-be going around killing people, either. But Father Duncan had said, often enough, that everything one did was predestined, and if that were true, Gavin didn't really see how God could complain.

He turned to look back the way he had come, into the sunset, because now he had reached the last high pass from which he would have a sight of his home. The mountains cut off all but a small triangle of the loch and blotted out the straggling cluster of peat-walled, heather-roofed hovels that made up the village. But he could still see Kinveil's tower perched darkly above water that, tonight, was all shades of saffron and flame and molten gold.

He stood and gazed at it for a moment, on his face a curious expression in which anticipation warred with a kind of surprised regret. Only a few more steps, and Kinveil would be behind him, not forever, perhaps, but for a long, long time. He felt a twinge, a very slight twinge, of loneliness.

Then, with a gesture that might have meant anything, he turned his back on Kinveil and the western sea and faced towards the east, and the wider world, and the other seas round which all history was made.

PART ONE

1426

CHAPTER ONE

I

ROME, in the summer of 1426, lay under a thunderous pall of cloud and heat and stone dust.

To breathe the trapped air was to choke on as pungent a combination of smells as Gavin could ever remember. Human sweat and horse dung, candle smoke from the Vatican and rotting vegetables from the market, burning lime from the builders' kilns and – stronger and more sickening than any of them – the vile stench of sewage from the Tiber.

The city was full of noise, too. It echoed off the hot, thick canopy of the sky, volleyed through the streets, bounced off the greasy surface of the waters, thundered its way round all Rome's seven hills and back again. The noise of hammering, sawing, shouting, swearing and praying. Of carts rumbling, donkeys braying, accoutrements jangling. Of half a thousand church bells all ringing at once, and all fortissimo. To Gavin's unaccustomed ear, it sounded like the ultimate, plate-armoured battle between the hosts of heaven and the legions of the damned.

But there was reason for the noise and the smells, or some of them. After a century of neglect, the half-ruined capital of western Christendom was being restored, in a hurry, to a state fit for the pope to live in.

IF ANYWHERE in Rome, there ought to have been silence and sanctuary in the great basilica of the Lateran, but there was none, because its spacious halls were full of workmen relaying floors and replacing ceilings. This had made it necessary to set up a temporary audience chamber in one of the side chapels, which was not only cramped but in a sad state of disrepair, its frescoes stained and faded, its marble pillars bruised, the glass gone from its windows and the stonework disintegrating.

Gavin, on his knees before the apostolic throne, his lips poised over the papal slipper and his eyes filled with the gold-woven scarlet silk of the papal robes, reflected that His Holiness might as well have chosen to hold court in the Forum.

Except that here, within the illusory shelter of these walls, the vulgar smells of the city were rounded out by other, more expensive smells, of a kind that any well-informed man could put a price to. Fumes of incense (five shillings a pound). The mustiness of rich vestments (£40, not a penny less, for that cloak of Cardinal Condulmer's). The tang of fresh, oak-gall ink on parchment (twopence a leaf, not counting the work of the scribe). The odour of sanctity . . . Yes, well. The price, there, might be open to negotiation, but it was never cheap.

Through the noise, Gavin tried again to catch what the voice above his head was saying, but the sonorous Latin reached him only by its rhythm, compelling and meaningless as some half-heard liturgical chant. He was mildly annoyed, as if he were missing something. Which was ridiculous, because whether they could hear the words or not, everyone in the audience chamber knew what the pope was saying.

Gavin knew because he had rehearsed the scene in his mind so many times during that journey through the years that had brought him here, in the end, to Rome. And all the cardinals, bishops, deacons, secretaries and other officials of the curia who – tonsured and discreet – crowded the chamber, knew too, because they had made it their business to find out. Gavin could feel their eyes on him, cold, inquisitive, calculating; busily assessing the implications, present and future, of Holy Father's unexpected surrender to the demands of a powerless little nation like Scotland. Which, he guessed, most of them had had to look up in the Catalan atlas.

'Wherefore,' the voice was saying, 'by virtue of the authority vested in us as Vicar of Christ upon this earth, and lending ear to the representations of our beloved cousin King James of Scotland, of whose devotion to Holy Church we have heard much, we are now persuaded that you, Gavin John Cameron, may be judged worthy to hold the high and exalted dignity of Bishop of the See of Glasgow. Be it known, then, by all men, that in you we place our trust, and that, in evidence of the same, we grant this day the faculty for your consecration. Go with God, my son, and so act that your light shall shine before all men.'

An eleven-year-old voice crowed triumphantly inside Gavin's head.

Then there was an unmistakable rustling of parchment and he could look up, and rise at last, and kiss the pope's ring and the proffered cheek. For a moment he stared into the sallow, heavy-jowled face and the dark, level eyes, faintly smiling and utterly impersonal, and then one of the officials signed to him and he dropped to his knees again and took the oath of fealty. His voice wasn't quite his own as he repeated the ancient formula, but it was clear and unhurried, and his features showed only the calm deliberation the occasion seemed to require. He had become very good, over the years, at guarding his expression.

Afterwards, the pope made the sign of the Cross before him, and it was done. The *cantore* raised their voices in a hymn of thanksgiving and Bishop-elect Gavin John Cameron was led off in procession to the altar of the Blessed Virgin.

3

AND after the ritual, the reckoning. In the makeshift privacy of an alcove off the great nave, the papal chamberlain raised the matter of the annates. The bishop-elect would know all about those, of course. It was customary, indeed – ahhh – mandatory, for newly appointed prelates to pay over the whole of their first year's income into the papal treasury, in recognition of the 'common service' due to His Holiness and the College of Cardinals. In times past the precise sums had been decided voluntarily by the donor. But such a system, as the bishop-elect would readily understand, could be productive of embarrassment, so it had been found more convenient to leave the assessment to the cashiers of the apostolic chamber. In the present instance, it was their view that the sum of two thousand five hundred gold florins would adequately cover the bishop-elect's common service. About £1100 Scots. If that was agreeable? It was? *Bene!* A few weeks' grace could be permitted. And in addition, of course, there were the five little services – another two hundred gold florins or so. But that was really all, except for the chancery's charges for copying and registering the documents, which was a matter of a few *scudi*, no more. Doubtless the bishop-elect would instruct his estimable dean to consult with the treasury staff over such details as how and when the moneys should be paid?

The bishop-elect said he would.

Released, Gavin picked his way back over the half-laid mosaics to the audience chamber, where he found his estimable dean crushed in a corner, hemmed in by two cardinals, one papal notary, and a referendary clerk who had no right to be there at all.

'Aye, aye,' murmured Dean Myrton, mopping his perspiring brow with the corner of an ample sleeve. 'It's all official now, is it?'

'It is. Can we raise £1100 in the next three months?'

The dean snorted. '£11, maybe.'

'That's what I thought,' Gavin said. 'Move over.'

The dean nodded his head gloomily. 'Yes, my Lord Bishop. Certainly, my Lord Bishop. At once, my Lord Bishop. Ye sanctified idiot, would I be standing here, d'ye think, if I *could* move over?'

But he managed it somehow. It was one of Tom Myrton's great talents, that he could always manage things somehow.

At last, Gavin was able to observe what was going on. More specifically, he was able to take a long, critical look at Pope Martin V, to try and see behind the gold-clasped scarlet cope and the famous Ghiberti tiara to the man who had been born Odonne Colonna, raised to the rank of cardinal deacon by Innocent VII, and now, at the age of fifty-eight, was undisputed head of a Christendom united for the first time in almost half a century. Gossip said he was a mild, gentle, humane man.

Certainly, he couldn't be other than an improvement on his immediate predecessor, who had been deposed from the papal throne on charges of murder, piracy, rape, sodomy, and incest. It was widely believed that there had been other, more scandalous charges, too, which had been suppressed.

Gavin pursed his lips, thoughtfully. For almost forty years, there had been two popes in Europe, one based at Avignon, the other at Rome. At one stage, there had even been three, all of them trading in benefices, selling indulgences, appointing cardinals and bishops, and issuing excommunications with a fine, free hand. The church had been reduced to abject confusion, and the papacy to little more than a bargaining counter in the game of European politics.

Then, in 1417, on St Martin's day, the Council of Constance had elected Cardinal Colonna to the throne of St Peter.

In the nine years since then, Martin V had brought all the nations of Europe to his side, crushed his rivals, embarked on the rebuilding of Rome, taken the field in person against the condottieri who had overrun the papal territories, swept the Roman countryside clear of bandits, and begun urging the Germans to arms against the heretics of Bohemia.

Mild? Gentle? Humane? Gavin didn't believe a word of it.

Which made it all the more interesting that Martin should have given in to 'our beloved cousin King James' over who was to be Glasgow's new bishop.

It had been Rome's right to decide, and Rome had known no more of Gavin Cameron, the king's nominee, than that he was twenty-six years old, fully qualified in canon law, and James's keeper of the privy seal. But that had been the least of the problems; Rome couldn't have, and didn't expect to have, direct knowledge of every candidate for every one of the five hundred episcopacies in the Latin church. The real problem had been that His Holiness had promised one of his Colonna cousins the next bishopric that fell vacant, wherever it happened to be.

Dean Myrton and the cathedral chapter of Glasgow, as horrified as James at the prospect of being landed with a foreigner who knew no more about the place than what its revenues added up to, had willingly agreed to the royal demand that they elect Gavin Cameron forthwith, if not sooner, and present Rome with a *fait accompli* – thus settling the matter once and for all.

It hadn't done any such thing, of course. Far from it. Because His Holiness, who had just won a battle of wills with England and another with France, was in no mood to permit the king of a ramshackle, third-rate little country like Scotland to poach on his preserves, and had said so in no uncertain terms when he quashed the election. James had been deeply offended.

For a while, it had looked as if nothing would ever be resolved, and it might not have been if Tom Myrton, diplomat as well as dean, hadn't been despatched to Rome and brought things to a satisfactory conclusion. Gavin still hadn't discovered how he'd managed it.

He was just mulling over ways and means of finding out – because Tom, clever as a cat despite his unexciting appearance, gave nothing away that he didn't want to – when that gentleman growled beside him, 'Mary Mother, but it's hot,' and then, on a chirpier note, 'Well now! Look who's here.'

Gavin looked, and saw that another in the long roster of clerics was taking his place before the tasselled throne, and that this time it was someone he knew. A man with the looks and build of one of the more substantial Roman emperors, a man who sank to his knees as if he didn't spend as much time on them as a good churchman should. A man who, twelve years ago at St Andrews, had abandoned the task of instructing students like Gavin in the principles of elementary logic, and had taken himself off, first to Paris and then to the papal court, in search of a richer living.

'Yes, indeed,' Gavin said thoughtfully. 'Columba Crozier. Our fellow-Scotsman – when he remembers. I notice you haven't told me what you've managed to arrange for *him*.'

4

IN THE elegant little French town of Villeneuve-lès-Avignon, roughly six hundred miles to the north-west of Rome, Ninian Drummond was scrambling her way, with furious haste, into a new blue gown with flowered silk sleeve linings, while one of her gentlewomen tried to comb out the heavy tangle of her red-gold hair, and another hovered close by, waiting to cinch the gilded belt round her middle.

Ninian knew it was going to be too tight. She longed to have a fashionable figure, slender enough above the waist to wear clinging bodices, and full enough below for the skirts to swell out the way they were supposed to before they cascaded to the ground. But she was plump all over. It was the despair of her life, even though with Sévèrine's guidance she had learned to dress in a way that helped to disguise it.

With a rush of panic, she wondered whether Harry might turn out to dislike her figure. Or dislike *her*. Sir Harry Graham, her husband-to-be, whom she had met at the betrothal ceremony when she was seven years old – and never since. Who was arriving at noon today to claim his bride.

They should have been married when she was thirteen, but Lady Drummond had died that February of the plague. It was an excuse that had served Ninian for more than two years, even though she had never been close to her delicate, detached, other-worldly mother. And then, when she was fifteen, her father, too, had died in one of the battles that, as a professional fighting man, were all he had ever been interested in, and Ninian had been granted another two years' grace.

But now she was seventeen and there were no more excuses. Her mother's friend, Sévèrine de Verne, who had taken Ninian's upbringing out of her ladyship's incompetent hands when Ninian was still a child, said it was high time she was married. She hadn't phrased it quite like that. What she had actually said was, 'It is high time that you ceased to be the only seventeen-year-old virgin in the whole of France.'

And Ninian's adored Columba – her guardian and her father's stepbrother, to whom she had always been closer than to anyone else in the world – had agreed. 'Sévèrine is wise,' he had said. 'And she is right. Besides, you know that in the eyes of the church a betrothal is as binding as marriage. God has given you four uncovenanted years of freedom; my pet, you cannot ask for more. It is time for you to honour your obligations.'

Ninian sniffed back a tear. 'Oh, Columba! Columba!' she thought. 'If only you were here now to give me courage.'

But he was in Rome. Perhaps at this very moment he was kneeling before His Holiness, being restored to all the honours that had been so unjustly taken away from him.

Ninian, reared in a town that, during the decades of the Avignon papacy, had been the country retreat of cardinals and popes, knew a great deal about the intricate manoeuvrings that went on in church circles, and some of them seemed to her highly reprehensible. She had always thought it very noble of Columba to say that Holy Father could not be expected to be aware of every minor detail and that, sometimes, there was bound to be injustice. Especially noble, when Holy Father's ignorance had meant that for two whole years Columba had been reduced almost to penury through being deprived of his benefices.

Though she had always thought that, for him, that hadn't been the worst of it. What had come near to breaking Columba's heart had been his exile from Rome and the curia, which were his spiritual home in far more than the obvious sense.

She said, 'Oof!' as her gentlewoman tugged at a thick strand of front hair, trying to weave it into the gold fillet on her brow while she herself held the rest of her hair back with one hand and, at the same time, struggled to fit rings on it with the other.

Just then, two things happened at once. From somewhere down the hill there came the flourish of trumpets that heralded the approach of an important visitor, and from much closer at hand Séverine's voice said calmly, 'Ninian, *ma petite*, it would make me so very happy if you could bring yourself, just occasionally, you understand – I try never to ask the impossible – to accept that time does not stretch like the strings of your clairrsack. Shall I ever cure you of being late?'

She waved Ninian's women away and, swiftly and skilfully, reduced the red-gold hair to order. Nothing and no one argued with Séverine when she chose to exert herself.

Breathlessly, Ninian said, 'Clarsach, pronounced clarsha. Anyway, you're thinking of a harp. It has gut strings, not brass wires, and . . .' Séverine looked at her, and she backed hurriedly towards the door. 'And gut has *much* more stretch!'

They had just reached the foot of the winding staircase when they heard Sir Harry Graham and his escort dismounting in the main courtyard. Ninian hesitated only for a moment and then, picking up her skirts, fled through the arched passageway towards the inner court.

Séverine, following more slowly, raised eyebrows that would have been strong and dark if they had not been plucked to modish invisibility, and opened her mouth to speak, but Ninian forestalled her. 'I know,' she gasped, hastily disposing gown and sleeves to their best advantage. 'It is not *comme il faut* for a lady to gallop!' And then she smiled rather weakly at Séverine, and Séverine smiled back.

She was ready just in time – a model of demure young womanhood, seated on a carved stone bench by a tinkling fountain, toying idly with a single rose as she waited for her lover.

There was the soft, leathery scuffing of footsteps on the cobbles, and a jangle of spurs echoing through the arch. Ninian could hear the cheerful, devil-may-care voice of Séverine's elder son, Adam, and another voice, less assured and unmistakably Scottish. She gulped, and waited to see the man who held her future in his hands.

And as she waited, she thought again, 'Oh, Columba! Columba! If only you were here to give me strength!'

5

COLUMBA lowered his lips to the papal slipper with some difficulty, resigned to the fact that his figure wasn't what it had been. But he didn't grudge the effort. All his mind, all his ambitions for the last two years had been directed towards this moment, and on his face was an expression of the most profound thanksgiving.

He was aware that dispassionate observers like Dean Myrton and Bishop-elect Cameron might think he was giving it too much play, but he knew Pope Martin V better than they did, and Martin had one very human weakness – he liked to be appreciated. Columba's own career as an official of the papal court, which had ended so abruptly two years before, had flourished not only because he was an able man and a clever one, but because he had a talent amounting to genius for conveying appreciation to the right person, in the right way, and at the right time. No one could ever have described him as obsequious; it was simply that he believed in giving honour where honour was due.

And now his moment had come. The moment when His Holiness would restore to him all that had been taken from him.

He raised his head and found that the pope was smiling, and in the sudden silence that followed the noon bells, the calm, compelling voice spoke the words Columba had been waiting to hear.

'To you, William Columba Crozier, our son and faithful servant, we restore all the benefices of which we deprived you two years since. The faults you then committed were faults not of the spirit but of worldly judgement, and we have been persuaded, through the intercession of our dear cousin King James of Scotland, that they have now been expiated.'

Columba knew, and he had often wondered whether His Holiness also knew, that his real fault had been that he had happened to be the only convenient scapegoat at the time. He had been accused of losing or misappropriating an important document. It wasn't true. He knew precisely where the document was, and under whose surplice it had

39

been smuggled out of the registry. But one of the cardinals was involved, and Columba knew better than to say so. There had been nothing he could do but throw himself on Martin's generosity, and because it had been one of those occasions when the curia seemed to consist entirely of wheels within wheels, his plea had been rejected.

Columba had never resented it. To anyone who was anyone in the church, loss of papal favour was as much an occupational hazard as loss of royal favour to those who consorted with kings. But now, on his knees, he made an implacable resolve. Never again would he permit anything that was his to be taken from him.

The pope, his smile still on Columba, extended a hand for the parchment his datary was holding out to him, and after a moment his voice resumed, 'We restore you, then, to the canonry of Dunkeld in Scotland, the rectories of Kirkgunzeon and Fetteresso, the archdeaconry of Teviotdale . . .'

The words rang in Columba's ears like a *Te Deum*, even though his thoughts were, shamefully, much more of the world than of the spirit.

He had first entered the church, as so many men did, not because he had a true religious vocation – that had come later – but because only the church offered any prospect of advancement to an ambitious, well-born, but impoverished youth. And despite the fact that he had done well, it was still the case that, after almost twenty-five years, not only his reputation but his entire income depended on the benefices the pope saw fit to grant him.

Popes had their own way of rewarding their servants. It would have been unseemly to offer anything as crass as money to men who had dedicated themselves body and soul to the glory of God, so those whom the pope wished to honour were endowed, instead, with one or more of such church livings as happened to be vacant at the time. No one expected the beneficiary to live in his benefice, or even to visit it if he didn't want to; all he had to do was appoint a proctor to look after his pastoral duties in his absence. In such cases, the responsibilities that went with a benefice were regarded as more symbolic than real.

But the income was real enough, and it was paid by the parish.

It was a highly ingenious system, enabling His Holiness to dispense the most tangible marks of his favour in a way that didn't cost the papal treasury a penny. Columba deeply admired whoever had first thought of it.

No benefice, however, was for life, and what could be given could as easily be taken away. For two years now Columba had existed on his reserves, which were not great, for he had always lived up to his income. The most painful part of it all had been his inability to give anything more than love to those who were closest to him, to that small group of people who inspired in him the kind of fierce and obsessive passion that a true son of the church was supposed to feel only for Christ. Columba knew that in this he sinned, but he was powerless to change it.

Now, with a warm and pleasurable excitement, he began to review his fortunes again, and to think, first and most urgently, what he could give his adored Ninian as a wedding gift. What should it be, what should he buy her with the tithes of Kirkgunzeon and Fetteresso, Dunkeld and Teviotdale?

Suddenly, he became aware that the pope's voice had ceased, and that there had been a note of finality in it. But there couldn't have been. He stared at the Holy Father, and went on staring. He willed him to say something more. Something like, 'We restore you also, William Columba Crozier, our son and faithful servant, to the position of trust which you formerly held here in the curia of the Holy See, that you may serve us once again as acolyte and nuncio, as judge delegate, as emissary to our vicar-general at Avignon, and in any other role in which we see fit to employ you. Our blessing be upon you. Go with God, my son.'

But the words remained unspoken, and the pope, still smiling, inclined his head dismissively.

The Ghiberti tiara was really beautiful, chased with gold leaves and elegant little figures in full relief. Columba wondered what had happened to the other, pearl-encrusted one that Martin had got back from Giovanni de Medici only by threatening to excommunicate him. You could never trust a banker.

Columba rose, and kissed the ring, and backed away from the throne.

His mind was reeling. If he had no position at the curia, it meant he had no excuse for staying in Rome. It meant that the rules had changed – that the responsibilities that went with his benefices were no longer just symbolic. Now, he would be expected to take himself off to Scotland and devote his life to ministering to a pack of illiterate peasants and their scarcely more literate overlords.

To Kirkgunzeon, under the bellicose thumb of the Douglasses; to Dunkeld, with that pig-headed old ruffian, the Earl of Atholl, meddling in everything he did; to Teviotdale, with Bishop Gavin's cold grey eyes watching every move he made. And in the rain, too.

Columba could have sat down and wept, but instead he summoned up all his dignity and charm and made his way slowly, and with many pauses to receive congratulation, across the audience chamber to where the Bishop-elect of Glasgow – Columba's erstwhile pupil, and now his master – was standing with the dean of his cathedral beside him.

6

TOM MYRTON didn't blink under Gavin's penetrating gaze, but said merely, 'Aye, weel. That's "our dear cousin King James" got both of you back into the pope's good books. Wonderful what a wee bit of family feeling can do.'

'Family feeling? Cutthroat bargaining, more like. How much did you have to pay?'

The dean was offended. 'Pay?' he said. 'I maybe mentioned that James had a notion of endowing a monastery or two . . .'

He glowered up into the lean, dark, formidable face above him. Gavin Cameron, with his austere manner, his sparing habit of speech and far from sparing efficiency, was very good at demoralizing people, but not Tom, who was twenty years his senior and loved him like a son, even if he was careful not to show it. Gavin could be a wee thing unpredictable in the matter of human relationships.

'Anyway,' Tom said, 'what have you got to complain about?'

'What have I got to complain about? You know damned well. Teviotdale's in my diocese, and what I do *not* require is an archdeacon who spends all his time trying to bribe his way out of it and back to Rome. He's supposed to be one of my two chief administrative officers. He's supposed to be "the bishop's eye" in the whole eastern half of the diocese. He's supposed to stand in for me when I'm away. But would you care to wager on what Columba Crozier will get up to the minute I turn my back? I thought we'd agreed you shouldn't ask for his reinstatement?'

'Aye, weel. We may propose, but others dispose. The Earl of Mar was awfu' keen, and our royal lord and master didn't feel it would be politic to say him nay.'

Gavin, his lips tight, watched Archdeacon Crozier smilingly acknowledge the felicitations of a grave, sharp-nosed, expensively-cloaked cardinal.

'Gabriel Condulmer. He knows all the right people, doesn't he. Have you worked out how much those benefices of his are worth to him? A hundred and fifty pounds a year?' A seventh, near enough, of what Gavin was going to have to run the whole Glasgow diocese on.

'Something like that,' murmured Tom, who didn't need an abacus to keep track of figures. 'He can go back to living in style again. But do him justice, Gavin. At least he didn't buy his benefices, or bribe his way into them, like most folk. He's done something to earn them.'

To Gavin, the mere mention of trading in benefices – what the Scots called barratry, and others called simony – was like a red rag to a bull. It wasn't the morality of it that riled him. It was the astronomical total in gold and silver that was drained out of a chronically insolvent Scotland every year by priests who spent it at Rome, buying preferment.

'You think so?' he said. 'Perhaps. But if that wily old bird *has* earned his benefices, it's only because he couldn't afford to buy them!'

Tom scratched the tip of his nose delicately. 'Prejudice, Gavin. Prejudice. That's no way to speak of a fine man like Archdeacon Crozier.' And then, because he himself had entered the world a good few years before Archdeacon Crozier, he added *sotto voce*, 'Forbye, he's not old.'

7

TOM could see at once that the archdeacon knew Gavin wasn't going to give in to the Crozier charm without a struggle. But he persevered. Mary Mother, how he persevered! As the two men made their way – one of them tall, lean and vigorous, the other an inch or two shorter and a foot wider round the middle – through the arcaded, spiral-columned cloister, past the chapter house, along the tree-lined path, and out at last into the reverberant city streets, Tom trotted along behind, enjoying himself hugely.

All cities smelled, and all were crowded, but Rome was in a class of its own. It wasn't just crammed with people; it seethed with activity like a wasps' nest on a summer evening. Sturdy, black-clad women haggled with food vendors over pastries and sausages and spices. Masons dripping with compasses, scabbling axes, and plumb-bob squares shouted at labourers perched unsteadily aloft with hods of mortar and buckets of bricks. Carpenters cut themselves a path through the throng with lengths of scaffolding borne like battering rams. Itinerant pedlars screeched their wares, and public criers bellowed the news of events past and to come. Pilgrims with scrips and burdons begged their bread – though Tom would have been surprised if even one in a thousand of those who carried palm branches had ever been near Jerusalem. The halt, the sick, and the blind clamoured pathetically from every church porch. And always, and everywhere, there were the bells.

Tom had his eyes on a big lout of a peasant, who had just slipped on a piece of soap and was waggling a threatening fist at its owner – one of the sick, frothing piteously at the mouth – when he heard the archdeacon remark to Gavin, 'How much I regret that force of circumstances should have kept me abroad during the period of your Lordship's – ahhh – meteoric rise to distinction.'

The sentiment was irreproachable, and so was the manner of its utterance, but it had not the slightest effect on the bishop-elect, who sidestepped a bad-tempered-looking mule lurching along under a mountain of herbs and greenstuffs, and replied briskly, 'We will, however, see much of each other in the future.' And that was blunt enough, Tom thought, inwardly smiling. Gavin wasn't one to waste time or energy beating about the bush.

It seemed, however, that the archdeacon had no intention of being put out of countenance by someone fifteen years his junior, however – ahhh – meteoric his rise to distinction. Bending a look of dignified melancholy on the begging bowl a cripple was holding out before him, he sailed majestically round it and said, 'What a stimulating prospect! I cannot tell you how much I look forward to it.'

Tom's snort of laughter was quickly suppressed, but it had been enough to attract the archdeacon's attention. He glanced back, and Tom thought what an imposing head he had, with its beak of a nose and the thick, grey brows overhanging eyes that, though shrewd and observant, were of a pale and almost innocent blue in the sun-browned face. The eyes crinkled, and the archdeacon said, 'I am ashamed. I seem to have omitted to thank the dean for placing my case before His Holiness. In fact, if it had not been for you, Dean Myrton, I fear I should have had to wait many more weary months before it was decided I had been punished enough.'

Tom hesitated, turning a dour eye on the water seller who was dripping all over his foot, and then succumbed to temptation. 'Och, dinnae thank me,' he said in his thickest Glasgow accent. 'Thank His Majesty and m'lord o' Mar. It wuz their view that a clever body like y'rsel sh'd be wurkin' at hame for his countrymen's souls, not footerin' aboot at Rome, runnin' the messages.'

The archdeacon's armour wasn't, it seemed, impenetrable after all. The smile still didn't falter, but Dean Myrton could see him mentally translating the half-forgotten tongue and disliking the result.

Reflecting that he could probably be had up for blasphemy for describing a papal acolyte as if he were an errand boy, Tom glanced at Gavin and very nearly disgraced himself. For on the face of the bishop-elect was an expression of the most profound displeasure. He was staring fixedly at a group of ladies, jewelled, painted, and inviting, who were heading purposefully for a corner of the piazza crowded with men in clerical robes, black, white, grey, drab, and scarlet. Only a babe in arms could have mistaken what they had in mind.

But though Gavin was staring at them, Tom knew that he wasn't seeing them. What his fearsome expression usually meant was that he was struggling with an insane desire to laugh.

Tom knew it, but Columba Crozier didn't, and he drew his own conclusions. Looking back many years later, he was to regret, very deeply, the estimate of Gavin Cameron he formed in that moment. But by then it was much too late.

Fortunately, perhaps, it was time for their ways to part. Columba, courteous to the last, said, 'Is it too soon to ask, or has a date yet been set for your lordship's consecration at Glasgow?'

'Early in the New Year,' Gavin replied. 'I have a few outstanding matters to deal with here at the curia, and then I return to Scotland by way of France. What of your own plans? I would like you settled in Teviotdale as soon as possible. There is a good deal to do there.'

'I am sure there is. But with your lordship's permission, I should like to spend a few days at Villeneuve on my way back to Scotland.'

'Villeneuve? Which Villeneuve?' France was even fuller of Villeneuves than Scotland was of Newtowns.

For the first time, there was a trace of genuine humour in Archdeacon Crozier's smile. 'The only one the Holy See can be relied on to recognize – the one across the Rhône from Avignon. I have a niece there who is very dear to me, and who is to be married soon. She has asked me to give her my blessing.'

'You have permission.' Without thinking, and without any real interest, Gavin asked, 'She marries a Frenchman?'

'No, no. A Scot. Sir Harry Graham of Dess.'

Gavin's expression didn't change, nor did his eyes even flicker in Tom Myrton's direction. All he said was, 'One of the Grahams? Indeed. We must wish her happy. And now, good day to you, archdeacon. Go with God.'

CHAPTER TWO

I

IT was twenty-three years now since Benedict XIII, ninth and last of the Avignon popes, had fled like a thief in the night from the massive, imposing, honey-gold palace on the heights above the Rhône. But not until three years ago had he obliged everybody by dying. He had been ninety-four years old by then, devout, indomitable, and crafty as ever – and still calling down anathemas on the man who had usurped his right to the throne of St Peter. All the nations of the Christian world had breathed one huge, collective sigh of relief.

Few people spoke of Benedict nowadays, and when they did it was with anger or contempt, and only by his personal name of Pedro de Luna. But Columba still thought of him as Benedict, still remembered the cold, dead hours of that cold, dark night in March 1403, when he himself had been nineteen, and a student, and one of the handful of men who had helped smuggle Benedict out of the Palace of the Popes, through the city gate, and away to the blessed refuge of the waiting barge with the fourteen oars that would carry him to safety. Another of the men had been Pierre de Verne, and it had been on that night that Columba had met Sévèrine for the first time.

Sometimes, even now, Columba felt sad that it had been Rome, not Avignon, that had triumphed in the end, because insofar as it was in him to idolize any man, he had idolized Benedict. But Christendom had united at last to depose 'the anti-pope', and even Scotland and Aragon, Benedict's last supporters, had abandoned him. As had Columba.

Now, he gazed out towards Avignon from the turret of the Vernes' *livrée* in Villeneuve, his eyes narrowed against the newly risen sun. Though his view was interrupted by the buildings that meandered round the river-washed skirts of Mount Andaon and up to the Fort of St André, he could just see the machicolated top of the bell tower of the great palace on the other side of the Rhône, still standing square and solid against the aquamarine sky despite the battles that had been fought around it.

Avignon was a mournful place these days, he thought, for when Benedict had gone, so too had gone almost a century of power and glory and riches. Now, the city felt like some vast, reproachful relic, a gritty sandstone monument to the divided past that Rome, which had inherited it, wanted only to forget.

Odd that Villeneuve had suffered so much less than Avignon – neat, smart little Villeneuve, the new town that was still on the itinerary of merchants heading for the great fairs of Montpellier and Beaucaire; still on the pilgrim route to Santiago de Compostela; still of the greatest military importance to France. And though the cardinals, no lovers of lost causes, had decamped from Avignon long before Benedict himself, the *livrées* they had built across the river remained – the 'country' houses in which they had found refuge from the constraints of life at the Palace of the Popes. The *livrée* now owned by the Vernes had belonged originally to Cardinal Guy de Bologne, and to other cardinals, later. Cardinals of the church came and went, as did popes, and bishops – and archdeacons.

From the church of Notre Dame, a few hundred yards away, the Ave Maria bell rang out – thick, metallic, unmelodious – drowning all the other bells from other churches that followed it, raggedly tolling out the same call to prayer. Small bells, large bells, sweet bells, strident bells, high-pitched bells, low-pitched bells, each of them sounding the three familiar strokes three times, and then the slow and measured nine. Columba's reverie was broken. Instinctively, he bent his head and began to murmur his prayers.

He was still there thirty minutes later when an exasperated Sévèrine found him. '*Mon Dieu!*' she exclaimed. 'I arrange for you a special and most charming breakfast of celebration so that you may break to us the happy news about the restoration of your benefices, which we know already. And are you there? No, you are not. Is my dear son

Adam there? No, he is not. Is my guest, the Lady Elinor, there? Alas, yes she is. I would be so very much obliged if you would come and deal with her. Blane is ignoring her, Harry Graham flinches every time she looks at him – as if she were about to bite him! – and she is by no means the kind of young woman who will permit another woman to guide her.'

He marvelled, as he always did, at how little Sévèrine had changed over the years since they had first met. She had been fifteen, then, a wife but not a mother; there had been something wrong with Pierre, so that the children they conceived had never come to birth. And now she was thirty-eight, her warm skin still clear and smooth, the heavy-lidded gaze as sardonic, the mouth firmer than it had been, but still shapely. Her black hair, with its betraying hint of grey, was hidden as usual under a fashionable headdress, a cloud of white veiling thrown over a wired framework that perched above her brow like the horns of a small but mettlesome bull. 'It is the mode,' she said when he remarked on it, as if that settled everything.

She was thin, still – too thin, he had always thought – in her low-necked black gown with the white-lined sleeves that fell from wrist and shoulder like the blossoms of some great arum lily. Since Pierre de Verne had died a dozen years ago, she had never worn anything other than black or white. It amused her, she said – shocking Columba just a little – to play the virtuous widow as she had always played the virtuous wife.

'The Lady Elinor?' he said, after a moment. 'Yes.' He had arrived late last night, and it had been a disagreeable shock to discover not only that Sévèrine had another, unexpected guest, but that it was the wife of the young man who – until King James's queen succeeded in bearing her husband a son – was second in line to inherit the throne of Scotland. In Columba's experience, close acquaintance with royalty was productive of more headaches than it cured, especially when the royalty concerned was a footloose and flighty young woman.

'Yes,' he said again. 'Tiresome, is she? From what I know, that is by no means her only failing. How in the world did Adam come to invite her here? And how in the world' – his warm, ironic smile robbed the words of offence – 'did she come to accept?'

Sévèrine shrugged. 'She was visiting the vicomtesse at Uzès, and found it boring. An insufficiency, I suspect, of knights and squires. But she cannot return to Scotland until her escorting party arrives – which should be any day now, I am enchanted to discover.'

Columba took her elbow, his rueful frown giving way to the expression of lofty benevolence he was in the habit of adopting when he intended strong men to quail before him. Which, as Sévèrine reflected amusedly, they usually did.

'Then, in the meantime,' he said, 'let us see what the power of the church can do.'

2

WHEN the cardinals had built their *livrées*, they had prudently re-inforced the divine protection to which they were entitled with good, sound, stone-and-mortar fortifications. The countryside then, as now, had been infested with freebooters – the Routiers – who were not only ambitious but uncomfortably well-disciplined, and as likely to hold a whole castle or town to ransom as to squander time and energy on a solitary wayfarer. Unless the wayfarer looked rich, of course. Sévèrine had absolutely forbidden Ninian ever to venture outside the walls of the *livrée* unless she was accompanied by half a dozen servants, armed to the teeth. It was the one subject on which she was inflexible.

At times, Ninian felt disagreeably hemmed in. There wasn't even space within the walls for a garden, and the charming little pleasance Sévèrine had created outside – across the road that linked Notre Dame with the Carthusian monastery of the Val de Bénédiction – was just as much out of bounds without an escort as anywhere else. But there at least, on special days like today, the armed retainers stayed discreetly out of sight.

It was to be a very intimate family party, with no knights or squires or yeoman servants, no gentlewomen, no ladies-in-waiting, no carvers or cup-bearers or servers, no marshal of the hall. Only Sévèrine, Columba and Ninian; Sévèrine's two sons, Adam and Blane; and the three inescapable guests – Lady Elinor, Ninian's husband-to-be Sir Harry Graham, and his twenty-year-old cousin Malise Graham, Earl of Strathearn. They were all, with rare informality, going to serve themselves.

Even so, everyone was in the finery suitable for a grand occasion, because Columba liked to see those he loved dressed richly and with style. Ninian was wearing her favourite gown of the rich, clear blue that matched her eyes. It was deeply V-necked and embroidered in gold, and her waist-long hair, intricately braided in front, fell loose and curling at the back under a cloud of gold veiling. Lady Elinor, herself an ethereal vision in creamy gossamer silks, had looked at the neckline with an absence of expression so complete as to be insulting, and Ninian had been sorely tempted to retaliate by commiserating with her on having no bosom to display.

Séverine's little pleasance was a true Paradise Garden, set in a natural dell where the ground dropped sharply away from the road, and she had filled it with sweet-scented roses growing on trellises, and with lemon and peach trees that at this season of the year were heavy with fruit. A sundial gleamed gold on its column of Parian marble, and a fountain sent up jets of crystal into the early-morning sun, misting the grass and the meadow flowers that starred it so that they shone bright as enamel against the carefully tended green.

At the end of the garden farthest from the road the steward was casting a final, critical eye over the table the servants had just finished laying, a table set with all the dishes proper to an alfresco breakfast – jellies and brawns, fruits and leavened breads, custards and fried creams, and a whole roast peacock in its plumage, its beak brightly gilt. Ninian didn't like peacock very much and neither did Séverine; it was always tough and dry, no matter what the cooks did with it. But it had a festive air and that, they had decided, was what mattered today. Seated on the grass among the flowers, Ninian wished Columba and Séverine – and Adam, too – would hurry up. She was hungry.

Harry Graham was sitting beside her, unrelaxed and clearly ill at ease. They should have been making merry, frivolous small talk, but Ninian, her mind half on breakfast and half on Columba, whom she had not seen since he arrived, was tired of small talk. In two whole weeks, she and Harry had not progressed beyond it, and little of it had been merry and none of it frivolous. Harry was a very staid young man. So she had sent a servant to bring her clarsach from the house and was singing softly as she played. Her breath control, thanks to the tightness of her bodice, was less than perfect, but she was managing to hit most of the notes she was aiming at.

'. . . The king of Scotland dreamed a dream, of the fairest maid the sun had seen . . .'

No one was listening but Harry.

Blane de Verne, Séverine's dark, boisterous, nineteen-year-old younger son, was standing over by the slope up to the road, fidgeting, tossing his dagger up in the air and catching it by the hilt as it fell. Lady

Elinor – Ninian couldn't understand why Adam should be so besotted by her – was leaning against the sundial with her mind ostentatiously elsewhere, looking as pale, willowy, and supercilious as a tomb effigy. And Harry's cousin Malise, having just had his nose snapped off by her ladyship – whose tongue was a good deal less refined than her looks – had speared a fat slice of brawn from the table and retired sulkily to the furthest corner of the garden to eat it.

Although Malise was bigger than Harry, and four years younger, they were very much alike. Both were fair-skinned, brown-haired, hazel-eyed and muscularly built. They carried themselves well enough, too, though Ninian couldn't judge whether the hint of slouch about their shoulders was a result of too much time in the saddle or simply an optical illusion caused by the bag-shaped sleeves of their low-waisted, full-cut, and frankly bourgeois-looking tunics. She had decided she didn't like northern fashions very much.

What she hadn't decided yet was how alike the two young men were in temperament. It wasn't difficult to read Malise, who was transparently kind-hearted – not to mention opinionated, inquisitive, sanctimonious, impossibly naïve, and as hard to ignore as an unschooled puppy. Ninian, striving for tolerance, thought that many of his failings might be put down to the fact that he had been orphaned at thirteen and neglected ever since by his guardian, the Earl of Atholl, who was his mother's uncle and also, by a typically Scottish quirk of fate, Lady Elinor's father-in-law. Malise, like Harry, had known and disliked her ladyship for years, and their feelings were only too obviously reciprocated.

Harry himself was more opaque. Ninian had no way of knowing what lay behind the rather oppressive propriety, the conscientious attention to doing what was right in everything – even to praising the insignificant talents of his wife-to-be. She didn't think anyone could be as correct as that all the way through, but suspected she wouldn't find out the truth of him until she saw him at home, in his own country.

Her country, too, though she hadn't been there since she was a baby and remembered it not at all. Columba had summed it up for her once, and it didn't sound very appealing. 'Moors and mountains, rain and snow. Edinburgh is its largest city, with about as many people in it as you might expect to find in a decent-sized French monastery. Most Scots live in turf huts and burn a kind of black stone to keep warm, because of the shortage of wood. A country, *ma petite*,' he had concluded sorrowfully, 'where a man of culture might die a lingering death from intellectual starvation if the climate didn't kill him first. It is very unlike France.'

The verse ended, and Harry said with impeccable promptitude, 'Play some more. You play so beautifully. You do everything so well.'

Ninian, wishing it were true, dutifully picked up the plectrum again. But before she could begin, he stopped her. 'What were you thinking about just now?'

It was so unexpected, so stiffly spoken and yet so prying, that she was momentarily at a loss. It hadn't even occurred to her that he might notice.

It wouldn't do – it most certainly wouldn't do – to say she had been feeling suffocatingly bored and wishing that Columba or Adam would appear. Séverine had warned her that her attachment to them was something of which Harry might easily become jealous.

'I was thinking . . . I was thinking about Villeneuve, I suppose, and Avignon. About the sun, and the colours and the – the clarity of it all. And about how little I remember of Scotland. I haven't seen it since I was a child.'

'You mustn't think Scotland is any less beautiful than France,' he said defensively. 'In fact, I believe it to be both more beautiful and more colourful, and it is certainly fresher and more invigorating. Though as for the sun . . .' It sounded as if he thought the sun was slightly immoral but didn't want to say so for fear of upsetting her.

Since the only choice seemed to lie between laughing and bursting into tears, Ninian laughed. 'My father always said that it wasn't duty, or money, or the joy of fighting that persuaded him to come to France in the Dauphin's service. Just the weather!'

Harry's 'Mmmm' suggested that he thought the late Sir Thomas guilty of something very near treason, but all he said was, 'Does it distress you that I'm taking you home, instead of staying here? I know there are a lot of Scots in the French service but, although you might not think it to look at me, I am not the kind of man who fights, either abroad or at home, just for the pleasure of it.'

Ninian couldn't imagine him doing anything just for the pleasure of it.

He went on, 'I also believe that it is a man's duty to look after his estates himself. But I would be sorry if you didn't like it. It may sound strange, considering that we are not very well acquainted yet . . .' He had been looking down at his hands, and when he raised his head again his face was scarlet and his expression that of a man steeling himself to say something shameful. 'But I think I am' – he cleared his throat loudly enough to cause Lady Elinor to turn a languid head – 'in love with you. And we must be happy, mustn't we, if you love me, too?'

Ninian blinked. It seemed to be the happiness he was asking about, not whether she loved him. Gloomily, she supposed he must be taking that for granted.

She should have answered at once, but she didn't. She would have been bound to come out with something like, 'We-e-e-ll – I hope so', and that wouldn't have done at all. Sévèrine was always imploring her not to say the first thing that came into her head. 'A sweet and deceitful tongue. A style that flatters. These are what society requires of a woman, and we cannot change it. Accept the reality, *ma petite*, for your own sake, and try to be more submissive. When you are as old as I am, you may be as frank and independent as you choose, but not until then.'

Since she admired and loved Sévèrine almost as much as she did Columba, Ninian summoned up a smile and began to play again and sing, her voice sweetly confiding as if she were giving Harry his answer through the song.

' . . . *Amo dioric badutala, etzaizia-iduri* . . .' Such love I feel for you, do you not know it?

She wasn't sure why the old Basque lyric had suggested itself to her, unless it was because a Scotsman who scarcely even spoke French couldn't be expected to understand it. It seemed to make it less dishonest, somehow.

If only it were true. She had always been romantic, had always believed everything the troubadours said or sang about chivalry and courtly love. Since as far back as she could remember, she had been captivated by the oft-told tale of the fair, handsome, impoverished squire who adored a high-born and unattainable lady. It was the squire's perennial fate to set out, with only his sword and his own high heart to sustain him, to brave all the perils of the known world and so make himself worthy of her, and Ninian had always shed tears enough to fill the well of Saint-Jean when he emerged from his final ordeal and swept the lady into his embrace at last.

When she was a child, it had confused her that the only reason why the lovely, high-born, unattainable lady *was* unattainable was because of her rank. No one seemed in the least concerned about the fact that she had a husband already. It was only a story, she had said to Columba once, so wouldn't it be much more satisfactory for all concerned if the squire and the lady were free to wed and live happily ever after?

She knew now that there were many answers Columba might have given her, but what he had said, with the infectious chuckle that only those who were dear to him ever heard, was, 'Well, you know, however brave this hero of yours may be, he doesn't sound to me like the kind of man the Medici or the Lombards would choose to extend credit to. And marriage is a commercial contract like any other. Rank and property are what matter, not love. Besides, my pet, love is a brittle plant, and it breaks if it's tied.'

What Columba said had to be true, because it was Columba who said it, but Ninian had a stubborn streak. Tilting her chin bravely, she had announced, 'Well, I am going to be different. If I can't marry for love, I shan't marry at all.' Columba had laughed, and hugged her, and his eyes had been wet.

But though it sounded all very fine to say she wouldn't marry without love, she was human, after all. Her parents had betrothed her to Sir Harry Graham when she was seven, but she had managed to postpone the marriage itself for four years, until, quite suddenly, the politely barbed remarks and ambivalent glances to which a seventeen-year-old virgin was inevitably exposed had become too much for her. She had begun to think that, since she was getting quite old and her ideal lover still showed no signs of materializing, perhaps Sévèrine was right and she ought to let the marriage go ahead.

And then Adam – who, for want of anything better to do, had decided it might be amusing to handle the negotiations – had told her carelessly that Harry Graham was tall-ish, and fair-ish, and good-looking enough, if you cared for the type.

And because she was Ninian Drummond, and romantic, she had instantly succeeded in persuading herself that when she saw her husband-to-be, she would fall in love at last.

She had been wrong, even though he was, indeed, good-looking enough, and twenty-three years old, and well born, and by no means poor. And abysmally dull. So here she was, in spite of everything, on the brink of an arranged marriage just like any other arranged marriage. It was very discouraging.

Sévèrine said she should be grateful Sir Harry wasn't forty years old, and fat, and incapable, which would have been more than possible when so many women died in childbed and so many men worked their way through three or four wives in a lifetime. It was perfectly true.

Just yesterday, Ninian had decided to try again; to stop comparing Harry with Columba, and with the incomparable Adam, even with tiresome but red-blooded Blane. It wasn't fair to an ordinary, inoffensive young man to judge him against that kind of competition.

Interrupting her song for a moment, she said impulsively, 'Of course we will be happy, Harry. For you truly are my Very Perfect Gentle Knight!' And then, with a faintly embarrassed giggle, she added, 'And I promise not to be your Lady Unattainable!'

He took it with a smile that had more than a trace of condescension in it, which Ninian found exceedingly irritating.

So, a little hastily, because the sun was getting hot and she didn't want her hand held in Harry's large, damp grasp, she resumed her singing.

'... *Zure gatic igaran nezake, itchassoa igheri* ...' For you I would swim the seas ...

Grimly, she hoped she wouldn't have to. It was a long, wet, weary, way to her new home in Scotland.

3

COLUMBA cast a single, comprehensive glance round the garden and smothered a grimace of amusement.

It should have been an idyllic picture, straight out of the pages of an illuminated manuscript. Everything was there under the pale, clear, cloudless sky – the silver and the gold, the jewel-bright colours, the damasked doublets and the broidered gowns, the whole reassuring ambience of formality and delicately ordered luxury. But despite it, and despite the flowery, fruity, spicy scents that floated so soothingly on the calm, warm air, the atmosphere was far from lightsome.

It was clear to Columba at once that Blane – always happier in a tavern or at a tourney than in his mother's garden – was on the *qui vive* about something. Which probably spelled trouble; it usually did. The boy hadn't even noticed that he had arrived.

Ninian had, though. She was smiling at him with that vivid, conspiratorial smile that always lit candles in his heart. He was an emotional man, he knew, even in a world that revelled in emotion, but he could not regret it. He smiled back at her with his eyes, and then bowed briefly to the young man by her side – Harry Graham, he assumed – who had struggled to his feet and was making a profound obeisance.

The other, larger young man with the sullen expression must be Malise Graham, Earl of Strathearn. The Graham family, although not one of the noblest in Scotland, had ramifications that, even in a country where second cousins three times removed were regarded as close kin, were very intricate indeed. Columba could think of several members of the family whom he'd be interested to have in the confessional.

And then Sévèrine led him towards Lady Elinor, who bestirred herself sufficiently to drop him a negligent curtsey. He raised his brows a fraction and was gratified to see the curtsey deepen. 'An honour,' he said, 'to have such a charming representative of the royal house of Stewart here in Villeneuve-lès-Avignon.'

Her head tilted a little, and she looked again at the priest in the orthodox cap and plain long robe, noting that the robe was of velvet and its sleeves trimmed with miniver, and that the high-nosed face was not the face of a pious ascetic. It was nothing unusual to find a Scots cleric who was experienced, but rare indeed to find one with polish. Most of them, in Lady Elinor's opinion, were impossibly crude. She liked men with style, and condescended to give Columba the faint curving of the lips that was her equivalent of a social smile.

His suave voice continued, 'I am, of course, acquainted with your father-in-law, my lord of Atholl.' And a rough old diamond he was, to put it charitably. 'I imagine your husband's continuing imprisonment by the English must distress him as deeply as it does you.'

It was a sadly commonplace remark, and Lady Elinor was disappointed. How would this worldly-wise priest respond, she wondered, if she answered with the brutal truth – that Atholl's distress came in fits and starts, like indigestion, and that she herself felt nothing but relief at being free from a husband who was inadequate on every count, in bed and out of it. Coolly, she made the conventional answer to the archdeacon's conventional remark. 'Of course,' she said. 'We both feel the lack of his presence very deeply.'

Sévèrine had heard considerably more than enough about Lady Elinor's paragon of a husband. 'I think,' she intervened, 'that perhaps we should not postpone breakfast until Adam arrives; the young people must be hungry.' Then, seeing her ladyship's pale mouth harden at the implication that Sévèrine did not consider her one of the 'young people', she went on smoothly, 'I imagine Adam will appear at the precise moment when we have decided to give him up. He always does. It is the one thing in which he is predictable.'

Neatly, she began to steer Lady Elinor towards the table. 'So sad that the king has been unable to arrange for your husband's release.' It was said in a tone designed to put an end to the conversation, but Lady Elinor disliked Séverine, as she disliked all women, especially when they were handsome and assured and tried to manipulate her.

So she ignored the tone and took up the words. Her bleached brows rising, she said, 'Not yet, certainly. But there are negotiations. There are always negotiations . . .'

And always would be, Columba thought drily, as her ladyship talked on, and on, and on. The Master of Atholl was in English hands not because he was a prisoner of war, but because he was King James's cousin; in fact, he wasn't a prisoner at all, but a hostage.

James himself had been captured by the English as a boy of twelve, and had spent the next eighteen years of his life in and out of the Tower of London until, two years ago, the English had grown tired of the game and decided to let him go. But at a price, and a high one. A ransom of £40,000 in English coin, payable in six annual instalments with, as surety in the meantime, a full £40,000-worth of hostages to be held in English keeping.

It was a clever notion. At one blow, it had removed twenty-seven of Scotland's richest, most distinguished, and potentially most belligerent barons from circulation, among them the Master of Atholl.

It seemed likely that some of the hostages, at least, would stay out of circulation for a good deal more than six years, because James had so far managed to pay no more than part of the first instalment of the ransom, and no one knew where the rest of it was coming from.

Even so, the English had magnanimously allowed the eleven least valuable hostages to return home last year in exchange for others of similar worth. Magnanimously? Columba wondered about that. The English were cleverer than most Scots gave them credit for. James had been forced to spend so much time bullying eleven of his other lords into agreeing to act as replacements, and so much more time negotiating with London over whether they were acceptable or not, that he'd been left with very little leisure for governing the country. Which suited the English admirably, because confusion and discord within Scotland relieved them of the need to keep one wary eye always on the Borders.

It was rumoured that more negotiations were in the offing, and

Columba – who thought it highly unlikely that England would consent to an exchange for the Master of Atholl, easily the most valuable of the hostages – wished the Lady Elinor, and the king, joy of them.

Séverine's voice said, 'Columba?' and, recalled to the present, he smiled, and raised the handsome silver-gilt goblet someone had put in his hand. This was, after all, not a political occasion but a celebration.

Looking round, he said, 'I had thought of making a speech, but one does not make speeches to friends. So I will say no more than that I want you all to rejoice with me that His Holiness has seen fit to restore my benefices.'

Glancing at Lady Elinor and the Grahams, he went on, 'Even you, who do not know me, must have some idea of what two years in the wilderness of papal displeasure must have meant to me. But I have been blessed in having had not only my beloved niece, the Lady Ninian, to sustain me, but also my dearest of friends, the Vernes, who have stood by me as staunchly as a loving family might stand by a man not vowed, as I am, to celibacy. They have given me a kindness and sympathy without which I think I could not have survived.' He paused for a moment, his eyes on Lady Elinor's bored and petulant face. He hoped she was taking it all in.

'On another level,' he resumed, allowing a wry note to creep into his voice, 'I have learned a good many lessons from these last two years, among them that I must never again permit anyone to take away from me anything that is mine, and never again permit anyone to get the better of me. I do not wish to live through such a time again. And I *will* not, if there is anything I can do to prevent it!'

Blane's voice rose, over-loud, against the polite murmuring of the others. 'And you will not, if there is anything *we* can do to prevent it!'

Columba smiled, touched by the boy's obvious sincerity, but said no more than, 'Thank you, Blane. And now, come – if I spend more time talking, we will find ourselves breakfasting in the full heat of the day. Lady Elinor, what may I serve you?'

Food and drink, as always, had their effect. The atmosphere mellowed a little. Séverine took Malise Graham efficiently in hand. Blane, slightly flushed, gave his attention to Lady Elinor. Harry devoted himself to the peacock with as much dedication as if he had never seen peacock before, which perhaps he hadn't. And Columba stood companionably apart with Ninian, laughing at the smear of bright blue paint that stained her forefinger.

As she tried guiltily to hide it, he said, 'Do you remember that day when you told me, "If I can't wed for love, I shall not wed at all. I shall devote my life to my art"? You were so young then, and so sure!' Sure that love and chivalry must be there for the asking. Sure that an ability to paint must be there, too, for the asking.

He could still remember how hard it had been to keep a straight face. A travelling painter, formerly apprenticed to the Limbourg brothers, had lately passed through Villeneuve, and in his satchel had been copies of some of the manuscript illuminations Pol Limbourg had done for the Duc de Berry a year or two before. They had been magical little things, their colours burnished and pure, their detail meticulous – pictures of pale, airy castles and lacy towers set amid green and leafy landscapes, of handsome lords and beautiful ladies riding and dining and hawking, of peasants doing all the things peasants did, like sowing, and reaping, and haymaking. And all of them wondrously clean. Ninian had been captivated. The only thing she had wanted to do had been to paint like Pol Limbourg. She still did.

Now, she said, 'Yes, well . . .' and then broke off, listening. Columba could hear it, too, a solitary horseman approaching from the direction of the river, riding at a breakneck gallop. It was no underfed country nag he was mounted on, but a big horse, and a heavy one.

Ninian said, 'Who can it be? A herald? It sounds urgent. But we would have heard if the Routiers had been coming this way!' It was always the Routiers everyone thought of first.

Silence fell on the garden, a waiting silence, although everyone made a pretence of continuing to eat and drink.

'Did you know,' Ninian murmured, her eyes turned towards the road and the tracery of leaves that veiled it, 'that they have a new captain? A Castilian called Rodrigo de Villandrando.'

The rider was close now. Columba wondered whether he would stop and shout his news outside the gate of the *livrée*, or ride on to the Val de Bénédiction? If it were the monastery, such haste could only mean that either His Holiness or the head of the Carthusian Order had died; neither of which seemed likely. They had both been in excellent health two weeks ago.

There was a flash of brilliant colour and movement through the foliage, and they heard the horse's pace slacken slightly. But no voice was raised, nor any trumpet sounded.

And then violence exploded into the Paradise Garden in a soul-searing blur of scarlet and black and gold.

With savage abruptness, the thin green veil that screened the road

60

was ripped apart by something monstrous and fast-moving and menacing, a nightmare vision of glittering metal and flailing hooves and bared teeth, a figure so towering and macabre, so unmistakably bent on havoc that, in the shock of it all, and the speed, there was scarcely time to recognize it as a great black Flemish stallion, its Roman head harnessed in gold and the huge, barrel-chested body blanketed in scarlet from withers to fetlock. A stallion with a knight on his back, as ferocious and frightening as he, a knight whose armour gleamed black under a brilliant red surcoat, and whose crest flew like a vermilion oriflamme over a helm hooked and malevolent as the beak of a questing eagle.

The knight's visor was down, and his twelve-foot lance, couched in the slot of a gold-embossed shield, was levelled at Columba.

The stallion stumbled as he landed, but his rider, with a jerk on the gold-fringed reins, had him hurtling onward again with scarcely a pause, pounding across the flowered turf even while the thin, diffuse crackle of breaking twigs still echoed beneath the thunder of hooves and the stallion's frantic, snuffling breath, and the creak of metal, and the wind-slap of crest and trappings.

The little party scattered, all but Columba. He could hear Blane yelling, and Lady Elinor shrieking, and the Grahams shouting. He could sense Ninian and Séverine breathing quickly, close behind him. But, moving only a step or two back, he continued to stand erect and motionless, a curious look of expectation, almost of pride on his face.

And then, at the last possible moment, the mailed glove hauled on the reins again and quarter of a ton of horse and armour and rider swung into a magnificently controlled turn to sweep down on their real target – not Columba, but the open-mouthed, immobile figure of Sir Harry Graham.

There was nowhere for him to retreat to, no shelter to be found. Blane, with a whoop, tossed him a knife, but he was too slow. He missed it, and then, diving too late, caught his foot in the brass strings of the clarsach, still lying discarded on the grass.

He stayed where he had fallen, measuring his length amid the meadow flowers, doomed, apathetic, waiting for the end to come.

But it didn't.

For the knight was dragging his horse to a slithering halt, its hooves digging long, brown, ragged scars in the turf, and the bunched muscles of its hindquarters sliding along the ground until they came to rest, at last, in the gentle haven of a clump of gillyflowers.

There was a sudden sense of farce in the air.

And then the knight, after a brief tussle with the hinges, tipped his visor up and spoke.

'Well, by all the sons of Satan!' he said disgustedly. 'You will have to do better than that, Harry, my friend, if you want to impress your Lady Fair!'

Silence settled on the garden, briefly, tentatively, as unstable as a butterfly at rest.

After a few moments, Columba gently cleared his throat and the knight turned, clumsily because of the high saddle bows, and Columba saw the familiar dark eyes smiling at him, felt the familiar blaze of vitality, and heard Adam's laughing voice breathlessly exclaim, 'I don't believe it! Did I alarm you? Surely not!'

Columba shook his head, and Blane, speechless with mirth, helped his brother down from the saddle.

Clanking faintly, Adam de Verne strode across the grass towards Archdeacon Columba Crozier, still standing motionless in his tonsure cap and plain long robe, and put his hands on his shoulders, and grinned down into his eyes, and then threw his shining metal arms around him in a powerful, loving embrace.

'Never mind, father,' he said. 'Welcome home!'

CHAPTER THREE

ADAM's tone of voice when he said 'father' had been quite the wrong one. For the rest of the day, Columba had gone about flying his priestliness like a flag and addressing every male within earshot as 'my son'. But no one knew whether or not Lady Elinor had been deceived.

Ninian was still fretting about it next morning as she sat perched on a rock near the Fort St André with her painting brush in one hand, her little dish of vine-charcoal ink in the other, a sheet of best Bambyx paper pinned to the board on her knees, and not a servant in sight.

She was wearing her oldest and most disreputable gown, which was very disreputable indeed because it was the one she wore for plucking poultry, sweeping the floors, gutting fish, and playing midwife to the pigs when they farrowed. Sévèrine, an unremitting perfectionist, held that it was impossible to keep servants up to scratch unless one knew precisely how to do the work oneself. It was not necessary to do it often, but an occasional demonstration had the most salutary effect. Ninian wished, sometimes, that Sévèrine would revise her definition of occasional, because most of the time she seemed to regard it as synonymous with frequent.

What with the gown and the limp and middle-aged wimple over her hair, Ninian didn't think any ransom-minded Routier would give her a second glance; in fact, she was much more likely to be in danger from

Sévèrine, if Sévèrine discovered that she had been out without a guard.

But she had wanted to be quite alone, so that she could concentrate on drawing the Palace of the Popes in the same true perspective as Pol Limbourg would have done. She had never managed it yet, and this was the last chance she would have. In a few hours there would be the wedding feast, and tomorrow the wedding day, and then the wedding night . . .

She began, as she always did, by sketching in the strongest vertical, the bell tower. But her mind kept wandering.

Columba, who was rarely angry, and never – ever – with Adam, had made up for it yesterday. He hadn't gone stiff, or scarlet; he hadn't shouted, or waved his arms; he hadn't even said anything particularly cruel or cutting. But there had been no mistaking how he felt.

The moment of reckoning had come as soon as the alfresco breakfast had limped to its strained, but blessedly swift conclusion. Sévèrine had taken Lady Elinor and the Grahams off to the stables to show them the new puppies, and Adam, Blane, and Ninian had gone with Columba to the private chapel for an informal rehearsal of the nuptial Mass. Ninian couldn't make up her mind whether it had been a very appropriate, or a very inappropriate, place for the scene that had followed.

'An explanation, if you please?'

None of them had been in any doubt over who was going to have to do the explaining, or about what. The jousting escapade had been so typically, so flamboyantly Adam that, after the first moment, when they had recognized the helm and the trappings and Adam's inimitable style on a horse, none of the family had thought much more about it. Only Ninian had been a little upset. She couldn't imagine how she was going to smooth down Harry's ruffled feathers, and wished Adam hadn't taken the joke quite so far; there had been a moment when she had thought he really was going to run Harry through.

'I'm sorry,' Adam said, his smile flashing. 'I was so delighted to see you back – and with all your benefices restored – that I didn't think.' It was obvious he didn't consider it of much importance.

'You didn't think that what you said might easily lead to my having them taken away again?' Columba's voice was expressionless.

'Oh, come, father! How could it do that? Anyway, every priest has his byblows, and Blane and I are proud to be yours!'

Columba had had his back to them, his hands firmly planted on the

64

altar and his head slightly bent. Now, he inhaled deeply through his nose, and swung round exclaiming, 'May God give me patience! Your mother and I have been devoted to each other – more devoted, I sometimes fear, than you are capable of understanding – for all the years of our adult lives. *I will not* have you speak to me of byblows!'

Some of the colour had drained out of Adam's face, but his voice remained light as he said, 'I'm sorry. I withdraw the byblows. But the church knows better than to damn a priest for lack of chastity. They make enough fuss about enforcing celibacy on you. That, surely, is enough.'

'It is enough for a priest in a provincial parish. It is enough, even, for a cardinal – or a pope! – provided that the children he fathers are fathered in a moment of weakness. Holy Church recognizes the fact that to be human is to be fallible. But for a man who has dedicated himself to God to love and live with the same woman for a lifetime is a most grievous sin, not only against his vows but against the whole sacrament of marriage.'

Never – never – Ninian thought, would she understand the church. That it should be better for a priest to father a child on a servant girl in a ditch than for Columba and Sévèrine to live in love and amity for twenty years and more . . .

Columba said, 'I had thought that, by now, you had grasped these things.' And then his voice hardened. 'In fact, I know you have, otherwise why should we all have taken such care, for so long, to conceal my sin from the world? No. When you said, "I didn't think", that was the truth of it. You didn't think – and you never do.'

Ninian watched the two men, wide-eyed, realizing suddenly that Columba was right. She had never thought about it before, because Adam was just – Adam – the brilliant, dazzling big cousin whom she had adored ever since she could remember. But it was true enough. He took too much delight in the airy flourish, whether of word or deed, to risk spoiling his fun by giving thought to the consequences. His self-absorption could be hurtful, sometimes. Ninian knew it hadn't even occurred to him that it would be she, not he, who would have to suffer Harry's shame and resentment over this morning's episode.

But if he weren't spectacular and selfish and devil-may-care, he wouldn't be Adam.

Ninian could feel the tears in her throat. Columba loved Adam so much, and Adam both admired and worshipped him in return. It seemed to her dreadful that the laws of Holy Church meant there must be trouble between them because Adam had shown what he felt for his own father!

She said, 'Is it really so important?'

Columba turned his eyes towards her, and then sat down heavily. 'It could be.

'Think about it for a moment. At present, I am in King James's favour. It was he who interceded for me with His Holiness. But James is unpredictable. In one mood, it might matter to him not at all if he were to discover – from Lady Elinor or someone else – that Archdeacon Crozier of Teviotdale is the father of two full-grown sons by a lady to whom he has long been attached. But in another mood, who can tell? He can be very zealous for the honour of the church. And what he has helped to give, he can as easily help to take away.'

'Oh, if that's all!' Adam said cheerfully. 'Elinor won't mention it! I'll make sure of that!'

And he would, Ninian thought. With his looks and style, with the kind of vitality one could warm one's hands and one's heart at, with all Columba's charm magnified to a sometimes overpowering degree, Adam could make any woman do what he wanted. Even Lady Elinor.

Even, come to that, Lady Ninian Drummond, although she knew he was not for her. He had always thought of her as a child, and always would. When she was younger, she had been heartbroken about that, but she had grown out of it.

It was several seconds before Columba spoke. Then he smiled, without humour, and said, 'Can you silence her for ever? Oh, Adam, Adam! Will you never learn to look ahead? Hasn't it occurred to you that Lady Elinor is in the position of Caesar's wife? Think of the Scottish succession! James's heir presumptive is Atholl, who is an old man and can't last for very much longer. And after Atholl comes his son, the Master of Atholl. And after *him*, the son of his marriage to Lady Elinor. Tell me, Adam, is Lady Elinor a good wife?'

Adam threw back his head and laughed. 'Faithful, do you mean? Chaste? Oh, yes – if you'd describe a bitch in heat as chaste!'

Ninian gasped aloud, and then tried to look as if it wasn't enthralled astonishment that afflicted her but a genteel and maidenly shock. Chilly, stand-offish, holier-than-thou Lady Elinor! So *that* was why Adam was besotted!

Columba said, 'And how do you think James would react if he discovered that the wife of one future Stewart king, and the mother of another, was behaving like a harlot – and with *my* son?'

66

There was a long silence.

Blane broke it, blustering in defence of his brother, who had no need for his advocacy. The trouble with Blane was that he regarded Adam almost as if he were a god, and yet still found it necessary to compete with him. It made life rather trying at times. For once, however, he hit the nail on the head. 'How would James find out? *We're* not going to tell him and, God knows, that wilting lily out there certainly isn't!'

It was such an apt description of her ladyship that Columba actually laughed.

Afterwards, he had chosen to let the matter rest. Adam had thrown his arm round his father's shoulders and said, 'Forgive me! And don't worry. Blane is right, James won't find out. Anyway, even if he did, what does royal favour matter when you have the favour of the Holy See!'

And Columba had replied, 'Yes, well. We must ensure that I keep it.'

2

NINIAN discovered that she had been staring blankly across the river for so long that the ink had not only dried on her brush but begun to thicken in the dish.

She sighed and, uncorking the little pots of charcoal paste and honeyed gum arabic, began to mix a fresh supply. It was a messy task. How fortunate that she had such a steady hand! She giggled, beginning to feel more cheerful. Her instruction book was full of dire warnings about putting the steadiness of one's hands at risk by 'heaving rocks around, or wielding crowbars, or indulging too much in the company of women'. She wished she could have known Signor Cennino personally, instead of just through a copy of a copy of a copy of the painter's manual he had written more than fifty years ago. He sounded like the kind of teacher who would have had her drawing like Pol Limbourg in no time.

She had already sketched in the Old Palace, and now settled herself, with some trepidation, to the New. Even the great Pol, she thought, would have been forced to admit that the perspectives were difficult, because the two buildings didn't join quite at right angles, and the New Palace also had a lot of blind arches and two little spired turrets that, she knew from experience, looked wrong however one drew them.

'Note where the shadows and half tones and highlights come. Apply your shadows with washes of ink. The tint of the paper itself will give you your half tones. For the highlights you must use white lead . . .' She took a deep breath, and raised her brush.

And then, gritting her teeth, she began to count to ten. When it didn't do any good, she went on to twenty. Because while her wits had been wool-gathering, the shadows had moved.

She couldn't ignore them, or it would throw the whole picture out. And she couldn't wash out the shadows she had already put in because a moment's inspection was enough to tell her that they had already soaked deep into the paper. And, most certainly, she didn't have time to start all over again.

She looked at the Palace, and then at her painting. And she thought, 'What does it matter? What *does* it matter?'

Because, if the truth were told, it wasn't much of a painting.

As she went on looking at it, almost unseeing, she felt her heart gradually beginning to pound, and all the tensions she had been trying so hard to control building up inside her until they came together in a tight knot at the base of her throat.

She had had moments of dejection before—of real depression, even —but they had never been very serious, because life itself had been too bright, too enticing, too full of warmth. This time it was different. This time she felt nervous all the way through.

The drawing was only part of it, and so was the trouble between Adam and Columba, and Columba's doubts about the future. And the new life that would begin for her tomorrow, alone with a husband she scarcely knew and didn't much like, in a land she had forgotten. She had been trying conscientiously to be good about it, and had succeeded quite well, here in the sunshine with the people she loved around her — but she didn't know if she could go on being good when she had to face the reality.

Yet even that was only part of it, and she didn't know what the rest of it was.

The wimple was drooping over her forehead and she pushed it back with stained fingers. Then, carefully, she began to pick up her brushes, and the ink dish, and the flasks; the maulstick, and the swan quills, and the scraping knife; the inky rags, and the spare paper, and the board with the sketch she would never finish now, and didn't want to. Her hands were shaking like aspen leaves. Signor Cennino wouldn't have approved.

And suddenly, it was all too much for her. Quite without warning, the tightness in her throat found release in a thin, ragged wail of misery, a wail that swelled and surged and exploded at last into a wild, uncontrollable outburst of childish rage. Raising her hands as high as they would go, she dashed their contents to the ground with all the strength she could muster, and then – sobbing and hiccuping as if she were seven years old again instead of seventeen – began to jump on them, stamping on them, drumming her feet on them, while the tears poured down her cheeks and dripped darkly on to the bosom of the thin, patched, drab-coloured, over-tight gown.

The drawingboard snapped and crunched, the brushes and the sticks splintered, the inkpot shattered and the ink oozed out from among the shards to creep glutinously round the soles of her slippers, while the honeyed gum spread over the torn paper in thin, streaky, grey-brown puddles with edges that looked frayed and rusty black, like the robes of a village priest. The cloying sharpness of it caught at Ninian's eyes and nostrils and the torrent of her tears became a cataract.

It took perhaps ten minutes for the tantrum to wear itself out, and it was just when it had subsided into anticlimax, just when, sniffling lugubriously, she was poised to kick the last sad remnants of her art to the uncaring winds, that she caught a movement out of the corner of her eye and realized that someone was watching her.

The distraction could scarcely have come at a less opportune moment. With a dreadful inevitability, her foot, already swinging, missed its objective completely and connected instead with a large, unyielding, and very hard outcrop of Mount Andaon.

She made no sound except for a rather squeaky moan, but it was some little time before she recovered herself sufficiently to pay attention to her audience. Then, collapsed on the grass with one leg folded under her and both hands inelegantly clutching the other foot, she forced herself to look up.

From the other side of the wall bordering the roadway above, two horsemen were watching her, the smaller and older of them shaking his head reprovingly, the suspicion of a grin round his mouth. The other man looked as if he were extremely displeased about something.

Ninian unclamped her teeth from her lower lip, opened her mouth to speak, closed it again, and gulped nervously.

Still shaking his head, the older man dismounted and vanished from her sight for a moment, then reappeared clambering over the wall with the long skirts of his gown bunched up neatly under his arm.

'*Vous permettez, madame?*' he asked in accents that, though far from French, were perfectly workmanlike, and leaned down to help her to her feet. He wasn't gentle, but the hand under her elbow was firm and reassuring, as if picking up damsels in distress was part of his daily routine. Perhaps it was, for despite the plated shin-greaves and the mailed gorget that showed above the neck of his robe, he was unquestionably a man of the church.

She had to lean on him for quite a while before she was able to stand by herself. For a good deal longer than was necessary, in fact. If it had been possible, she would have postponed for ever the moment when she had to look the second horseman in the face again.

But in the end, miserably aware that her own face was swollen with tears, scarlet with embarrassment, and probably streaked with ink as well, she had no choice.

He was tall, as tall as Adam, and equally black of hair. But there the resemblance ended, for whereas everything about Adam was luxuriant, everything about this man spoke of control and command. Ninian couldn't guess at his age; he might have been anywhere between twenty-five and thirty-five.

Feeling unnaturally short of breath, she met his rather chilly grey gaze, noting the rest of his face and imprinting it on her memory without even being aware that she was doing it. A thin, aquiline nose; flat cheeks tinged with russet against the tawny skin; and a long, firm mouth, deeply indented at the corners, that looked as if it would laugh beautifully but never did. Then she dropped her eyes, and saw that the hands on the reins were long-muscled and competent, neither cared-for and soft like Columba's, nor yet hard and calloused like those of Adam and Blane and other men who spent most of their lives in the saddle.

In excellent French which sounded as if it might have been learned in Paris, he said, 'If you are recovered, madame? We are looking for the Chartreuse du Val de Bénédiction, and we seem to have missed our way. Can you direct us?'

He wasn't – he couldn't be – a priest, but neither was he a knight or a merchant. Like his companion, he wore a chainmail gorget to protect his neck and shoulders, but instead of a long robe he had a fine white cloak over a short black brigandine, the lightweight, padded-leather tunic reinforced with metal plates that some men preferred to conventional armour. A shallow, wide-brimmed traveller's hat hung from cords over his shoulders, and there was a steel bonnet at his saddle bow. Ninian could just see the belt at his hips and the sword hilt projecting from it. As the daughter of a soldier, she had no difficulty in putting a nationality to the sword, even if she couldn't to the man. The quillons and the langet were Scottish.

For several moments she had been conscious that the two men were not alone; there was a subdued clinking and shuffling that signified a large but well-disciplined escort somewhere nearby. Now, the horseman turned his head briefly towards them, and the movement was enough to show her two things, that the cords attached to his hat were heavily tasselled, and that he looked as if he might, until very recently, have been tonsured. It wasn't possible! Surely it wasn't possible? But the hair on his crown was just like Columba's, when Columba didn't trouble to have it cut as often as he should. Columba said he was tired of scissors the size of sheep shears and razors as big as a carving knife, and when someone invented better ones he would consider mending his ways. In the meantime, keeping his face shaved was penance enough.

Ninian stared at the stranger, utterly bewildered.

He turned back to her. 'The Chartreuse du Val de Bénédiction?' he said again, crisply, and she gathered herself together and gave him the direction. That they were on their way to the Charterhouse didn't mean very much. No one of importance lodged at a hostelry if there was a monastery within reach.

They were gone at once, with a parting grin from the older man and no more than the briefest of nods from the younger, and Ninian stood there motionless and listened to the rattle of hooves fading into the distance.

After about ten minutes, and surprisingly clearly, she heard the trumpet flourish announcing their arrival at the monastery gate.

3

SHE was still lost in thought as, half an hour later, she limped back along the road to the *livrée*, and it wasn't until she was almost there and could hear the bustle in the courtyard that she woke up sufficiently to consider how she was going to get back inside without being seen.

The Verne *livrée*, like most of the others in Villeneuve, was a thick-walled, rectangular structure built round a main courtyard in whose centre was the well that ensured the water supply. On the ground floors of the surrounding buildings were the Great Hall, the stables, the kitchen, the storerooms, the woodsheds, and the long, barn-like living quarters communally and odoriferously shared by cooks, hens, scullions, pigs, carpenters, spit-boys, dogs, bakers and brewers, and a large and heterogeneous collection of their human and animal dependants.

The only external access to the courtyard was by way of an arched corridor that tunnelled through the whole depth of the buildings fronting the road, and Ninian was already halfway along it, reflecting that, if there was no one around except the servants, all would be well, when she became aware of a special quality in the bustle ahead of her.

There were alcoves in the corridor wall where the gate porters sat when they had nothing better to do, and Ninian slipped into one of them that had a window overlooking the courtyard. She had to stand on tiptoe to see what was going on.

She should have been surprised, but she wasn't, because she had been brought up to believe that everything that happened was pre-destined, that God's will was paramount. What would happen, would happen, whether one sat with one's hands folded and waited for it, or went out and fought to bring it about. The waiting and the fighting were equally aspects of God's will.

And God had, it seemed, ordained that the two horsemen she had so recently directed to the Val de Bénédiction should have gone there only briefly, to arrange a lodging, and then turned back again – to the Verne *livrée*, where their real business was.

They were here now, in the courtyard, with a dozen other men already dismounted, whose air of privilege marked them as members of the visitors' riding household.

Adam was standing by the stirrup of the white-cloaked man, speaking with unnatural and rather exaggerated civility while the rider listened coolly, and then bowed slightly, and dismounted without effort and without fuss.

Ninian, her eyes huge and her mouth slightly open, watched as Adam nodded to Sévèrine's steward, a dignified man with a heavy gold chain round his neck, who stepped forward and ceremoniously de-livered his wand of office to one of the visitor's attendants, equally dignified and similarly garlanded in gold.

The visitor, it seemed, was a man of rank. Ninian waited breathlessly to hear who he might be – though she wasn't sure she would be able to hear anything at all above the pounding of her heart.

But Adam's voice rang out with deliberate clarity, so that the words of protocol could be heard not only by the man in the white cloak but by everyone in the Verne household who needed to know, especially the servants. And what he said was, 'My mother's house is yours – my Lord Bishop.'

4

BECAUSE Tom Myrton had a moderately shrewd idea of what was going on in Gavin's mind, he hadn't complained – or not much – about the speed at which they had been travelling since they left Rome.

They'd started with a hell-for-leather, five-day ride north, which in the height of summer was a great way to lose weight and gain a sore arse. Then they'd taken passage in a Genoese trading galley, westward over the bright, blue, sultry, scentless sea to the dead-water port of Aigues-Mortes at the mouth of the Rhône.

Tom had been there before, and he didn't like it – everything was so neatly squared up that being inside the ramparts felt like being locked up in a clothes chest; an *old*-clothes chest, for the moat and marshes stank only a degree or two less than the Tiber. Tom didn't like the mosquitoes, either, though they welcomed him as if he were the Prodigal Son; he'd rather have had a good, honest Scots midge any day. He had been every bit as anxious as Gavin to get out of the place, even on to the oily, endless flats of the Camargue, with nothing to see but birds and beasts, and nothing to do but sit and sweat.

They'd joined the Rhône proper at Arles and sailed straight on up river, heat-parched France on the left and independent Provence, reeking of lavender, on the right. By the time they disembarked at Beaucaire, Tom had had a thirst on him like a Highland drover.

Then they'd had to find and haggle over horses, not to mention eighty trustworthy men-at-arms to supplement the riding household. And that had been no joke with Gavin grilling every last one of them as if he were the Grand Inquisitor in person.

Tom had made a sly comment about an escort worthy of the Bishop-elect's episcopal dignity, but he knew very well that wasn't the reason. In obedience to King James's inconvenient command, Gavin had escorted the Master of Atholl's lady out to France when he was on his way to Rome, and he was supposed to be convoying her home, too. A touch acidly, he had pointed out to Tom that, since he hadn't time to waste defending either his purse or Lady Elinor's person from any marauding Routiers – though he thought that being kidnapped would do her ladyship nothing but good – the only solution seemed to be to travel in enough force to discourage them. 'Let's have it both ways, shall we?' he had said. 'That surplice of yours to deter the godly, and the escort to deter the ungodly.'

It had been two full days before they were able to go dashing off to Uzès to collect her ladyship, and Gavin had been very much annoyed to discover that she wasn't sitting there virtuously waiting for him with all her boxes packed.

She had gone, it seemed, to stay with acquaintances at Villeneuve. Tom had sighed quietly to himself as they had turned and ridden back – hell-for-leather again – to Villeneuve-lès-Avignon. Which was the place, if Tom remembered rightly, where Archdeacon Crozier's niece was about to marry one of the Grahams. Queer coincidence!

5

BUT it wasn't coincidence, of course.

Gavin, restraining his desire to ask the young man in the blinding doublet and hose what the hell her ladyship thought she was doing vagabonding around the French countryside, said merely, 'It was most kind of Madame de Verne to invite the Lady Elinor to be her guest. Her ladyship's friends will be much indebted.'

Adam de Verne stood back to allow the visitor to enter the Grand Tinel, a vast and handsome room so lavishly hung with tapestries that scarcely an inch of wall space showed; the tapestries were good ones, too, from Tournai or Arras, Gavin thought.

'My mother's house is her ladyship's, as it is yours, my Lord Bishop,' the young man replied formally. 'Tomorrow we celebrate the marriage of my cousin to a Scottish gentleman of the Lady Elinor's acquaintance. Her ladyship expressed a desire to attend.'

Gavin swung round. It was as much as Adam could do not to cannon into him, but Tom Myrton, still on the stairs, wasn't so lucky.

'A Scottish gentleman?' Gavin said, his eyebrows raised a little. 'Sir Harry Graham?'

The young man nodded in a way Gavin didn't much care for, as if he were one jump ahead. Which he probably was. If he were acquainted with Archdeacon Crozier, he must know something of Bishop-elect Cameron, even if Bishop-elect Cameron knew nothing of him.

With the greatest cordiality, Gavin said, 'Then, since the bride is niece to Archdeacon Crozier of Teviotdale, and you describe her as your cousin, you must be – what?'

There was a fractional hesitation before the young man's mouth curled into a smile. 'There is no real relationship. I use the word "cousin" loosely. My mother was a dear friend of the late Lady Drummond's, and she has always encouraged Lady Drummond's daughter to regard our house as her home.'

As an explanation, it left a good deal out – including Archdeacon Crozier – but Gavin didn't pursue it. All he said was, 'I see.' His interest in Columba Crozier's family and friends was tepid, and wouldn't even have been that had not Adam de Verne appeared to him to be the kind of flashy young devil who trailed trouble around with him like a cloak.

But he wasn't thinking about Crozier or the Vernes or the unknown niece when, a few hours later, he stood in his white-washed cell in the Val de Bénédiction and allowed his usher to robe him for the unavoidable eve-of-wedding supper that was to be held at the *livrée* after Magnificat. His mind was too much occupied with the reflection that, when he left Villeneuve – which wouldn't be tomorrow, if Lady Elinor had any say in the matter, but certainly the day after – he would really be on the way home.

This whole journey would stay in his memory forever, not only because it was his first direct experience of Europe, not only because he had learned so much at first hand about Holy Church and the men who ruled it, but because it marked the start of the most glorious and most rewarding challenge of his life. Being appointed Bishop of Glasgow was not the end of his ambitions, but the beginning.

It was for this that he had struggled through the lean and hungry years of adolescence, when he could afford either to eat or learn, but not both; for this that he had persevered through the scarcely less hungry years of holding minor legal office; for this that he had waited with ever-growing impatience, first as secretary to the Douglasses, and then to the king. And now, after all the years, not so long in time but very long in the living, the day was approaching when at last he would know the reality of power.

Ever since the ceremony in the Lateran chapel, he had been possessed by an intense inner excitement, a driving impatience to get started on all the things it would now be possible to do. For too long the world had suffered from a sickness that was both emotional and political. Bad government, the cupidity and violence of the great, war and brigandage, scarcity and pestilence – these alone would have been enough to drain ordinary people of their will, even if the situation had not been aggravated by the widely held belief that the Day of Judgement was at hand.

Gavin didn't know whether it was, but he did know that the belief itself was as good an excuse as any for not doing anything to improve matters. Apathy was easier.

But apathy wasn't one of Gavin's failings, and it certainly wasn't one of King James of Scotland's. James's reforming zeal was as great as Gavin's own, and in some ways more urgent. Life was short for most men, and shorter still for kings. James was already thirty-two, but in his eighteen years of enforced idleness in England, he had had time enough to dream of what he would do to set his country to rights when the opportunity came. And now the opportunity had come, and there were to be no more delays.

All the way from Rome to Villeneuve, Gavin had been suppressing a mad desire to laugh aloud. But it would have been impolitic to allow the men he travelled with to know that he was human; except Tom, perhaps, and Tom knew, anyway.

Ordinarily, Gavin had little difficulty in sustaining the air of cold detachment that was at once his most useful weapon and most valuable defence in dealings with his fellow men. He had had enough practice, God knew, for he had learned very soon that the rough, avaricious world of the fifteenth century equated civility with weakness. By the time he was sixteen, he had begun cultivating the distant, forbidding style that by now was second nature to him. It even put the garrulous barons off their stride sometimes, though there had always been a note of condescension when they marvelled at it, or at his superhuman efficiency. He was, after all, only a clerk.

But a laconic and energetic minor official was one thing. A laconic and energetic bishop who had the king's full confidence was quite another. The unregenerate son of Kinveil who still lurked inside the

Bishop-elect of Glasgow was looking forward to teaching the barons a lesson or two.

He reflected that, if he could drag her ladyship away the day after tomorrow and make best speed across country to Bordeaux, they ought to be able to arrange a passage with the first of the wine fleets. Perhaps it was too much to hope that one of the Leith merchants might be there, but Scarborough or Newcastle would do almost as well.

Privately, he damned his servants, and his fellow travellers, and those with whom, sedately, he was about to dine. Only once in his life before, on that day, fifteen years ago, when he had left Kinveil for the first and last time, could he remember feeling such exhilaration. If only he could have been alone, he would have done as he had done then. He would have laughed, and sung, and shouted his pleasure to the heavens. And, childishly, would have felt the better for it.

Why should he suddenly remember that day, that other beginning? That day when even his body had been stirred for the first time by a pair of tear-filled eyes, a quivering, innocent mouth, and a promise of beauty hidden under the folds of a drab, ill-fitting gown. He smiled to himself. Little Moragh was twenty-one years old now, married three times and widowed twice, and the innocent look was long, long gone. Why should he suddenly remember?

He shrugged, nodded dismissively to his usher, and strode out of the cell into the cloister, and then along the mulberry walk to the stables.

CHAPTER FOUR

I

'WHAT a hateful man!'

That sounded more like her. The little folds of flesh at the corners of Columba's mouth deepened in amusement. Ninian had been looking alarmingly superior all evening, so much so that he had begun to think her eyebrows had taken up permanent residence in her hair. She had been behaving, in fact, in an exceedingly ladylike way, her manner demure to people who mattered and gracious to people who didn't, and her smiles looking very much as if they had been stuck on with pins. She hadn't giggled once. It was almost as if she had been taking lessons from Lady Elinor.

Columba wondered whether the imminence of matrimony had anything to do with it. For everyone's sake, and especially Harry Graham's, he hoped not. The boy was looking as confused as if someone had pulled the ground from under his feet.

'Well, but look at him, Columba!' Ninian went on. 'Has he no idea how to behave? Standing there glowering at everyone!'

Columba didn't need to look. He had already observed a beleaguered Gavin Cameron on the far side of the Grand Tinel, with his back to a tapestry of the Virgin and the Unicorn and his unamiable gaze bent on the stone-deaf old Knight of Montfavet who, having cornered a bishop, wasn't going to let him go easily.

Columba said thoughtfully, 'I'm not sure that he is glowering, you know. It's the only expression I've ever seen; it may be the only one he has.'

A new voice spoke beside them. It was Adam, magnificently turned out in tunic, doublet and hose of his favourite scarlet, and wearing an intricately draped red and gold turban over his curling black locks. 'He is annoyed, I am told,' Adam said. 'He is in a hurry to return to Scotland. He would have spirited Elinor away this very day, except that she had the vapours when he suggested it. *Peasant!*'

He threw a possessive arm round Ninian's shoulders. 'But don't complain, *ma petite*. He has agreed to give you and Harry his episcopal blessing tomorrow.'

'I don't know that I want it!' She tried to shrug off the embrace, but Adam's grip tightened, and he laughed.

'What? Worried about Harry? Surely not. I cannot see him running me through for a cousinly hug – or anything else, if the truth be told. In any case, I assure you that I do not intend to abandon the habit merely because you are being married tomorrow.'

Sévèrine's voice spoke quietly from behind. All she said was, 'Adam!' but it was enough. Carelessly, he removed his arm from Ninian's shoulders.

It always amused Columba, the delicate war between Sévèrine and her sons, which Sévèrine invariably won. But she was far too clever to pursue her advantage. Her smile didn't change at all when she asked, 'Who is it you are all so busy disliking?' and Adam answered, 'What a foolish question, *ma mère*! Our uncivilized new lord and bishop, of course.'

'Oh, is he uncivilized? From what little conversation we have had, I should not have thought so.'

Columba said, 'I feel that perhaps "provincial" would be a better word. Our good bishop-elect is, in essence, a provincial churchman playing at politics. However, he has the king's ear, so it would be unwise to offend him.' He sighed, faintly. 'A pity that he seems not to approve of me.'

'Columba, no!' Ninian exclaimed, genuinely horrified. 'Surely you must have misunderstood something?'

He couldn't help but be touched. She was still so very young, and disturbingly naïve at times. They had all conspired to spoil her and protect her, and he was afraid that the reality she would so soon have to face was going to bear hard on her.

Dropping his voice to a dramatic whisper, he breathed, 'No.

But what does that matter, when I – do – not – approve – of – him!'

Just so had he teased her in her childhood. She should have unwound and giggled mischievously, but Columba was taken aback to see that, instead, her lips were beginning to tremble.

Then Sévèrine's voice, gently malicious, claimed his attention. 'Because he is more eminent than you – and younger?'

'Certainly not.' But, after a moment, he smiled ruefully. 'Well, perhaps there may be something in that. Though I have never wanted to be a bishop.' The distinction of ruling over one of western Christendom's five hundred episcopal outposts had always seemed to Columba much over-rated. To be a cardinal, on the other hand . . . But one had to be blessed at birth with all the gifts of fortune if one were to join *that* select fellowship. It was a pity. Columba had always thought he would make a good cardinal.

'No, it is more than that,' he said. 'He's not a real churchman. He has no Christian tolerance, for one thing. He's a moralist, the kind who gives Holy Church a bad name. You should have seen his face in Rome, when he was watching some – er – *filles de joie* on the prowl!' He shook his head censoriously. 'And aside from that, well . . . He's an administrator, a lawyer. It's reason, not faith, that drives him. His first duty is to the king, not to the church.'

'Is that so very reprehensible?'

Columba stared at her. 'But, my dear Sévèrine, of course! All kings want to reign supreme within their own dominions, and since the power of Holy Church knows no frontiers they see it as a direct threat. Every time a king tries to bestow the mitre on a man whom he, not the pope, has chosen, he strikes a deliberate blow at the whole fabric of the church. If Cameron had been a man of faith, he would never have consented to being "elected" by the Glasgow chapter without the prior consent of His Holiness. That he did so was as good as an open confession that his primary allegiance is to the world, not the spirit, to the flesh, not the faith.'

Her eyes widened in mock horror. '*Vraiment*? And to the devil also, instead of to God?'

He ignored it. 'But never mind,' he went on. 'Many men have risen as Gavin Cameron has, only to vanish as swiftly. I don't doubt that our young friend will very soon find himself riding for a fall.'

Sévèrine's brows rose quizzically. 'And you hope to be there when it happens?'

GAVIN was enjoying himself in his own inscrutable way, though the supper had been tedious. It had amused him once, when he had been an undistinguished clerk eating at the low table in other people's Great Halls, to watch the nobles at the high board, strung out in a sour-faced row like figures on a frieze. But he had learned since that it was enough to make anyone sour-faced to have to sit for three hours or more in a stiff-necked, lordly line, staring down enviously at the cheerful anarchy that reigned on the floor of the hall – especially when one had no one to talk to except one's immediate neighbours, who were neighbours not from choice, but because they happened to be next in rank or precedence.

Not that he had wanted to talk, this evening, or not to strangers. What he wanted to do was listen and observe, and now he had found an admirable way of contriving it. And just in case anyone were to take pity on him and come to rescue him from the old chatterbox from Montfavet – which seemed unlikely – he had adopted his most unapproachable expression.

It had no effect, fortunately, on his captor, who was elderly, single-minded, ignorant of any language other than French, and very deaf indeed. Frequently, as he rambled on, the old man paused and glanced up at the bishop-elect, and as long as he saw Gavin's lips move in what seemed to be reply, he was satisfied. Neither he, nor anyone else in the Grand Tinel, had any reason to suspect that Gavin was availing himself of the opportunity to carry on a private and pleasantly slanderous conversation with Tom Myrton, anchored at his side.

'Since seventy years they have despoiled France, the Routiers!' the old knight was complaining. 'Seventy years!'

Gavin shook his head sympathetically, and opened his mouth. 'What do you think, Tom?' he said. '*Are* they Crozier's sons?'

Tom had his arms folded and his chin propped on his hand, the fingers fanned to obscure his lips. 'I don't see any great resemblance. Or not physically.'

'. . . the Routiers are soldiers with no war to fight, so they resort to pillage . . .'

Gavin nodded gravely, and said, 'No, they look like their mother. But there's something there, though it's hard to put a finger on.'

'. . . and they have ideas of the most grand . . .'

Gavin looked disapproving. 'Anyway, watch them together, Tom! That's not old family friendship. They're far too close.'

'Well, it's likely enough,' Tom grunted. 'Crozier's not the kind to muddle up priestly chastity with priestly celibacy.'

In other circumstances, Gavin would have grinned and said, 'Just like some others we could name!' Tom was the doting father of six children by four different mothers.

There weren't many priests nowadays whose chastity would have raised a cheer from St Augustine or St Jerome, but the church didn't regard an occasional lapse, or even relapse, as any great cause for concern. What did worry it was when a priest who had abandoned all pretence of chastity went on meting out penances of anything up to ten years on the bread of affliction and the water of tribulation to parishioners whose sins of the flesh were far less reprehensible than his own. It was a clear case of one law for the shepherd, and another for his flock, and in recent years a good many sheep had begun to rebel. Clerical celibacy, which Holy Church regarded – though without any divine justification – as the symbol of moral authority, was on the verge of becoming a mockery.

And that, Gavin thought regretfully, was as dangerous in lay terms as in ecclesiastical, because nowhere in Europe was there any system of law enforcement worthy of the name, and the only thing that could be relied on to operate consistently in the interests of law and order was the moral authority of the local priest. No one could afford to have it undermined, however feeble it might sometimes be, and if Rome didn't take steps to bring its erring ministers to book, kings might have to.

Unless Gavin had misread the situation, it looked as if Columba Crozier might be one of those who suffered as a result. Smothering a grin, Gavin thought he must remember to remind him that one of the main duties laid down for an archdeacon was to report to his bishop on the lives and behaviour of the clergy within his jurisdiction, with particular reference to the keeping of concubines. Satan rebuking sin!

And then he found himself, to his surprise, reflecting that it would be a pity if Madame de Verne were to be hurt. Perhaps it was lucky that such a woman as she had never come his way before.

He had always preferred not to give hostages to fortune. In some ways, he knew, he was as single-minded as the old knight who stood there rambling on before him. Single-minded in his driving ambition, and single-minded in the idealism that still, despite everything, possessed him. He had never been in love and didn't intend to be. He had more important channels for his energies. Even in these days, it was still possible for one man of passion to accomplish miracles, provided that his passion stayed single-minded, and seamless, and safely impersonal.

'. . . they abducted him, and took him up to the mountain fortress at Les Baux . . . D'ye know Les Baux?'

Gavin looked thoughtful for a moment, and then shook his head.

3

THEY disengaged at last from the Knight of Montfavet when he showed signs of launching into a different monologue, this time on the misfortunes of Charles VII, the not-yet-crowned king of France – or as much of it as the English and Burgundians hadn't yet stolen from him. Both Gavin and Tom knew far too much already about the one-time Dauphin, and even Tom was prepared to admit that, if only the Routiers would kidnap him as well as the Lady Elinor, a good many folk would have cause to be grateful to them.

Austerely, they set off on a tour of the tapestries. Next to the Virgin and the Unicorn, there was the Pursuit of Fidelity. Then Hercules on his way to the Olympic Games, and then the Wild Man of the Woods.

Standing immediately in front of this last were Harry Graham and Blane de Verne, both smelling strongly of hippocras and engaged in an acrimonious argument over whether a knight errant setting out on the dragon trail should put the Loch Ness Monster at the top of his list, or the Ravening Beast of Tarascon. Called upon to arbitrate, Bishop-elect Cameron suggested they might care to marshal their cases rather more lucidly and present them to him at some future date.

The Grand Tinel was insufferably hot and noisy and crowded, even though the rowdier guests had been left downstairs in the Great Hall when supper ended. But the tumblers and the minstrels and musicians were here, earning their wages, and there were a licensed fool, and a man with a talking bird on his arm, and a great many dogs squabbling and yapping and scratching in the rushes.

Gavin's eyes searched the throng, and after a few moments he saw

Archdeacon Crozier pouring charm, like cream, over a minor member of the royal house of Anjou. Nearby, Lady Ninian and Lady Elinor were whispering together. Surprised, he said, 'Tom, did you overhear that exchange at supper, when our supercilious little bride put Lady Elinor in her place?'

Tom shook his head, the creases in his face deepening into a smile. He was still trying to work out why Gavin and the Atholl woman disliked each other so much, though he was beginning to have an inkling.

'They were talking about the succession – what else? – and Lady Elinor said her husband had no desire to inherit the throne. Where-upon the bride leaned over and said, bland as you please, "But even if your husband doesn't want to be king, surely your son does? He must be old enough by now to have his own opinions on the subject." If looks could have killed, we'd be officiating at a wake tomorrow instead of a wedding.'

Tom grinned. Her ladyship was twenty-eight years old, and her son thirteen, but she never called him anything other than, 'My baby'. He said, 'Aye, well. The Master of Atholl may not have ambitions to be king, but I'd like to see her ladyship refusing the role of queen. She's a funny lassie, is she not? Looks like a saint, and acts like a whore. Let's hope Queen Joan's next child is a son, then we can all stop worrying.'

Gavin, reduced to speechlessness for once, stared at Tom with his mouth slightly ajar, and then closed it again.

Tom stared back at him benignly. So he was right, and her ladyship *had* made a pass at the laddie! Well, well. He said, 'There's something afoot. I think the bride's coming over to talk to you.'

And sure enough, the Lady Ninian was beginning to drift, uncon-vincingly casual, in their direction, pausing only to condescend to a few women on the way, and brandish her eyelashes at a few men.

Gavin said, 'Yes, indeed. Radiant and innocent as a bride should be.'

'Maybe she is.'

'What? Innocent? Damn it, Tom, she was brought up in Avignon!'

Tom sighed. 'Och, you're half a century out of date, man. It's not the hive of iniquity it was when Benedict and Clement and Gregory were up there in the Palace of the Popes!'

'Isn't it? I wonder.'

He had been watching her off and on during the course of the evening, because there was something familiar about her and he couldn't think what. He was moderately sure they'd never met before.

She wasn't unattractive to look at. Big blue eyes, and brows widely set under a high, broad forehead; a nose too positive and a mouth too wide for beauty; and prettily rounded cheeks bracketed with unusually strong creases that ran from curling nostrils to the equally curling corners of her mouth. But she was certainly too plump, and the almost indecently deep V of the rich blue gown didn't disguise it. Her hair, trailing virginally down her back under the gold veiling, was an unusual colour somewhere between fair and russet, with a sheen on it like satin.

No, he didn't object to her looks. It was her manner he didn't care for, arrogant one moment, oppressively sweet the next. A true product of the courtly tradition. He thought her a calculating little minx and wouldn't have trusted her an inch.

'Brought up in Avignon,' he said again. ' "Cousin" to Crozier's bastards. And now marrying into the Grahams. I shouldn't have thought it was humanly possible for her still to be innocent.'

She wafted to a halt before them and it was clear that she wanted something, because she began by thanking him with a cool graciousness for the promised blessing.

When he gave her no more reply than a slight inclination of his head, she took a careful breath and went on, lashes fluttering winsomely over downcast eyes, 'I hope that you will continue to favour us with your presence for the entertainments we have planned for the next few weeks. I am sure the Lady Elinor would be loath to see you ride off without her.'

So that was it, was it? He might have known. 'Then there is a simple solution, madame. She may accompany me when I leave tomorrow evening.'

It threw her off balance; clearly, she wasn't used to such bluntness. The big blue eyes flew up to his and the artificial smile faltered, but she recovered quickly enough. 'Surely not, my Lord Bishop! You cannot deprive me of her ladyship's company so soon! I quite depend on her.'

My Lord Bishop raised one satanic black brow. 'Indeed?' he said. 'How very sad! I was not aware that your friendship was so deep and of such long standing.'

It gave him malicious satisfaction to observe the sulphurous glance she threw at Lady Elinor, now hovering a few feet away, staring at the Massacre of Saint Ursula and her Maidens as intently as if it had some undisclosed relevance to the present situation. Gavin wouldn't have cared to bet on which of the two ladies was going to massacre which.

He deduced, without much difficulty, that Lady Elinor had put the bride up to this, knowing very well what his reply would be if she herself were to do the asking.

The bride inhaled deeply. 'Our acquaintance is short,' she said, the honey flavoured now with pepper, 'but that has nothing to do with it. Chivalry does have its rules, you know, and it would be quite ungallant of you to refuse a bride's request made on the eve of her marriage!' Her chin was somewhere up in the air, and she appeared to think she had made a point that was quite incontrovertible.

Chivalry, to Gavin, was something so meaningless and so irrelevant that he stared at her for a moment as if she were talking a language he didn't understand. And then, mellifluously, he replied, 'Ah, I see. You believe that all the public business of Scotland, the meeting of parliament, the passing of laws, the service of the king, the care of all the thousands of souls in my diocese – that all these should be held up for weeks, purely to satisfy some archaic law of chivalry?'

It was pitching it a bit high – parliament and diocese were more likely to be grateful for his continuing absence than his invigorating presence – but he went on, 'No, madame. I fear that I have more urgent things to do than attend banquets and mystery plays and riding parties. I leave immediately after your marriage tomorrow, and the Lady Elinor with me.'

It was too much for Lady Elinor. Turning towards them, her lips tight, she drawled, 'I really have no need of your escort, my Lord Bishop. I shall stay on.'

Gavin merely looked at her. She was impossibly thin, and as fair as if she had been hung out in the sun to bleach, with hair and lashes that were nearer white than blonde, and eyes of a dilute blue that added no more colour to her face than the pale and unexpectedly full lips. Another woman might have resorted to tinted salves and rich clothing to rectify the balance of nature, but Lady Elinor did the opposite. The gowns and headdresses she wore always looked as if they had been snipped out of some floating patch of sea mist, and the effect of ghostliness was so pronounced that, once or twice, Gavin had caught himself feeling surprised that he couldn't see right through her. Though only in the physical sense. In other senses, seeing through her presented no problems at all.

He said, 'Unfortunately, the decision does not rest with your ladyship. You will remember that it was the king's command that I escort you back to Scotland.'

And then he turned to Lady Ninian again and saw that her cheeks were flaming and her lips quivering. It didn't seem to be temper this time. The uncertainty in the gentian-blue eyes suggested that she was – very properly, in Gavin's opinion – suffering from acute embarrassment at having landed everyone in such an awkward situation. She couldn't be expected to know that my Lord Bishop was thoroughly enjoying himself.

It was at that precise moment that he realized why she looked familiar.

It couldn't be! The girl in the countrywoman's wimple who had been having a tantrum near the shore this morning? The girl, flushed and tearful, whose bosom had been heaving so much that he had thought it was going to burst out of its bodice? The girl who had told them how to get to the Charterhouse? He had taken her for an over-developed twelve-year-old.

It couldn't be the same girl, but it was.

Surprise and a mildly conspiratorial amusement assailed him, and just for an instant he had the feeling that it showed.

But no one, it seemed, had noticed. The girl exclaimed, 'I think you are . . .' and then bit the words off. He would have been interested to hear her opinion in more detail, even if the general tenor of it was obvious enough. But she drew herself up in a way that, if she had been older, he would have described as disdainful, and said, 'If you will forgive me, my Lord Bishop?' And then she stalked off.

Gavin hoped she wouldn't spoil it by tripping over one of the dogs.

4

IT SEEMED as if they would never leave her alone. Her women fussed around her for hours, fidgeting and gossiping, laying things out, hanging things up, folding this and unfolding that. And when at last she had succeeded in convincing them that there was nothing more they could usefully do, the heavy wooden door opened and Séverine came in to see that all was well.

Séverine had no reason to think other than that her ward, like any virgin bride, was nervous over what tomorrow would bring; it was a subject about which she had already spoken to her, coolly, sensibly, and at some length. But for the first time in her life, Ninian derived no comfort from the dry reassurance in those dark, heavy-lidded eyes.

Years later, she was to wonder how different all their lives might have been if, that night, she had poured her heart out to Séverine, who would have understood so well, so very well. But the cause of it was too new, too private, too fragile, and much too painful.

Séverine left, in the end, and the women settled down on their pallets after drawing the heavy curtains round Ninian's bed, shutting out the room with the painted borders and the tiled floor, the wall fireplace with its empty summer grate, the table with the gilt basins and ewers, the convex mirror, the alcove shrine, the clothing and the bedding chests – shutting them all out, so that she could be alone in the stuffy, airless little damask-hung space that was at once her bed and her only refuge.

She took a deep, silent, sobbing breath, and gave herself up to her misery. Because now, when it was far, far too late, she had fallen in love. She was to be married tomorrow to someone she didn't even like, just when the man she had dreamed of, and waited for, had come into her life at last.

She didn't know what to do. There was nothing she *could* do. She was seventeen years old and her whole life was in ruins.

And would still have been in ruins, she thought, feeling as if her heart was breaking, even if she were not to be married tomorrow. Because she had fallen in love with a man she could never have.

She lay in the hot, soft darkness with one question skittering around in her mind, erratic and insistent as a mouse in the wainscotting. Why him? Of all the men in the world, why him?

It was a pointless question, like a condemned man asking whose hand had fashioned the executioner's sword.

Struggling to answer it, as if putting everything into words would put it into perspective, too, she acknowledged that it had something to do with the lean, formidable face, and the deep-toned voice with its faintly accented French. With the smile she had never seen and had to stop herself from trying to imagine. With the tall, easy-moving figure that even the bishop's robes couldn't hide. With the way his hair grew, heavy and short, and curving a little over his forehead and round the smooth, incongruously youthful nape of his neck . . .

But she had met striking-looking men before and felt not even the mildest *frisson* of attraction.

Her response to Gavin Cameron, on the other hand, had been

nothing short of cataclysmic, and she was still half stunned by the shock of it.

When she was growing up, she had dreamed dreams of finding herself alone some day in a magical wilderness, or a mysterious forest, or on a moonlit shore. Perhaps she would be hurt or frightened a little – but not much. And then, riding to her aid out of nowhere, would come a man who was tall, and dark, and a few years older than she, and he would raise her up, and hold her by both hands, and gaze into her eyes – and in that moment both of them would be possessed by knowledge of a love that was destined to last until life's end.

And she *had* been on the shore, or near it, and a tall, dark stranger *had* come riding up. And then she had stubbed her toe excruciatingly, and had been picked up and brushed down by someone short and square and fatherly, and asked how to get to the Val de Bénédiction. And left to find her own way home.

She smothered a little hiccup of hysterical laughter, in case her maids should be awake and hear her.

For her pride's sake, she had tried, this evening, to be the opposite of that futile girl on the shore. She had made sure she was exquisitely arrayed, completely grown up, impeccably wellbred, as self-assured as a lady of courtly love should be. She had spoken of him and to him as if he were a stranger, trying very hard to impress him as he had impressed her, hoping and praying that he wouldn't recognize her. But she had been quivering with nerves all the time, and he *had* recognized her in the end, and had laughed. He had made it quite clear that he didn't like her at all.

Adam had called him a peasant. Columba considered him provincial. Lady Elinor said he was as cold as a fish and didn't like women.

And none of it mattered. What mattered was that she had fallen in love with a man who frightened and fascinated her at the same time, who, despite the cold, controlled exterior, seemed to radiate excitement, and power, and something else she couldn't even begin to identify. A man who was also a bishop of Holy Church, and vowed to celibacy.

Briefly, she thought of Columba and Séverine, but it didn't help, because she knew, without knowing why, that such a relationship could never be for her.

She was seized by a dreadful frustration. It wasn't fair, *it wasn't fair* – any of it – she thought, ignoring the shocked little voice in her head that said it was wrong to complain about what God had decreed. It wasn't fair that she should have fallen desperately in love with the wrong man. It wasn't fair that she should have been shown the reality of all she had ever dreamed of, only to have it snatched away from her as everything else was being snatched away. Until now, she had only had to ask in order to be given, but now it seemed that no amount of asking could give her the only things she longed for in the world.

It wasn't only this new and doomed desire, desire imbued with a pain that she didn't think would ever grow less until it merged into the greater pain of death. It was so many other things, too – her realization, this very morning, that she still couldn't paint as she wanted to, and probably never would; she had resolved never to lift a paintbrush again. She was convinced that she would never be happy again, either – with no Columba, no Sévèrine, no Adam or Blane, no one but dull and boring Harry and Harry's dull and boring cousins for company. In a draughty, dreary castle, and a Scotland cold and damp. She, Ninian Drummond, for whom sunshine and cheerful company and a knowledge of loving were the very breath of life.

What, now, was she condemned to? Dully, she recognized that falling in love had changed very little of what lay ahead, except the extent of her heartbreak.

All she wanted to do was die. But somehow she suppressed the self-pitying tears, and somehow, her face buried in the goose-down pillow, she lived through the long night without weeping until the sun rose on the day when she was to be married.

5

IT WAS a beautiful day, and since there hadn't been a fashionable wedding in Villeneuve for months, the whole town was in a festive mood.

Sévèrine came to see Ninian dressed, and she and the Comtesse de Thouzon and the Vicomtesse d'Aubanel exclaimed over how pretty the bride looked in her blush-pink gown with its all-over embroidery in gold, and the narrow, flattering, paler pink panel set into the front of the bodice.

'A picture, a perfect picture!' gushed the fat comtesse, her hands clasped admiringly over her stomach.

Ninian, staring into the polished mirror on the wall, saw her own unhappy face stiffen for a moment, and then soften again as a slow tide of gratitude begin to ripple through her. A picture?

The covered litter in which the women of the bridal party were carried the few hundred yards to the collegiate church of Notre Dame was indeed a picture, enchantingly decorated with garlands of flowers and gilded leaves, and when it arrived at the church all the guests were gathered outside, so artistically grouped that it might have been intentional.

Even the church itself was neat and fresh and crisp after the spate of building work that had culminated in its reconsecration less than three months ago.

Ninian told herself that, correctly, it ought to be a serial picture. Pictures of weddings always were. In the right foreground, the painter – a real painter, of course, not an amateur like herself – would show the marriage rites outside the church, and to the left, a little further up, the sacrament before the altar. And then, above the two main scenes and very much in the background, there would be representations of the feasts and gift-giving, the cakes and the bride-wine.

As she stood by Columba's side while the rings were blessed and the deed of settlement read, she concentrated on deciding which detail of the ceremony would illustrate best, and she was still thinking about it when Columba gave her hand into that of the Bishop of Avignon who, in turn, placed it in Harry's.

She went on thinking about it while Harry slipped the ring on and off three successive fingers of her right hand – in the name of the Father, the Son, and the Holy Spirit – and then placed it finally on her left.

Only when, still holding her hand, he made his pledge – 'With this ring I thee wed, with this gold I thee honour, and with this dowry I thee endow' – did she finally make up her mind. It would have to be the pledge, she thought, because all that remained after that was for her to sink to her knees before her newly wedded lord and master, and if she were to figure in a painting she didn't see why she should figure as a suppliant.

She was glad someone had put a carpet down on the steps of the church; she didn't want her pretty dress covered with marks.

There was no real choice when they moved inside. It could only be the benediction, with herself and Harry kneeling together under the canopied veil. But she was able to occupy her mind by choosing the best of several possible viewpoints.

All through that interminable day; through the ceremonies, and the feasting; through Columba dispensing the guest-gifts of velvet-collared greyhounds and enamelled bottles of wine and other such trifles; through the music and the dancing and the spectacles; through it all Ninian clung to sanity by translating everything into pictures in her mind, the kind of pictures Pol Limbourg might have painted. Pictures beautifully designed, beautifully disciplined, beautifully polished. Everything that she and her life were not. Was that, perhaps, why she couldn't paint as he did?

And then the Compline bell rang out, and the pictures turned to reality.

Like rag-stuffed dolls, she and Harry sat in the great fourposter, their hair still gritty from the seeds the guests had showered upon them. The room was full of giggling women and sottish men, and even the holy water and incense with which the priests had drenched the bedclothes couldn't disguise the sickly smell of wine-heavy human breath. Blane and Malise and two of Blane's cronies were playing tennis across the bed with a stuffed leather ball. Two or three pretty young squires were romping in a game of ring-a-ring-o'-roses. And Adam, throwing dice on the counterpane against the Abbot of Jaurès with one hand, had his other arm round a flushed Lady Elinor, his palm clamped possessively over her breast.

Standing beside the bed were two churchmen. The gown of the taller man was austere, but Columba's was his favourite and his best, the one of fine-cut velvet trimmed with miniver. He was smiling, even while two thin rivulets of tears ran down the sides of his nose and into the creases round his mouth.

Ninian knew he was trying to say, 'I would have spared you all this, if I could,' and her eyes clung to his, trying to draw strength from him as she had so often drawn strength from him in the past.

Slowly, the noise began to diminish in response to repeated calls for silence, and after a few moments the second churchman, frowning a little, bent cool grey eyes on the young couple in the bed. Somehow, Ninian succeeded in keeping her own eyes downcast. If she hadn't, they would have flown to his as if they were her lodestar.

He raised his hands, saying, 'God of Abraham, Isaac, and Jacob, bless these young people . . .' and then broke off.

Into the pause, Columba murmured, 'Bless them, oh Lord,' and at once the bishop resumed, 'And sow in them the seed of eternal life, that it may spread throughout the length of days and down the ages . . .'

She heard the words, but didn't hear them. They were the formula words, the words she knew he had to speak, words that meant nothing – and everything. Words that, despite their sanctity, were no less suggestive than the tiny symbols of fruitfulness tangled in her hair and trapped between the sheets. Words that had more to do with life physical than life eternal.

Her eyes began to blur so that everything was distorted, and her tired mind, too, saw and heard everything twice over. Twice over, and not quite the same. Not 'eternal life', but 'eternal love'.

That was much better! she thought. 'Eternal love . . . throughout the length of days and down the ages.' It expressed exactly how she felt – and in words she could clasp to her as passionately as a martyr the arrows in his flesh. Oh, yes. That was *much* better.

And then it was over, mercifully – mercilessly – brief. Immediately afterwards he bowed his head, unsmiling still, and left.

It was more than an hour before the bedchamber was at last empty of revellers, and Ninian was alone with Harry, to face what the night still held. Sévèrine had told her what to expect.

But she had left out the one thing that mattered. She hadn't told Ninian how to deal with a man who found himself impotent for the first time in his life, and who blamed her for it. Her, and the Vernes, and French customs, and French wines, and the terrible, torrid heat of the southern French summer.

He had no thought for her at all during that endless, sweating night, no thought for anything but the manhood he couldn't prove. Drily, hurriedly, arbitrarily, he kissed her mouth, and her neck, and her breasts through the fine linen of her shift, and when he couldn't undo the ties of the shift he pulled it up by the hem until it was bundled round her chest, half choking her. He didn't hear her protests as he threw the whole weight of his body on top of her and began to jerk, and rub, and swivel, to knead with his hands, and clench himself between her thighs, to push against her desperately, this way and that, again, and again, and again.

But although he tried for a long, long time, nothing happened, except that, in the end, he wept, and so did she.

THEY set off for Scotland four weeks later, Ninian as if it were heaven they were leaving behind, Harry as if it were hell.

Ninian shed tears all over Sévèrine, hugged Adam passionately, and kissed Blane very much less passionately. They had never been close, and it was unflatteringly clear that Blane was only waiting to see the little cavalcade out of sight before he hurried off to join his friends at the vintaging.

Columba had left a week after the wedding, Bishop-elect Cameron having made it clear that any longer delay in taking up his duties would be viewed with disfavour. But it did mean that he would be in Scotland when Ninian arrived, even if Teviotdale was separated by half the length of the country from her new home at Dess.

All Ninian knew about Dess was that it was a traditional tower house, high on the moors. Columba had said it wouldn't be quite what she was accustomed to, a little spartan, perhaps, so she should take a few small comforts with her.

It had been difficult to persuade Harry that all the things on the sumpter mules and the spare baggage cart were absolutely essential to her wellbeing on the journey, but any hint that she expected to need them at Dess would have been fatal. Furniture, tapestries, bed curtains, bed linen, serving vessels and plate, cooking pots, wine, spices, and a whole pharmacopoeia of medicinal herbs; it did add up to quite a lot. However, as she pointed out to him reasonably, it was going to be a long journey and one never knew what might happen, or where one might have to stay.

She herself was to travel, as befitted a lady of rank whose husband hoped that she might soon be in a delicate condition, in a four-wheeled covered waggon with cushioned seats, accompanied by her two gentlewomen, and with a pair of the new hunting puppies curled up on the painted azure dower chest at her feet. Harry and Malise were to ride alongside, and the cavalcade would be surrounded by armed retainers. Harry said that when they reached Scotland, where roads were few, she would either have to ride or be carried in a litter.

They didn't expect to average more than about twenty miles a day, perhaps less, so it was going to be a long time before they saw even the North Sea, far less Scotland.

And yet, and yet . . . Once Villeneuve and the honey-gold towers of Avignon were out of sight, once Ninian was able to stop looking back, she felt her spirits rising. However unpromising things looked, it was, after all, a new adventure.

And, reprehensibly, she caught herself thinking that in the country she was going to were the two men she loved most in the world.

PART TWO

1427

CHAPTER ONE

I

'NO!' said the bishop forcefully. 'He may judge cases of petty assault, he may adjudicate on the election of parish clerks, he may even – with my goodwill! – rule on actions for defamation of character. But he most certainly may not deprive priests of their parishes or fill my nice clean dungeons with his grubby little lechers and poachers.'

He held out his hand. 'Thank you.'

Dean Myrton surrendered the mitre he had been twirling on the tip of his forefinger and said peaceably, 'I'm not arguing.'

Three months of Archdeacon Crozier had been enough to try any man's patience. It wasn't that he'd been idle, or incompetent, or contumacious. Far from it. In fact, he'd gone out of his way to be charming, especially to the dean and chapter. But he had also pro-ceeded with the business of his half of the diocese as if he were sole and supreme arbiter of its destiny. Gavin, himself working at full stretch, had left him to get on with it. He'd even said, in a fair-minded way, that Crozier was an experienced and clever man who couldn't be expected to enjoy acting as deputy to one of his own former students. 'Though if he makes mistakes . . .'

Which he very soon had.

In Scotland, as everywhere else, there were not only civil courts but ecclesiastical courts, handling all cases involving clerics as well as secular ones that were thought to touch, however distantly, on matters of faith or morals. The Archdeacon's Court was supposed to deal only with the minor cases, the kind that earned the offender no more than a fine or a stiff reprimand, and anyone who took exception to the sentences handed out there had the right to appeal to the bishop.

But the Archdeacon of Teviotdale hadn't only been meting out deprivations and imprisonments. He had also been refusing his incensed victims permission to appeal.

Crozier wasn't a qualified lawyer, of course, as Tom had pointed out. He was a philosopher, a logician, a theologian. Maybe he didn't know. Gavin had told Tom not to be a fool, and had despatched a brief and unequivocal message to the archdeacon requesting him to desist.

The archdeacon had refused, just as unequivocally though a good deal less briefly. The general tenor of his message had been that only in the most backward countries, nowadays, was there centralization of justice. The Holy See had found that allowing independent jurisdiction to the archdeaconate had contributed greatly to administrative efficiency. Perhaps my Lord Bishop, as a recent – and most welcome – recruit to the higher ranks of the clergy, had not been aware of this? But now that he was, Archdeacon Crozier could not doubt that he would wish to conform with enlightened practice.

Gavin, justifiably irritated, had demanded chapter and verse, and had been even more irritated to receive it – and to discover, moreover, that the leading exponents of 'enlightened practice' were Scotland's oldest enemies, the English.

'What now?' he had asked Tom when he had begun to cool down. And Tom, delicately scratching the tip of his nose, had said, 'Do you think you could persuade him to fetch you a clout?'

'To *what*?'

'Ye'll maybe not remember, but there was an occasion a few years back when an archdeacon laid violent hands on his bishop, and the bishop excommunicated him. I thought at the time it was a gey good way of getting rid of an archdeacon ye didn't like.'

Gavin looked at him. 'Oh, I remember! I wasn't Judge of Lothian for nothing. But if that's the best idea you can come up with . . .'

The merest trace of a grin on his lived-in face, Tom had said, 'Yes, well. Maybe arbitration would be more reliable.'

It had been agreed, and the dean and chapter were to meet to arbitrate a week from today. A week from this very day that had seen

Gavin consecrated by the Bishops of Dunkeld and Dunblane and formally installed, at last, in his cathedral, the strong, sturdy twelfth-century building that dominated the busy little market town of Glasgow from its high ground on the north side of the river, the very spot where St Mungo was said to have built his original wooden church.

Gavin was going to make very sure that the arbitration went the right way, because he wasn't having his authority challenged at this stage by anyone, least of all Columba Crozier.

For the second time, he held out the hand with the big, new amethyst ring on it, and his usher gave him the pastoral crook. All that remained of the ceremonial was the induction banquet in the chapter house, and then he was bishop indeed.

He took a deep breath and, in full panoply of mitre and crook, amice and maniple, stole, alb, dalmatic, tunicle and cope, strode out of the robing room to confront four fellow bishops, three earls, an indeterminate number of church and civic dignitaries, and a three-course banquet whose first, twelve-dish course was to include venison and frumenty, swan's neck pudding, blancmanger, eels in saffron, porray of leeks, bruet of capon . . .

He remembered, with nostalgia, the days when bannocks and stoorum and salt herring had been all the banquet he had ever needed.

2

NINIAN, shivering even in her furs, said disparagingly, 'Goodness! I doubt if the Bishop of Gap would think much of *that* for a defensive position!'

Harry, who had been explaining things to her at great and boring length ever since they left the Rhône, interrupted his flow to say, 'Who? What?'

It pleased her inordinately that Harry not only knew little about military matters, but had never even been involved in a battle, whereas she herself had been at the siege of Avignon when she was only two years old.

Well, not *at* the siege precisely, because she had been in Villeneuve at the time. And if the truth were told, she didn't remember a thing about it except that her father and Pope Benedict had been among the besieged. But, later, she and her mother had spent two or three years following papa around until the perpetual noise of cannon had become too much for her mother and they had fled back to Villeneuve. Where it hadn't always been peaceful.

'The Bishop of Gap,' she repeated. 'You remember, I told you. In 1417, when the Comte de Chalon attacked on behalf of the Burgundians and we all had to take refuge in the Fort St André. The bishop was in command, and very competent he was, too. But, of course, Fort St André was defensible.'

Angrily, Harry said, 'So's Dess!' but Malise, who had decided to see them all the way home, was moved to protest. Stickler for accuracy that he was, he said, 'Well, but, Harry, what about yon time when your father . . .'

Ninian, as it happened, had been criticizing only in order to keep her spirits up. Because Dess was one of the most depressing places she had ever seen.

Her first view of Scotland hadn't been too bad, quite pretty in fact, although any dry land would have looked pretty to her after the cockleshell ship that had dipped and rolled and shivered its way queasily across the wild grey sea. But she had come to think of it, almost at once, as an unfriendly countryside. In France, although much of it was empty and ravaged by war, it still seemed as if, round every curve, there might be habitation, whereas in most of the Scotland that Ninian had seen, it was a glaring shock to come across any such signs. It was as if the place was meant to be deserted.

The nearer they had come to Dess, the bleaker everything had become, especially now, at the turn of the year, when the sun skimmed the southern tops for no more than a couple of hours at noon, and today not even that, for the sky was heavy with sleet.

They had been climbing for quite a while before they emerged onto the moors and Harry said they would see Dess soon. All around them stretched a landscape that, neither highland nor lowland, lay bleak and inhospitable in its winter covering of rusty black vegetation and streaky, yellowing snow. Every rock was blanketed in moss and lichens, and the few leafless trees were lichened, too, twisted green skeletons against the dirty sky.

There was a small tubby mountain on their left, wearing its cloud like a coronet of curly, greasy fleece, and as they skirted it Harry and Malise exclaimed simultaneously, 'There's Dess!'

It wasn't more than a few hundred yards ahead and if Ninian hadn't already seen several tower houses of the kind, she thought she would probably have fainted clean away at the first sight of her new home.

Tall, crude and menacing, it rose, single room above single room, to a height of four storeys, where it stopped – just like that, as if the builders had given up in disgust and gone home. At the foot of the tower, adjoining it on one side, was what Ninian had already learned to call the barmkin, a kind of courtyard of makeshift wooden buildings that included the bakehouse and brewhouse, storerooms and stabling, the hawking mews, and a guest room or two for benighted wayfarers, of whom Harry said there were quite a few, because in this part of the country, there wasn't anywhere else for them to go.

As they drew nearer, Ninian looked up and almost lost her sense of balance because the tower loomed over them in such a way that she had the feeling that, if it were vertical, then she couldn't be. The stonework looked very uneven, as if the stones had been gathered at random, rather than properly hewn. They had been set in rough courses – a few feet of thin, slivery ones, then another few feet that were square-ish, then some that were large and lumpily rectangular, and finally thin ones again. This practical but unbeautiful method of construction was the tower's only claim to architectural distinction.

There was a rickety wooden staircase set against one of the walls of the tower, but Harry said that was only for tenants and peasants and anyone coming to see him in the Speak-a-Word room, where he dealt with estate business. To reach the main entrance they had to go through the barmkin – which acted, he said repressively, as a kind of defensive perimeter.

So they rode into the barmkin, and dismounted, and they were home.

3

ALL the way from Villeneuve, Ninian had succeeded in being bright and cheerful and amenable, which had been very necessary, especially at first, with Harry heaping on her shoulders most of his dislike for Adam and Blane, who had treated him with a casual dismissiveness that – she was perfectly prepared to admit – hadn't been very nice. On the other hand, it wasn't a very nice world, and she felt that Harry ought to be adult enough to accept it. But it meant that she had to take care never to mention the Vernes, and that she couldn't even wonder aloud how Columba was faring at Teviotdale. Malise was no help to begin with, because Adam had impressed him enormously and she had to have a serious private talk with him before he could be persuaded to stop going over and over every single thing his hero had said or done.

After the first two or three weeks of the journey, however, with so much that was new to divert Harry's mind from all the slights, real and imagined, of Villeneuve, he had begun to treat her more civilly, and by that time, too, she had been learning not only how to avoid offending him, but even how to please him.

And that had been equally necessary. Stupidly, she hadn't foreseen that Harry would hold the orthodox view of women and wives, and expect her always to be patient and obedient, concerned only with making him happy and with no thought at all for herself. Life in Sévèrine's household hadn't been like that, because Sévèrine held that women had just as much right to their individuality as men did.

The first time Ninian had answered Harry back, he had quoted St Thomas Aquinas – of all people! – at her.

'You must never contradict me, Ninian,' he had said reprovingly. 'You must always remember that woman is by nature inferior to man, because man is guided by reason, not whim.'

It had been a very serious struggle, but she had managed to apologise and he had graciously forgiven her.

Mentally, she had added yet another to the long tally of her good resolutions, though the temptation to cross it off again was great when she saw that Harry was congratulating himself on how well he had handled her. He even went out of his way, a little later, to say how pretty she was looking.

She was glad, however, that she had been sensible enough to go to Sévèrine for advice after the disaster of her wedding night, because Sévèrine had told her what she could do to help Harry in bed.

'You must take it gradually, p'tite, and with tact,' she had warned her. 'It is most necessary that Sir Harry should think himself your only teacher. You must give him no excuse for claiming that you are what Holy Church believes every woman to be – a daughter of Eve, a temptress, the devil's decoy. Because if you do, nothing but trouble will come from it.'

By the time they were nearing Paris, Ninian had been managing quite well, although she hadn't experienced, and couldn't even imagine, the beauty Sévèrine had told her might be found in the act of love. However, it had done wonders for Harry's moodiness and that was what mattered.

The journey had taken almost four months, and Ninian had lived through it from day to day, resolutely refusing to look ahead, which hadn't been too difficult. Even more than Harry was she ready to be beguiled by new experiences and new sights. But it meant that it was more of a shock than it need have been when, at last, she came face to face with her new life.

Because what happened when they reached Dess and Harry led her up the stairs into the huge, bleak, draughty High Hall of her new home – smelling strongly of the cattle stabled on the floor below, and pungent with smoke from the fire that had been kindled in her honour – was that she had a sudden memory of the white, sophisticated, sun-blessed beauty of Provence and the warm, lovely, toasted scents of the south, and all her carefully nurtured brightness drained away with a single horrible gurgle, like water into a hole in the ground.

4

SHE took up her household duties immediately, and efficiently. It was what every gently bred girl was trained for. But she knew, even as she smiled at the four-score unknown faces of the servants lined up in the barmkin, even as she said all the right things, that her whole manner must seem as false to them as it did to her. Through the black depression that had taken her in its grip, she wondered if she would ever be able to tell one from the other. She would have to, because there weren't really very many of them, and Dess was their only home. It had been different at Villeneuve, where there were more than two hundred servants, with friends and ties and an active social life in the town, not just the *livrée*.

But Sévèrine had taught her well. She was able to confer with Master Lindsay, the starchy, expressionless, middle-aged steward, as if she were perfectly accustomed to ordering the day-to-day affairs of a much larger household; to suggest improvements to the baker and the brewer and the cooks – who were sadly in need of instruction; to supervise the yeomen of the buttery and the pantry; to see that the gardener supplied fresh rushes for the floors every few days; to teach the watchman to blow several short, crisp notes on his horn at the approach of strangers instead of the long, ear-splitting wail he was used to; and to recommend the almoner not to gabble the grace at meals and to draw breath in more logical places when he was chanting Matins or saying morning Mass in the chapel. She could see that he didn't like being corrected; none of the servants did.

The 'chapel' at Dess was in the gallery at the very top of the tower under the roof timbers, and was the only room in the place that wasn't subject to constant coming and going. Within days of her arrival, Ninian had decided to appropriate it for her own; certainly, there was nowhere else to hang her tapestries or put her few pieces of fine furniture.

Harry objected, of course, as if there was something immoral about covering up nasty, dirty, damp-stained walls and sitting on cushioned chairs instead of hard stools. To him, Dess was perfect as it was, and he didn't want it, or anything about it, altered. But she knew she would go mad unless she had some active, positive outlet for her frustrations, so she rushed ahead, changing everything she thought needed to be changed, and explaining it all very sweetly to him afterwards.

Immediately below the gallery-chapel was the private floor of the castle, with two small bedchambers for important guests, and the Laird's Hall, which served as her and Harry's bedchamber and also as an informal reception room. It wasn't very welcoming, but when Ninian had put a furred rug on the splintered wooden floor, hung her little shrine and mirror on the walls, and laid out the silver-gilt basin and ewer on her gaily painted dower chest, it began to look better.

Down the turnpike stairs from the Laird's Hall were Harry's Speak-a-Word room, which she wasn't even allowed to enter, and the enormous High Hall, the centre of activity at Dess, where everyone lived and ate during the day and some of the servants and squires slept at night. Within a week, Ninian had a stiff neck from the draughts that shrieked in through the glassless, shutterless windows, so that, ignoring Harry's demonstrably false claim that fresh air never did anyone any harm, she summoned the carpenter to construct some wooden frames filled, in the absence of glass, with oiled parchment that served almost as well. It made a big difference.

She had to resign herself to doing nothing, just yet, about the stone-vaulted ground floor where the cattle and sheep were housed, but she promised herself that she would some day. The animals could perfectly well be stabled in the barmkin outhouse where the kitchen now was; then the kitchen could come indoors and they could all have the pleasure of hot food instead of cold. She couldn't imagine why no one had thought of it before.

But it was false, all of it, her own housewifely fervour, Harry's grudging complaisance, Malise's kind-hearted approval – for Malise was still there, snowbound as they all were, as cut off from the out-side world as if Dess were some island in the unknown seas round Cathay.

The crisis came unexpectedly, precipitated by something so minor that Ninian was totally unprepared. She was talking to Master Lindsay about teaching some of the women servants how to make proper candles instead of the rushlights that were all Dess had ever had in the way of illumination, and Harry, who had been growing sulkier for several days past, overheard and suddenly erupted.

'*Candles!* You'll be wanting beeswax for them next, I suppose, instead of good honest tallow!'

'That would be nice,' she said wistfully, ignoring his tone, 'but I don't suppose it's possible here. Unless – perhaps there's some monas-tery that might let us have some?'

Beeswax smelled sweet when it was burning, which was why it was used for ecclesiastical candles. Séverine had had an arrangement with the Val de Bénédiction so that they had never had to have tallow at Villeneuve.

'No, there isn't, even if I could afford it. Bees don't do well here. What's wrong with tallow, anyway?'

'It smells horrible.'

'No, it doesn't.'

'Yes, it does. It smells just like what it is, burning mutton fat. And it doesn't give much light, either.'

'Yes, it does.'

'No, it doesn't. But at least candles would give more than those miserable little rushlights.'

'No, they wouldn't.'

'Yes, they would.'

'What do you want more light for, anyway?'

Ninian wondered whether to scream. There were scarcely six hours of daylight at Dess in winter, and even daylight was gloomy enough under these overcast skies. Rushlights, which were made from the pith of rushes dipped in melted fat, burned themselves out in no time, smoked nastily, and gave scarcely more than a pinpoint of light, so that they had to be used in considerable numbers if they were to be any use at all. It was an almost fulltime occupation for two of the servants, fitting new ones into the special pincer holders every few minutes.

With some asperity, she said, 'I have to see in order to be able to sew!'

'What do you need to sew for? I should have thought you had enough gowns to last you for life.'

She took a deep and slightly shaky breath. 'And what about your shirts? Have you enough of those? And Master Lindsay's shirts?' She nodded towards Master Lindsay, still standing there looking as blank as if he had been stuffed. 'And all those tunics with the little poked sleeves that you like your yeomen to wear when they are riding out with you? The women can't manage everything by themselves, you know. And I have forty-five ells of napery to make up into sheets and towels . . .'

'Have you, by God? And how much did *that* cost that I haven't heard about yet?'

'At two shillings an ell, you can work it out for yourself. But it didn't cost anything. It was a wedding gift.'

'Oh. Well, why don't you do your spinning at night, and sew during the day?'

'Because in this terrible, awful, dreadful country of yours, I can't see to sew during the day, either!'

'Well, you shouldn't have filled in the windows with that oiled parchment stuff!'

And then she did scream at him, 'Oh, stop it, stop it, *stop it!*' and fled from the High Hall up to the sanctuary of the gallery.

It was their first quarrel, and that wasn't the end of it, because he followed her upstairs. She was sitting with her lips clamped between her teeth, trying not to cry, telling herself that it had all been silly – childish and spiteful – and that it didn't matter. But she knew that it did, because Harry was her only anchor in this new life, and without him she would be quite alone. In these last weeks, she had been relieved to find him trying so hard – or so she had thought – to be tolerant, and civilized, and prepared to put up with what she did, even though he couldn't always approve. Her mind and feelings numbed by the life-denying depression that gripped her, she had tried to persuade herself that they might rub along quite well. He was pleasant enough, much of the time.

But now – it had taken very little to turn her numb unhappiness into abject misery.

There was no door to the gallery, so he walked straight in.

'I've been meaning to say,' he began, without preliminary, 'that this "terrible, awful, dreadful country" of mine is yours too, now. I haven't liked hearing you chattering away in French to those two women of yours, and I've made my mind up. They'll have to go back to France, as soon as the roads are open. We'll find some decent women for you in Perth, and in the meantime you can fetch a couple of lasses up from the laundry shed to maid you.'

Her gentlewomen, her only link with France, her only confidantes, however little she confided in them.

She opened her mouth, but he wouldn't let her speak. 'No. I've told you my mind is made up. And even if it hadn't been, arguing with me in front of the servants downstairs would have been enough to decide me. It's time you learned. I'm your husband, you know. I'm the master.'

And then he turned and walked out.

After a while, she dragged herself from her chair and went up to the parapet walk on the roof of the tower, hoping the fresh, biting air would settle the sickness in her. But it didn't. All that happened was that she looked down, and thought how easy it would be . . .

Suicide, *felo de se*. A sin of unimaginable proportions, a path to everlasting damnation – a rejection of God as sacrilegious as heresy, the greatest sin of all.

It shocked her back into something near normality, shocked her into trying to look at things sensibly, unemotionally, as if through someone else's eyes. Sévèrine's, perhaps; not Columba's, because he was never detached where those he loved were concerned.

She thought, fighting down a wave of self-pity, that even Sévèrine might sympathize not with her but with Harry, who had believed himself to be marrying a bright, biddable girl and had found himself, instead, tied to a bride whose heart was as remote from him as the moon. It wasn't his fault that, on the day before their marriage, she should have fallen victim to the kind of love that some poet or other had called a folly of the mind, an unquenchable fire, a hunger without surfeit and without surcease. Nor was it his fault that she hadn't known, and didn't know, how to deal with it.

There were potions to induce love. Was there, perhaps, some magical elixir that would take love away? And would she drink it, if there was?

She wouldn't have loved Harry, anyway, but she hadn't meant to cheat him. Her thoughts should have been wholly on him, and his happiness and welfare her only concern. Perhaps, if she had behaved better, she might even have succeeded in giving him the one thing he passionately wanted, for he was impatient that, after almost seven months of marriage, there was still no sign of a child. He blamed her for it, and perhaps he was right. She had done nothing to stop herself conceiving, but in her prayers night after night, she had been giving thanks for it. It wasn't that she didn't want a child – she did – just that she didn't want Harry's. And that was very wrong of her.

She turned away, in the end, from the parapet walk, and descended the turnpike stairs to the chapel, knowing she had to gather herself together and try to make the best of things for both of them.

And she would manage it somehow, as long as she could blind her eyes to a future that would be like this, for ever and ever, until she died.

5

NINIAN'S nose was delicately tinged with blue, and Columba couldn't tell at first whether the moisture round her eyes came from the biting east wind or from pleasure at seeing him.

His own eyes were streaming, and he had been sniffing continuously for the last mile because it seemed a lesser evil than having to halt the little cavalcade, and dismount, and search under all his outer layers of clothing for the purse that contained his handkerchief. He envied his retinue, who cared nothing for such modern pretensions.

It had been a long ride, and a weary one. Harassing, too, because he still wasn't accustomed to travelling with only a handful of men to protect him. But seven was the maximum entitlement of archdeacons who hoped to beg a free night's lodging from abbeys and monasteries along the way, and Columba was being careful with his money.

Worriedly, he hoped he could afford the time this visit would cost him, but he hadn't seen Ninian since they had parted in Villeneuve six months before, and the two brief messages she had sent him had been cheerful to the point of inanity. He had reassured himself with the thought that she was happy and optimistic by nature, capable of facing up to most of the problems likely to beset her, but, even so, he had felt he couldn't sail for Rome without seeing her. And the nearer they had come to Dess, the greater had grown his doubts.

His first, distant sight of the castle with the small, solitary figure standing outside the entrance to the barmkin had confirmed them – for it was one of the tower houses of a kind he knew only too well, perched in the middle of a moor and open to every wind that blew. It must have been built, he thought, about sixty or seventy years ago, with an eye not to convenience but to defence against the Highland caterans who, year in and year out, raided down through the mountain passes to replenish their cattle from among the fat, pampered stock of the cultivated lands. Not that Dess looked as if it were much cultivated.

As they drew near the last shallow rise to the castle, Adam, cantering easily along beside him, raised a satirical voice to say, 'Ah hah! It seems that Harry intends to welcome us after all!' And that was a relief, because at Villeneuve Harry had scarcely even tried to hide his jealousy of his new wife's family and friends.

But the young man who greeted them at the gate to this, his 'castle' of Dess, was very much on his home ground and far more master of the situation than Columba would have believed possible.

Master, too, of his wife, the Lady Ninian Drummond, who – following the Scots custom that was a source of such confusion to foreigners – had kept her own name but, it seemed to Columba in the first few dismaying hours, nothing else of herself at all.

6

SHE hadn't realized that her lips and hands were so cold until she kissed Columba sedately on the cheek and he gave a tremendous mock shudder and exclaimed, 'By all the saints, child! Take yourself indoors. We'll follow in a moment!'

But she had been waiting eight shivering weeks for his visit, so she kept her grip on his hand and said, 'No, no. I'm used to it.' She was able to say it smilingly, as if it were something of no importance, just as she was able to control her desire to throw her arms round his neck and hug him as if she would never let him go. Harry didn't like her being impulsive.

Watching Columba now, as he and Harry exchanged civilities, she reflected that, a few weeks ago, his mere presence would have been enough to smooth away all her sorrows; she would have listened for a decent interval to what he had to tell, waiting eagerly for the moment when it would be her turn and she could pour her heart out to him. But not now.

She would tell him, of course, something of how she had been faring; never in her life had she kept anything from him. But she would tell it lightly, because he had troubles enough, she suspected, without her adding to them. There was a touch of strain in his face, and Adam, whom she had thought still in France, raised his eyebrows at her in a way that spoke volumes.

Harry insisted on taking Columba on a tour of the house and barmkin, so that it was from Adam, following behind with her, that Ninian heard a brief and disconnected version of what had happened. His voice, whenever he spoke of Bishop Gavin, was filled with dislike and contempt.

And then Columba himself concluded the tale as they sat down to their evening meal in the High Hall.

'So,' he said, pensively surveying a dish of roasted salmon in verjuice and cinnamon sauce, 'I lost. And Cameron won. The dean and chapter have not the slightest interest in what is practised elsewhere. They have decreed that I have no right to deprive or imprison anyone without a direct mandate from the bishop, and that any offender who objects to my rulings can go straight to him to appeal.'

Ninian said, frowning, 'But Columba, what will you do?'

'I have no choice but to fight, otherwise the position is impossible. If Cameron can overrule me in the courts, he can overrule me in other things, too. And he will.'

Her own voice, blankly repeating, 'He will?' was overridden by that of Malise Graham, who was still there and was beginning to seem as if he always would be. Ninian had resigned herself. At least he kept Harry company, and in the evenings, while she sewed by the light of the candles – she had won over those, in the end, even if they were tallow and not beeswax – the two of them were able to talk about cows, and sheep, and parliament and the law, and the treaties with Norway and Flanders, and all the other things she knew nothing about and had no interest in.

'Well, you know,' Malise said in his most infuriatingly moralizing tone, 'I've no wish to criticize, but, however much you girn about them, the rules *are* the rules and you ought to bide by them. And so long as justice is done, does it matter whether it's you or the bishop that does it?'

Columba looked at him, more in surprise than anything else. 'Oh, yes. It matters very much. I have already spent two years in the wilderness of papal displeasure because a particular person – someone with more power than I – willed that it should be so. You may remember that, at Villeneuve, I swore that never again would I permit anything that was mine to be taken from me. And *I will not.*' It wasn't said belligerently but as a plain statement of fact.

Malise replied sulkily, 'That wasn't what I meant,' but he didn't pursue it, and Ninian, confused, said, 'Anything that's yours? Are you talking about having the right to imprison people? But is that really yours? I mean, surely it's not a personal thing. Isn't it a matter of – of episcopal policy? Of a bishop limiting the powers of an archdeacon, not of . . .' To speak the name was almost too difficult. 'Not of Gavin Cameron *taking* something from Columba Crozier.'

Columba shook his head. A servant had just poured some wine into his cup and he raised it and swallowed a mouthful. An involuntary spasm crossed his face and Ninian suddenly remembered that she had meant to tell the yeoman of the cellar to have some hippocras or clary prepared. Harry, who preferred ale, always economized on wine and bought new, raw wine-of-vintage instead of a mature wine-of-rack. It was scarcely drinkable without honey and spices.

'I don't mean the jurisdiction,' Columba said. 'Or only in the sense that it's an omen. Cameron doesn't approve of me. He doesn't want me as his archdeacon. And if I have no authority of my own, if all the power is his, and he is as conscienceless as I think, he could have me dispossessed with very little difficulty.'

She couldn't let it go. There was a dreadful fascination in saying again the name she had so often forbidden herself even to think of. 'But why are you so sure that Bishop Gavin is a danger to you? He seemed to me a perfectly – a – a perfectly reasonable man.'

It was strange to be carrying on such an adult, such a serious conversation with Columba. She had never heard him speak like this before, with no lightness in his tone, no warmth in his eyes. If it had not been Columba, the word she would have thought of would have been 'implacable'.

'Oh, no. Cameron is a clever man, and a man in a hurry. Only a driving ambition would have got him where he is, so young. Nothing will do for him but to have everything done his way. He knows my judgements would be judgements according to the laws of the church, whereas he wants them to accord directly with those of the realm. You would almost think he didn't believe that the laws of Holy Church are one and the same as the laws of God. No, he is no good priest, whatever the robes he wears. I have said it before, and I say it again – he is the king's creature, first and foremost.'

Unexpectedly, Harry intervened. Ninian hadn't even thought he was listening. 'Oh, well, if that's the case, you haven't much choice but to fight if you want to survive. If James supports Cameron, you'll have to get Rome on your side, because James is ruthless!'

Ninian knew what was coming next. It always did.

'Well, you remember,' Harry went on, 'he'd scarcely been back in Scotland a year before he had Albany's head on the block. The regent! His own cousin! The man who'd been keeping his throne warm for him! *And* two of Albany's sons, *and* his father-in-law. Treason, he said. Hah!' Harry glared at Columba as if it had all been his fault.

'But you know about that! What you probably don't know is that anyone he suspected of favouring Albany got pretty rough justice, too. Including my Uncle Robert. It was straight into prison for him, just because Albany had given him some lands that James said belonged rightly to the crown.'

'Oh, dear,' Adam remarked, emerging from his abstraction. 'What a sad want of tact!'

Harry had no sense of irony. 'Yes. Well, Uncle Robert escaped, of course. But he's had to keep his head down ever since.'

Ninian hadn't met Sir Robert Graham yet, but she had heard a great deal about him from Harry, who quoted him as if he were the final arbiter on everything. He had studied, it seemed, at the university of Paris, but that alone wouldn't have been enough to overawe Harry, and Ninian had the feeling that there must be a lot more to Uncle Robert than mere book-learning.

'Outlawed? How exciting!' Adam's voice was dulcet, and Malise Graham cast an uneasy look at him from pale-lashed hazel eyes. Even though Malise was fascinated by him, he still wasn't comfortable about Adam's open contempt for all legally constituted authority. The only authority Adam acknowledged was Columba's.

Adam grinned at the boy, and flashed him a cheerful wink.

Harry, vaguely dissatisfied, said, 'Well, no, not precisely outlawed. But it's a gamble every time he shows his face at court, in case the king's in one of his moods.'

Although Ninian had learned to make allowance for Harry's extremism on the subject of his sovereign lord, she had still, almost insensibly, begun to think of James as an unstable and unpredictable tyrant. The reminder, now, made Columba's peril suddenly seem much greater. She exclaimed, 'But Columba, what *can* you do? If the king chooses to back Bishop Gavin, how will fighting the decree help?'

Columba's lip curled. 'If this were a civilized country, there would be an archbishop who could rule on the matter but, as it is, I have no alternative but to go direct to Rome. The bishop has been so obliging as to give me his permission. He is, of course, sending his own representative to make sure my arguments don't go uncontested. However, I hope to arrive before his emissary does, and I think I'll win.' His chill smile deepened. 'I have a good case and, even if I hadn't, I still have the advantage of knowing the ways of the Holy See better than most.'

He twirled the horn cup in his fingers, studying the wine but making no further move to taste it. 'Both the bishop and the king will be bound to accept Rome's decision, however little they may like it.

'But I wish . . .' He raised his eyes. 'I really *do* wish that our young friend Cameron was at the bottom of the deep blue sea. Because as long as he bears the title of Gavin Glasgow, I have the feeling that I will never be entirely safe.'

7

THERE was a light fall of snow that night – the lambing snow, the last of the winter, Harry said. But it wasn't deep and Columba couldn't afford to delay, so, leaving Adam behind, he set off at first light on the following morning. As he kissed Ninian at parting, he murmured, 'Remember, I never stop thinking of you. This is not the life I would have wished for you, but, you know, the trials will seem less as you come to know your husband better. God be with you.' It was never an empty phrase, the way Columba said it.

Her eyes stinging, she watched the little party out of sight across the waste of the moors. She had never thought that, some day, there might be something she would have to keep secret from Columba. What an irony that both of them should be obsessed, in such different ways, by the same man.

Harry, his dislike at war with the laws of hospitality, was less than gracious to Adam at first, but even he soon began to mellow as, under the influence of Adam's explosive vitality, life at Dess improved beyond recognition. Ninian found herself laughing for the first time since Villeneuve, and Malise followed along at Adam's heels like a large, faithful, and rather didactic spaniel.

Adam, accustomed to hero-worship, had no hesitation in leading him on – baiting him, giving him orders, mocking him, testing the full extent of his devotion. It was something he was very good at, and he soon discovered that Malise would yield on almost anything except his belief in law and order and his fondness for Harry's old peregrine falcon, Sibella.

There was nearly a crisis in their relationship one day when they went out after rook and Adam, impatient with Sibella's fidgetting, said, 'Tip a bucket of water over the old bitch. That should quieten her down.' But Malise protested furiously, and Sibella, spared her second bath of the day, went on to make two beautiful kills, which had the fortunate effect of allowing Malise to say, 'I told you so,' and thus restoring him to temper.

With his company so much sought after, Adam was soon constrained to point out that he was not at Dess for a rest, but on serious business. The business of Columba's income.

As it happened, Dess was situated not far from a district whose tithes were supposed to account for a goodly part of this. Unfortunately, said Adam astringently, the local peasants' piety did not extend to turning up on the doorstep with a bag of gold labelled 'Annual contribution to the benefice income of Columba Crozier, Archdeacon of Teviotdale and Canon of Dunkeld.' Someone had to collect it, and that someone was to be Adam. Nor was it gold he was fated to collect.

'Lambs and calves! Kids and piglets! Eggs, milk and butter! Leeks and kail!' He clasped a dramatic hand to his forehead. 'A tithe is . . .'

'A teind,' Harry interrupted helpfully, 'and we don't have pigs in Scotland.'

Ignoring the pigs, Adam stared at him. 'My friend, when you are capable of pronouncing *dîme* so that a Frenchman can understand it, I will undertake to pronounce whatever it was you said, so that a Scotsman can understand it.' Then, giving in to Harry's frown, he went on grandly, 'Very well, let us call them *decimae*! Tenths. How, will you tell me, do I collect a tenth of a lamb? Or, *mon Dieu*, a tenth of an egg?'

'You don't,' Malise said. 'The law reckons that every hen lays twenty eggs a year, so you take two eggs per hen.'

'*Merveilleux!* And what, then, do I do with the eggs? Considering that, by the time my master has returned from Rome, they will no longer be perfectly fresh.' Since that disastrous day in Villeneuve, Adam had been very careful to maintain the fiction that Columba was no more than a family friend, even among those who knew better. Harry had had to be told, but not Malise.

Ninian giggled. 'You sell them.'

'Sell them? You mean I am not only to be a collector of tithes, and a herder of sheep, but a merchant, also?'

He was playing the fool, of course, but Harry took him seriously. 'It may not be so bad, you know. Most of the poorer folk don't have ten of anything. In that case, you just demand a halfpenny for each of their lambs, and a farthing for a kid. That's what the priest does here, anyway.'

'The difficulty arises,' Malise said, 'when the folk don't deal in coin at all. In these airts, most of them rely on barter. I'm not sure what you do then.'

Adam had been teasing one of the puppies, but now he looked up, his eyes blazing with laughter. 'Don't you? I do! I excommunicate them!'

Malise let out a hoot of mirth. 'You can't! You're not a priest!'

'Pfui! A matter of a robe, no more. And a bell, a book and a candle.'

He leapt to his feet in a swirl of scarlet, and, whisking a candle from its sconce on the wall, threw his arms wide and began to intone, 'Cursed be ye sitting, standing, riding, going, sleeping, waking, eating and drinking; from the crown of your head to the soles of your feet.'

He was tall and magnificently built, and he towered over them all like some bat-cloaked figure from the abyss, every muscle taut and his eyes darkly glittering.

Then, suddenly, he swung his free hand round so that a long, hard, predatory forefinger was pointing straight at Harry Graham's heart, and went on, his voice rising in both pitch and intensity, 'Few be your days! Your dwelling be with Dathan and Abiram for whose sins the earth swelled! And as this candle is cast from the sight of men' – the thrilling voice ceased for a moment, and he pitched the candle the whole length of the chamber – 'so be your soul cast from the sight of God into the deepest pit of hell, ever to remain with cursed Nero the wicked emperor, and all his cursed fellowship!'

The thought of Harry doomed to an eternal *tête-à-tête* with one of the nastiest of the Caesars was almost too much for Ninian who, repressing an almost irrepressible and entirely impious desire to applaud, picked up her skirts and ran to the other end of the gallery where the floor rushes were already beginning to smoulder.

When she had stamped them out, she salvaged the candle and, walking with exaggerated decorum, restored it to its place. She and Adam, brought up within the orbit of the church, had a down-to-earth view of religious ritual that was common enough in ecclesiastical circles but hard for a layman to understand, and she could see that both Malise and Harry were very shocked indeed.

But Adam was smiling upon them all with the greatest amiability. 'I have done my homework, you see! And in the "cursing for tithes", as in all else, Scotland is unique. If this were England, you would be condemned to share eternity not with Nero but with Judas. Who would, I feel, be not at all such stimulating company!'

For an extended moment, Harry said nothing, and Ninian could see the struggle going on inside him as he busied himself relighting the candle with a taper from the fire. But the rules of hospitality won, and when he spoke it was only to say – albeit a trifle uncivilly – 'These grand gestures are all very well, my friend, but please remember that although the High Hall floor is of stone, this one is wood. There may be no shortage of timber in France, but here, if the floors or roof were to take fire, I would have a very hard time replacing them.'

Malise, ponderously tactful, broke in, 'That's why we build high rather than wide in Scotland, Adam. Did you know? It takes a fair bit less wood, especially in the roof.'

And Adam, to Ninian's relief, had enough sense to allow himself to be drawn into a discussion of building practice. But she wished that he wouldn't always choose Harry as the victim of his more extravagant jokes. It was just the same here as it had been in Villeneuve. When Adam offended, it was she who suffered.

Her mind was still occupied with thoughts of how she was going to persuade Harry that Adam hadn't really been guilty of blasphemy, when something Malise was saying caught her attention.

'But do you not think I should put in an appearance at court? Uncle Atholl says I could do with a bit of polish.'

It was the most extraordinary thing. Harry gaped at him for a moment and then threw back his head and laughed as if he were never going to stop. And after a moment Malise was laughing, too, reluctantly at first, and then, as the mirth built up inside him, so uncontrollably that it looked as if he were about to have a spasm.

Ninian stared, open-mouthed. Harry and Malise laughing? Laughing in real, honest, irresistible amusement?

When they had calmed down a little, Ninian said, 'Harry?' and Harry, still snuffling and gasping, replied, 'Wait till you see Atholl! For *him* to talk of polish!' And he was off again.

Adam, one quizzical eyebrow raised, looked at Ninian and murmured, 'Well, well! It seems that the Earl of Atholl is someone one should meet for more reasons than one thought.'

A little later, a cup of ale in his hand, Harry had recovered sufficiently to say, 'Well, it's up to you, Malise. I don't much care for court myself, though I'll have to take Ninian there soon. I grant you there's a feeling of being where important things are happening, but Uncle Robert says it's all a fallacy, and I think he's right. He's spent a bit of time in the Highlands these last years, off and on, and he says it gives you a different perspective. He says it used to trouble his soul that he was never able to find God in the haunts of men, whereas in the empty glens he finds Him everywhere, even in the – what was it, now? – oh yes, even in the wind that blows from out the wilderness.'

It was an evening of surprises. Ninian found herself staring again, with her mouth slightly open. She hadn't imagined Uncle Robert as the kind of man who concerned himself much with his soul, or with flights of poetic fancy either. If only Harry didn't make 'Uncle Robert says' into quite such a litany!

'And Uncle Robert says,' Harry went on, 'that you don't realize how loud and garish and spiritually slothful what we call civilized life actually is until you've experienced the sacramental purity of the glens.'

For good or ill, the only immediate effect of this pronouncement was to remind Ninian that she had been entirely unmoved by the sacramental purity of any of the glens she had seen so far, and that there was nothing she wanted more in the world – apart from what she could not have, and was schooling herself never to think of – than for Harry to fulfil his promise and take her to the loudest, most garish, most shamelessly civilized and spiritually slothful haunt of men in the whole realm of Scotland, the court of King James I.

When, later, she excused herself and retired to bed, Adam's eyes followed her and there was satisfaction in them. It seemed to him that his little cousin, who had so clearly been unhappy when he and Columba arrived, was already much more like herself, which he attributed, not without reason, to the stimulating effects of his own presence. She had always worshipped him.

He estimated that he could afford to stay on at Dess until perhaps the end of April, although he would have preferred not to; these godforsaken moors would have been enough to drive him to drink – if Harry's wine had been drinkable. By that time young Ninian's cure should be complete. He wasn't leaving Scotland, anyway, so he could ride over occasionally and keep an eye on her. Given, of course, the time and the inclination.

He turned a reflective eye on Malise Graham, Earl of Strathearn. Earls, however tiresome, had their uses, and this one was related to Scotland's premier lord. He'd take the boy with him when he went.

8

ALWAYS, before, Columba had found spring the most congenial season in Rome. Warm, but not too hot; the air bright and freshly rinsed; the foliage green instead of grey; even the Tiber smelling more like a river than an open sewer. And the people correspondingly healthier and better-humoured than at any other time of the year.

But it was different in 1427. Such was the sickness in his heart that he scarcely saw the city at all except as a blurred, wavering frame round the living portrait of Pope Martin V, his friend and executioner.

Columba, as was his Christian duty, revered the Holy Father above all men. But to Martin he also owed a personal debt of gratitude, because when Martin had invited him, nine years ago, to join the papal court, it had been like an answer to his prayers. He had known by then that he was not cut out to spend his life either wresting the souls of serfs and villeins from the embraces of Antichrist, or initiating fledgling priests into the intricacies of logic and philosophy. What he had been born for, what both intuition and intellect passionately cried out for, was to be at the centre of things. And the papal court was more than the centre of Christendom. To every man of faith, it was the centre of the world.

The debacle of three years ago, and Martin's failure, last year, to reinstate him at the curia, had scarcely changed Columba's attitude. A pope was not invariably his own master, nor subservient only to God.

During these last months of exile, Columba had persuaded himself that it was only a matter of time, that before very long he would find himself recalled to the papal court, to become once again a member of the papal 'family'. His own mind and Martin's had always been perfectly attuned, and it seemed to Columba that Martin might even be missing him. All thrones were lonely places, and the throne of St Peter loneliest of all.

So, although he had arrived in the Holy City with the ostensible object of having the Glasgow ruling overturned, he had hoped in his heart that it didn't matter very much, that the time might be opportune for His Holiness to suggest that Archdeacon Crozier return to the curia permanently.

Almost at once, he had discovered that he was right about it not mattering very much. But for all the wrong reasons.

The moment he walked into the Rota to register his plea, he sensed that there was something amiss. Two of the judges, whom he had known for years, scarcely even nodded to him in passing. One of the scribes glanced up at him, and then shiftily away. And the notary who attended to him was so cursory that Columba not only had to emphasize, but re-emphasize, the importance of the three key points in his argument.

As he made his smiling way out again, along corridors bustling with legates and petitioners and lawyers, through a courtyard stuffed to bursting point with pilgrims waiting for the pontifical blessing, his mind was racing. Clearly, he must find out what was going on. So he did what everyone did who wanted to know what was happening in the Holy City. He went to a courtesan.

His devotion to Séverine, though lifelong, had never been exclusive, and he had been acquainted with Vittoria d'Aragona for years, a handsome, voluptuous, clever woman for whom harlotry was neither more nor less than a commercial venture at which she happened to excel. Her house, rented from the monastery of S. Maria in Capitolio, was one of the most luxurious in Rome, and much frequented by prelates, high-ranking noblemen, and adherents of the new doctrine of humanism.

Columba found there was no need for him to manoeuvre round to what he wanted to know. She had lost none of her acuteness, it seemed, for, 'Columba!' she greeted him from under the gilt-encrusted canopy of her chair. 'My dearest man! My long-lost dove! And with a hawk in pursuit! Will you take some wine with me?'

No one but Vittoria had ever made play with the derivation of his name, and that she should have taken the trouble to discover that Gavin was the old Celtic word for hawk surprised him not at all. She was that kind of woman.

He kissed her, and gave her the four ells of crimson velvet he had bought for her that morning, and said, 'What do you know? And how do you know?'

'*How* do I know? You would have me betray the secrets of the confessional?' She primmed her lips, and drew in a deep, scandalized breath that strained her silken bosom almost to splitting point.

Despite himself, Columba laughed. 'Take care, woman. You should know that I am not too old to fall for such tricks!'

Releasing the breath, she grinned at him. 'But you have more important things on your mind. Very well.' Laying the velvet aside, she said, 'Sit, then, and tell me first. What do *you* know?'

'Nothing, except that I have a jurisdictional dispute with the Bishop of Glasgow, and that I hope to persuade the Rota to rule in my favour.'

'Why am I not acquainted with this bishop of yours?' she asked, raising her brows in mock perplexity. 'Has he not been to Rome? Or is he a hawk that will not come to a woman's lure?'

'He might be a eunuch, for all I know. But I can tell you that he disapproves most strongly of your profession.'

'*Santo cielo!* What a very odd thing for a bishop! But I am told he is quite young. Young – and intolerant? He will grow out of it.'

Then she frowned and leaned forward, the unbound hair swinging dark and heavy against her cheek. 'Columba, my dove. I do not wish to tell you what gossip says, but it is better that you learn from me, I think.'

He waited, his face expressionless, and after a moment she went on, 'Gossip says that your case will not even be heard because there will be no need, since you are again to be deprived of your benefices.'

He had expected something unpleasant, but not that. He continued to sit, cold and disbelieving, aware of nothing except that Gavin Cameron must be behind it.

Vittoria placed a plump, compassionate hand over his. 'I do not know if it is *all* your benefices. Listen, and I will explain. So that Tee . . . Teevee-oht . . .'

'Teviotdale.'

'*Si.* So that that place could be restored to you last year, it had to be taken away from another man, the one who had held it since you were deprived. I cannot say his name – Bov . . . Bovmakkar?'

'Bowmaker. John Bowmaker.'

'*Sto imparando!* Well, this man wishes to have it back. He has been in Rome for three weeks arguing his claim.'

Three weeks? Three weeks! If, after the arbitration at Glasgow, Columba had not gone back to Teviotdale to arrange for someone to look after things while he was away . . . If he had not then gone on to Dess . . . If he had not had to wait for a ship . . .

'I know nothing of the worth of his case,' Vittoria went on, 'but it is said he has invoked the *Execrabilis* against you.'

The *Execrabilis* was the papal bull of 1317 that forbade any priest to hold more than one benefice, and it was infringed every day of the week with the active connivance of the Holy See itself, which was not only willing but eager to make exceptions to it. For a fee, of course. Columba knew of one man who had been rich enough to be 'excepted' to the tune of two archdeaconries, one abbacy, seven canonries, five rectorships, and a cardinal's hat.

He himself had been unable to afford the fees last year, but he had been told unofficially that there was no urgency.

Slowly, he said, 'The *Execrabilis*? But no one ever invokes that, because it cuts both ways. If Bowmaker uses it against me, he must abide by it too. Are you quite sure?'

'Oh, yes. He says that the sum of all your benefices comes to more than £160 Scots a year – I did not know you were so rich! – and that you hold too many other cures to be able to look after Te . . . Teevee . . . that place as well.'

'Teviotdale,' he said automatically. 'And – rich? On paper, perhaps. I suppose Bowmaker *might* regard Teviotdale as profitable enough to make it worth while giving up the chance of other benefices, but I doubt it.'

And then something occurred to him and, almost to himself, he said, 'But there could be a friendly little local arrangement. When a benefice falls vacant, it can be a year, two years, before it is filled from Rome. If Bowmaker were to be promised any such Glasgow livings, on a temporary and unofficial basis . . . The income from vacant benefices *should* go to the curia, but I am not at all sure that Scotland even has an official Collector of First Fruits at the moment.' He looked at her narrowly. 'Why did you speak of the hawk?'

She shrugged. 'I heard that Archdeacon Crozier had been rash enough to challenge his bishop, whereas Master Bom . . . Bomakker has a more ingratiating disposition.' The painted eyes looked at him consideringly. 'It is not like you, my friend, to invite trouble.'

'I was defending, not attacking.'

She could see that his mind was working furiously, and that she herself scarcely existed except as someone to be questioned. It didn't trouble her. It was from men in this mood that she learned many things that were lucrative to her.

He said, 'What more have you heard?'

'Only that your Bishop of Glasgow – Columba, where *is* Glasgow? – is soon to be named chancellor of Scotland.' She shook her head. 'An ill man for an enemy, my dove.'

Abruptly, he rose to his feet. 'His enmity was not of my seeking. I must go now.'

She, too, rose after a moment, and went towards him. 'Must you?'

Delicately, she turned the heavy outer robe back from his shoulders, but no more. She neither touched his flesh, nor pressed her own magnificent body against his. She was Vittoria d'Aragona, and she was never vulgar. The invitation had been given. He could accept or refuse it, as he chose.

He felt the familiar, enticing quiver in his loins but then, even as he placed his hands on her hips – the hips that were not, nor ever had been slender, but always soft and yielding – he knew that however well she understood him, however seductive her arts, he would find no oblivion in her embrace this day. Nor did he want to.

So he shook his head, smiling a little, and said, 'I will not insult you. When one is young, the act of love is all-absorbing, but as one grows older, only one's body is involved. And my mind, today, is not fit for love.'

She smiled back at him, drily amused and in no way resentful. He thought, as he had often thought before, that she and Sévèrine would like each other very much.

Later, alone in his lodging, he wrote a letter to Adam, ready for the moment when he could find a courier to take it. There was no language that was entirely safe, neither French, nor Scots, nor Latin, when he might have to use a papal messenger. So he was very cautious with the wording, making it sufficiently opaque to be more or less meaningless to a casual reader if the letter were to go astray on the long, hazardous journey to Scotland, but still clear enough for Adam to understand all the implications of it.

'I have to stay, of course, and it will be expensive,' he wrote. 'Some of the moneys you must by now have collected would be most useful. It seems Master B has already pledged himself for certain sums and I must be able to better them.

'You know my views. Everything that has gone wrong since that false dawn last summer can be laid at the same door. I wonder now whether it was he who ensured that I was not then restored to the post I desired, and still desire, above all others. But however that may be, I believe it is no longer possible for the two of us to co-exist in the church.'

The last three words were too explicit. Columba crossed them through several times until they were illegible, and then sat staring at the lime-washed wall for a long while, nibbling gently at the feathered quill, before he set down what remained to be said.

'The minor skirmish I came here to win is unimportant now. If we are at war, as it seems, then he loses all who does not win outright. I do not intend to be the loser. For all our sakes, we must find some way of bringing the hawk down.'

CHAPTER TWO

I

IF THE circumstances had been different, if Adam's mind had been less preoccupied by the piece of travel-stained parchment tucked away inside his tunic, he might have laughed when he saw Ninian standing in the doorway of the royal apartments at Perth. For she had an expression on her face that he remembered very well from her childhood – an expression which meant she was feeling not just seditious but downright mutinous.

She was dressed to kill, too, in one of the gentian-coloured, gold-embroidered gowns he knew from Villeneuve, with what looked like every piece of jewellery she possessed, and her hair hidden in a tall, blue, cone-shaped hennin from whose tip fell a cloud of rich golden gauze. It was an outfit worthy of the court of the Emperor Sigismund himself, and to match it she had adopted a faint upward curl at the corners of her lips, and eyebrows superciliously raised over fashion-ably heavy lids.

French manners! Adam thought impatiently. They wouldn't do for Perth. He knew already that the men would sniff and the women would sneer. The Scots liked finery well enough – very well, in fact – but on themselves, not on outsiders; and, priding themselves on being a plain-spoken, blunt, and down-to-earth folk, they hadn't much time for airs and graces, either.

Harry, standing beside his wife, was wearing a slightly hunted look, as if everything had got out of control, but Adam had no sympathy with him. He was a fool not to have brought Ninian to court weeks ago, when things were relatively quiet, instead of putting off until parliament was due to sit and he had to come anyway, along with every prelate, earl, baron and freehold tenant-in-chief in the land. Though not, perhaps, *every* one. But those who hadn't turned up by tomorrow were going to have some pretty ingenious explaining to do to His Majesty.

Her chin high, Ninian surveyed the crowd and, catching sight of Adam, acknowledged him with the merest flicker of a superior smile before her eyes moved on. Adam waited sardonically, and, sure enough, the blue gaze passed over the man at his side, and then stopped, and moved back again, and stopped again, and there remained.

Adam had learned, during the few brief weeks of their acquaintance, that most people stared at their first sight of the Earl of Atholl, uncle to the king and heir to his throne – to which, in fact, he had a more convincing entitlement. For the king's father had been born a bastard, and legitimized only after the marriage of his parents, Robert II and Elizabeth Mure; whereas Atholl was one of the two indisputably legitimate sons of Robert's second marriage.

Few men, in these barbaric, plague-ridden days, expected to live much beyond the age of thirty-five, and it was toughness of mind, not body, that made the difference. For that reason alone, Adam would have had the very healthiest respect for his lordship, who should have died thirty years since. But there were other reasons, too. For Adam knew a villain when he saw one, and although Atholl might look like a manic escapee from Bedlam, might behave like an aged and pampered *enfant terrible*, he was a cold, calculating, crafty old serpent at heart.

About his face there was nothing very unusual. He had the long Stewart nose, thickened at the tip with age and open pores. His eyes were Stewart, too, pale, round, wide-set and slightly protruberant, cradled in soft, sagging folds of flesh. Even the demented white hair and brows, and the tough white stubble that was the nearest his barber could get to a close shave, would scarcely, in another man, have been worthy of remark.

But the clothes . . .

With what was undoubtedly malice aforethought, the earl still clung to the style that had been fashionable when he had stopped being interested in fashion more than quarter of a century ago. His tunic, bulbously padded and elaborately belted, was little short of indecent by the standards of the 1420s, for it reached down no further than the crotch, which was protected by an oxhide codpiece of obscene proportions. Below this, tailored cloth hose covered a pair of legs that ended in leather slippers with toes so extravagantly elongated, so ruthlessly stiffened, that they might well have served for digging badgers out of their setts.

And all this antiquated splendour was embellished, whatever the occasion, with a random selection from the earl's wardrobe of armour – today an ill-polished corselet consisting of the breastplate part only, metal splints on his upper arms, and chainmail chausses on his legs. His lordship rarely wore a helmet. What he crammed, instead, over the rampaging jungle of his hair was one of the knitted woollen hats known as toories, shaped like a pudding basin, coloured a virulent magenta, and topped with a fluffed-out pompom in a baleful shade of saffron.

The only fault Adam had to find with Atholl's appearance was that it was so very much more eye-catching than his own.

The earl's elbow dug him in the ribs. 'Who's the wumman giving me the eye?' he muttered, and when Adam told him, cackled, 'Oh ho? Young Harry'll huv tae watch *her*, eh? Jings, aye! She looks tae me as if she'd lead him a fine dance, and yon laddie couldny keep a pussycat in order.'

Adam grinned, as was expected of him. Even before Columba's letter, whose final sentences confirmed what his own instincts had already told him, he had recognized that the Earl of Atholl could not be anything other than a valuable ally. And indeed, he had shown his worth already by introducing Adam to court.

Reflecting that he would have to send for Blane, Adam watched Malise Graham shouldering through the crowd towards them and decided he would also have to get rid of that young man. He'd served his purpose by introducing Adam to his Uncle Atholl, and Adam already found his perpetual, clinging presence an embarrassment. It would have been another matter if he hadn't been so obsessed with law and order, but Adam had no intention of having his style cramped by a sanctimonious young puppy like the Earl of Strathearn.

'Malise,' he drawled, embarking on the process of severance. 'Why the heaving bosom? Why the maidenly blush?'

At his side, Atholl sniggered, but Malise, hot and breathless, was used to his great-uncle's contempt and ignored it. Only Adam could hurt him. His rather loose mouth quivered, and some of the light left his eyes as he stammered, 'I thought you'd want to know that Robert Graham's here, and Patrick, too – my cousin, the Lord of Graham's son. You ought to meet them. Though I wanted to warn you about Patrick. He's – uhh – he's . . .'

Atholl clamped his hand over his toorie, groaning. 'That I should huv a sumph like this in the family! What he's ettling to say, my very *dear* Mishure de Verne, is that Patrick Graham's a bonnie wee sweetheart that wouldny know what tae do if ye put a naked wumman before him. No' unless she turned her back, of course.'

The pouched eyes stared expressionlessly at Adam. 'And *you're* such a muckle great honeypot that Malise is feared Patrick might be wanting a share in you.'

Adam already knew that Atholl's friendship would have to be paid for, and putting up with the old man's gibes seemed a small enough price. But he wasn't accustomed to being insulted, and he didn't like it at all.

2

NINIAN had been bracing herself for days, so that by the time she and Harry entered the Blackfriars priory in Perth, where the king had his Lodging and parliament its Hall, she was sufficiently wrought up to do battle not just with a few dozen provincial Scots barons and their wives, but with all the serried ranks of Tuscany, and more besides.

After the low, dark, tunnel-vaulted cloisters, her first glimpse of the King's Lodging came as something of a shock. It was huge, and bright with hundreds of candles even at this midsummer noon, candles whose pitiless brilliance illumined a gathering predominantly male, high-complexioned, unkempt of hair, and clad in all the unseasonable, and indefinably slovenly splendours of wool and fur and velvet, of roll-brimmed hoods and high felt hats. They were making enough noise to deafen a bellringer, shouting at the pitch of their voices against a sweet, drowned background of music that sounded as if it might be worth listening to, if only one could hear it properly.

She wrinkled her nose involuntarily, trying not to sneeze, for though the music might be sweet, the air was not. It was thick with the smells of smoke and wine, dampness and dogs, stale sweat and flea-repelling herbs, and something else she couldn't quite place for a moment, until the chill underlying the warmth of the candles reminded her that the king and queen must only have moved here from Edinburgh a day or two ago and would have brought their household comforts with them. What she was smelling was the elusive, characteristic odour of wall tapestries that had been rolled up for a while, and then shaken out and rehung; a compound of dust, and musty linen, and dyed wools. Just so had her own tapestries smelled when she had unpacked them at Dess.

There was no one in the room whom she knew, except Adam and Malise. She would have felt it – surely she would have felt it? – if he had been there. But the fluttering under her heart wouldn't be stilled.

And then she saw a third familiar face. Although the chair of state on the high dais at the far end of the room was empty, the other canopied chair beside it was occupied by a grave, rather maternal young woman who must be the queen. She looked as if she were bored, which Ninian didn't wonder at, because one of her ladies was sitting beside her, talking ceaselessly, and it was none other than the Lady Elinor, as wraithlike and, no doubt, as pettish as ever. The Master of Atholl, Ninian knew, was still in the Tower.

Today's reception was an informal one, an occasion for general conversation rather than the restricted intercourse of the table, but although the dining boards and trestles had been dismantled and stacked against the walls out of the way, due provision had been made for the lubrication of throats dry with talking. The buffet recesses, which would normally have been full of gilt and pewter plate, had been cleared to make space for great tierces of wine and ale, and royal squires bearing pewter flagons were passing and repassing among the crowd, replenishing empty cups.

'Right, then,' Harry said abruptly. 'I'd better start introducing you to folk.'

She had thought it all through very carefully beforehand. She recognized that most of the courtiers must have known each other for years, that even those who disliked each other must have a common outlook, common memories, and an intimate acquaintance with each other's personal tastes, quirks of character, and family relationships. Harry had warned her, too, that, though a good many of the men were widely travelled, their stay-at-home wives would be, at best, suspicious of her, and at worst downright jealous. It was going to be an ordeal, but she didn't care. After the cold, economical emptiness of Dess, almost anything would be an improvement.

She glanced at Adam again, hoping for a grin of encouragement, but all his attention was on the extraordinary old man at his side, and his eyes, suddenly, had a glitter of anger in them. Wondering what on earth had happened, she stiffened her spine and followed her husband into the throng.

It was worse than she had expected. Everyone was polite enough, but after they had acknowledged her and, with insulting brevity, assessed her, they went back to their original conversations – conversations couched in what might as well have been Babylonian, every word full of nuances that didn't need to be expressed, every casual remark as mysterious to Ninian as the Number of the Beast. And because she had made up her mind that she was not, under any circumstances, going to be ignored or condescended to, she began brazenly to interrupt, laughing and chattering about anything and everything that occurred to her, from the astonishing elegance of the new French styles of architecture to the amusing antics of the little monkey she had once seen in Villeneuve. She could hear herself being brittle. She knew she was working too hard. But somehow she couldn't stop.

And everyone listened, and waited for her to finish, and then went back to speculating about the forthcoming exchange of hostages or the growing threat from the Highlands, whose most powerful hereditary chief, the Lord of the Isles, had recently begun to style himself *Magister*. Ninian couldn't see what was wrong with a man calling himself 'Master'; if he'd chosen to call himself 'King', that would be different.

As she and Harry progressed slowly down the length of the room, she became aware of one or two people watching her, unobtrusively but with more than ordinary interest. She didn't flatter herself that they were admiring her; she was still raging inside over Harry's failure to warn her that, in this company, she would be as overdressed as a butterfly in a roomful of moths. Also, she was cold because, summer or not, the rarely-used chamber was like an ice-house.

One of the watchers was a man of middle age, unusually tall, with a powerful physique that ought to have been impressive but wasn't, because there was so little life either in his movements or in his face – a face that was unnaturally white, the flesh flat and almost doughy over the big bones. He didn't look as if he had been ill, more as if he spent all his time indoors and took care to travel, when he had to, in a covered litter. Nettled, she succeeded in fixing his elusive gaze, and gave him her most brilliant smile, receiving a returning smile that was open and surprisingly innocent. But afterwards, when she glanced at him again, his eyes merely slipped over her face without really seeing her, and certainly without acknowledging her breathing existence.

She tugged at Harry's sleeve. 'Who is it? Who's that man over there – the big, pale man who keeps watching me?'

Harry looked, and said, 'Oh, Ninian! Oh-h-h-h, Ninian!' He shook his head lugubriously. 'Your sins have found you out.' He had been in quite a reasonable mood for weeks now, but Ninian found his idea of humour more than a little trying.

'*Don't* be so exasperating. Who is he? Do you know, or don't you?'

He laughed. 'Of course I know! That's our Grand Inquisitor of Heresy. That's Master Laurence of Lindores.'

She could feel the blood draining from her face. 'It can't be. I mean, it isn't – is it? Why is he watching me? I haven't done anything!'

'Haven't you? Then you must be unique among women.'

'It isn't funny. That's the man who sends people to the stake! That's the man who has people burned alive when he doesn't approve of them!'

'Well, of course. He can't have them beheaded, after all. The church abhors the shedding of blood.'

'That wasn't what I meant.'

But Harry had lost interest. His gaze elsewhere, he exclaimed, 'My God, there's Patrick Graham and Uncle Robert!' and, gripping her firmly above the elbow, began to force his way through the crowd to where Adam and Malise were standing talking to a curly-haired, effeminate-looking youth whom Ninian hadn't seen before, and a thin, sinewy, red-haired man of whom she had been aware for some time. She was faintly disappointed to discover that he, at least, had a legitimate reason for watching her, even if now he didn't vouchsafe her so much as a glance.

She stood, silent and ignored, while Harry fussed – no, fawned! – over his uncle. So this was Sir Robert Graham, the not-quite-outlaw. The clever man, the man of principle, the man who found God not in the haunts of men but in the wind that blew from out the wilderness. So what was he doing here, at court?

He looked at her and said, 'I am here only to discover what is to be discussed in parliament tomorrow.'

She didn't realize, until afterwards, that the play of expression on her face must have been perfectly easy to read, if one were as experienced as Robert Graham. But Malise had told her once that he was reputed to have the evil eye, and Ninian, startled out of her wits, was almost prepared to believe it. Even if it wasn't evil, she reflected nervously, it was certainly disconcerting – the eye of a man who might, perhaps, be prepared to go to the stake for his beliefs, but looked much more likely to send other people there, for theirs. She wondered whether Master Laurence of Lindores ever employed him as an assistant.

'Uncle Robert' was somewhere in his thirties and Ninian could see in him no family resemblance at all to the Grahams, neither to Harry, nor Malise, and most certainly not to the chubby, rather pretty young man who appeared to be cousin Patrick.

And then she thought suddenly – the sign of the Cross! She had held neither brush nor charcoal-stick in her hand since the day before her marriage, but she still could not rid herself of the painterly habit of looking for a pattern, and in Robert Graham's long, rather slack-muscled face the pattern was concentrated with almost startling intensity around eyes and nose; eyes that – narrow, straight-set, unblinking, and very dark – formed a strong, powerful horizontal line crossed at its centre by the scarcely less powerful vertical of a narrow-boned nose with two deeply-etched clefts in the forehead above it. Everything else was subsidiary to the cross; the wide, indeterminate mouth, the lax cheeks, the unemphatic jaw. As symbolism went, Ninian didn't care for it greatly. She hoped she wouldn't have to see very much of Uncle Robert.

He said, in his flat, inexpressive voice, 'I have to wish you well, I believe. I hope that you will soon become adjusted to our customs and that Harry is teaching you everything you ought to know about your new homeland.'

Her response was cut off in its prime, for no sooner had her mouth begun to curve into a gracious, if somewhat gritty, smile than he abandoned her completely and was off on a different tack, leaving her with her mouth half open and her cheeks pink with annoyance and embarrassment. She was to learn in time that, however pedantic his speech, Robert Graham's mind was always a jump or two ahead of other people's.

To Malise he was saying, 'It is convenient that you should be here, because I wished to speak to you about the matter of the hostages.

Why are you looking surprised? I suppose you have given it no thought?' He sighed, scratched his jaw absently, and looked as if he were suppressing a yawn. Suddenly, he seemed a good deal more human.

'You did not know, I imagine,' he went on, 'that Thomas Roulle took a list of fifteen possible replacements to England at the beginning of the year, but only five of them were acceptable. The others were not sufficiently rich. So the question is still open. And since James has no great opinion of you, I imagine he would as lief see you go as stay.'

Malise, offended, opened his mouth, but Robert Graham said in exactly the same flat tone, 'Don't interrupt. The only thing in your favour is that, though Strathearn is a distinguished earldom, it is not, in fact, a rich one. So you may escape that way. However, I believe you would be advised to ask your Uncle Atholl to speak to James on your behalf, unless, of course, you wish to spend the next few years in the Tower of London.'

There was a brief silence, during which Sir Robert watched Malise, and Adam watched Sir Robert. It seemed to Ninian that Adam's face wore an arrested look, as if here was a new acquaintance worthy of his notice.

After a few moments, he said very quietly and rather as if he was thinking of something else, 'Sir Robert, for someone who is no friend to the king and who avoids the court, you are very well informed.'

Sir Robert turned his cruciform gaze on the younger man as if something in Adam's words or tone had given him pause. When he spoke, however, he didn't reply directly, but said, 'You are known as – Adam?'

Adam smiled faintly. 'An abbreviation. I was named after St Adamnan, the ninth abbot of Iona.'

And author of a life of St Columba. Ninian sometimes thought that Sévèrine's habit of mockery had gone a little too far, there.

Sir Robert said thoughtfully, 'Indeed. Yes, well, in reply to your question, I make it my business to know what is going on.'

Adam raised a quizzical eyebrow. 'On the principle that you may discover something you can turn to your own advantage?'

'Not only my own. Don't think I am opposed to the king purely because of his injustice to myself. I believe him to be a tyrant. On grounds of political principle alone, I would be his sworn enemy.'

'I see,' Adam said. 'Thank you.'

Belatedly, there came a wail from Malise. 'But I don't want to spend the next few years in the Tower!' It was impossible not to laugh.

And then one of the queen's ladies was at Ninian's shoulder, and she was being led off to be presented to Her Majesty.

3

JAMES'S queen was English, not royal but descended from the royal line. Part of the dowry she had brought her husband had been the remission of one sixth of his ransom, but other things she had been forbidden to bring. Ninian knew that, of the dozen gentlewomen who surrounded her, some sitting, some standing, one strumming idly on a harp, only two were English. It had been thought impolitic for her to employ more, and the barons had further insisted that those two should be widows. Not even in time of truce did anyone want a pair of English husbands running tame at court, privy to everyone's secrets.

Ninian curtsied before the canopied chair and then, eyes downcast, hands loosely folded, stood and waited to be addressed. But the queen's voice, when it came, was so soft against the general level of noise that she found herself stammering, 'I – er . . . I'm afraid that I didn't . . .' And then, with reckless aplomb, 'I am afraid that I didn't quite hear you, Madame.'

And that, she thought, was probably *lèse majesté* at the very least. From the corner of her eye she could see a swift, smiling disdain cross Lady Elinor's face.

The queen wasn't offended, however. On the contrary, she raised her voice and said, 'Don't be nervous, my dear. So many people pretend to have heard, when they have not, and it makes sensible conversation quite impossible!'

Ninian, resisting the temptation to flash her sweetest smile in Lady Elinor's direction, curtsied again and looked into the queen's clear hazel eyes, calm and friendly under brows as perfectly arched as segments of a circle. The relief was considerable, for though royal favour might bring the envy and spite of others in its train, royal disfavour – or even indifference – was a sure passport to oblivion.

She had expected to be honoured with some gracious, time-worn words of welcome and then dismissed, and so was very much surprised to find herself, within minutes, seated at the royal feet being subjected to a full-scale catechism. As the Lady Joan Beaufort, it seemed, Her Majesty had been in attendance at Windsor when Henry V brought Catharine de Valois to England as his bride; now, after three years in Scotland, she needed to be brought up to date on all things French. 'For although we have many visitors here from France,' she said, 'most of them are fighting men who know little of fashion or culture.

'Now tell me, do you play on any instrument? Can you sing all the latest airs for us? For one of the king's greatest pleasures is music. And laying out gardens is another. And, of course, he is a poet, too, as you must know.' Ninian, who didn't know, floundered a little. None of it fitted the picture of James that the Grahams had painted for her. And that a royal lady – especially a royal lady with such a very firm chin – should love and admire her husband, as the queen so obviously did, was almost as startling.

Ninian chattered on obligingly, answering when she could, admitting ignorance when she couldn't, sensing not only the queen's reactions but those of her women. Some of them were listening carefully, others – equally carefully – were not. If only, Ninian thought, one of them might turn out to be a kindred spirit. It seemed a very long time since she had been able to talk freely to anyone, and she missed Sévèrine more than words could say. But there was only one face – amber-and-rose coloured, handsome, and heart-shaped – that looked interesting, and the expression on it was far from encouraging. Its owner, clearly, was engaged on summing Ninian up.

Ninian was just reflecting that it would be a help if she could put a name to all these people, when there came a resounding blast of trumpets, a surging draught from the doorway, and a loud and ragged rustle as all the women in the room curtsied and all the men removed their hats and dropped to one knee.

Then, waving the trumpeters to silence and the company to its feet, a vivid, sturdily-built man with a short, dark red beard, a brimmed and bejewelled hat, and an inordinate weight of velvet and bullion on his shoulders, strode into the chamber and made a bee-line for the chair of state. The impression of energy and forcefulness was so strong that, for a moment, Ninian thought he was going to walk right through it. It couldn't be anyone other than the king.

Brushed aside with the other ladies, Ninian retired a few paces and watched as her sovereign embraced his blushing wife gallantly, addressed a few private words to her, and then turned to survey the assembly. He nodded to several of the men, craned his neck to see who was round the side of the musicians' staging, and then caught sight of the extraordinary old man who had been talking to Adam. Shooting one hand in the air, he roared, 'You're in health, uncle, are you?' and the ridiculous saffron pompom pirouetted in acknowledgement.

But by that time His Majesty was already marching back towards the door, where another figure had appeared, tall and dark in the shadows. Another fanfare sounded, and the king flung both arms wide in greeting, before swinging round again to face the company. His hand resting proprietorially on the newcomer's shoulder, he bellowed, 'Your devoirs, my friends, if you please! For we wish to make known to you the man you will obey from now on as if he were my second self! Our legal guide, our spiritual preceptor – our newly appointed chancellor of the realm! Bishop Gavin of Glasgow!'

4

WHEN he stepped out into the light, her heart was hammering so hard and her lungs so empty of breath that there was nothing she could do but look, all thought suspended. And then her mind woke again to the single question that had obsessed her ever since she had admitted to herself that she might see him again.

Had she been right about him all these months, or wrong? She had fallen in love with a face, and a voice, and a personality, had exchanged a few words with him, and never seen him since except in the dreams she had tried not to dream. Had she created someone who didn't really exist, cherished a hopeless desire for someone who was really just an ordinarily good-looking man with a certain amount of style? She had been so overwrought on those days in Villeneuve that anything was possible.

If, seeing him now, she felt no tremor in her heart, she would be free again, even though she died a little. But if she felt the same wild, fateful stirring as she had felt then, she didn't know what she would do. Because if that happened, she thought, there would be no freedom for her ever.

And then the mist over her eyes receded, and for a few brief moments nothing mattered at all but the tiny nucleus of warmth inside her that grew and spread, gratefully, all through her, until it was like being in Villeneuve again, in the sun. For the reality and the dream were the same.

Her memory had played her no tricks. She had held him in her mind's eye not as some figure from a Book of Hours, brightly coloured, smooth and polished, but with the urgent, black-and-white vitality of a blockprinted image on a playing card. And she had been right, it seemed. Right about the heavy, springing black hair, the fine-boned, positive nose, the saturnine brows and the long, firm, curling mouth. Right – almost – about the eyes, for they looked darker than she remembered, dark as a winter sea, whereas in Villeneuve the sun had lightened them to the clear, translucent grey of washed ice. There were little lines of tiredness round them, now, but they were bright still, because of the candles that lit them from without and something else that lit them from within. And she had been right, above all, about the tight-leashed excitement she had sensed in him. She could sense it now, flowing from him in waves. Was she the only one who felt it? She glanced around her, almost as if she expected to see the same magic reflected in other people's eyes.

She had been half prepared for the encounter, so that after the first fraction of a second she was able to school her face, even if her legs still felt horribly unreliable.

Her expression one of politely detached interest, she stood with the other ladies and watched him survey the company almost as if he were a player scanning his audience for the first time, and seeing it only as a featureless blur.

She could understand that, but the understanding didn't help when his gaze passed over her without so much as a flicker of recognition.

It hurt abominably. Often enough, fighting her lonely battle, she had told herself that he was too important even to remember her if he saw her again. In a life so full of people, she was only one – an insignificant stranger, briefly encountered, as briefly spoken to, and then forgotten. Except, perhaps, as a Frenchified young woman who had made a fool of herself. She had told herself all this, but she hadn't believed it. Surely, surely, some of her own awareness must have communicated itself to him!

And then the hurt was lost in a sudden wave of indignation. How dared he forget her? How dared he! 'I *will not* be ignored!' she thought. '*I will not* be forgotten! I *will* make him take notice of me!'

IT WAS easy enough to think, less easy to contrive when half a roomful of people was intent on claiming his attention, and the other half equally intent on avoiding it.

'"The man you will obey from now on as if he were my second self!"' Robert Graham was quoting acidly to Adam as Ninian rejoined their little group. 'Well, we shall see, no doubt. It is all part of James's plan to try and bring the barons to heel. But I will be much surprised if they are prepared to give their obedience to a man who, were it not for the king, would be no more than a clerk in the head-court of one of the shires. *I* certainly shall not, any more than I bend my neck to James himself.'

Malise, his face flushed, exclaimed, 'But that's wrong! You can't disobey the rules just because you don't like them!'

'Oh, for God's sake!' Harry said disgustedly, but Robert Graham took the boy up seriously enough. 'Why not, if the rules themselves are wrong?'

Adam said, 'Is there no possibility of changing them in parliament?'

His eyes, however, were not on Robert Graham. The Lady Elinor had drifted to his side. It gave Ninian much satisfaction to observe that her ladyship's neckline had slipped a little, revealing that her ethereal draperies covered an undergown of cosy, practical homespun.

Neither she nor Adam gave any sign that they were more than casually acquainted. Ninian wondered how much they had seen of each other in these last weeks.

'Parliament?' Sir Robert was saying. 'Parliament exists only to ratify the royal will, and always has done. No, there is little possibility of changing the rules in parliament.' And then, without any detectable change in face or voice, he added, 'But that does not mean that I do not intend to try.'

Ninian, her nerves unnaturally sensitive, felt for the first time the sheer magnetic force of Sir Robert's personality, all the more compelling for being kept in check. A clever man, she knew, and subtle-minded. An eloquent man, she had been told, and expert in the law. No one had said he was dangerous.

Adam's eyes were alight, and his smile shone white in the warm-skinned, handsome face. 'A declaration of war?' he murmured. 'Against the king – *and* Cameron?'

'Oh, yes!' Lady Elinor breathed yearningly. 'Oh, *certainly* against Bishop Gavin!'

Ninian wanted to exclaim, 'No!' but she didn't dare. Instead, being entirely human, she leaned over and, murmuring, 'Your undergown is showing,' helpfully twitched Lady Elinor's neckline back into place.

And then Adam was laughing, not at the daggers in Lady Elinor's eyes, but at Ninian, because she had shied like a startled filly when there was a sudden, powerful clearing of the throat just behind her. It turned out to be the extraordinary old man whom she now knew to be the Earl of Atholl.

'G'day to you, Sir Robert,' he said. 'And to you, young Harry. You, too, Nell.' But it was Ninian he was leering at.

Adam said smoothly, 'Ah, yes, of course,' and transferred his gaze back to Ninian. 'My *dear* cousin . . .' He placed his arm round her waist and looked down into her eyes with the slow, intimate, provocative smile she had seen him bestow on his mistresses – including Lady Elinor – but never on her.

It was acutely embarrassing. Blushing furiously, she wanted to move away, she knew she should move away, but her limbs refused to obey her.

'Verne!' Harry muttered between clenched teeth, but Adam didn't even glance at him.

And then Atholl gave a snort of laughter and said, 'Och aye, my dear Mishure Honeypot, but it doesny *prove* anything, does it? Except that Patrick here can get awfy excited just frae looking.' And Patrick Graham was, indeed, noticeably pink about the cheeks and shiny about the eyes.

Lady Elinor, unlike her father-in-law, was not amused.

Completely at sea, Ninian looked up at Adam again and found that his eyes, a sudden glaze of anger over them, were still staring into hers, while he resumed what he had been saying as if no one else had spoken.

'Cousin Ninian, you must permit me to introduce you to my lord of Atholl, who is anxious to make your acquaintance. He has been most kind in lending me assistance in one or two cases where his tenants were reluctant to subscribe to Archdeacon Crozier's tithes. I am sure you will be as grateful to him on Columba's behalf as I am.'

The old man grinned. 'Canny have folk refusing to pay their dues, can we! That's a' they're good for, most of them.'

Then Adam released her, and the old man took her hand and enveloped it warmly in his own, and Ninian stood there smiling a little tremulously while he said – loudly enough for his daughter-in-law to hear – what a pleasure it was to have a bonny wee hen like herself at the court instead of nothing but a wheen o' stringy old boiling fowls. The pompom on his toorie wagged lecherously, and Ninian wished she were a hundred miles away.

Why didn't Adam rescue her, instead of standing there looking sarcastic? Why didn't Harry rescue her, instead of hanging like some cringing acolyte on every breath his Uncle Robert drew? Why didn't Robert Graham rescue her, instead of holding his unreadable gaze on her while he lectured Harry and Malise about some Act or other that had been passed in 1424?

But, at last, a squire appeared with a cup of wine and she was able to repossess her hands. As she raised the cup to her lips, still smiling at Atholl over the rim and trying, urgently, to think of some way of changing the subject, he said bracingly, 'Aye, that'll warm ye, lassie! Ye'll be cold wi' nothing on but that skimpy wee bit gown.'

Then his face creased from ear to ear and he rubbed his palms merrily together and added, 'Or d'ye not need any more than that bonny, plump flesh tae keep ye warm?'

And with all the vigour of sixty-seven vigorous years, he gave her a whack on the buttocks that resounded from one end of the royal audience chamber to the other.

Completely unprepared, she jumped like a rabbit, and screeched, and dropped the cup, while Atholl cackled happily, and Adam laughed, and Harry glared at her as if it was all her fault.

She stood for a moment, shaking like a leaf, staring down at the dark purple stains spreading over the blue and gold silk of her skirts, and hearing the rustle of barely suppressed amusement from everyone within range. It was more than her nerves, already strung to snapping point, could stand. She would not – *she would not* – give way to hysterical tears, and there was only one other outlet.

Choked with rage and misery, she forgot that she was at court in the presence of the king and queen, forgot that the man responsible for her discomfiture was the country's premier earl, rich and royal, and licensed by age and public favour to play the buffoon whenever and wherever he chose. To Ninian he was no more than a vile, vulgar, loathsome old man, and she had only one thought in her mind, to retaliate. Eyes and cheeks aflame, breath rasping in her throat, she raised her arm to strike back with all the strength that was in her.

But someone stopped her.

Her stiff, open palm was scarcely halfway to its objective when another, stronger palm covered it from behind and closed it firmly and decisively. Almost at the same moment a linen handkerchief was pressed into her hand and a deep-toned, matter-of-fact voice said, 'Was this what you wanted? You will need something to mop up those stains.'

To master the shivering that threatened to possess her took every ounce of her fortitude. She didn't dare look round, but after a moment she managed an unsteady 'Thank you', and began dabbing at her skirt while everyone watched in restive silence. Then at last Harry said, 'For God's sake, the privy boy'll get you some water, if you need it! Outside, down the main staircase, and on your left.'

6

THE privy boy brought her a bowl of water, and cloths, and some salt, and she retired into the little cubicle set in the thickness of the outside wall of the priory and did what she could to repair the damage.

The marks would never come out . . . Was it only ten minutes ago that she had thought, 'I *will* make him take notice of me'?

The salt would take the colour out of the silk as well as the stains . . . Was it a judgement that he should never see her except when she was behaving like a fool?

She would have to have a new panel set in the front of the skirt . . . How he must despise her. He had saved her from disaster, but she wasn't even sure whether that meant he had remembered her. Perhaps he would do as much for anyone.

Was it a judgement?

It was a sin to love where love was forbidden. A sin to feel such uncontrollable physical desperation even at a passing touch of his hand and the sound of his voice.

She remembered the big-boned, pallid, watchfulness of Master Laurence of Lindores, and shuddered. Love couldn't be heresy – or could it? One never knew. Anything could be heresy, if the Grand Inquisitor chose to call it such.

She knew she had been away for too long, and that it was time she went back to the hall. Racked by desire, and despair, and the beginning of nausea, she leaned her head for a few moments against the cool, thick wood of the door and prayed that Bishop Gavin John Cameron would be gone when she returned. Then she prayed that he would still be there.

But he had gone.

There was a great deal of movement in the hall, a shifting about, a forming and reforming of groups, an atmosphere of whispering.

'An accident . . . an accident . . . dead . . . he is dead . . . *is* he dead? . . . an accident . . . the chancellor . . . an accident on the tower stairs . . .'

7

GAVIN had not stayed long talking to the Grahams. His purpose there had been swiftly accomplished, and it had had nothing to do with the little bride. Though he wished she would grow up.

It had been purely instinctive, saving her from turning a piece of typical Atholl skittishness into a full-scale drama. When he had caught sight of her a few minutes earlier, sparkling busily at the old man, he had been surprised into a private smile. Not many women amused him, even by mistake.

But she had been asking for trouble. However elderly noblemen might behave in France, in Scotland they were of the earth, earthy, and, where women were concerned, constitutionally resistant to anything remotely resembling chivalry or even courtesy. He had been able to see Atholl's hands itching all the way across the room, and wondered whether anyone had warned her.

When it came to the crisis, he had felt mildly sorry for her – for the second time. The first had been when he had been forced to bless her in her marriage bed. It was a task he never enjoyed, but even her patent discomfort had given him no reason to revise his first opinion of her as a spoilt little madam, with a neat ankle and no self-control. He wondered whether she always lived in such a high state of tension. But since most of the women at court were damsels demure to the point of paralysis, or middle-aged crones with nerves of Carinthian steel, she at least had the merit of being different.

As she left them, sped on her way by her unsympathetic husband, Gavin saw Moragh watching them with that familiar, calculating look on her heart-shaped face. If it had been permissible for the chancellor of the realm to wink at a childhood friend, he would have winked. Instead, he looked her straight in the eye until, after a moment, her mouth twitched and she turned her attention back to Master Laurence again. Gavin suspected she was up to something in that direction, but he couldn't think what. Information, probably; she had the most inquisitive nature of anyone he had ever come across. But even Moragh's feminine wiles were unlikely to extract anything from the Grand Inquisitor, whose tastes lay in quite another direction.

He inclined his head to Lady Elinor – whose return to Scotland had transformed her into an unassailably virtuous wife again – and then to Atholl, still chittering gleefully to himself. He was a terrible old man, but only on a personal level. Politically, thank God, he caused a good deal less trouble than he might have done. He didn't approve of Gavin, of course, because, appearances to the contrary, he was as stiff-necked as if the Stewarts had been kings since time immemorial, instead of a mere fifty-odd years, and had nothing good to say of a chancellor who had emerged from some Highland hovel and was a radical, to boot. It didn't worry Gavin unduly. His swift rise to prominence had given him enough enemies to make any increase in their number more or less irrelevant. He thought, sometimes, that no one except James was on his side. But James was the one who mattered.

He turned to the Grahams, and waited cynically for the congratulations on his appointment that didn't come. Then, politely, he asked Adam de Verne whether he had any news of Archdeacon Crozier.

The young man wasn't used to straight questions, and there was a fractional hesitation. Then he said, 'None. I expect he is preparing his case at the Rota – in the matter of that jurisdictional dispute between your lordship and himself.'

'Ah, yes. An expensive business. I imagine he must be writing urgently to you for funds!'

'No.'

He was lying. Columba Crozier had been spending money like water, and Gavin was annoyed about it. He was annoyed with Tom Myrton, too, because he had just discovered that Tom, in a spirit of regrettably private enterprise, had sent John Bowmaker off to Rome a few months ago with instructions to buy himself back into the archdeaconry of Teviotdale – and blow the expense. Which was all very well, Gavin had pointed out, except that it meant the Bishop of Glasgow, through his dean, was encouraging someone to make hay of the law against spending money abroad that the chancellor of the realm was going to be seeing through parliament this very week. 'Aye, well,' Tom had said shiftily. 'Ye wanted Crozier out, did ye not?' But Gavin wasn't altogether sure that he did. Crozier, at least, had brains, which was more than could be said for Bowmaker.

To Adam, he remarked merely, 'You surprise me', and turned his attention to Robert Graham. His presence today almost certainly meant that he was proposing to attend parliament tomorrow, but it was as well to know. He was an unpredictable devil.

Gavin didn't dislike him personally. Indeed, he sometimes regretted that they were on opposing sides. But where Gavin, like the king, believed that reducing the liberty of the barons was the only way to give the rest of James's subjects any liberty at all, Sir Robert believed that royal attempts to discipline the barons were an attack on the foundations of liberty itself. It was a point on which they would never agree. But, apart from that, Robert Graham was a formidably intelligent man, witty in the right company, and stimulating always. It was unwise to let one's thoughts wander when he was present.

Once Sir Robert had confirmed, readily enough, that he would indeed be present on the morrow and at the other two sittings on the 7th and 11th as well, there was no need for Gavin to stay. None of the Grahams was going to say anything to the purpose in his presence. Not before him would Malise or Patrick mention their hope of being exempted from the next exchange of hostages. Not before him would Harry Graham admit that he had been trying without success to borrow money from the English branch of the Strozzi bank. And certainly not before him would Robert Graham reveal that he was in regular touch with the disaffected clans of the isles.

He was saved the trouble of farewells by the king's hand on his shoulder. James was anxious to settle a point about Mr Boudin van der Poele and the proposed Flemish treaty, and wanted to see the papers. It seemed simplest for Gavin – more than willing to grasp a few minutes' respite from the crowd – to go for them himself, so, pausing only to nod to the Grahams and exchange a few words with the royal chamberlain, Sir John Forrester, he made his way towards the stairs that led down to the monkish cell currently serving him as an office.

The spiral stone stairs were wide enough only for one, and the treads narrow on the inside, where they joined the massive central post, but since there were a number of convenient alcoves incorporated in the post it was perfectly possible to pass if two people happened to meet. Gavin, running lightly down, had no thought of trouble until he discovered that one of the flares had tipped over in its socket and gone out.

And by then it was too late. He just had time to see the glimmer of oil on the edge of the step right under his foot, just time to grab for the rope handrail and have it fly loose in his hand, and then all was blackness.

When he hit the ground again, it was head first and with two violent, skull-splitting cracks that restored him to consciousness for just long enough to think, 'This is it!' before everything went black again.

It was a surprise to discover that it hadn't been 'it' – not the end, or not yet. For he was sitting up, his fingers spread over his temples, with a musty-smelling, musty-tasting emptiness pervading his head, a disgusting, familiar-unfamiliar sensation as if he had blown his nose much, much too hard. There was someone trying awkwardly to pull him to his feet and he was saying, as forcefully as the vacuum inside his skull allowed, 'Just a minute! *Just* a minute!'

And then he was back in the world, with Sir John Forrester bending fussily over him, and an aching head and some thick, sluggish, black blood trickling down one cheek.

And no other harm worth mentioning, except for the certainty that it hadn't been an accident.

CHAPTER THREE

I

ATHOLL's laugh was loud and staccato, a succession of short, sharp hoots that beat against Gavin's headache like a jack-o'-the-clock's hammer on the midday bell.

'Witchcraft, that's what!' the old man chortled. 'It's nae wonder Mariota canny conceive. Yon wee bugger would cast a bane on any coupling!'

'Ummm!' the king replied, rattling his fingers on the table top. His sister's two previous marriages had been fruitful enough, but her recent union with Patrick Graham's father was still barren. 'It's a queer thing, I grant you, though I doubt whether having a womanish stepson about the place would be enough to put Mariota off her stroke. What do you think, Bishop Gavin?'

Controlling, for more reasons than one, a desire to laugh immoderately, Gavin said, 'I would not claim to be an expert.'

'What?' And then, observing the displeasure on the bishop's face, the king hurried on, 'Oh, no. No, of course not. Anyway, that's by the way. Personal considerations shouldn't be allowed to influence our selection of replacements for the hostages. It's not a good enough reason for choosing Patrick Graham.'

He chewed thoughtfully on a fingernail. 'On the other hand, as the Lord of Graham's eldest son, Patrick *would* be acceptable to the English.' He made up his mind. '*Right, then!* We're getting on. We've got Patrick Graham, and Logan of Restalrig, and Douglas of Loch-leven. Who else? We've still got another seven to find.' He clapped his hands together and rubbed them busily.

Just like his uncle. Gavin wished the Stewarts weren't such a noisy family.

Hopefully, Atholl said, 'I wouldny mind seeing the back o' Malise. I'm getting gey tired o' him telling me what's right and what's wrong! I don't know where he gets his notions from.'

James looked at him in exasperation. 'Did you not hear what I said, uncle? No personal considerations. Besides, he won't do. Strathearn's only worth £147 a year in rents, and it's not enough.'

'Och, but it's a *bonny* wee earldom. It was one of my brother's.' Two tears welled up and trundled pathetically down into the pouches under the old man's eyes. 'My dear, lamented brother. Earl of Caithness and Strathearn . . .' His voice trailed off wistfully.

James was unmoved. 'Bonny or not, it makes no difference to the English. And you've got Caithness already; you can't have Strathearn, too.'

The discussion was taking place in the privacy of the royal bedchamber, while the reception still went on outside, and His Majesty now hopped to his feet and, striding to the door, opened it and shouted for a flask of wine. On his way back to his chair, he gave Gavin a vigorous clout on the back. 'How's your head? All right? Good. Well, let's get on, then.'

An hour later, they had settled another six names and disposed of two flasks of wine, but still no one had mentioned the reason why Atholl had been invited to join the discussion in the first place. Gavin could see that James wasn't going to if he could help it, and neither was Atholl. The old man knew how to wait.

Resignedly, Gavin opened his mouth. It had been a trying day, and it was by no means over. He still had work to do in preparation for tomorrow's opening of parliament and the following day's church council. He wondered whether the council had ever been presided over by a bishop with a black eye before.

'The Master of Atholl,' he said firmly, whereupon the Master's father sniffed loudly. 'Oh, aye?'

'We have been informed by the English wardens that there is no Scots nobleman of sufficient consequence for them to accept in exchange. Whatever we may have hoped, they are not prepared to release him.'

148

'They said that, did they?' The old man wasn't disturbed. 'Aye, well, they would, would they not? The next-but-one heir to the throne isny someone ye let go lightly. They didny suggest taking me instead, did they? Or are they feared I'm so old I'd go and die on their hands?'

Ignoring this unblushing demand for flattery, Gavin said, 'That appears to be the situation, my lord, unfortunate though it is. We are sure you will understand.'

James, busily combing his beard out with his fingers, muttered, 'I'm sorry, uncle. I know how much you miss David, but there's nothing we can do about it.'

But it wasn't, of course, so easy.

It suited James very well to have his cousin out of the way. No king, denied a son of his own, could be blamed for being suspicious of his heirs. Atholl himself was too old to be a threat, and didn't in fact seem to be much interested, but David was only in his thirties and might very well succeed in rallying the disaffected if he chose. Even after only four years of James's rule there were a goodly number of disaffected, and would be more. No, James didn't want the Master of Atholl home.

But he was getting no cooperation from the English, who were being unwarrantably helpful. They had said they would take three – possibly just two – lesser men in exchange for the Master, and James had snorted. 'Yes, they would like that very well, to add to my troubles. They're not fools.'

He and Gavin had settled, days ago, who the replacement hostages were to be – although they were still stuck for the last one – and these two hours of humming and hawing had been no more than a performance mounted for Atholl's benefit. It had been necessary to drive home to him how difficult it was to find ten replacements, and how impossible it would be to find more – just in case the English solution occurred to him, too.

It had been James's plan, and Gavin had doubted that it would work. Now, with honest regret, he discovered that he had been right.

'Nothing ye can do about it? "No Scots nobleman of sufficient consequence to accept in exchange for the Master"? Well, there's an answer to that, is there no'? If one won't do, send two. Or three. Or four. I tell ye, Jamie, I want my laddie back, and I'll have your guts for girth-straps if ye dinny arrange it.' Slapping his hand resoundingly on his breastplate, he concluded, 'And I *can* make trouble for ye, as ye ken very weel!'

The tinny echoes followed him as, stubbly chin high, pompom rampant, he stalked from the room in a right royal huff.

James removed his jewel-crusted bowl of a hat and threw it, with an oath, on the table, knocking over cups, flagons, and a whole ribbon-tied pyramid of account rolls. 'Has he not been listening at all for the last two hours? Where does he think we're going to find the extra hostages – where *are* we going to find the extra hostages – if he insists? We still need one more, even as it is.' Then he stopped short, swore again, and said, 'No, no, no. I won't have the Master back, whatever my uncle says or does. Gavin Cameron – *think of something!*'

2

BUT it wasn't Gavin who thought of something.

Just before curfew, when the reception was beginning to thin out, and he and the king were closeted once more in the royal bedchamber finalizing the wording of one of the next day's statutes, there was a discreet knock on the door.

' "... all justices to swear to judge faithfully and lawfully all causes and complaints laid before them without favour or hatred and without fraud or colour" ... Yes, that seems to cover most things. Come in!' bellowed His Majesty. 'And who may you be, young man? What do you want?'

Adam de Verne smiled with a nice mixture of charm and deference, first at James and then, less convincingly, at Gavin. 'My name is Verne, sire. I am – er – proctor to the Archdeacon of Teviotdale.' He glanced at Gavin again, but Gavin's face was merely thoughtful. It gave Adam no sorrow to see that it was beginning to turn a rich, patchy purple down one side.

'But I am not here about Teviotdale. My concern is with the affairs of his lordship of Atholl.'

The king's eyebrows shot into his hair. 'An emissary from my uncle? Why should my uncle need an emissary?'

'Ah, no. Not an emissary. Not quite. I have no wish to speak out of turn, but some of the present difficulties over the hostages have been confided to me, and it has occurred to me that there might be a solution that would satisfy almost everyone.'

'Yes, yes!' barked the king. 'Get on with it, man!'

The candles were guttering, and Gavin caught a whiff, not of hot wax, but of brimstone. He had wondered about Verne. The accident on the stairs – the spilled oil, the faulty knot on the hand cord – had had a flashy, impromptu quality about it that seemed to fit no one else Gavin could think of. But there was no reason. Certainly none worth trying to kill for. And would even Adam de Verne have the nerve to draw attention to himself now, like this, quite so soon?

Adam said, 'It appears to me that his lordship is much attached, sentimentally attached, to Strathearn . . .'

The king groaned. 'Not that again!'

' . . . so much attached that, if Strathearn were by some means to be transferred to his possession, it might perhaps compensate him for the – er – continuing imprisonment of his son, the Master, in England.'

James stared at him and after a moment said, ' "By some means"? Yes?'

'As I understand it, Strathearn is what you call a male fief?'

'Yes.'

'But Malise Graham inherited it through his mother, his grandfather having begotten no sons?'

'Ye-e-es.'

'So it could be argued that Malise Graham has no true entitlement, because his mother had none. Strathearn should correctly have passed to the nearest male, his grandfather's brother. My lord of Atholl, in effect.'

It sounded to Gavin much more like Atholl's own idea than Verne's, and he wondered why the old man hadn't come straight out with it before. The mere fact that he was proposing to rob his greatnephew of all he possessed didn't account for it; in Atholl's view, that would be no more than a bit of commendably shrewd profiteering.

'Legally,' Gavin said, 'you are in the right. The title was not, however, contested when the Countess Euphemia inherited it almost forty years ago, nor when she transferred it to Malise's father twenty years ago. There is such a thing as natural justice. It would be highly improper, now, to strip the young man of his title and lands.'

Adam de Verne turned gleaming dark eyes on him. 'But if that impropriety were to be offset by very substantial benefits to all concerned?'

'To *all* concerned?'

Verne's excellent teeth flashed in a smile. 'You did not think, I trust, that I was suggesting that Strathearn's present earl should be reduced to penury? On the contrary. It has always seemed to me sadly uneconomical to kill only one bird with one stone.'

There was a very long silence, while the king and his chancellor studied the blindingly dressed, handsome and entirely self-assured young man before them, and tried to see how his mind was working.

At last James said impatiently, 'Well, go on!'

Adam bowed. 'There are, I am told, several earldoms that have reverted to Your Majesty's keeping in recent years.' It was a tactful way of putting it. When James had executed his Albany cousins, he had declared all their titles and lands forfeit to the crown, to the considerable augmentation of the royal rent rolls. There were some people, Robert Graham among them, who believed that it was James's avarice, not the Albanies' treason, that had been directly responsible for their demise.

'It seems to me,' Verne went on, 'that if Your Majesty were to give the present Earl of Strathearn one of these vacant titles in exchange for his own, it might suffice to placate him.'

With heavy sarcasm, the king said, 'Which would you recommend?'

'I had thought of Menteith.'

There was another silence. 'Why?' James said.

Verne's gesture was gracefully deprecating. 'Because it is worth £350 a year.'

Gavin's brain cleared suddenly, but James was slow to see the point, too busy being shocked at the thought of foregoing £350 of his own income, and wondering how much less he could get away with.

Gavin rose carefully to his feet and, picking up the list of replacement hostages, scanned it briefly and quite unnecessarily. He knew exactly what was written there. Then he raised his head again, equally carefully; it still didn't feel properly attached to his spine. 'Since we appear to be engaged in horse-trading, Monsieur de Verne, do we assume that Menteith is an integral part of the deal?'

Monsieur de Verne, suddenly looking very French, shrugged, and spread his hands again, and said nothing. His Frenchness, Gavin had noticed, was a variable quantity, brought into play only when it suited him. Most of the time, give or take an occasional mannerism or expletive, it was quite unobtrusive. He spoke English extremely well, thanks, no doubt, to his 'old family friend', Columba Crozier.

The king said, 'Eh? What?'

Gavin looked at him. 'Malise Graham, Earl of Strathearn, is worth

£147 a year – not rich enough to be acceptable to the English as a replacement hostage. But Malise Graham, Earl of Menteith, would be worth £350 a year.' He had no choice but to add, 'And we are still one hostage short.'

James, who had been stalking round the room, hands tucked under the tail of his gown, threw himself on the great fourposter bed and bounced thoughtfully for a few moments.

Then, addressing the canopy, he said, 'I see. We give Strathearn to my uncle, which silences him on the subject of the Master's continuing imprisonment. And we give Menteith to young Graham, which may or may not silence him over the loss of Strathearn, but we won't hear him complaining, anyway, because he'll be four hundred miles away in the Tower of London.'

He didn't add – or not aloud – 'And for so long as he remains in England, Menteith's rents can continue to be administered by the crown.'

He screwed his head round. 'Was this my uncle's idea?'

'Indeed no. It is entirely my own suggestion – and, pray believe me, a profoundly respectful one – for smoothing out some of the difficulties that seem to be besetting everyone. I would add that I should be sufficiently honoured if the idea were of interest to you to desire no other credit for it. Truthfully, as an outsider, a foreigner, I believe it would be best if I did not appear in the matter at all.'

Gavin said drily, 'It is rare to find such selflessness in these covetous days.'

Robert Graham wasn't going to like it, he thought. Two of his nephews, Patrick and Malise, shuffled off to England for a period of years, and Malise deprived of his title for another that, though nominally richer, was far less distinguished. A hard blow at a family that, though of no great political influence, was large, close-knit, and possessed of far more retainers than any king, unsure of his throne, could contemplate with equanimity.

Even so, from the crown's point of view it was an excellent bargain.

'You have no motive in all this,' Gavin went on, 'except to be of service to His Majesty and the Earl of Atholl? It does you credit. Yet I am surprised that you should choose to be involved. You have personal connections with the Grahams, have you not? If I remember, your cousin, Lady Ninian, is married to Sir Harry, and Malise, I am told, is your own constant companion.

'He is the only one to suffer from this arrangement. I cannot think he will be grateful to you for the suggestion that he should be torn up by the roots.'

It had all been said with Gavin's usual icy objectivity, but he allowed himself the pleasure of a thoroughly artificial pause before he concluded. 'But of course – you require no credit for it! So the question of gratitude does not arise.'

James, still staring up at the canopy, didn't see the challenge in Adam de Verne's eyes as he replied, 'The good of the kingdom must always come before personal inclination, I believe.'

And that was too much. Gavin, turning away, said coldly, 'I hope you will feel the same when you hear of the new legislation that is to go before parliament on the 7th. For it will not, I fear, be at all compatible with the personal inclinations of your – er – "old family friend", Archdeacon Crozier.'

3

PERTH was a thriving little town, moated and walled, and set in the heart of the fertile valley of the river Tay. For metalwork, cloth, and leather it was pre-eminent, and its harbour in the sailing season bustled with ships trading with half the ports of the North Sea.

The wind was most often from the east, and for that reason the town's castles and monasteries, like the households and lodgings of the rich, were safely located to north or south. It was well known that infection could be transmitted by smells carried on the wind, and there were infections and smells enough among the close-packed wattle houses of the town, with their thatched roofs and sanded floors, and their open yards that were at once cesspit and midden, workshop and cattle pen.

The priory of the Blackfriars, the Dominicans' principal school in Scotland, was on the northern fringes, in a pleasantly open position with an undulating view towards the hills and nothing between it and the river but marshes and water meadows that, in this dry summer, provided pleasant strolling for the ladies of the court.

After almost a week, Ninian had begun to feel more at home, even to the extent of recapturing part of the self she had lost in this last year. The first two or three days had been difficult, but the queen's favour, and the fine weather, and the coming and going of all the most important men in the kingdom, had combined to put everyone into an agreeable frame of mind. It made such a welcome change, Lady Moragh said, from being cooped up in one's castle all the year round.

The lady with the heart-shaped face, slanting brown eyes, and amber-and-roses complexion had disturbed Ninian at first. She was about three or four years older, small and neatly built, but very handsome and self-confident. The wings of hair that just showed under her tricorne headdress were heavy and gleaming black, and though her firm mouth turned down at the corners it lent no hint of dejection to an expression that was pleasant enough, and looked as if it might be habitually so.

But Ninian had been certain that the slanting brown eyes were calculating. It was as if their owner was impersonally ticking off all Ninian's smiles, frowns, gestures and mannerisms against some master list, and marking her pass, borderline, or most often – Ninian was convinced – fail. Ninian didn't like it in the least. Several times, on the first day, she had smiled directly into the woman's eyes, trying to establish some sense of contact, but though the woman smiled back quite merrily, her eyes continued to pass judgement.

And then, a few hours after the Atholl episode, and when everyone's morbid excitement over Bishop Gavin's accident had begun to die down, she had come over to Ninian and complimented her on her success in removing the wine stains from her gown. She hadn't known that salt was the answer – if one was quick enough – and very soon they were talking quite easily.

The Lady Moragh had turned out to be amusing, sympathetic, and most interested in knowing all about Ninian's likes and dislikes, her upbringing and background. In no time at all, it was as if they had been acquainted for years. Except that the Lady Moragh was very much more reticent about her past than Ninian was. But that, Ninian had discovered, was characteristic of the Scots.

'You are in good hawking country at Dess,' Moragh said now. She had a lilt in her speech, and a softness that drew 'Dess' out into something more like 'Teh-eh-ssss'. Harry said it was because she had been born somewhere in the west Highlands. 'How I envy you! At Laggan the countryside iss too enclosed to giff the birds free flight.'

Ninian knew very little about falconry. Adam and Blane enjoyed it well enough, but Sévèrine had always said that, having steered her infant sons, of necessity, through an endless succession of near-fatal illnesses and accidents, nothing would induce her to repeat the experience – and from choice, *mon Dieu!* – with birds whose sole ambition appeared to be to pine away and die of cramps or apoplexy, frounce or fractures, ticks or bumblefoot. 'And if I must ply my needle, I prefer to employ it on something inanimate, not on mending the tail feathers of some ungrateful fowl which, while I am so engaged, thanks me by depositing before me droppings of a pungency quite inconceivable.'

Now, her eyes following the Lady Moragh's out to the high, free hills, Ninian wondered whether falconry might be the answer. What she needed at Dess, she thought, was something to occupy not her mind – for that, or the everyday part of it, was kept busy enough by domestic routine – but her emotions. Not passion, or love, or hate or misery, but gentleness and caring. She could feel the warmth that had always seemed to her the most important part of love dying within her because there was no Columba, no Séverine, on whom to lavish it. A warmth less than she would give to a wanted child; different, in quality, from what she gave to Adam; more, much more, than she could ever give to Harry.

A wanted child. She was confused every time she thought about it. She had always believed, romantically, that a child ought to be the product of two people's loving, so that in the early days of her marriage she had been terrified of finding herself pregnant. It hadn't seemed right that she should bear a child to Harry Graham, whom she didn't love and who didn't really, she thought, love her. Then she had begun to think that perhaps what mattered was not so much the feeling between the parents, as how much love they could give to their child. And she had so much love to give, a love that would nourish her baby most richly – and nourish herself, too, in the giving of it.

But she was beginning to despair. Was it she who was barren, as Harry claimed – or he? Was it a judgement on her, for loving where love was forbidden? She didn't know, and she tried not to think about it because it frightened her. Perhaps keeping a falcon might divert her, give her some living thing to care for, something to cherish. It would be better, much better, than nothing. And nothing was all she had.

She was depressed by the thought of going back to cold-spirited Dess. If she hadn't given up painting, it mightn't have been so bad, but there was nothing to paint at Dess, anyway. Nothing, even in spring, but threatening skies, and starved trees, and a rolling, featureless landscape in colours that were scarcely colours at all, but almost *grisaille*, too drab, too neutral for her bright French palette. No flowers but wildings that, tiny and frail, died when they had scarcely opened, all their strength in the roots that sustained them through the long, long months of winter. No buildings but the high, forbidding stone tower that was her home.

She had been trying to persuade Harry to build a proper wall round the barmkin and a small turret to enclose the outer stairs, but he didn't have enough money and it seemed he couldn't borrow it.

She said to Moragh, 'Hawking, is it interesting? Is it absorbing? We have an old peregrine at Dess. Could I fly her, or must I have a young one of my own?'

'A peregrine!' Moragh exclaimed. 'Take care who sees you flying her. It iss only kings and earls who iss allowed to fly peregrines. Country lairds iss supposed only to haff common goshawks.' She smiled. 'Though it iss only at court that anyone iss paying attention to *that*. But it iss better to haff your own bird.' Her eyes wandering towards the crowd of churchmen pouring like consecrated ants out of the monastery gate, she went on absently, 'It iss important to catch him young.'

'Him? Not a female?'

Lady Moragh didn't answer for a moment, and then said, 'It iss a matter of preference.'

There were bishops and abbots, deans and archdeacons, prelates of the collegiate churches, and priors of convents, and all – as laid down by the rules governing provincial councils of the church – ceremonially arrayed in albs and amices, copes and surplices, gloves and staffs and 'solemn mitres'.

'What do they discuss?' Ninian asked curiously, and Moragh chuckled. 'Efferything! They start with a service, and then they haff a grand, stirring sermon and then they iss going on to the general excommunication. That iss when they curse everyone, known or unknown, who iss even thinking of doing anything wrong – perjurers, thieves, robbers, incendiaries, poisoners, those who clip the king's coins.' She turned her head to Ninian, her mouth prim. 'It iss a terrible cursing, you know! "May their part be with Dathan and Abiram, whom the earth swallowed up quick. May their days be few. May their children be orphans!" It iss enough to put you off clipping the king's coins for life!'

Ninian laughed. She was fairly sure that she liked Moragh.

'And then they iss going on to argue about tithes, and assessments, and testamentary dispositions. And the violation of sanctuaries, and the right to confer benefices. But . . .' her tone was mischievous, 'but if our new chancellor iss haffing anything to say in the matter, they will *not* be arguing about what parliament iss to decree tomorrow about speeding up litigation in the spiritual courts. They will chust be meekly accepting it. The arguing about that will come later, at Rome!'

Ninian glanced at her sideways, impressed to find her so well informed. She herself, knowing a great deal about Rome, knew very little of its influence on everyday affairs in Scotland, and had made no effort to find out. Perhaps she should. And not only because there was a small voice whispering in her head that it would be nice to be able to talk intelligently to Bishop Gavin, if ever the opportunity should arise.

Following the direction of Lady Moragh's eyes, she began hastily to try and think of something to say, now, at once, so that she didn't have to just stand breathlessly watching as he came towards them across the grass.

She had spoken to him more than once since her first day at court. Not from choice – she could feel herself going scarlet every time she saw him, and would have been much inclined to crawl under a stone if there had been one handy – but because trying to avoid him had been like trying to avoid the air she breathed.

Everywhere she had gone, Bishop Gavin had been there, discussing treaties, arbitrating in disputes, drafting laws, celebrating Mass, debating the most recondite subjects in the most recondite terms. And even when he was not physically present, everyone at court seemed to be gossiping about him, about his influence with James, his intolerable efficiency, even his impossible good luck. For had he not escaped, alive and whole, from an accident that should have resulted in days of endlessly tolling bells and the kind of spectacularly woeful obsequies that were guaranteed to put the mob in a good humour for weeks?

The first time they spoke, she had thanked him, in a subdued way, for rescuing her from the awkward situation with Atholl. It had been very hard for her to do, and he had seemed surprised, almost as if he had forgotten, and then said, 'I think one may take it as a rule of thumb that assaulting the heir presumptive to the throne is not good policy.' And that had been that. The whole side of his face had been purple and yellow, and she had wanted to weep for him, from fright or gratitude, she didn't know which.

The second time, remembering that she had been remiss, she had said, 'I don't know whether one congratulates a bishop on being

158

elevated to chancellor? Rank in the church must be superior to rank in the state, mustn't it? But . . . but – please – if it is appropriate to offer congratulations, I would like to do so.'

He had looked, for a moment, as if this was a view of the situation that had never occurred to him, and there was a ragged edge to his voice, almost as if he were laughing, when he said, 'Congratulations are perfectly appropriate. Thank you.' And, again, that had been all. He had moved on with no more than a nod.

But although the ice had been broken, she was still nervous as a cat at the prospect of bidding him even a passing good day. It was all part of being in love, she supposed, but it didn't help that she had to wind her courage up to sticking point whenever she encountered him, and found herself unable to act naturally in his presence. The truth was that he made her feel quite insignificant, which she wasn't accustomed to and didn't enjoy. But he still fascinated her and frightened her, and she had no idea how much of the one depended on the other.

Standing quietly and apparently calmly in the mild Scottish sun, she felt a sudden anger with herself. It was so stupid, the whole thing! To be in love, consumingly in love, when there was nothing there for her at all, and could be nothing!

He was bowing before the queen, whom he respected and admired. After six days of intense awareness, Ninian was learning to read the almost invisible movements of the muscles round his eyes which betrayed a little – a very little – of what he took such care to disguise.

He respected the Lady Egidia, too, the most favoured of Her Majesty's women; very small, very thin, very brisk, no longer young, wearing a plain cloth gown, a fortune in gold chains, and a velvet-banded hennin that was almost as tall as she was. But when the bishop's gaze was transferred to Lady Elinor, it cooled rapidly. Moragh won a glance that was unquestionably warmer and, to Ninian's puzzlement, almost conspiratorial. And then his gaze came briefly to rest on Ninian herself, and he responded to her overbright smile with a look of detached and rather quizzical amusement.

She made an astonishing discovery after that. As his eyes travelled on, she saw that every single one of the women, however hard she tried to hide it, was waiting breathlessly for her moment of attention.

Incredulously, Ninian watched, and it was true. There was a heightened sensitivity about them all, shimmering like the air over a fire in the sunlight. Even the queen; even the uncompromising Lady Egidia. A kind of illicit excitement.

A dozen worldly-wise women and one striking, unforthcoming, celibate priest. Ninian blinked nervously, aware of a prickling at the back of her neck.

And then he moved on, taking up his interrupted conversation with the Bishop of St Andrews, and the ladies began to chatter again with great vivacity, and Moragh said, 'You might still be able to get an eyass – a nestling – if your falconer iss quick. It hass been a late season, and in the north it iss possible they haff not yet all flown the nest.'

4

'AND in order to save expense for any poor litigant who may bring a case against a cleric . . . the defendant shall be cited to appear on a day appointed . . . proofs to be adduced within forty days . . .

. . . which Act to be duly set down in the record in the Latin tongue . . .

. . . *et quod istud statuatur de praesenti auctoritate consilii provincialis.*'

The parchment rolled itself up with a satisfying crack, and a hundred or so prelates, earls, barons and freeholders shifted restlessly, while the king settled back in his chair of state and Gavin unrolled the next statute on the agenda, which related to the property of Scots who died abroad.

No one had anything to say about this one, either, which was fortunate, because James was determined to propose the next measure in person, and he had no gift of brevity when it came to an argument. They would probably still be talking at Compline. Gavin glanced round the hall and wondered how many of the barons would last until then. Most of their faces, patterned in red, blue and green by the mote-filled light that poured through the stained glass windows, were either half asleep or else only too irritably awake. It gave him a good deal of satisfaction to reflect that they would soon have something to be irritable about.

'*Now!*' James began, explosively enough to wake the dormant from their rest. 'You all know that Scotland's not rich and we've got my ransom to pay. It's a big drain, so we have to husband our resources. And that means gold and silver. In our last three parliaments, we've passed a fine collection of laws putting duties on things, and regulating the tenancies of land, and improving trade and exports, and trying to curb imports. But it's not enough.'

Gavin wasn't sure whether the blunt, brisk, man-to-man style which James affected in parliament was a good idea. Certainly, it meant that most of those present understood him, and were thus more inclined to listen, but in the present case a good, thick smoke screen of legal jargon was what was really needed.

'There's far too much gold and silver still pouring out of the country – *and not coming back*. Why? I'll tell you why. Because there's too many folk going off abroad and spending it.'

Swivelling his head, the king rested accusing eyes on the clergy. 'Holy Kirk isn't the least offender. The curia at Rome is littered with Scots priests wanting their benefices confirmed, or buying graces and pensions, or litigating about this, that, and the other. *And all with gold and silver that should never have left Scotland.*

'Now, as a devout son of the kirk, I don't believe all this accords with the will of God. But it's up to Rome to sort that problem out for itself, because no one else can, certainly not me. But what I can do, and what we are going to do today, is put our foot down where the drain of gold and silver is concerned.'

Purposely, Gavin hadn't let any hint of all this slip to the church council and he sat, now, with his eyes on the quill he was twirling gently in his fingers, and wished that he could have given himself the pleasure of studying the expression on his fellow churchmen's faces. There was a great deal of shocked, if muted, comment emanating from the benches of the lords spiritual.

And then James swivelled his head again and wiped the smile off the faces of the lords temporal.

'And that's only the kirk,' he said. 'The rest of you aren't blameless either. Just for a start, there's a good few folk spend more time away jousting in tournaments in England and France than they do at home looking after their lands, and that's an expensive game, as we all know. And there's far too many sending their sons to French universities, too, when we've got a perfectly good university here in Scotland.

'So, from now on, there's nobody – churchman or layman – to go abroad without exchanging money for their foreign expenses before they go. And they'll have to prove to the chancellor or the chamberlain that they've done it. *And* they'll have to explain why they're going, too.'

It was the churchmen, of course, who were the real offenders, but to have applied the law only to them would have been akin to declaring war on the Holy See. Seventy-odd years ago, the English had solved the problem by making it illegal for clerics to take appeals to Rome – and had got away with it – but in James's view that had been carrying things to extremes. So Gavin had reminded him about Philippe le Bel, who, determined to undermine the pretensions of Pope Boniface VIII, had banned the export of gold from France with what were reported to have been highly satisfactory results. 'Fine!' James had said. 'What was good enough for the Iron King ought to be good enough for me, too.'

Now, running his fingers through his beard, James concluded, 'And if that doesn't sort things out, we'll just have to make the laws stronger next year. *Right!* Does anyone have anything to say?'

He might better have asked, 'Does anyone *not* have anything to say?' for to His Majesty's very evident surprise the whole hall was in ferment.

Gavin, glancing round, saw that John Crannoch, Bishop of Brechin, was on his feet; he had got rid of a good few handfuls of gold at Rome last year buying preferment for two of his brothers. Nicholas Tunnok was on his feet, too, frantic at the thought that he mightn't be allowed to go on with that interminable case about Ingram Lindsay's pension. And John Benyng and John Winchester, who still owed the curia for their dispensations to hold benefices in plurality, were equally agitated. As were a whole host of others.

Including Master Laurence of Lindores, whose pallid, big-boned face was uncharacteristically flushed. Why? Gavin wondered. Was he objecting to parliament meddling in the affairs of the church, or to the effect the law would have on free movement of students and teachers between the universities? He was Dean of Arts at the University of St Andrews, as well as Grand Inquisitor. Or – *or* – was it because he was a lifelong friend and crony of the free-spending Archdeacon of Teviotdale, Columba Crozier?

All the barons were talking at once, too. Not one of them who hadn't been thinking of sending his son to school at Paris. Not one who hadn't at some time or other considered taking a private army across the Channel to see what loot there was to be picked up in a divided France. Not one who didn't see the whole idea as another example of royal interference with his age-old right to do as he damned well pleased.

Except Atholl, who had his feet on the bench before him and

appeared to be snoozing peacefully, his chin cuddled down on his breastplate. And Sir Harry Graham, clearly bored and wondering what all the fuss was about. And Malise Graham, an earnest furrowing on his brow as he absorbed yet another law he was going to have to remind everyone to observe.

And then a flat, unemotional voice cut through the din, and suddenly everyone was sitting down again, and the silence was absolute.

It was Robert Graham.

Gavin put his quill down gently, distributed his robes more comfortably about his knees, and waited.

He had never seen Robert Graham in a rage and knew only from Tom Myrton's gossip that he was capable of it. And it was interesting — for though Sir Robert's voice might be flat, his face was suffused under the red hair, and the tight-focused gaze was fixed and staring, like some Christ Pantokrator on the tympanum of a cathedral. The thought flashed across Gavin's mind that he might already have heard what had been decided about Patrick and Malise, but he rejected it because the decision hadn't yet been made public and neither Atholl nor Adam de Verne, who knew, would have told Sir Robert, of all people.

He stood facing the chair of state, feet planted a few inches apart, fists clenched on his hips, and his voice echoed through the waiting silence, effortlessly audible to everyone in the hall.

He began on a level above the comprehension of most of the barons.

'*What is a king?*' he demanded rhetorically. 'Is it one who stands outside and above the people whom God has entrusted to his government? Do they receive the law as a gift of God through his mouth? Have they no liberties save those granted to them by *his* grace and favour, or the grace and favour of his predecessors? Is his governance to be unfettered by all human laws and human agencies?'

A thin, sinewy hand sliced through the air in a gesture of violent negation. 'No, I say! The king does not stand outside and above the community. He is a member of it. The link between him and his vassals is one of simple contract, and for the keeping of a contract two parties must agree. The law of the land is not what the king *issues*, but what is *approved* by both the king and the barons.'

It would, Gavin thought, be a perfectly tenable argument if the barons weren't blind and deaf to everything except their own self-interest.

Robert Graham swung round to face the company. Behind him, James was no less scarlet in the face than he.

'And we – barons, prelates and freeholders – will *never* approve that the king shall curtail our liberty!'

And then, so swiftly, so unexpectedly, that no one had time to move, he had turned again and leapt towards the king, and laid rough hands on James's shoulders and, even as James struggled with all the power of a trained and athletic body, Graham shouted, 'I arrest you in the name of all the Three Estates of your realm. For as your liege people are bound and sworn to obey Your royal Majesty, in the same way are *you* sworn to care for your people, to do them no wrong, but in every way maintain and defend them.'

But by the time he had finished the king's secretaries were tearing him away, and the king was shouting, too, and his household officers were rushing to his aid, and Gavin was giving swift, purposeful orders to the captain of the royal guard who had come running at the sound of the king's cries.

And all the while, the prelates, and earls, and barons, and freeholders simply sat, tight-lipped, and did nothing. Nor did they move or remonstrate when Sir Robert Graham, who had had the courage to say what every last one of them had been thinking, was ruthlessly searched and then flung to the ground at the royal feet and held there, his arms twisted behind him, and a swordpoint at his back.

James seated himself again and settled the jewelled hat firmly back on his head. He was breathing fast, but the flush was beginning to die down.

Gavin stood by the lawyers' bench and hoped very much that the king was going to make the right decision. James was neither as volatile nor as headstrong as he liked to appear – it kept everyone on their toes, he said – but he could be vindictive when his temper did desert him. On the other hand, he had the true statesman's talent for calculating the odds.

He flashed Gavin a glance, and then stared coldly down at Sir Robert Graham.

'Let it be seen,' he said in carefully measured tones, 'that I *do* care for my people, and that I *do* defend them, from themselves as from others. You have laid violent hands upon your king, and I know of no country in the world where such a crime as that would be punished by anything other than a traitor's death.'

There was a rustle of movement throughout the hall, as if every man there had caught his breath.

James waited, and then resumed, 'While I was imprisoned in England, for eighteen long years, my Uncle Albany and then his son maintained themselves as regents by giving in to every demand of the barons, just or unjust, so that you have all come to think you have rights that, in God's sight, *you – have – not*. You must learn again what it is to bend the neck to your sovereign lord.'

There was a very long pause indeed, during which no one moved so much as a finger. Gavin could sense the change of feeling in the hall. They were all thinking now, he knew, that Graham's fate was sealed. They were thinking, too, that Graham had been a fool.

James raised his eyes and slowly scanned the company. 'But because I understand all this, and because I too know what it is to lose my temper . . . Because I know also that Sir Robert Graham, however rash and ill-advised, was moved today by honest belief and not by common spleen . . . And because, fortunately for him, he carried no weapon . . . For these reasons, I will lighten the hand of justice, and let him live. But I give the sternest possible warning to you all. Next time, there will be no reprieve.'

He nodded to the captain. 'Release him.'

Sir Robert rose to his feet and stood, lips compressed, waiting. Gavin thought he must be expecting life-long banishment, or ten years in the galleys, at the very least.

But James said, 'Sir Robert, this is the second time you have crossed your king. Let there be no third.' And then, magnanimously, 'You are free to go. Only do not let me see your face either at court or in council until at least five years have passed.'

The most brutal of punishments, or a complete pardon – Gavin sometimes thought that these were the only two levels of justice the world was capable of understanding. Yet his sigh was one of relief. The barons might be in need of a lesson or two, but executing them solved nothing. James was a good king, and might some day be a great one.

HARRY was beyond rational thought, almost beyond speech, the bones of his face showing through the flesh so that one could see what he would look like when he was old.

'Harry!' Ninian said. 'Harry, please!'

'Why should they spare *me*? Why should I be the only one left at large? Am I not important enough? Am I a nothing? Should I change my name to Nimmo?' His laugh grated too loudly on the air of the Blackfriars' guest hall, and Ninian, half her attention on him, and half on the chamberers who were packing her travelling chests, said again, 'Harry, *please!*'

After Sir Robert Graham had made his exit, the king, with admirable *sangfroid*, had moved straight on to the next business on the agenda.

It was the revelation of that next business, more than Uncle Robert's disgrace, that had reduced Harry to impotent, incoherent rage, because he had a blind faith in his uncle's ability to control his own destiny, and, however one looked at it, he had invited trouble.

Not so Patrick and Malise. The king's announcement that Malise was to be deprived of Strathearn, and that both he and Patrick were on the list of replacement hostages who were to be ready to set off for England in the course of the next two months, had come as a shock of such magnitude that Harry couldn't at first believe it.

'Why? Why us? Why should James hate the Grahams so much that he wants to destroy us? I tell you, Ninian, I sat there for the length of a Miserere before my mind so much as began working again!'

Ninian, genuinely upset about Malise and, indeed, Sir Robert, said, 'Harry, what did you *do*?' and then wished she hadn't spoken. The reason why he was suffering such an extremity of anger now was only too obvious. He hadn't even had the courage to get up and speak.

Adam, lounging in the doorway, asked, 'More to the point, what will Sir Robert do?'

'What?' Harry said. 'Oh, I don't know. What he always does, I suppose. Spend some of his time at Kincardine and some in the Highlands.'

'How sad,' Adam said.

'Sad?'

'That James chose not to put him in prison for a while.'

'*What?*'

Ninian said, 'Really, Adam! Must you be so irritating?'

Harry was glaring at Adam with all the old dislike. 'And what is sad about that, pray?'

Adam waved an arm expansively. 'We are robbed of the pleasure of rescuing him!'

'You may consider it a pleasure! Not I! I wouldn't even know how to go about it.'

Adam didn't trouble to disguise the contempt in his voice. 'Then I must remember not to ask for your help if the occasion should ever arise. Or you might become Nimmo indeed.' Harry, he reflected, was nothing but a bag of wind, and he was beginning to think he should have done something to save young Ninian from him. Perhaps, after all, he should have run him through that day in the garden at Villeneuve.

Even so, Sir Harry might still have his uses. Adam detached himself from the wall and moved forward, saying, 'Let us not quarrel, however, especially since I have a few days to spare and had thought of spending them at Dess.'

Ignoring Harry's look of disgust and Ninian's qualified enthusiasm, he went on, 'But I am here, at this moment, for another reason entirely. I have discovered something that you, Harry, and perhaps Sir Robert, ought to know. It is not the king we have to blame for all this, but Cameron. I have it on the best authority that it was he who instituted the law against spending Scots gold abroad. That it was he who had the idea of taking Strathearn away from Malise. And that it was also he who insisted that Patrick and Malise should be among the hostages. It seems he has mounted a full-scale attack not only on Columba but on the Grahams.'

Ninian, her hands full of veiling and gloves and girdles, said distractedly, 'Why, Adam? I don't see why!'

'You don't see why, when you know how he hates Columba, when Columba himself has told you how ruthless and ambitious he is? Today's anti-barratry law is only the beginning, and it is aimed directly at Columba because Cameron is frightened of him – because anyone can see that Columba would make a far better bishop and chancellor than he.

'And he's frightened of the Grahams, too, in a different way, because Sir Robert wants to curb the power of the king, and that means that Cameron's power would also be curbed. Which is why he will do anything to harm Sir Robert, either directly or through his family.'

Adam paused hopefully. Sir Robert Graham was just the kind of man he wanted for an ally; but Sir Robert had to be persuaded that the king's chancellor presented as great a threat to everything he believed in as the king himself.

Ninian said, 'Adam, I don't believe any of that! You make it sound as if Bishop Gavin thinks of nothing and no one but himself, whereas I don't think I've ever met anyone so – so *im*personal. I am sure he has far too many things to do to spend time working out ways of upsetting us and making life difficult for Columba! You should know better than to listen to such rumours.'

Fortunately, neither Adam nor Harry was very perceptive. Harry, typically, said, 'If you can't maintain a decent womanly silence, Ninian, at least spare us your opinion on matters you know nothing about!'

But Adam raised his brows satirically. 'Not even when the source of the rumours is – er – uniquely well informed?'

'What does that mean?' Harry asked irritably.

'You wouldn't wish me to betray a confidence! But who, besides Cameron and the king himself, would you expect to know everything that goes on?' He thought, for a moment, that he was going to have to spell it out. Harry could be impossibly obtuse.

Harry's frown deepened, and he said, 'You mean Atholl? Well, why didn't you say so!'

Ninian, watching Adam, recognized the smile that meant he was reaching the limits of his tolerance, and suddenly caught the memory that had been eluding her – of Adam saying, a few days ago, that Malise's devotion had ceased to be amusing and that he must think of some way of discouraging it. And of herself replying blithely, 'Short of murder or abduction, I can't see what, can you?'

But she couldn't believe that Adam could have had anything to do with something as drastic as this. And if the Earl of Atholl said Bishop Gavin was behind it all, he was probably right.

She felt a thin, miserable, familiar anger wash through her. How could she – *how could she* – be in love with a man who seemed to have declared war on everyone in the world who mattered to her!

She said, 'Harry, don't you think it would be a good idea to invite Sir

Robert to come to Dess with Adam? Perhaps if we could talk about things sensibly, we might find some way of putting a stop to all this nonsense.'

Dear Ninian, Adam thought. What a clever girl she was, sometimes.

6

ADAM and Sir Robert Graham, free from the encumbrance of sumpter ponies, reached Dess only a few hours after Harry and Ninian, and Ninian came flying in to the High Hall to greet them. But her welcome to Sir Robert was cursory, to say the least, and she looked, for a moment, as if she couldn't think why he was there.

'Adam! A letter from Columba. It was waiting for me, and there is another one for you. For heaven's sake, come upstairs. Perhaps he has said more in yours than he has in mine. It's dreadful! Oh, *do* come! You will excuse us, Sir Robert, I know. Harry will be with you immediately.'

She would say nothing more as Adam followed her up the privy stair to the gallery that served also as the chapel, but he knew what it must be. He, unlike Ninian, had had warning of it. Columba's premonitions must have been right.

And it was so. The letters confirmed that the pope had taken Teviotdale away from Columba and restored it to John Bowmaker.

Columba's wording was restrained, factual, a little obscure in parts. It was clear that he had fought very hard, even though he had been expecting to lose. It was clear, too, that much of his pain came from having to tell those he loved – again – that he had lost. Again.

Adam had been reading his letter aloud, but he stopped halfway through the last paragraph, just after the sentence that read, 'Cameron is behind all this, as I suspected.' He needed to think. If he was to do what Columba seemed to want, he had to move with care. But he could do it – indeed, his plans had already begun to take shape – and it would give him great pleasure. For a moment he came near to smiling.

The tears were pouring down Ninian's cheeks. 'Oh, Columba! Columba! Why should you be hurt so?' She turned away and leaned her forehead against the wall by the window. Then, suddenly, she burst out, without any logic that Adam could see, 'It doesn't mean that I don't care about Malise and Patrick and Sir Robert! It doesn't, because I do care. It's just' – and the tears threatened to choke her – 'it's just that I care more about Columba!'

Light dawned, and Adam said, 'Harry?'

'It was awful. He said why should he worry about Columba, who always survives, when his own family is under attack. He said Patrick and Malise are his first concern, and should be mine. He said I still love Columba, and you, and Séverine, and Blane, and Villeneuve, far more than I love him or Dess. Oh, *Adam!*'

She threw herself in his arms.

Poor, plump, pretty little cousin. His mind elsewhere, he wrapped her soothingly in his embrace, and stroked her hair, and rested his lips on her cheek somewhere to the south-west of her eye, and murmured a few meaningless endearments.

And then, gradually, it became more complicated than that.

She filled his arms most comfortably, and her cheek was soft, and the tears sweetly salt. He moved his hand until it was under the falling hair, his fingertips resting quietly at the nape of her neck, cradling her unresisting head, turning it slowly until her face came up a little and her lips were raised to his. Her eyes were closed, and as he looked at her, lonely and vulnerable, he felt a violent, wholly unexpected shudder run all the way through him, so that he couldn't stop himself from sliding his other hand swiftly down her back and pressing her body to his.

A stabbing, beautiful ache shot through the muscles of his thighs and he flexed them voluptuously, with a sensual joy that he hadn't felt since his very first adventure, when he was a boy. Breathing with care, so as not to put his pleasure at risk, he lowered his lips to hers.

But she did no more than start, very slightly, because she had found sanctuary and had no wish to leave it. She had been so tired and so forlorn in this last year; she who, before, had never been anything but given in to and pampered.

When she was a child, Columba had often taken her in his arms to comfort her, until suddenly, just when she was at the age to need him most, he had stopped. She had been heartbroken for a long time until she had summoned up the courage to speak to Séverine about it, and Séverine had told her why. The little buds that had become breasts, the child who was becoming a woman. But, ever since, there had been an emptiness in her and a hunger for the special kind of warm, reassuring physical closeness that she thought of as the essence of love. A hunger that neither her dreams, nor almost a year of marriage had done anything to assuage.

She couldn't remember a time when she hadn't looked up to Adam, loving him only fractionally less than she loved Columba, and – she had always thought – in not too different a way, despite the dangerous extra current of excitement she felt in his presence. Columba was the calm, Adam the storm.

So, now, when he accepted her into his arms, it was like coming home again, and all tension and all willpower were drained out of her by the longed-for comfort of it.

The first, gentle embrace lulled her just as Columba's had always done, blinding her senses to everything except the security and tenderness she craved. Even when she felt him shudder and press his body against hers, she thought vaguely that she needn't pull away from him because she couldn't bear to and, besides, this was Adam, who wouldn't hurt her.

His lips were warm and kind, first on her mouth, and then sliding softly down to touch the skin above the wide, low neckline of her gown, moving over it so gently that she felt no more than the harmless whisper of a caress. And then, easily and naturally, his hand followed where his lips had led; and further, too, slipping under the silk to cradle one breast in a hard, calloused, horseman's palm.

At the touch, harsh flesh against soft, she felt her body begin to tremble, quietly and independently, in a way that was completely strange to her, and the trembling spread and grew when he took her breast in his lips, teasing it with his tongue, while his hand moved free and downwards, slowly, slowly, smoothing over her stomach and the inward curve of her thighs, skin over silk over skin.

And then he held her for several moments, in a state of bemused suspension, and she felt almost as if there were two of her in his arms, one observing curiously while the other experienced the strangest sensations, as if all her muscles were melting, inside and out. She would have fallen if there hadn't been two hard arms holding her up.

Completely absorbed, she didn't see Adam's eyes flicker or the satisfied smile lift the corners of his mouth as he looked at her and knew she was ready to be led on in a direction that, he suspected, might be new to her. It had always pleased his vanity to give his mistresses as much satisfaction as possible, provided it didn't interfere with his own, and the thought of teaching Ninian what she ought to know held a special, rather whimsical charm for him.

It was a relief that Harry's unquestionably loutish attentions hadn't ruined her. Her body, indeed, responded with unexpected swiftness to the practised caresses of his lips and hands. He thought, 'Starved, *pauvre p'tite*, without even knowing it.'

So he fastened his mouth on hers and allowed a hint of passion to replace the tenderness of moments before, while his hands took up their movement again, the long, repeated, compelling strokes that ran from waist to thigh and then inwards, and inwards again, and again, hard palms over slippery silk, over the skin he would reach when the time was right, his own hips moving always in rhythm, his body no more than inches away from hers so that she could feel the warmth of his every pulse-beat.

She stood, breathless, devoid of will, as the tantalizing sensations became stronger and more urgent, until she scarcely recognized her own body, possessed suddenly by a nerve-strung agony, an aching ecstasy, a hollowness of waiting – for what? Were these the feelings Sévèrine had spoken of, when she had said that love could be beautiful? But this wasn't beauty, it was desperation, a yearning after something that should be there, but wasn't, a . . .

In a single fluid movement, Adam dropped to one knee and buried his face between her thighs, and then his hands were resting lightly on her ankles and beginning to glide upwards, swiftly and surely, his wrists carrying the weight of her skirts with them as they went.

She had no warning, no idea then, or ever, what nerve it was in her that he touched at that moment. But suddenly, every muscle from neck to calf went into spasm, and she tore frantically away from him, and inside the envelope of flesh that was her earthly shape a raging fire exploded into life, a molten fire whose flames raced through her veins, searing, purifying, retreating, and as swiftly dying, so that everything was over almost before it had begun.

After a long, stunned, terrified moment, she straightened up and stared at Adam, her eyes enormous and her hands crossed before her throat, while he, still on one knee, drew in a single, raging breath, and exclaimed, '*Merde!*'

When he had risen and recovered himself a little, he said brutally, '*Dieu de Dieu*, woman! There's no need to look like a saint who's seen a vision. There was nothing divine about that little experience. From where I stand, it looked more like the work of the devil.' And as she went on staring at him, he laughed, without humour. 'Oh, well, I suppose that puts an end to our little frolic for today. Perhaps it's as well.'

She wasn't completely sure what he was talking about. All she knew was that he had been deceiving her, that his tenderness and gentleness hadn't come from the heart but had been only a way of bewitching her.

He had done it so well that he must do it often, with all his mistresses. Of whom she had no intention of being one.

From the welter of emotions possessing her, the one that came to the surface was a swift, white-hot anger, a need to hurt back. He had condescended to her all her life, and because he was Adam, whom she loved, she had never retaliated. But that didn't mean she didn't know how.

So she, too, laughed. 'I think I should apologise. It seemed a good opportunity to discover how you compared with Harry, but perhaps it's not the best time, when I am having these abrupt attacks of the colic. Yesterday's fish, I suspect.'

She knew the insults would sting, even though, deep down, she didn't expect him to believe her. But their effect went far beyond what she could have imagined.

He was quite unused to being challenged, certainly not by his adoring little cousin, and she had caught his vanity on the raw. The reflex was immediate. The deep red spreading like a tide under his sun-browned skin, his brilliant eyes glittering, his lips clamped into an invisible line, he took a lunging pace forward, his hand coming up, flat and violent, reaching for her.

But even as she leapt back, catching her slipper in the hem of her gown and stumbling, he remembered who she was and stopped himself. Instead, unsmiling and breathing unevenly, he said, 'A good try, little one. How fortunate that I can tell when you're lying, otherwise I might be angry. But don't test me too often.'

She looked at the Adam who, for a flicker of time, had turned into a menacing stranger, and realized that never before had she seen him lose his temper. His impatience, his occasional flashes of anger, were familiar enough – but they were nothing like this. She wondered if there were other things about him she didn't know.

But she had to say something – anything – to put an end to this frightening interlude. This instructive interlude. What she had learned of her own motives, and of her own body, she couldn't even begin to think of now. That was for another time and some other, private place.

With a superhuman effort of will, she asked, 'Test you? Would I dare?' and smiled mischievously.

Then she said, 'Oh, Adam! We're wasting time. The thing that matters, now, is what are we going to do about Columba?'

7

ADAM had handled Sir Robert Graham very carefully on the ride north, unaware that the only reason why Sir Robert had accepted the invitation to Dess at all was because he was curious to know what young Verne wanted of him.

He undoubtedly wanted something. Sir Robert wasn't the kind of person to whom men of his type gravitated naturally. But Sir Robert had the feeling that there was more to Adam de Verne than met the eye – much more than the hunting, tourneying and womanizing that his appearance suggested. The young man had been careful to let slip that Archdeacon Crozier, in the past, had occasionally seen fit to employ him as a papal messenger, and had larded his conversation with so many casual references to the courts of Europe that even a stupid man, which Sir Robert assuredly was not, would have been bound to recognize that he was unusually well informed.

Unless it all turned out to be mere parade, Sir Robert had reflected, he and M. de Verne might find cooperation to their mutual advantage.

Which was precisely, it seemed, what M. de Verne had in mind.

Adam wanted Harry out of the way while they were holding their council of war, but Harry wasn't to be shifted, or not until it was time for him to do his evening rounds of the cattle, and the gates, and all the other things that it seemed he alone was capable of doing. So Adam took an inordinate length of time telling Sir Robert every detail of Archdeacon Crozier's career, from his days as a theology student at Paris up to Rome in 1424 and the case of the missing document, and when he had finished with that, he went on to supply all the minutiae of the controversy with Bishop Gavin.

When he could protract the tale no longer, Sir Robert, who knew very well what he was up to, obligingly embarked on the scarcely less interminable history of the Grahams' relations with James, and James's father, and his grandfather, despots to a man, it seemed.

Ninian, distaff virtuously in hand, sat spinning her wool and

174

wondering when, if ever, they were going to get to the point, while Harry, whose attempt to hurry Adam along had been cut off in its prime by one glance from his uncle's compelling eye, relapsed into lofty indifference.

In the end, he rose to his feet and said, with heavy sarcasm, 'Since you seem to have no need of my presence, I shall go and attend to all the things that need to be attended to. You will tell me, perhaps, if you reach any conclusions?'

'Well . . .' Adam said when he had gone, and wasted no more time. 'Sir Robert, I believe we are natural allies. Archdeacon Crozier is under threat from Gavin Cameron. Your family is under threat from the king, and you yourself, despite His Majesty's apparent lenience, must live on a knife-edge from now on. Or so it seems to me. Neither of us has any defence except attack.

'I suggest that, if you were to join me in striking a blow at Cameron, who is the king's right hand, you would avenge much of the damage that has been done to your family. According to my information, it is he who has been directly responsible for a good deal of it. And however you care to look at the matter, if we strike a blow at one, we injure both.'

Sir Robert nodded. There was no visible movement in the muscles of his face. 'I would not dispute that. However, much though I resent the wrongs done to my family, I am more concerned about the wrongs James has already done – and will continue to do – to the country. My quarrel is with him. I cannot afford to squander my energies on his servants. So, although I can see that an alliance might be of value to you, I cannot see that it would greatly benefit me.'

Uneasily, Ninian interrupted. 'Adam, I . . . Why are we talking about "striking blows"? I thought *our* object was to persuade Bishop Gavin that Columba isn't an enemy, but a good and clever man whom he has misunderstood? And that yours, Sir Robert, was to soften the king's attitude towards yourself and the family?'

Adam, it seemed, was still angry with her. 'Don't be naïve,' he said. And almost without thinking, she snapped back, 'What is naïve about expecting people to behave in a civilized fashion?'

Sir Robert was watching them both, his mouth slack as always under the dark line of his eyes. He said nothing.

Dismissively, Adam drawled, 'Make no mistake, Ninian. It is either Columba or Cameron.' Then he turned back to Sir Robert. 'I fully expected that you might not see the benefits of an alliance at first. So let me approach the matter in another way. When I spoke of striking a blow at Cameron, what did you think I had in mind?'

Sir Robert shrugged and didn't even trouble to smother his yawn. 'Catching him alone on a dark night?'

Neither of them even noticed Ninian rising to her feet and going to stand by the window, to look out blindly on the evening landscape, all deer-grass and bracken, where a few undernourished sheep grazed, and two of the milk goats. There was no other sign of life at all. She hadn't thought, when she had talked of saving Columba, that it might lead on to physical violence against Gavin Cameron.

Adam shook his head. 'You think me as crude as that?' There was a note of mockery in his voice. Then, his eyes on his hands, he added, 'And perhaps you haven't noticed that, since his accident ten days ago, he hasn't moved without an armed escort?'

'I noticed.'

Ninian's mind didn't grasp the implications at first. Even then, all she thought was, '*Not* an accident?'

'So,' Adam resumed lightly, 'it would scarcely be worth the risk, would it? It would be poor satisfaction to cut down an enemy if one's own head promptly landed on the block. No. Only the Inquisition can get away with murdering a bishop.' He grinned suddenly. 'You don't happen to know where Cameron stands in matters of doctrine? How convenient it would be if he turned out to be a secret Lollard! Then we could persuade Master Laurence to light the fires!'

For the first time, Robert Graham's mouth twisted in amusement. 'I have no idea. But, as to murder, there is a better argument against it. Murders make martyrs, and James would not hesitate to justify every future act of tyranny by reference to the wishes of his lately deceased – and instantly beatified – chancellor.'

Adam threw back his head and laughed. 'According to the will of Saint Gavin, you mean? I hadn't thought of that!'

Ninian wondered dizzily how much of this conversation was real, and how much designed merely to shock her. Was it just that Adam was still intent on paying her out? Because he couldn't mean it. Whatever Columba felt about Gavin Cameron, it was impossible that murder should even have entered his head.

It occurred to her that, if she let Adam think he had won, that she was still as much his adoring little cousin as she had ever been, perhaps they could all go back to being sensible again.

Drifting over to the table, she sat down and said artlessly, 'Adam, you know you have some ingenious plan in mind that will settle everything. You always do. Put us out of suspense!'

She knew him very well, most of the time. One eyebrow rose, quizzically, and he grinned and said, *'Merci du compliment!'*

It turned out that his plan, though spaciously conceived, was really quite simple. If they could succeed in discrediting Cameron in James's eyes, he would be of no further use either to the state or to the church. And, deprived of his offices, he would be deprived also of his power to harm Columba.

'The principle,' Sir Robert said, 'is admirable. But I am still at a loss to understand how all this can be of benefit to me.'

Adam looked slightly impatient, as if Sir Robert were being stupid. 'If the king loses his right arm, he loses half his strength. True? And if Cameron were gone, is there anyone else who could fill his place?'

'None of the same calibre, I agree. But you are still being much too nebulous, M. de Verne. I deduce that you have some specific action in mind, and I believe we would proceed more rapidly if you told me what it was.'

Adam stretched luxuriously and clasped his hands behind his head. 'Is there some wine coming, *p'tite*?'

She nodded. 'Soon. I told them to bring it just before curfew.'

'What about Harry?'

'Not for a little while yet.'

'Good. Very well, then, Sir Robert, I believe we understand each other. What I have in mind is to attack Cameron from all sides. I have no doubt that Archdeacon Crozier will already be busy at Rome, undermining his reputation in the church. Here at home, I believe we ought also to be able to wreck his reputation for personal integrity; we will come to that in a moment. And politically . . . Well, when a man is chancellor of the realm, he has another, secondary role – as scapegoat. *All* civil and religious troubles can be laid at his door. And if we stir up the kind of trouble I have in mind, your cause, Sir Robert, might well benefit even more than Archdeacon Crozier's.'

Sir Robert waited, the sinewy hands lying loose and relaxed on the table.

Adam took a deep breath. 'Trouble in the Highlands,' he said. 'As I understand it, a mere sixteen years ago the father of the present Lord of the Isles set out at the head of the largest army ever to come out of the Hebrides to try and turn the whole of northern and western Scotland into an independent state, under his governance. The battle of Harlaw put an end to the affair for the time being, but I am told that the issue is by no means dead.'

Sir Robert said nothing.

'I am told, also, that the present Lord, Alexander, is a fiery young man with more energy than he can find outlet for, and a desire to prove his mettle.'

Still, Sir Robert said nothing.

Adam grinned. 'And you, Sir Robert, are not without influence in that quarter. It must have occurred to you that, with guidance, Alexander . . .'

Ninian, who had heard the scuff of a servant's feet on the stairs, rose and went to the door to admit him. It was a new door, and Harry had taken a lot of persuading to have it installed. In the subdued bustle that accompanied the laying out of the hippocras and spice cakes, she missed Adam's last words, and when the servant had gone there was only silence.

When the wine had been poured, Sir Robert said, absently scratching the stubble on his chin, 'I had not thought it justifiable until now.'

Ninian saw the satisfaction in Adam's eyes as he raised his wine cup, but she had the feeling that something that had been said earlier must have escaped her, because he and Sir Robert certainly couldn't be sitting here drinking Harry's wine and coolly discussing whether they should start a civil war.

Since she had no desire to be snubbed again, she didn't ask for enlightenment, but sat with a cheese-filled wafer in her hand and waited.

Adam said, 'Excellent! I am glad we are agreed. We need not go into detail here and now, I think. Perhaps we might both take time to consider.'

Sir Robert inclined his head and sat back in his chair – Harry's chair, the one with the cushioned seat and the cloth-covered back.

'Let us instead,' Adam continued, 'turn our attention to the other matter I mentioned. This is where the Lady Ninian comes in.'

The brilliant eyes flashed at her. He was himself again, all the familiar charm and vitality back in full force, and she couldn't help but smile back with the relief of it.

'Ninian, p'tite. We are agreed that we must attack our adversary's private as well as his public reputation. Now, even Sir Robert must know what a dull dog Harry is, so I doubt if he will be shocked when I suggest that you set your mind, and your undoubted charms, to seducing the bishop. Wouldn't that amuse you?'

She stared at him for the length of several heartbeats. Then, without being aware of it, she was on her feet, unable to disguise either her horror at the idea itself, or her shame that Adam should suggest such a thing before someone who was almost a stranger.

And even as she struggled to find words, Adam added cheerfully, 'You need a man, you know – and it would be interesting to find out whether friend Cameron *is* one!'

All those women, she thought suddenly. All those women at court, and their almost palpable awareness of him the other day by the water meadows. Was *that* what they had been thinking? She herself, brought up in a society where every other man was a priest, hadn't thought until then that in a different kind of company a handsome, celibate churchman might have a very special kind of attraction. The charm of the unattainable, she had decided unhappily. But perhaps it hadn't been that, after all.

It wasn't bearable. Any of it. It – was – not – bearable. She *would not* be in love with him.

If only she didn't have to see him, she knew that she could break herself of it. But the queen had been gracious enough to say that she would like the Lady Ninian in regular attendance at court, which meant that it would be impossible to avoid him.

Unless . . . Unless Adam's plot, whatever it was, succeeded. Then, a discredited Gavin Cameron would vanish from public life and there would be an end to all her troubles. And Columba's, too, of course.

But she could never do what Adam had suggested.

She sat down abruptly and succeeded, somehow, in looking straight into Robert Graham's eyes and saying, 'What you must think, Sir Robert, I cannot imagine. Adam and I had a small disagreement earlier today. I can only assume he is having his revenge.'

She had no idea why she should be so upset about it, because it was just like Adam to come out with an idea like that, regardless of anyone else's feelings.

Injured, he said, 'Revenge? When my sole intent was to demonstrate to Sir Robert what a very perfect, moral wife his nephew has?'

Robert Graham said, 'There was no need.'

Adam picked up his cup and surveyed its contents. 'No? How dull you must think her. Ah well, I suppose that respectability must have something to recommend it, though I have never been able to see what.

'However, it seems I must think of some other way of ruining the bishop's reputation.' His face creased into one of his most spectacular smiles. 'Which shouldn't be difficult. There are more ways of killing a cat than stuffing it with cream.'

And then he drained his cup, threw back his head, and laughed as if he were enjoying some extravagant private joke.

PART THREE

1427–1428

CHAPTER ONE

I

THE fourteen days between Christmas Eve and Epiphany were a sore trial for anyone who liked his privacy and was trying to get some work done, for the king was holding court at Edinburgh, and its castle, perched on a damned, cold, draughty crag, was bursting at the seams with people.

Gavin, his mind on the overdue ransom payments, and the £600 repair bill for the palace of Linlithgow, and the £2,000 James had managed to spend on siege engines from Flanders – not to mention fur-lined mantles, ostrich feathers, and a fine new standing salt made of solid gold studded with pearls – had protested, without much hope of being heeded, at the scale of the entertainments planned.

But James had said what he always said, and scarcely less quietly, even though they were in the castle chapel hearing Mass at the time. 'Nonsense, man! A parade of wealth and luxury is essential for a king. No one believes you're powerful unless you look it.' It was true enough, but it was also true that James was dangerously extravagant, though Gavin could understand why. Remembering only too well how ignominious it felt to be poor, he could imagine what it must have been like for an exiled king to grow up at another king's court, beholden to his royal jailer even for the clothes on his back. It wasn't surprising that, now, James felt no urgent need to repay his ransom – especially when it was, nominally, a refund to England of the cost of his niggardly board and miserly lodging during his eighteen years' involuntary exile.

'Anyway,' James had gone on. 'What'll it cost? £20 for wine and ale! A few barrels of salmon at £1.10s. a time! A few shillings for the players!'

The first course at the Christmas Day banquet had consisted of umbles of venison, blancmanger, brawn with mustard, chines of pork, roast fat capon, roast swan, roast heron, venison cutlets, swan's neck pudding, meat slices in gravy, and a custard with a gold-leaf lion on top. And that had been only the first course. The wines had been Rhenish, Gascon, and a Spanish Osey compounded with spices. The players had included minstrels, trumpeters, choristers, verse-makers, bear-leaders, tumblers, and mimes, the latter brought all the way from Flanders for the occasion.

James, cornered, had admitted he wasn't sure how much it would all add up to in the end, and since, where money was concerned, he seldom allowed his right hand to know what his left hand was doing, Gavin believed him.

It was too late to repine and, in any case, royal finance was the business of the chamberlain, not the chancellor, although James was intending soon to introduce the English-style offices of treasurer and comptroller. So, quietly, Gavin began to enjoy himself, even if he took care not to show it.

Royal banquets had their compensations. There was an undoubted pleasure in having his capon carved for him by his former employer, the fifth Earl of Douglas, and his wine poured by that old reprobate, the Earl of Mar, who had acquired his title almost thirty years ago by the simple expedient of making a widow of the Countess of Mar, besieging her in her castle, and then carrying her off and forcing her to accept him as her second husband. There was scope for some new legislation there, Gavin had always thought.

There was something about Christmas and, more especially, New Year, that seemed to put people at ease. Even that little minx, Ninian Drummond, normally on edge when the king was present, was behaving naturally for once. In the last few months, she had become very popular with the younger knights of the court, who had swooned, to a man, at all her French tricks – the smile in the astonishingly blue eyes, the long, flirtatious eyelashes, the demure playfulness, the inviting plumpness, the outrageous decolletage. Even some of the older men, like Walter of Lithgow, weren't immune to her busy sparkling. If Tom Myrton had been here, Gavin would have reminded him of their conversation on the night before the girl's wedding, when Tom had said she was probably an innocent. Innocent? Ha! But at least her husband was having enough sense to pretend that he didn't mind. Gavin was reasonably sure that he must be jealous, but he would have looked a fool if he had allowed it to show.

Gavin was faintly surprised that she hadn't tried her tricks on him. In his experience the mitre was no protection against a predatory woman; rather the opposite, he sometimes thought. But the Lady Ninian, after behaving like some novice from a convent during their first few encounters, had subsequently become exceedingly sprightly, so that he had found it necessary to take a repressive tone with her. He couldn't have a chit of a girl being impertinent to the chancellor of the realm.

Tonight, however, he had been sorely tempted to laugh, and she had caught the displeased expression on his face and looked suddenly as if she were about to weep. It hadn't occurred to him before that perhaps he was being unfair to her. She must be about eighteen, he supposed, but she was a very young eighteen.

She had been singing, to a small circle of admirers, a nonsensical, punning little snatch of a *rondeau* that was obviously – and most improperly – aimed at James, who had just dropped something and, as usual, gone scarlet in the face and started breathing fire and smoke as if all the inanimate objects in the universe had been designed specifically to annoy him.

> . . . *Fumeux fume par fumée*
> *Fumeuse speculacion!*

'He who fumes, and lets off steam, provokes – hot air!'

It was fortunate that the king was well out of earshot, because it wasn't respectful, and it certainly wasn't genteel. But, coupled with the mischief in her eyes, it was irresistible.

A pity she was involved with so many suspect, possibly dangerous people. The other Verne boy had just turned up from France to join his brother Adam, and Gavin wondered why. He wondered, too, about Adam de Verne and the Lady Elinor. That was a relationship that didn't seem to have ended at Villeneuve, although they were being extremely careful, and Gavin supposed that anyone who didn't already know about it would be unlikely to notice. There was nothing surprising in Atholl's daughter-in-law being on relatively easy terms with a young man who had become one of Atholl's most constant companions. But Gavin would have liked to know what the two of them were talking about in such an apparently indifferent but suspiciously low-voiced way.

It was New Year's Eve and time for the bonfire, burning the old year out. And then for the entry of the 'first foot', the dark-haired, handsome, dark-complexioned outsider whose role it was to enter the Great Chamber a minute after midnight and, in total silence, place a peat on the fire as an augury of peace and plenty for the coming year. Gavin hoped it wasn't some kind of omen that Atholl should have suggested Blane de Verne to do the royal first-footing.

And after that, everyone present had to have his or her health separately drunk.

There were well over a hundred people in the Great Chamber, and none of them impeccably sober even to begin with.

2

IT was Gavin's unsocial habit to be wakeful at the hours when most other people were decently asleep. So, as he retired to his chamber somewhere between three and four in the morning, wending his intricate and slightly too careful way along corridors and passages full of unimportant guests bedded down on makeshift pallets, he decided that, before he laid his head down, he might as well have a look at his final notes on the erection of Strathblane into a prebend. It still seemed to him that one markland and fourteen marks a year for the vicar ought to do, with an added sixteen marks for the maintenance of four choirboys; though the prebendary would have to be responsible for maintaining the church fabric as well.

Absently dismissing his usher, Gavin shut the door and, fixing his eyes undeviatingly on the clothes chest that served as his desk, made his way towards it. It was the only way he had ever found of treading a straight path when his head and legs were imperfectly coordinated. Then he lit another couple of candles and found the parchment he was looking for.

His nostrils full of the smells of people and wine, he didn't at first sense the presence of the intruder, but when he did, he was still sufficiently master of his wits to give no sign. There was only just space in the room for the chest, and a stool, and the bed. So the intruder was either under the bed, in the gap against the wall, or on the bed itself behind the part-drawn curtains. Who? One of his own servants, overcome by drink? Some hopeful squire, looking for a place to sleep? Or someone whose motives were less innocent?

Not someone already sleeping, for whoever it was was holding his breath. Yet Gavin felt no serious prickle of danger, even though, poring over his document, his back was open to the knife.

Casually, after a moment, he put the scroll down and, tossing off his long, heavy tunic, went to the door and as casually shot the bolt. There was nothing wrong with his balance now.

Then he turned.

Pale face, pale lips, pale eyes, pale hair. But no pale draperies, or none that he could see. The Lady Elinor, languid as always, was wearing nothing at all except a small corner of his bedcover drawn coyly over the place where thighs and torso met. Her skin was so transparent that he could see the veins and arteries shining through, bright and blue, and branched like rowan saplings. There were two or three bruises on the bones of her pelvis, and another, livid one on her breast that looked as if it might have been made by teeth.

He said politely, 'And a happy New Year to you, too. Can I be of assistance?'

'I don't know.' Deliberately, she scanned the body revealed to her by shirt and clinging breech-hose. 'Can you?'

'You wished to make your confession, perhaps?'

The trouble was, he didn't like her and he didn't want her, but he couldn't think how to get rid of her. If the corridor hadn't been full of revellers, he would simply have picked her up and dumped her unceremoniously outside, and her clothes after her. But not tonight. She would have to leave fully dressed, and unobtrusively.

'Not your confession? Ah, I see. The castle *is* full, I agree, and as it happens I have some work to do. You may borrow my bed, with pleasure, for an hour or two.'

Decisively, he sat down on the stool again, with his back to her. But it wasn't easy to concentrate on the markland and how much it cost to feed a choirboy, when the figures were multiplying themselves before his eyes.

It was appearances that counted, however, and he succeeded in looking engrossed, even though he was sensitive to every smallest sound and movement.

She shifted restlessly after a while, and sighed once or twice. By the time ten minutes had passed, she was breathing audibly through her nose.

'You can't,' she said in a bored voice at last, 'expect me to come to you. It's up to you to make the first move. If you know how, of course.'

He let it go for a moment, and then said abstractedly, 'I'm sorry. Did you say something?'

'If I did come, would it be worth my while?'

Bitch.

There was a pause and then, indifferently, she went on. 'I don't suppose it would. How futile you are, in spite of those exciting looks. I thought so on the journey out to France. You annoyed me then. I'm not used to being turned down. But I suppose it's natural that you would turn a woman down, if you're incapable.'

To his intense exasperation, he was becoming more capable by the second. He clenched his teeth and, telling himself that he was not a callow boy to have to respond to such a challenge, picked up his quill, and made a decisive marginal gloss on the parchment. The quill was bone-dry and the note invisible. He uncorked the ink pot.

'Is it only women you're incapable with?' the world-weary voice resumed. 'Someone tried to make a wager with me about that the other day.'

In a moment he really would pick her up and throw her out of the door, and to hell with the consequences.

'How boring,' she went on pettishly, 'always to have one's suspicions confirmed.'

And then there was a faint, slithering sound, and the light voice said, right by his ear, 'But I suppose one *should* make a final effort.'

She was behind him, pressing the thin body against his back, her breasts small and soft against his shoulder blades, her hands reaching forward, caressing his flesh, unlacing his shirt, and her stomach just touching the base of his spine, skimming it, undulating with a slow, intolerably lascivious motion that brought him abruptly to his feet, backing away from her, his face and body stark as a saint in a Byzantine mosaic.

He stared at her, at the white, flawed skin, and the long, pale, silken hair, and the colourless mouth, smiling and spiteful. At the salacious ripple of movement running through shoulders, arms, stomach and legs. At the erotic, quivering thrust of her pelvis, and the valley between her slightly parted thighs, open, experienced, flagrantly inviting.

He said, 'You have missed your way,' and had to clear his throat before he went on. 'Following the Act of 1426, all the whore-houses have moved to the outskirts of the town.'

She half-laughed, and said, 'A lawyer. A priest. Not a *man*! But don't think — don't think for a moment — that I can't manage for myself.' And then the space between her legs widened and, deliberately, rhythmically, her pelvis began pushing forward and back, forward and back, and her hands were hovering and darting between her thighs, and her breathing began to change. And all the while, her eyes remained fixed on his, gleaming with a mixture of sensuality and triumph and the uttermost contempt.

It was the wine, it was the wine. He should have laughed at her. But instead, possessed by a furious, uncontrollable rage, he took two strides forward, picked her up, and then threw her not out of the door as he had intended, but across the high bed so that the edge caught her behind the knees.

Then, still standing, he ripped the ties of his breech-hose, and spread her legs wide, and did, with violence, what she wanted him to do.

3

WITHIN hours, everyone in Edinburgh knew about it.

The cold, formidable Bishop of Glasgow — and the glacial, touch-me-not wife of the Master of Atholl?

It was the finest scandal anyone had heard of for a generation.

No one knew how the rumour had started, but no one doubted its truth. There were some who said, 'Like unto like', and shrugged. Others speculated shamelessly. One or two were outraged. Some of the queen's ladies were aghast; others, like Lady Moragh, monosyllabic; but there was a feverish note in all their whispering.

Ninian fled to the only place where she could find privacy, in the highest, furthest corner of the battlements, and stared out over the countryside with tears pouring down her cheeks and her heart breaking.

All the dreams, bidden and unbidden, of eighteen turbulent months reformed themselves before her eyes. Dreams that had been no more than a simple image at first, of a face and figure and personality that obsessed her, a kind of icon to be worshipped from a distance. He had seemed as far above her as the stars. But after a while, as she had seen more of him at court, the dreams had progressed until she was in them, too, and the stern eyes were smiling at her.

It hadn't been enough, of course, and she had found herself one night lost in the most beautiful dream she had ever had, when the voice that sent such sensuous shivers up and down her spine took on a different tone, and the deeply reserved manner was cast aside, and he told her how passionately he admired and loved her.

But he was a man of God, he said, and human passion was not for him. He took her in his arms and kissed her once, gently, and that was all. It had been very romantic, and she had understood the renunciation perfectly, and accepted it, and dreamed the lovely dream often until the day when Adam had embraced her, in all too real reality, and she had discovered desires in herself that she hadn't known before.

Since then, through all the weeks of pretending to herself that he was just another priest, for whom she felt nothing very much – except perhaps dislike, on Columba's account – she had held on to the belief, in a secret corner of her heart, that he was a man of principle whose vows were sacred to him. And it made life easier to bear – though it was both sinful and vulgar to think in such terms – to know that, even though she couldn't have him, neither could any other woman.

And now, and now . . .

4

THE king was very nearly apoplectic. Rampaging round his bed-chamber like the ferocious wee bullock Tom Myrton always likened him to, he gave Gavin the tongue-lashing of his life.

It was a full fifteen minutes before he paused to draw breath, by which time he had dealt comprehensively with his chancellor's morals, manners, upbringing, ancestry, effrontery, stinginess, ignorance of music, poor taste in poetry, and several other matters besides.

Gavin, angry enough to begin with, stood in a vibrating silence throughout, until the king, reaching his peroration, yelled, 'And for a *bishop of Holy Kirk* to seduce an *innocent woman* . . .'

It was too much. Gavin's temper snapped and, with lungs trained to carry from apse to porch of a sizeable cathedral, he yelled back, 'Damn it to hell! Bishops do it all the time! And as for innocent – *bollocks*!'

For a full minute James stared at him, on his face a wild conflict of emotions. And then he sat down with a thud, planted his hands on his knees, and began to roar with laughter.

'Was she any good?'

Gavin, breathing deeply, said, 'You don't expect me to answer that?'

'But I do, I do! She always looks as if she'd freeze your cods off!'

Appearances could be deceptive, but Gavin wasn't going to be drawn into that kind of discussion.

Anyway, there was something he wanted to know. 'I have no idea how this became public property. I have said nothing, as you may imagine. I can scarcely believe that the Lady Elinor has. And no one saw her leave.' That had taken some arranging, but he was sure of it. 'Who told *you*?'

It was enough to send James off into a tantrum again. 'Who told me? My uncle! Who else? I'm fond of the old man, but God knows there are times when I think his only ambition in life is to worry me to death. And you, Gavin Cameron!' He flung round and stabbed a short, muscular, accusing forefinger at him. 'Have you *any* idea what you've started? Well, I'll tell you. No, on second thoughts, I won't. You tell me something first. Is the woman experienced?'

Levelly, Gavin said, 'She is a married woman, with a son. Surely that answers you.'

The king snorted disgustedly. 'Don't be a fool. You were clear enough, a moment ago, that she's no innocent, and you're no virgin yourself, I take it. *Is she experienced?*'

'I – have – no – idea – whether she is experienced with other men than her husband. I do not, after all, know how experienced *he* is, or what he has taught her.' The lie didn't worry him; he was beginning to have some idea of the repercussions the truth might bring in its wake.

Atholl being troublesome. Atholl, knowing. Atholl, with Adam de Verne always by his side. And Verne and Lady Elinor, whispering together yesterday evening.

Adam de Verne – the *deus ex machina*. But what in God's name was behind it all?

There were two things Gavin would have been prepared to swear to. That the Lady Elinor herself had been motivated, last night, by sheer, simple spite. Her surprise, when he had proved to be capable, had been unquestionably genuine. And secondly, that she had told no one except Adam de Verne.

Abruptly, James said, 'All right. I'll see you again, here, after Magnificat.'

5

MASTER Laurence of Lindores, who Ninian now knew to be an old friend of Columba's, was putting her through a stiff examination on the spiritual competence of the almoner at Dess, when the queen sent for her.

'His Majesty wishes to speak to you,' the queen said. 'I will accompany you myself.'

Even after all this time, Ninian was still terrified of the king. Not just because he had been painted to her as an ogre long before she had met him; not because he was so volatile that no one ever knew what he was going to do or say next; not even because of what he had done to the Grahams.

Patrick and Malise, in fact, were very comfortably settled in the Tower of London now, and seemed to be having rather a good time, while Robert Graham had retired to somewhere on the edge of the Highlands, to commune regularly with his soul and, almost as regularly, with the disaffected clans of the Isles.

There was something more in Ninian's reaction to James. She had heard it said, once, that for every person on earth, however self-confident, there was one other person, somewhere in the world, who could shake that confidence to its foundations. She hoped never to meet anyone else who could shake hers as ruthlessly as James did.

She was trembling inside even before he started to bully her. She had no idea, at first, what he was after when he began asking her about Villeneuve, and her upbringing, and her marriage. The Bishop of Avignon had celebrated the nuptial Mass? Excellent. And Bishop Gavin had blessed her marriage bed? Good. And among the guests had been the Lady Elinor? How had it come about that she had been staying with the Vernes?

With growing horror, Ninian realized that the king was trying to discover whether Lady Elinor and Gavin Cameron might have begun their affair in France, more than a year ago. Confused, cornered, she hardly knew what to say. Forgetting that she had her own reasons, reasons that were not Columba's or Adam's, for wanting him discredited, she thought only of saving him. She knew – Columba had said it often enough – that a churchman could be forgiven an occasional lapse, but not a continuing liaison, and she knew, too, that there was no possibility of such a liaison having begun at Villeneuve, where her ladyship's eyes had been only for Adam. On the journey home, perhaps? But Ninian didn't think it likely and, anyway, that wasn't what the king was questioning her about.

His questions became ever more detailed. 'Did Bishop Gavin arrange to meet Lady Elinor at Villeneuve?'

'No.'

'Then why was she there?'

'She was invited.'

'By Madame de Verne? How did they come to be acquainted?'

'No, by Madame's son, who is a friend of the Vicomte d'Uzès. The Lady Elinor was a guest of the vicomtesse.'

'Where did Bishop Gavin stay during his visit to Villeneuve?'

'At the monastery of the Val de Bénédiction.'

'When he was at the Verne *livrée*, was he ever alone with her ladyship?'

'No.'

'How do you know?'

She floundered. How could she say that Lady Elinor had been with Adam every moment of the time?

'*How do you know?*'

'She was with other people all the time.'

'Which other people?'

Which other people? *Which other people?*

She floundered again.

'Come along!' the king exclaimed. 'If you are so sure she was with other people, you must know *which* other people!' It was like being hit not once, but again and again, with a bludgeon that numbed every faculty so that to think was impossible.

She stammered out a few names, none of which meant anything to His Majesty.

At last, he interrupted her, sturdy and indefatigable, his shoulders massive under the furred and embroidered dark blue velvet of his gown, his shirt open at the neck to reveal his powerful muscles, and his mouth hard and ireful in the shadow of his beard. 'This is useless,' he exploded. 'Perhaps Monsieur Adam may have been more observant. I will ask *him*.'

Ninian thought she was going to faint. Her head was spinning and her insides in turmoil. She swallowed, and swallowed again, trying to control herself, and the hand at her throat was shaking as if she had the ague.

The queen led her gently to a stool and then, turning to her husband, said quietly, 'Enough, surely? I think you have what you want?'

It was then that Ninian discovered how wrong she had been. The king, who was an observant and clever man under the callous exterior, had tricked her. He had not been asking about Gavin Cameron at all.

'Yes,' he said. 'It's clear enough. Adam de Verne also. Two men we know of. How many more has the slut lain with?'

6

RELEASED, Ninian weakly thought that she ought to warn Adam. She didn't know what the penalties were for bedding the wife of a king-to-be – exile, execution, or just the rough edge of His Majesty's tongue?

She found Adam with Blane, the pair of them crammed into something little bigger than a closet, trying to dress for the banquet. Hurriedly, she poured out her tale.

Adam, lacing his doublet with controlled ferocity, said, 'Thank you, *ma petite*. Thank you very much. You have successfully wrecked a very neatly conceived plot.' One of the points jammed in an eyelet; he pulled viciously at it, and it broke.

'Adam, I couldn't help it! I had no idea why he was asking me such questions. I thought it was Bishop Gavin he was interested in. Wouldn't it be wise for you to vanish for a while?'

Blane, going to his brother's rescue, exclaimed, 'Why the devil should he?' and Adam echoed, 'Vanish? Why should I? I can scarcely be hanged for bedding a woman. She'll be the one who pays, and serve her right, the stupid bitch!'

Ninian, already queasy, stared at him. Chivalry! The knight who would protect his lady – his sweet, submissive, loving lady – through

194

all the fires of hell, and back. She remembered her childhood dreams, and the troubadours' tales, and knew what they were worth.

She couldn't bring herself to speak but, chin high, turned and left.

Adam, watching Blane thread the new lace through the eyelets for him, said thoughtfully, 'I will, however, have a word with Atholl. Confession, they say, is good for the soul, and it might at least stop him calling me "*Malise*'s big honeypot".'

7

'I WANT rid of her! I'll no' have my only begotten son wed to a whore!'

Atholl meant his only *legally* begotten son and, tactfully, no one took time to count how many other sons he had, or how many of them had been mothered by whores. Most of them were now settled in comfortable church livings scattered around the country. Bastards or not, there were advantages to having Scotland's premier earl for a father.

'I ask you, whit's the world coming to?' The magenta toorie waggled malevolently. 'The way morals huv gone oot the window these last years, you wouldny think the Judgement Day was nigh. Women? Serpents! Daughters of Eve, every last one o' them! Though I tell you! In my young day, nae man o' birth and breeding would've laid a finger on a wumman who wasny his, nae matter how she tempted him.' His pale, choleric eye lighted on Gavin. 'But it's maybe different wi' peasants.'

He was almost unbelievable sometimes. Gavin was sorely tempted to laugh.

James said, 'Yes, well, uncle. We all know about declining morals, don't we! But leaving them aside, we're in a quandary.'

The quandary wouldn't have existed if Her Majesty's recent lying-in had produced a son, instead of a third daughter, but, as it was, the royal succession remained with the Stewarts of Atholl – father, son, and grandson; Earl Walter, David, and young Rob. And if young Rob's mother had been unchaste during the early, as well as the later days of her marriage, the boy might not be a Stewart at all. His physical resemblance to her ladyship was too strong for looks to be any guide.

Gavin, gloomily contemplating the waste of time and money that would follow from what Atholl all too clearly had in mind, tried without much hope to put a damper on the proceedings. 'If her ladyship has been distributing her favours over a long period,' he said, 'would there not have been some – er – evidence of it?'

Atholl laughed harshly. 'Jings! Ye're a priest in some things, after all. Did ye no' learn anything at school? Wi' a skinny lassie like that, it's a wonder she ever conceived at all. And forbye, if she lies wi' every man she meets, she'll know a' the whore's tricks – douching herself out, jumping up and down, herbal drinks, and a' the rest of it.'

Removing the toorie, which clashed nastily with today's embroidered grass-green doublet, he scratched his scalp energetically with both hands, and then, his hair standing out all round like a dandelion clock and his breastplate winking dully in the candlelight, he added shrewdly, 'And whether Rob's legitimate or no', it doesny matter. The whole town's blethering aboot his mother. If he were ever to come tae the throne, he'd be known as the Bastard King.'

It was true. And that would threaten not only the Stewart dynasty, but the whole stability of the realm.

James said, 'Well, she's your kin, uncle. It's up to you to say what you want done.'

'Divorce, what else! I want my Davie free to remarry and get a son no one can question.'

Gavin could see how James's mind was working. He was convinced that, in the end, the queen would present him with an heir, and, meanwhile, there were undoubted benefits to Atholl's plan, though not the benefits the old man had in mind. If young Rob Stewart, now on the edge of manhood, were declared illegitimate, it would mean one less potentially troublesome heir to contend with. And freeing the Master to remarry – in or out of the Tower – was a procedure that could be spun out for years, since there was no divorce without the consent of Rome. By the time everything went through, James was reckoning, he would have sons of his own and the Master of Atholl's marital problems wouldn't matter any more.

'Bishop Gavin,' the king said, 'you're the lawyer. What about grounds for divorce?'

'Only the ones everyone knows about. Consanguinity – kinship – is the simplest. The church forbids marriage between persons related up to the fourth degree, so if, for example, it were suddenly discovered that Lady Elinor's great-great-grandfather was also the Master's great-grandfather, that would fall within the prohibited degrees and His Holiness could dissolve the marriage.'

Atholl snorted. 'Aye, weel. I doubt the wumman herself even knows who her great-great-granddaddy was. So ye can rule that out, for a start.'

Gavin, straight-faced, said, 'It doesn't have to go as far back. Even if the husband's father and the wife's grandfather were one and the same, that would do very well.'

James glared at him, but Atholl missed it completely. His features were screwed up in concentration as he said, 'Mind you, everyone in Scotland's related, one way or another. Maybe we might be able to find something.'

Gavin said, 'There is one disadvantage in the present instance, however. Even after a divorce on grounds of consanguinity, the children born of the marriage remain legitimate.'

Atholl crammed his toorie back on his head. 'Then what are ye wasting our time for!'

'Because the only alternative is an annulment based on a plea of non-consummation. If there had been no children, there would be no great difficulty. As it is . . .'

'"As it is . . . as it is . . ."' the earl mimicked. 'Come on, laddie. There's a way round it. There's aye a way round things.'

'If both parties swore on oath that the marriage wasn't consummated, that might do.'

'That's more like it,' the old man said. 'They'll swear, all right.'

Gavin raised his brows. 'Do you think so? Regardless of the truth of the matter, you'd be asking Lady Elinor to make a public confession that the child she bore was not her husband's. I would have thought it better from her point of view to be an erring wife with some protection under the law, than a divorced, self-confessed harlot. Unless, of course, you would be prepared to make some financial provision for her?'

But Atholl was a Stewart through and through. 'Money?' he yelped. 'She'll no' get a penny piece from me, I tell you!'

James had been unusually silent. Now, he said maliciously, 'Well, Bishop Gavin, we can but try. And it seems to me that, since it was you that started all this, it's up to you to put an end to it. The Lady Elinor is at Doune castle, under guard. So you may have the pleasure of going to her and asking her for the statement we need. You can draft it beforehand. You're a lawyer. You know what needs to be said.'

SOON after the New Year, Ninian knew that she was pregnant at last. Her first disbelief was followed by something that wasn't so much happiness as a sense of nervous, breathless longing. So many babies died before they were even born; so many others didn't survive the process of birth or the dangers of infancy. Her own mother had laid three babies in the grave before Ninian herself had been born. Séverine had had two miscarriages before Adam came into the world, and two more between Adam and Blane. Ninian didn't know which was worse, to know one's child and then lose it, or never to know it at all. But she did know that no mother expected more than one in three of her babies ever to grow up – and she was frightened.

Harry, on the other hand, was ecstatic, his virility proved beyond doubt. He even began to behave like a loving husband with only her welfare at heart – even if she suspected that he was concerned less about *her* welfare than about the welfare of the woman who was carrying his son. She didn't dare think what he would say if it turned out to be a daughter.

'We'll go right back to Dess,' he announced. 'Now. You need to be in your own home, with all your comforts around you!'

Comforts? At *Dess*?

'No,' she said, stoutly ignoring the nausea that was plaguing her. 'I'm perfectly well. I don't want to sit about like a broody hen for the next seven months. If the queen can go on with her duties until the last two weeks, surely I can, too? She would think me a very poor thing if I gave up at this early stage. What if it gave her a dislike for me, so that I wasn't invited back to court?'

It was the wrong question. Harry hadn't enjoyed spending most of his time at Perth or Edinburgh these last months, but nothing would have induced him to leave Ninian there while he went back to Dess on his own, to see to the work that needed doing. It had flattered his vanity at first to have all the other men envying him his wife, but that had worn off very soon, especially when one or two of the stiffer courtiers, and rather more than one or two of the women, had begun to remark on it. He knew perfectly well that she wasn't playing him false – quite apart from anything else, as she took care to point out to him, the court was so crowded that anything like a private assignation would have been impossible – but it didn't stop him nagging. She had been making a very serious effort, lately, to appear more staid and sober, and it had depressed her, because being bright and popular and surrounded by people had helped to take her mind off other things.

However, as far as Harry was concerned, if the queen decided his wife's presence at court was no longer required, he would be delighted.

Fortunately, there was another and more conclusive argument against an immediate return to Dess. It had begun snowing hard in the north and report had it that, while an active, well-mounted man might still get through, the passes would be closed as soon as the wind got up. Harry, foiled, agreed sulkily that the journey might be better postponed, and Ninian was granted a temporary reprieve.

She didn't know whether she ought to be feeling so ill, but tried very hard not to let it show in case it worried Harry into going to the queen and begging her to release his wife from her duties. To be condemned to spend most of her time in her bedchamber would be worse than anything. So she tried to persuade herself that her sickness had something to do with the rich food, the stuffy atmosphere, the lack of exercise. Lady Moragh gave her a brew of herbs that helped a little, though not for long. But, doggedly, she went on taking it, trying to persuade herself that, even though she was losing weight, even though her skin was becoming dry and flaky, even though her head ached and her throat burned, she would be better soon. The first few weeks were always said to be the worst.

And here, at court, at least she knew what was going on, or some of it. It was common gossip that the king had sent Bishop Gavin to Doune to extract proof of all Lady Elinor's infidelities, and that her ladyship had laughed in his face. The king was furious, and so was the Earl of Atholl, but no one could do anything. Her ladyship had the upper hand. The bishop hadn't been seen since he left Doune, because he had gone on to Glasgow, where there were matters urgently awaiting his attention.

Then the door of the Great Chamber opened, and he was back and making straight across the room to where Ninian was standing, alone, tightening the wires of her clarsach and trying to remember all the details of the story of Patient Griselda. The queen and her ladies seemed to have done nothing but play cards and backgammon for days, and the queen had said it was time Lady Ninian amused them with another of Mme de Pisan's edifying tales.

Without preamble, the chancellor said, 'I need Adam de Verne. Do you know where he is?'

She hadn't spoken to him since before the cataclysmic day when she had heard that he was human, after all. Her heart pounding, she said, 'Is it urgent?'

'Moderately.'

The rawness in her throat was troubling her, and she had to turn her head aside, and cough a little.

When she turned back, he was looking at her with unexpected concern. 'You're not well,' he said matter-of-factly. 'Have you had attention?'

She shook her head, and succeeded in smiling as if it was nothing, and could almost see him thinking 'women's ailments' and dismissing the whole thing. She wondered briefly how he would have responded if she had said, 'I am pregnant, and sick, and terrified, and I love you beyond hope of redemption, and always will.'

'Adam de Verne,' he said again, and this time she answered. The sooner she told him, the sooner he would leave her in peace. Not until years later, looking back, did she recognize that this was the first time he had spoken to her as if she were a real person, and not just a tiresome chit of a girl.

'He set off two days ago to try to get through to Blair Atholl, on some errand for his lordship.'

'Damn!' said the bishop. 'That means another week at least before he is back. Thank you, Lady Ninian. I hope you will soon be recovered.'

But the sickness persisted, and became almost constant, until she could scarcely drag one foot after another. The queen, concerned, insisted she retired to bed for a few days, but it was worse in bed, so she dragged herself up again.

And then, one terrible night, in an agony of loneliness and fear, the real pain began, and the bleeding. It was as if her flesh was being torn apart, piece by piece, carefully and in stages, with intervals between, intervals just long enough to allow her mind to begin to climb out of the pit, so that when the pain struck her again it was inconceivably, impossibly, worse. She must have cried out, in the end, and woken Harry, who always slept like the dead, because when next she emerged from a brief, blessed spell of blackness, she was aware of people in the room and hands on her body and, once, a cool cloth on her forehead. Once, too, a voice said to her – Moragh's, she thought, but she wasn't sure of anything now – 'Where is it hurting?' and the question was so irrelevant in the context of the pain that consumed her that, if she hadn't known she was dying, she would have laughed.

'Poor Harry,' she thought in a moment of lucidity. 'No wife, no son. Poor Harry.' And then the pain began again and the raw, tearing fire inside her, and she couldn't bite back the screams any longer, and she wondered, before all thought was blotted out, how long this could possibly go on.

9

NINIAN knew nothing of Adam's return to Edinburgh, nor of his brief interview with Gavin Cameron.

'I am sure you know,' Cameron said, 'of the projected annulment of the Master of Atholl's marriage to the Lady Elinor. Her ladyship has refused, unequivocally, to discuss the matter with *me*, but during your absence in the north, I received a message from her saying that she is prepared to talk to *you*, and to no one but you. What she wishes to talk about, she does not say.'

Adam stared thoughtfully into the cold grey eyes, so exactly on a level with his own, and said, 'How interesting.'

'His Majesty has granted you permission to visit her ladyship, and his lordship of Atholl wishes to speak to you before you go. I will myself supply you with a copy of the document she is required to sign.'

'Must I go at once?'

Cameron's brows rose.

Adam very nearly choked on the words of explanation, when all his inclinations were to stick a knife in the man. But he needed time – time to get a message to Robert Graham, whom he had met, by appointment, near Blair Atholl. Graham was going to hook south by the Trossachs on his way home, and Adam calculated that, with luck, a messenger might catch him not too far from Stirling, which, in turn, was not too far from Doune.

'The last few days have been tiring,' he said stiffly. 'My men and my horses must have rest.'

'Such consideration! You may have one day's grace. My lord Atholl will see you now. You will find him in his bedchamber.'

Adam was in a vile temper. His neat plan to discredit Cameron by sacrificing an unsuspecting Lady Elinor had failed, at least in part, even if it would all be remembered against the bishop next time he made a mistake.

But if it had failed, it had failed. It was no longer of the slightest interest to Adam, whose sole concern now was to move on to the next, and more important stage of his campaign. He deeply resented being dragged back into the affair.

Atholl said, 'Yon Cameron couldny get anything oot o' her. Seems it's one thing jabbing his wee stick into the wumman in a nice, cosy bed, but when it comes to thumping some sense into her with those big, hard fists of his, he's too bloody perjink. So it's for you to put pressure on her, and I dinny mean just lying on her.'

And thank you very much, Adam thought. She's going to be scratching my eyes out, anyway.

'I want rid of the wumman, one way or the other. But it's an awfu' long-drawn-out performance, this divorce business. What would suit me fine,' and Atholl's pouched eyes stared at Adam expressionlessly from under the rumpled white thicket of his brows, 'would be to get Davie married again straight off and fathering some more sons. Time enough, then, to think about having young Rob declared illegitimate. I'm a great one for keeping my options open. Trouble is,' he went on ruminatively, 'I canny quite see how tae manage it.'

Can you not, you old sinner? Adam thought sourly.

When he repeated this exchange to Robert Graham, Sir Robert's immediate reaction was to rein in his horse and say tersely, 'I'll take my leave. Murdering women isn't in my line. If you are too lily-livered to do it yourself, find a hired assassin.'

Adam, his head down against the sleeting wind, mentally cursed the man's quickness, and wished he had brought Blane instead. But Blane wasn't reliable when it was a question of using his brain as well as his fists.

'You're jumping to conclusions,' he said. 'Whatever Atholl may be talking about, what *we* are talking about is the probable need to beat the woman up. And frankly, if she gets hurt, I want to be somewhere else at the time, with plenty of witnesses. James has some damned old-fashioned ideas about chivalry, even if you mightn't think it sometimes.' He glanced round. 'God be praised, there's a shepherd's hut over there. Let's get out of this wind.'

It took some hard talking. 'We have to keep Atholl sweet,' Adam said. 'You know very well that we need either his cooperation or, at the very least, a benevolent neutrality. And it won't help Columba if I lose the king's favour. If we can get Elinor to sign the paper, it'll satisfy the king and – if I handle it right – Atholl, too. Then we'll be rid of the whole stupid business.'

Robert Graham said coldly, 'It can't have escaped your notice that, once Atholl has the paper with the proof of young Rob's illegitimacy, he can have the woman killed any time he feels inclined, regardless of any promises we have made on his behalf?'

Adam's attention was all on the wineskin he had unstrapped from his saddlebow. 'Mmmm? Oh, I suppose so, but that's no concern of ours. The reason I asked you to join me was that . . .' He offered the wineskin to Sir Robert and, when he refused it, raised it to his own lips.

'The reason is that there's not the remotest likelihood of Elinor signing the paper if the request comes from me, for I don't doubt that she puts down all her troubles to my account. Not without justification. However, she has nothing against you – has she? – and you are fluent enough, and clever enough, to stand some chance of persuading her. You don't even have to lay hands on her. I'll leave a man of mine with you. You will need him, anyway, to bring me the paper afterwards.'

10

ADAM'S interview with Elinor went very much as he had anticipated. She stared at him palely, a vision of purity in her floating draperies, every inch the haughty, high-born lady. He told her, in straightforward and entirely impersonal terms, what was required of her. She said, 'Indeed?' and then again, 'Indeed?', and finally, 'No.'

And then, despite the fact that the captain of the guard had come with him as chaperon, she did indeed make a spirited attempt to claw his eyeballs from their sockets.

Later, as he extracted his escort from the guardroom in the big drum tower, he said to the captain, 'Her ladyship looks tired. The strain, no doubt. But I imagine she will decide to sign in the end, as His Majesty requires. She has a copy of the necessary document. I rely on you to forward it to me.'

The captain, who didn't like thin, arrogant women, and did like spectacular gentlemen with large retinues and free-spending habits, accepted what was offered and said, 'It will be a pleasure, my lord.'

Some of the coins went towards a firkin of good, strong ale, so that when Robert Graham and Adam's man-at-arms emerged from their hiding place on the upper staircase some hours after dark, the only signs of activity from the guardroom were a drowsy murmur and an occasional burst of song.

There was no sound at all from Lady Elinor's chamber, which had a new, smooth-running bolt on the outside of the door. The dim line of light framing the door from inside was unbroken, which meant that there was no gentlewoman's pallet set across it as a bulwark against intruders. The man-at-arms slid his dagger through the gap, silently lifted the latch, and pushed.

The pallet was to one side of the door, out of the draught, and the woman on it was fast asleep. The man-at-arms had a gag round her mouth and her limbs half tied before she even began to wake. They bundled her outside into one of the alcoves on the unlit stairs.

Then Sir Robert drew back the bed curtains and stood, her ladyship's furred dressingrobe on his arm, and waited for the Lady Elinor's unsleeping eyes to widen, and her mouth to open and close, for her to sit up, and then to rise and slip into the offered robe. She looked at the man-at-arms with her almost invisible eyebrows raised, and Sir Robert sent the man out, since he had no intention of resorting to violence.

Then he revived the almost dead fire and, turning, said, 'You may guess why I am here.'

She guessed wrongly, and it was to shape everything that happened after. Because she thought he had come to rescue her.

'Why should you think that?' he asked in the flat voice she had known, off and on, for years, the voice that gave nothing away.

Her reasoning was interesting, considering that Robert Graham had always thought her a basically stupid woman. 'You hate James,' she said. 'You must wish to overthrow him. And to do that, you must have someone else with a legitimate claim to replace him on the throne. The Master of Atholl will never leave the Tower alive if James has anything to do with it. So you need my son, do you not?'

'Go on,' he said.

She sighed faintly, as if it were all some tiresome kind of guessing game. 'And since I am a poor, weak woman, you are afraid that, if I stay here, I might give in and sign the document they want me to, the document that says Rob is a bastard. Which would spoil all your plans.'

'That depends. If the Master were free to marry again, he could beget a dozen other sons who would do as well.'

She stared at him with the first honest amusement he had ever seen on her face. '*Him?* Davie Stewart? When it took him a year of trying, twice a day, every day, for three weeks out of four, to get Rob on me? When it took him another eleven years, not twice a day but often enough, to get – nothing?'

She shook her head, and said, 'Don't rely on it, my friend. Don't rely on it! And anyway, could you afford to wait so long? You cannot put a babe in arms at the head of an army. Whereas my Rob, in another year or two, will be every inch a king!'

'Perhaps!' he said, recognizing her dream but quite untouched by it. 'However, the question does not, at the moment, arise. It is my lord Atholl's wish that you should sign the document which has already been shown you, and that is why I am here.'

She couldn't believe it at first. She stood there facing him, a tall woman, and strangely impressive with her emaciated figure mantled in fur and her fine-boned face a mask of astonishment and freezing anger. 'What have you to do with Atholl?'

'That need not concern you. But if I were you, I would sign. If you do not, I think you will not live long.'

She was too enraged to listen. 'And I thought you a man with principles! A man who did what was right, regardless of others.' She gave a high-pitched laugh. 'How wrong is it possible to be? For it seems you are nothing but a cringing lackey, after all!'

Contempt was something Robert Graham would take from no man; from women, with whom he had little to do except when he wished to assuage his bodily appetites, he had never encountered it.

He said, tightly, 'Did you hear me? If you refuse to sign, you may not live long enough to regret it.'

She laughed again, the same high-pitched, meaningless laugh. 'Live? *What is living?* A few men? A few hours of pleasure? And who is to kill me, pray? Not you. Not a lackey. When Atholl comes to me himself, then I might be frightened. He may be old, but he is worth a hundred – a thousand – of the mediocrities who serve him!'

Beside herself with disappointment and fury, she could not have read his eyes even if she had been able to see them in the slow, sporadic glow from the fire.

But he felt a stirring of curiosity. Before he left, as he knew he must before the tide of his temper rose too high, he wanted to know why she wouldn't sign. He said, 'But even a few hours of pleasure must be worth living for. There can be no pleasure in death. Why do you choose to put everything at risk?'

She misunderstood. '*Choose* to put everything at risk? I?' Her voice rose several tones, almost to a screech. 'Do you think I ever expected any of this to come out? *Oh, no.* It was my handsome knight, my fine French lover – my fine French bastard! It was a game, a wager between us. We were going to settle whether Gavin Cameron was frigid or not!'

She turned and paced the length of the room and back. 'I should have known. But one doesn't expect a man to use his own mistress to bait a trap for his enemy. My fine French lover had spread the news even before I left my room the next day.

'But I could have saved myself. I would have looked racked, tortured. I would have claimed I had been raped. Except that Ninian Drummond – *Ninian Drummond* – told the king I was already her cousin's mistress, and then it was too late. She always wanted Adam for herself, the little whore. She wanted Cameron, too. I could see it in her face.'

The pale eyes were glittering now, and she had lost every vestige of the control that had enabled her to keep up her pose of coolness throughout her adult life. 'But I've paid her! I have paid her, the bitch! Mandrake, and henbane, and belladonna, and a few other things besides. She should be dead by now. Why has no one sent to tell me she is dead?'

It was then that Robert Graham put his hands on her ladyship's throat and, neatly and without compunction, strangled her.

CHAPTER TWO

I

IT WAS June before Ninian was herself again, and it was not the same self.

She would have died if the anonymous message hadn't come, if they hadn't found out in time that even the lukewarm bouillon that was all she could swallow had been laced with deadly nightshade. It was the queen herself, mercilessly questioning everyone who fell under suspicion, who discovered that the guilt lay with a twelve-year-old chamber page, a boy who had served and obeyed the Lady Elinor in everything – not only for gold, it seemed, but from calf-love.

Justice had been done. They had branded a P for poisoner on the boy's forehead, and put him in the pillory for a day and a night, so that the people of Edinburgh could wreak their own rough justice on him. They'd had to nail him to the board by his hands and ears because his feet didn't reach the platform and they didn't want him throttled by mistake.

He was hanged the next morning, with the king and queen and all the court watching. Harry had carried Ninian to a window, so that she could see, too, and that had been the worst moment of all.

She had felt at first as if she would never recover, as if all the life that remained to her would be lived out in this same, changeless, burning torment, this prevision of hell. The Lady Egidia had brought the queen's physician to see her, and he had said that the poisoning and the miscarriage had left her body raw inside, and that healing was only a matter of time, but she didn't believe him. When he said he would bleed her to drain out the last of the pestilent humours, she had made no objection. She had no passionate desire to live. But the Lady Egidia – small, plain and implacable – had refused to permit it. The girl had no blood to spare, she said, and when the physician refused to listen she had picked up Harry's second-best scabbard and laid about her to such effect that he had fled from the room and never shown his face again. Ninian had tried to whisper the gratitude she didn't feel, and Lady Egidia, staring at her from under the pointed headdress that was as tall as she was, had said brusquely, 'You don't want to live now, but you will. Believe me, I know.'

And then, as soon as the thaw came, Harry had insisted on taking her home to Dess, and despite all the cushions and quilts in the litter and the care of the men who carried it, she had been unconscious for most of the journey, and for two weeks afterwards scarcely able to turn her head on the pillow.

Her physical recovery was neither swift nor sure, but came in a tiresome, discouraging series of fits and starts. For days there would be no improvement, and then suddenly she would wake to the knowledge that the hurt, in one place or another, was less than it had been. It didn't help that, when her mind emerged from the limbo into which it had retreated, it promptly rebelled against the whole, impossible situation. She had never been ill before, nor had her patience ever really been tested. It would have done her more good than anything if she had been able to give vent to her frustration by kicking or screaming or throwing things at Harry, but she was too weak even for that.

Harry had fussed around her like an old hen at first, until he was sure she wasn't going to die. And then, bit by bit, the truth had come out. He thought everything that had happened to her was her own fault – everything from having a womanizing cousin like Adam, and an uncle like Columba, who insisted on making enemies of people who mattered, down to letting herself be bullied by the king, and then poisoned – without even being aware of it, for God's sake! – so that his son, the future Sir Harry Graham, had died in her womb. It was time she learned not to meddle in other people's affairs.

She knew, in her mind, that the silly, bitter, cruel words sprang from disappointment, but it didn't help.

Even without Harry, her thoughts would have been gloomy enough, because she was convinced that the long unrelenting violence of her pain, the awareness of death, the sense that every breath she drew was still in some way tainted by the hatred of the woman who had tried to kill her – that all these things would stay with her for as long as she lived, lying like a thin skin of fear under the surface of her mind so that she would always recoil from anything that, however remotely, might bring danger in its wake.

But the days passed, and the weeks, and as her bodily pain diminished, so the memory of it changed. The knowledge that it was over, and that she had survived it, showed it to her in a different perspective. And death? Death was always at one's elbow in this year of Our Lord 1428, and in every other year, too. It was the hatred that was harder to tidy away.

But though she became more resigned, she still had too much time to think and found herself thinking almost exclusively of people. She had always been happy to accept others at their own valuation – with an occasional private giggle, perhaps, at some of their wilder eccentricities – not because she was naïve, or because her upbringing had been so sunny and sheltered, or even because Sévèrine said life was more *confortable* if one refrained from criticizing. Rather it was something inside herself, something that had always predisposed her to take a cheerful, friendly view of the human race. Which was why, she supposed – trying to set her thoughts out logically before her – the experience of these last weeks, this last year, had borne so harshly on her.

For the first time in all her life, she began to measure those around her against the yardstick of her own needs. Harry's sulky resentment, his furious busy-ness about the estate, so that he had time to spend no more than a few minutes with her during the course of the day. Adam paying an occasional cheerful visit, giving her an arrogant, not-quite-cousinly embrace – as if that alone should be enough to set everything to rights – and then saying, 'Well, I must be off. I want to be a Blair Atholl by nightfall.' And Blane, noisy, clumsy, competitive as ever, arriving once on his own and once with Adam, and so busy extolling the virtues of his new pony that he quite forgot to ask her how she felt.

She knew that he and Adam were at odds about something. Before they came in to her, she had heard Adam's voice, unfamiliarly curt, saying, 'You will do as I tell you!' and Blane's heated reply, 'And be branded a craven? You do as you choose, brother. I shall stand forth with my friends.' But although she tried worriedly to find out what was going on, and although they must have seen that she was concerned, neither of them would tell her.

If those who were closest to her assumed that a cursory sympathy was all that her pain and weakness, all that the residual horror of what had happened to her required, what did it say of them? Not just that they were men, and this was a man's world, though that was some of it. Not just that they saw her only as an appendage of themselves – Ninian-my-wife, or Ninian-my-cousin – though that was some of it, too. She had always thought that, even if they rarely showed it, they really did love her, deep down, but now, miserably, she began to feel that love was much too strong a word. If she had died, they would have made a great drama out of it, she knew; but she hadn't, so normal life could be resumed. She shouldn't have been surprised, because the world itself was a world of extremes – right or wrong, good or bad, dead or alive, and nothing in between.

Although she told herself that she shouldn't, because of this, make the mistake of overvaluing the kindness shown by others on whom she had no real claim, she couldn't help but be touched, and a little heartened, by it. The queen, so gentle, and yet so relentless when there was cause, sent regular messages enquiring after her progress, and twice a little silver box of sweetmeats. The Lady Moragh who, like most women, could write no more than her name, sent one of her gentlewomen to tell Ninian all the gossip of the court. And the Lady Egidia, who had no patience either with gossip or general expressions of goodwill, forwarded a receipt for a good, strengthening pottage that was worth all the rest put together.

But the surprise was Bishop Gavin. A few days after Ninian's return to Dess, he had sent a messenger to make sure that her ladyship had reached home safely. Harry had been offended, and was offended all over again a few weeks later, when another messenger arrived with a bald enquiry as to how the Lady Ninian did. 'What business is it of Cameron's?' he demanded, and Ninian said wearily, 'He probably has a list, Harry. You know – March 24, negotiate a peace treaty; March 25, rehearse the choirboys at Polmadie; March 26, ask after the Lady Ninian's health; March 27, look for woodworm in the cathedral rafters. . .'

Duty, she wondered, or an unexpected pity? Or guilt, that he had been the catalyst of the whole sorry business?

She was lonely, and it was Columba she needed, not only for the warmth of his loving, but because there were things that she needed to have explained to her. She knew that everything happened as God ordained it, but she couldn't understand why He ordained so much that was dreadful. It was the first time in her life that she had ever wondered about the beliefs in which she had been brought up.

But Columba was still at Rome, and Harry broke it to her crudely, and with a certain satisfaction, that he might never be able to return to Scotland again.

'Parliament's passed new statutes against barratry. Anyone who's proved guilty of taking gold or silver out of the country without permission – in the past as well as the future – is liable to banishment. Your uncle won't dare to come back now. He'd have a hard time proving that the gold he's spending at Rome isn't Scots gold! And there's something else. Adam won't be able to send his tithes to him in Rome, either, because that's been forbidden, too. Everyone's saying that the whole thing's been deliberately aimed at your uncle, and Ingram Lindsay, and one or two others like them. No, I think we can safely say Columba's lost and Cameron's won, after all.'

Adam, arriving unexpectedly, walked in just in time to hear the tail-end of Harry's remarks and said contemptuously, 'That pleases you, Harry, does it? The thought of Columba losing? But wait just a few more weeks and then you will find out who wins and who loses!'

Ninian stared at him, her upset over Columba – and, indeed, over Harry's undoubted malice – translating itself into an unusual asperity.

'Don't bother to knock! And is it absolutely necessary for you always to snipe at Harry? You're both as bad as each other.'

'Well, well,' Adam replied, his eyes suddenly laughing. 'Our little invalid has grown claws in my absence, has she?'

'She would have to be very quick to grow them in your presence, wouldn't she! Or do you intend to stay long enough this time to say more than, "How are you, and goodbye"? I do wish,' she went on crossly, 'that you would tell me what's going on. Are you quite sure it's something Columba would approve of, because all this secrecy is beginning to give me very serious doubts?'

But it didn't have the slightest effect. Airily, Adam said, 'Have no fear, *p'tite*. I have everything in hand – with the aid and cooperation of the good Sir Robert, of course. He sends you his respects, by the way, and wishes you well. No, not you, Harry, just Ninian.' It was said with such cheerful effrontery that even Harry was coaxed into a grudging half-smile. Ninian remembered when Adam had always been like this, able to charm the birds out of the trees whenever he felt like it, but where it had once been an honest expression of high spirits it seemed in this last year to have become something to be used deliberately and with calculation, although only someone who knew him as well as Ninian would have recognized it.

He stayed for no more than an hour, and then said it was time he was off again.

'Where to?'

'Mingary, *ma p'tite*, if you know where that is!'

Harry knew. 'In Ardnamurchan? James is raving angry over that blood feud between Alexander MacRuairi and John MacArthur. Says not even in the west will he have folk killing each other off whenever they feel inclined. He'll have law and order, or else! You're not mixed up in that, are you?'

Adam looked superbly innocent. 'I? Involved in a business as bucolic as pruning the vines? My dear Harry, it is only the vintage that interests me.'

And with that enigmatic utterance they had to be content.

Ninian went back to her Book of Hours, the only thing she had to read, but found no comfort in its psalms or stories of the saints, nor even in the illustrations that had once attracted her so much, the floriated initials, the fantastical figures of monkeys and minstrels, pedlars and priests, rabbits and roe deer, romping their way around the margins in perennial flight from the demons and dragons that pursued them. There was one sweet little demon who looked exactly like the Bishop of Avignon and Ninian often wondered whether it had been drawn from the life.

She rang her handbell furiously. She would get up, she must get up. Even if, today, she managed to take no more than two steps, it would at least be something.

2

THE first half of 1428 had been without respite for Gavin Cameron, fitting in the business of his diocese with following the king from Perth to Linlithgow to Edinburgh and back again, preparing plans for a House of Commons on the English model, framing and seeing through parliament not only the anti-barratry law but a whole new ragbag of statutes covering everything from the control of merchant shipping, craft wardens, beggars, lepers, and the size of a nobleman's entourage, to the declaration of open season on wolves and close season on partridge, plover, greyhen and blackcock.

After that there had been the exchequer audit, and after that the French marriage negotiations.

Charles VII, the still uncrowned king of a rapidly shrinking France, was at the end of his resources, with Orleans, key to the Loire valley, besieged by the English and only too likely to fall. Rumour had it that, if the worst came to the worst, he was thinking of fleeing to Scotland for sanctuary. Whatever the truth of this – and Gavin, like James, devoutly hoped there was none – Charles was anxious to revive the Franco-Scottish alliance. In exchange for military assistance, he was ready to offer his eldest son, Louis, as husband for three-year-old Princess Margaret.

He had sent an embassy to James, with Alain Chartier, his secretary, as spokesman. M. Chartier was a poet of some repute – even Gavin, who had little time for empty rhetoric, had heard of *La belle dame sans merci* – and this had lent a certain piquancy to his opening harangue. For James, himself a poet, had listened at first with respect that merged after a time into puzzlement and eventually into an irascible recognition that what he was hearing was the purest farrago. It had been necessary for Gavin to cross-question M. Chartier very closely indeed before they discovered what he was actually talking about.

James had become thoughtful, his eyes on the painted ceiling, his lips soundlessly whistling, his fist opening and closing rhythmically under his chin so that his beard flip-flopped like a sheet in the wind. Gavin knew very well how his mind was working. The Stewarts, late arrivals on Europe's royal scene, badly needed a transfusion of properly authenticated blue blood to give them respectability. But far more interesting, at this stage, was the fact that a renewed alliance with France would give James a bargaining counter in his negotiations with the English, who were becoming increasingly fractious not only over his failure to pay the ransom but his inability to control the Border barons – who considered their right to raid into England as not only unarguable but inalienable.

Better still, if James were to despatch a force to France, England might be angry enough to breach the truce that had been one of the conditions of his release. If they declared war, he wouldn't need even to think about the ransom again. The hostages could buy their own way out. Best of all, with most of England's armies already tied up in France, it might be possible to snatch back out of English hands the long-contested Border towns of Roxburgh and Berwick.

It was a tempting proposition. Briskly, James summoned a council-general to meet at Perth on 12th July to discuss it.

On that same day, the Lady Moragh – whose three marriages had carried her from Highland hovel to lordly hall, but who had never lost touch with her beginnings – privately went to her childhood hero, Gavin John Cameron, to tell him something that she thought might be of interest.

'Is it important?' he demanded, his hands full of documents and his mind on land grants, and then, with a rueful grin, sat down again and said, 'Tell me.'

She smiled back at him, with the merry, slanting smile that disguised her feelings more than it displayed them. She didn't mind when he spoke to her briskly, but the rage was like a fire in her heart when he was in relaxed mood, and talked to her and treated her as if she were an old friend. Some day she would teach him that she was not a friend, and never had been. Some day she would have him for her own.

'It iss important. It iss trouble, Gaffin, but you can stop it. The fiery cross iss gone round the clans.'

Gavin dropped the documents unceremoniously on his desk. He and the king had been expecting trouble in the Highlands for months. There had been mysterious rumours of activity, but nothing to put a finger on. 'Yes?' he said. 'And what summons does it carry?'

'The clans iss to gather at Strath Conon at the full of the August moon.'

A few miles north-west of Inverness. And what they were gathering for didn't matter. There were laws against more than a handful of people gathering at all. 'Where did you get your information?'

'Och, Gaffin, you know that I haff the sight. I haff seen it all as clear as I see you now.'

Gavin's lips twitched. He was enough of a Highlander to believe in the second sight, and he knew Moragh had it. On the other hand, the sight didn't usually run to providing such factual details as time and place. That sounded more like the Macraes or the Macleods.

'Have you?' he said drily. 'Well, well. You have no doubts about the authenticity of your – er – prevision?'

'I am as sure as if someone had told me in words.'

'Ah, well, in that case . . .'

THE council-general was whisked through the French business at a speed that left it gasping – jointures, embassies, oaths, expenses, titles, penalty clauses, wages for the soldiers, and shipping to carry them.

But the reason became clear when someone heard that the masons had just completed another stage in the reconstruction of James's castle at Inverness, which had been burned almost to the ground in 1411. It explained a lot. Everyone knew that James had a passion for building, and was probably wild with impatience to get off and have a look at it.

And it was so. By the 19th, he had put his seal to letters patent agreeing to the marriage treaty, and within a week he and the queen and most of the court were off on a royal progress to Inverness. There were no signs of undue haste; indeed, His Majesty went miles out of his way to deal with some business at Aberdeen. But by 10th August, with the moon in its third quarter, they were in sight of the three thatched towers of Inverness castle, perched on the river bank with the wattle and daub houses of the little town clustered around it.

It had been a surprisingly pleasurable journey, especially for Gavin, whose heart always lifted at sight of the mountains and the lochs. The weather had been kind, the pace leisurely, the countryside attractive, even if the size of the royal cavalcade forced it to move always by the low roads, never the high. This, however, had the advantage of leaving the mountain tracks free for the urgent, unobtrusive, comings and goings of the most trusted of the royal messengers. Few, if any, of the unusually good-humoured, brightly clad throng who followed the king had any idea of the conferences that were held behind the silken flap of the royal tent during the three or four hours of the northern summer dark.

The company itself changed almost every day, some leaving, some joining. The Earl of Douglas rode no further than Scone, and then made his excuses and turned south for Lanark and home. Gavin watched him go, thoughtfully, wondering whether he was still in regular communication with the Lord of the Isles. The Douglasses might be knaves sometimes, but fools never.

Then Atholl cut off westward, not far from Dunkeld. He wanted to get back to Blair, he said; he was too old to go stravaiging aboot the country; Inverness wasny worth the bother, anyhow.

At Blairgowrie, Ninian Drummond rejoined the ranks of the queen's ladies. She rode into the camp on a neat white pony, her husband at her side and her smile calm.

She had changed. All the immature plumpness had gone from face and figure, as had the artificial demureness from her manner. She had been no more than ordinarily pretty before – though appealing, in spite of her faults – but now she was . . . Gavin couldn't make up his mind. Not beautiful in the accepted sense; striking was a better word.

And it seemed that she was no longer at the mercy of every emotional wind that blew. The large, attractively placed blue eyes now gazed levelly out on the world, and she looked as if every muscle was under strict and unfaltering control. Suddenly, it was an interesting face, perhaps even an intelligent one.

They spoke briefly. He complimented her on her recovery, and she thanked him with apparent sincerity. Then the queen summoned her and she moved away.

It was ten days before they reached Inverness, and by that time there was no doubt in Gavin's mind that Ninian Drummond was deliberately avoiding him. He wondered why.

He was also very slightly piqued.

4

GAVIN interviewed the Gaelic-speaking chiefs, and James the ones who could manage some English.

Plain, vulgar curiosity with a strong admixture of misplaced vanity had been enough to bring them all, secretly and one by one, to the castle. The king, they had been led to understand, was considering calling a parliament in the north, and he (or his chancellor) would be obliged if Angus of Moray (or Kenneth Mor Mackenzie or Angus Dubh Mackay) would present himself, with the strictest confidentiality, at Inverness at such-and-such an hour on such-and-such a day, just for a private word. The messages had all gone out in good time, so that the chiefs had received them before they left home for Strath Conon. They had no reason to suspect that the king knew more than he should about what they were up to.

They arrived like lambs to the slaughter, having given their followers the slip and ridden the few miles from Strath Conon to the castle with only one or two clansmen for bodyguard.

'Well, well, Kenneth Mor,' Gavin said pleasantly. 'I am sorry to be putting you to all this trouble, but the king, you know . . .'

'Och, aye, he will be having his own ideas, will he not? Kings iss never anxious to say what they iss thinking, not straight out.' The pale, sea-rover's eyes stared out at Gavin from a curling red jungle of hair and beard and eyebrows, and Kenneth Mor licked his lips hopefully.

Gavin, filling a horn of heather ale for him, said carelessly, 'Just so, just so. No doubt he would be talking to you about the feud in Ardnamurchan when his mind was on something else entirely.'

The pale eyes blinked.

Gavin said, 'Indeed, and since we are on the subject, I would be interested myself to know what the chiefs are going to do to settle the feud. The *Magister*' – it went very much against the grain to dignify that randy young devil, Alexander of the Isles, with such a title – 'the *Magister*, I am thinking, can not be pleased to have the chiefs cutting each other's throats like that. And the king is not liking it either.'

'Och, no. He would not. We was thinking we might be having a meeting, just a few of us other chiefs, you understand, to see if we could be talking some sense into them.'

'Just "thinking"? And "talking"? Och, Kenneth, Kenneth. When you know very well that every last one of you is sitting there at Strath Conon this very moment, and none of you with a tail of less than two hundred folk! It is a terrible lot of men just for "talking sense" into people.'

The Highlander was on his feet, knife in hand, and his two followers the same. But Gavin had no need even to raise his voice. From behind the stiff new linen of the wall hangings, a dozen men-at-arms appeared.

'My apologies to you, Kenneth Mor Mackenzie,' Gavin said formally. 'But you know well that banding together is most strictly forbidden by the law, and for good reason. There are too many of you gathered at Strath Conon for the king to put anything but an ill construction on it. Eight thousand in all, I am told, or something like. It will not do.' Then he nodded his head to the men-at-arms. 'Take him away.'

And so it went on.

If it had, truthfully, been a council intended to settle the Ardnamurchan affair, things might have been different. Highland chiefs had a habit of taking half their kinfolk with them whenever they went anywhere; the size of a man's 'tail' was an index of his status. But the fiery cross didn't go out just to summon men to peaceable tribunals, even if some of them were thick-headed enough to believe that it might. The problem was to discover which of them were deluded and which actively dangerous.

It was the king's opinion that Alexander – who had a strong claim to the earldom of Ross – had been intending to try and force his sovereign to rule in his favour by the traditional method of consigning Inverness to the flames and then marching on in force to lay waste the countryside, thus provoking the king either to battle or settlement.

James had said he would have been very happy indeed to thrash the boy. But he couldn't raise an army even quarter the size of Alexander's, or not in a hurry, though his would be better armed and more scientifically led. He was as passionate a student of modern warfare as of everything else he set his mind to, and Gavin knew that, if he'd had enough men, he would have been there himself, in the thick of it.

Lacking force, they'd had to resort to guile. Between them, the king and his chancellor interviewed and arrested fifty Highland chiefs, including the Lord of the Isles himself.

The only surprise was that when Alexander MacRuairi of the Siol Gorrie – one of the main protagonists in the Ardnamurchan blood feud – presented himself before James, he was accompanied by his bodyservant, one of his clansmen, and a foreign gentleman, 'a friend and advisor', whom both the king and his chancellor had met before.

5

NINIAN was charmed by Inverness, which resembled Perth in that it was set on the bank of a river, but in nothing else at all. There were no suffocating town walls, no narrow, overhanging houses in the streets, no solemn, respectable seats of theology and learning, no marshes, no smells, no sludge in the gutters, no raucous voices, and no thick motionless mists on the water. The river was sparkling clean and scarcely less turbulent than the sea into which it merged, and even in

August the whole countryside breathed a freshness and vigour that acted on her like a tonic.

It was like no town she had ever seen, for it was little more than a cluster of makeshift dwellings set on a spacious estuary, with real mountains – not just hills – to north and west, mountains that were a miracle of colour and shade and shadow, their sides threaded with glittering streams and rich with the brilliant hues of heather, bracken and myrtle, and grass of an unimaginable green. As the sun moved, as the white clouds fled across the sky, so all the contours changed, as if by some magic the whole scene had moved into another place, another time. She stood on the river bank, and gazed out over the water, and for the first time in almost two years of misery, sickness, and isolation, felt alive and free.

There were three days of the purest pleasure before the blow fell.

The queen and her ladies were riding slightly inland, along paths half hidden in a green haze of birch saplings, the faint breeze off the islands in the river bringing them a tang of salt, and warm juniper, and the soft dampness of moss.

The queen, the trace of a frown around her eyes, beckoned Ninian to ride beside her, and said after a moment, 'Do you know why we are here?'

Ninian was surprised. 'To admire the castle?' She was smiling.

But Her Majesty didn't smile back. 'I believe you must be aware that the king has been expecting trouble in the Highlands ever since he ascended his throne. And it has been very near. Even now, there is an army camped only a dozen miles away that could have brought the whole country down in ruins.'

Ninian could feel dread settling around her, cold and clammy.

The queen was watching her closely. 'The leaders of the conspiracy have all been arrested. There is no need to be afraid.'

Was that what her face had shown? Deliberately, she relaxed her muscles, and waited for the blow to fall. This conversation hadn't been begun without reason. One word, one name only, possessed her mind. Adam.

Abruptly, the queen said, 'I do not believe you knew anything of it.'

Shaking her head almost imperceptibly, Ninian murmured, 'I . . . Of what, your grace?'

'One of the conspirators is an acquaintance, a close acquaintance, of yours. M. de Verne. M. Blane de Verne.'

The astonishment in Ninian's voice was as unmistakable as the horror. 'Blane? *Blane?* No. It's not possible!'

But it was. She could hear him still. 'I shall stand forth with my friends.' She should have known that it wouldn't be Adam, who was probably miles away and in immaculately respectable company.

'Oh, *no!*' she said again, her voice almost breaking. 'But what has he done? He has been in Scotland no more than a few months – what *can* he have done?'

'He has involved himself in something that was none of his concern. And now there is blood on his hands.'

'Blood on his hands?' The world tilted a little on its axis, and then, for a moment, Ninian was aware only of acute exasperation. What an infuriating boy he was, never happier than when he was in a fight! She said, 'What will happen to him?'

The queen hesitated, and then said gently, 'He is to be executed.'

6

ALTHOUGH the queen listened patiently and sympathetically to Ninian's arguments, it was with absolute finality that she said she could not possibly intervene with His Majesty, not even for the sake of one of her ladies whom she held in the highest regard. Justice and the safety of the realm were at issue, and personal considerations were irrelevant. When Ninian asked permission to go to the king herself, the queen unequivocally forbade it.

She didn't forbid her to go to the chancellor.

Ninian gave herself no time to think. Her own concerns were unimportant when Blane's life – and Columba's and Séverine's happiness – were at stake; when there was no one else she could turn to but Gavin Cameron.

His manner was not encouraging when she presented herself at the hour he had appointed, although she had thought last week that his attitude towards her was beginning to become more human, which was ironical, when she had made up her mind that, for her own peace, she must learn to avoid him.

She sat on the stool he offered her and then, when he too was seated behind a table piled with documents and note blocks and vellum-bound books, he said, 'Yes, Lady Ninian. You wished to speak to me.'

His voice was crisp, as always, his eyes cold and almost inimical, and she suddenly realized that she had no idea how to begin.

'M. de Verne,' she said after a moment. 'I understand he is under arrest.'

'M. *Blane* de Verne? Yes.'

She noticed the emphasis, but couldn't afford to be distracted by it. 'Can you tell me why? For what crime?'

'Murder.'

She had thought a quarrel, some argument that had gone too far. But it didn't sound like that. She sat with her lips folded together for a moment, steadying herself before she spoke again. 'Surely not. We have known each other since we were children, and I cannot believe he would do anything as culpable as murder.'

The chancellor wasn't sufficiently interested to argue. 'Then let us say that he has killed a man. Whether intentionally or not, the result was the same. A man is dead by M. Blane's hand, and that is against the laws of this realm.'

'It must have been an accident.'

He raised a sardonic brow. 'When a group of men go out with the stated intention of destroying other men's homes and driving off their cattle, there is no such thing as "accident". The possibility of physical violence is implicit from the start.'

What was he talking about? Pressing her fingers against aching temples, she said, 'But . . . I was told that he had been arrested along with the Highland chiefs. And I thought their crime was to have made congregation – is that the expression? – by bringing together an army that might have threatened the peace of the kingdom. What on earth has this to do with attacking people's homes and driving off cattle?'

'*Congregatio* is the word. It means unlawful assembly.' He laid his hands flat on the table before him, palms down, and surveyed them with detachment. 'There is nothing at all mysterious about it. M. Blane was foolish enough to take part in an unlawful assembly at Strath Conon, thus enabling us, quite coincidentally, to discover that he was guilty of killing a man, some weeks ago, in Ardnamurchan. That is all there is to it. I really think, Lady Ninian, that if you insist on going into all the intricacies of the business, you would be better advised to ask M. Blane himself. A visit can be arranged.'

He paused briefly, and then added, 'Unlike me, he has nothing better to do with his time. Or not until tomorrow morning.'

The careless indifference of it brought her to her feet, and the ill-judged words sprang to her tongue almost without conscious thought. 'How dare you! How *dare* you be so callous, when we are talking about a man's life?' She had been so sure, in these last months, that her temper had died with her unborn child, but this was the first time it had been put seriously to the test. Perhaps things might have been different if it had been some other man sitting before her.

'I came here to persuade you that Blane de Verne is guilty of no more wrongdoing than the vast majority of his fellow men, to beg you to intercede for him with the king. And you will not even tell me the full circumstances of his crime!'

'So that's why you are here? I wondered. But as to the circumstances,' he said, the long mouth curling, 'surely you have known all about those – including the Strath Conon gathering – since long before the royal retinue was within sight of Inverness! And knowing, you must have recognized that something like this might happen.'

Her brow furrowed, she exclaimed, 'But, but . . . You think I knew? How *should* I know?'

He shrugged. 'M. Blane, perhaps. Or others.'

'No,' she said. '*No, no, no!* I knew nothing at all until Her Majesty told me what had happened.'

It was clear that he didn't believe her, clearer still that he wasn't going to help her. It would have been sensible to accept it, and go. But she was the only person trying to save Blane's life, and she didn't know who else to turn to other than this implacable man with whom she had rarely exchanged more than a dozen words in all the two years she had known him.

She sighed, a little shakily. 'Why should you think I knew?' It wasn't the same as asking how, but if she expected an answer at all, she expected him to say much the same as he had said before. 'You are a cousin of M. Blane's, isn't that enough?'

Instead, he smiled obliquely and replied, 'Because ever since you rejoined the court you have been very careful to avoid me.'

She stared at him. After a long moment, and not without difficulty, she said, 'No, I haven't. I . . .'

He must think that she had been afraid of dropping some ill-considered remark that might give the game away. He must think that she had been in the plot herself. Again, she said, 'No.'

He was shaking his head at her reprovingly, as if she were a stubborn and not very bright child, and she found she resented it. But her brain had begun working again. If her evasiveness had been his only reason for thinking she knew about the plot, all she had to do was find some other explanation. Then perhaps he might be prepared to listen after all.

She stood there, with no real sense of time, and thought and thought. He made her nervous? But he had made her nervous ever since the day they first met, and she had never avoided him before. He frightened her? The answer was the same. She disliked him? Why, then, should she expect him to help her now? As explanations went, they all sounded totally unconvincing – and they weren't conspicuously tactful, either.

But she could think of nothing else except the truth, and she couldn't tell him that.

As if he were tired of waiting for her to invent some story that he had no intention of believing, he rose to his feet and began to move round towards the front of the desk, saying, 'I cannot think that there is anything further to be gained from this conversation, Lady Ninian. Perhaps I may open the door for you?'

It was a massive door, new, pale, and ill-finished, and whoever had put the wooden pegs in hadn't made a very good job of it.

Ninian reached it first, and put her back to it. She could feel the rough, splintery surface through the thin fabric of her gown, and her voice, too, scraped a little as she forced herself to say, 'Yes, I have been avoiding you. But not for the reason you think.

'I have been avoiding you because my feelings for you are of a kind that no woman should have for a man who has dedicated his life to God.'

7

THE silence lasted for no more than a few seconds.

And then Gavin said, 'Ah. That explains why it is you and not your husband who is here now. Would you like me to ensure that we are not disturbed . . .' He leaned past her and shot the bolt. '. . . or perhaps you'd rather we were? Is this to be another well-publicized seduction? Perhaps you, too, have been making wagers about me with someone? I confess I would be interested to know with whom, since he – or she – seems to be indecently curious about my private life.'

The words were ironic, but there was a harsh undertone in his voice, and his eyes were unfriendly as he waited for her reaction.

If everything hadn't fitted so neatly, he might have been readier to believe her. The lovely gentian eyes could scarcely have been more innocent or the hesitation more plausible when she said, 'Wagers? What are you talking about?'

'But surely you know? The late Lady Elinor swore most convincingly that it was a wager that brought her to my bed.'

The girl's chin went up and, colour heightened, she said, 'I have never heard such nonsense, and I am not a – candidate for your bed. You asked why I had been avoiding you, and I told you. It has nothing to do with the present situation. Blane de Verne's life is all that concerns me at this moment. I am here only to persuade you to intercede for him with the king.'

She said it with a certain dignity, despite the resentment which, he thought, was real enough. No more than anyone else did the Lady Ninian enjoy being made to look a fool.

No more than he did. 'To persuade me, yes,' he nodded. 'By any means within your power.' It came out as a statement, not a question, because it rankled. By God, it rankled. And then, his voice overriding her angry denial, he went on, 'You must have a poor opinion of me if you think not only that I can be bought so cheaply, but that, because I fell into a trap once, I am likely to fall into the same trap again. Oh, no. I can assure you that, when I want a woman, I am perfectly capable of making my own arrangements.'

He should have left it there, he knew, but he couldn't. He had become acutely conscious of her in these last ten days. He had thought, when he saw her first after so many months, that the flirtatious child of the past had been transformed completely, but it seemed that she hadn't been, after all. His anger, now, was exacerbated not only by a frustration that was entirely human and unambiguous, but by a kind of rage that she should demean herself in this way, and by an inexplicably deep disappointment.

And so he went on, tightly, 'Arrangements that are unlikely to include a lady reared in a society as notorious for immorality as that of Avignon, especially when she is niece to a churchman who has broken the laws of this land, as well as cousin to one young man whose criminality has been proved and to another whose activities are suspect.'

Her face was white as a cerecloth, but she surprised him by refusing to be diverted by his extraordinary outburst.

'Why will you not listen?' she exclaimed. 'Forget your opinion of me. Forget what I have said about my feelings. They don't matter. What matters is that a young man is to be executed tomorrow for something that is not his fault! Even if it was murder, as you say . . .' She stopped for a moment as if she were groping for the idea as much as the words. '*You* should know, if anyone does, that everything that happens in this world is predestined. One cannot help what one is, or how one behaves. It is in the stars. It is God's will, isn't it? So how can *anyone* be blamed for *anything*?'

It was so unexpected, and so appallingly logical in its way, that he could do nothing but laugh. 'So we are into the realms of higher philosophy, are we? Oh, yes,' he said drily. 'If everything is pre-destined, why struggle? Why fight against cruelty and injustice? Why try to leave the world better than you found it, when it is so much more comfortable just to do as you please and claim that everything is "ordained"?' He shook his head. 'No. It's too easy an excuse. As far as your cousin is concerned, he became involved of his own free will. He chose and he must pay.'

To speak his mind openly had been forbidden to him for so long that, lost in the self-indulgent luxury of it, he scarcely even noticed the change in her expression.

And then, wonderingly, she said, 'But that's heresy!'

It brought him back to reality, not at all gently.

Less than half a dozen years ago, he had managed to piece together the theological arguments of the fourteenth-century Franciscan, William of Ockham, which hadn't been easy, because the church was very good at suppressing opinions of which it disapproved, and it disapproved as violently of William's as William did of the church.

Gavin had been no more than curious, to begin with, but William's views had struck him with all the force of revelation, because in the course of proving that man could never know what God *might* will, the redoubtable Franciscan had made nonsense of the whole concept of predestination. Gavin suspected that some of his arguments were misconceived, and hoped one day to have the time and leisure to go into them more deeply, but in the meantime the conviction that free will was real, something quite apart from predestination, had acted on him like a tonic.

There was something else of which he had become convinced, that the priesthood to which he belonged – and which the church claimed as the only bridge between man and God – was a poor and inadequate thing, and that seldom did the laws of Holy Church march with the laws of God.

Most of what William had said was unorthodox, and some of it heretical. A good deal of it had been taken up later by John Wyclif, whose Lollard followers had gone, and were still going, to the stake for their beliefs. But Gavin was already committed to his own path. He knew that, if he were to abandon the cloak of orthodoxy, there was no hope at all of achieving the objectives on which his heart was set – the secular reforms Scotland so urgently needed. If he were to succeed there, if he were even to survive, it was essential to guard his tongue.

And now, to Ninian Drummond of all people, he had let slip what he had never before hinted to anyone. To Ninian Drummond, niece of Columba Crozier, whom Gavin suspected of being his enemy; to Ninian Drummond, protégée of Crozier's oldest friend, Master Laurence of Lindores, Grand Inquisitor of Heresy.

He couldn't imagine what had possessed him.

Just one hint in either of those quarters, and that would be an end of Bishop Gavin and all his works.

Coolly, he said, 'Heresy? To talk of free will? No, predestination can encompass that, as it encompasses everything else. And perhaps you have not thought that, just as M. Blane's crime was ordained, so also, we may assume, is the penalty he must pay for it.'

But the blue eyes under the wide, disturbingly intelligent forehead were still suspicious, and he didn't dare allow their encounter to end on such a note. So he turned away from her and moved the few steps towards the window. The sun was low, and the satin-gold gleam on the river and the purple shadows that clothed Ben Wyvis reminded him of Kinveil, which he hadn't seen for seventeen years but now, suddenly and unaccountably, had begun to miss.

With a deliberate impatience in his voice, he said, 'It appears you will not be satisfied until you have an explanation of why Blane de Verne is to die while others suffer no more than a few days' imprisonment. Very well. He is, if you will, a sacrifice. You must understand that while the king is justifiably angry over the present situation, he has no desire to put the chiefs in an impossible position. He wants not their enmity, but their friendship, or at least neutrality. However, what they have done is illegal and he cannot ignore it. He must make an example, and the men whose blood feud has held the whole of Ardnamurchan in thrall for these last six months are the obvious scapegoats. Even their fellow chiefs recognize that their behaviour has been beyond what can be tolerated. So Alexander MacRuairi and John MacArthur, with their closest adherents, are to be executed, and honour will be satisfied all round.'

'*Honour?*'

'Yes. Expediency, too, of course. Perhaps, as you say, your cousin is being condemned to bear a greater burden of guilt than he deserves, but the plain fact is that the peace and safety of the realm are more important than the life of one troublesome young man.'

He could see that at least she understood what he was talking about. This kind of moral manoeuvring was common enough in papal circles, and she must have heard a good deal about it from her uncle. Abruptly, he was reminded that Blane de Verne was Crozier's son, which would, no doubt, mean further trouble from that quarter.

She said flatly, 'So there is nothing you *will* do, and nothing I *can* do.'

She still had her back to the door as he approached and made to lean past her to release the bolt. But his hand brushed against her arm as he did so, and a violent shudder ran through her.

Slowly, he withdrew his hand. He still didn't believe that she had come innocently, and perhaps it would do no harm to teach her a short, sharp lesson. It might help to wipe that unpleasant word 'heresy' from her mind.

Treacherously, forgetting all that he had said earlier, he murmured, 'Nothing you can do? I wonder . . .' and putting one hand under her chin, forced her mouth up to his.

She resisted bitterly, her hands pushing violently at his shoulders, her body struggling under his as he held her pinned against the door, her lips shut tight as a prison gate. But he was tall, hard-muscled, and in perfect physical condition, and he was not in the mood to be crossed.

They were stubborn, both of them. It didn't even strike Gavin at first, fully occupied with the virago in his arms, that she was fighting much harder and longer than she would have done if this had been her aim all along. And when he recognized it, it was too late.

By then her strength was beginning to fail, and he was able to settle his arms more easily around her, and raise his head from hers and look down into her face. Her eyes were closed, and the long red-gold lashes were dark and heavy from the tears that lay on her cheeks. He couldn't read her expression.

He buried his fingers in the hair shining under the gold mesh coif, and then set his mouth again on hers, with a feeling he had never known before and was afraid to try and identify.

She lay in the circle of his arms, passive and exhausted at first, because she had been more ill than he knew, until the firm warmth of his touch began to reassure her and the no longer harsh pressure of his lips became more eloquent, hungrier and more insistent. And then, with a little moan far down in her throat, she began to respond.

It was a long, deep, measureless embrace, changeless and changing, a kiss unrelated to time or space, body or spirit, past or future, a kiss that was neither a beginning nor a continuance nor an end, but something magically self-sufficient, mystically complete.

Neither of them had any idea how long it lasted. But after a moment, after an eternity, Gavin had to find the strength to put a stop to what he had so dangerously begun, because the only alternative to going on was to go nowhere, and there was, it seemed, an alchemy between them that could lead only to disaster.

He dropped his arms and stood back. It was one of the most difficult things he had ever had to do, but it was necessary to kill what had happened between them, now, and finally. The risks were too great. He remembered once, as a boy, bending to crush the soft, tender leaves of some wild herb between his fingers, and being left with only a dead stalk in his hand and a tantalizing memory of fragrance.

After a moment or two, her eyes opened, dark in the failing light, and by then he was in perfect command of himself.

On exactly the same courteously ironic note as when he had last spoken, he said, 'I think, on the whole – no. We should not suit. But thank you. Now, do you wish me to take you to visit M. Blane?'

8

SHE watched Blane for a moment through the grille. He was throwing dice against three of his fellows in the crowded dungeon, shouting and laughing as if he hadn't a care in the world. And then the man-at-arms brought him out, and Gavin Cameron took them to the guardroom, which was empty, and left them there with a man on the door.

Ninian had never been very close to Blane, whose whole being had always been focused on the brilliant elder brother who was both idol and enemy. She knew that, if he had any feeling for her, it was jealousy, because it was she, not he, on whom Séverine and Columba had lavished all the warmth they had to spare from Adam. But that was because Blane was a prickly boy, and it hadn't meant they loved him less.

She kissed him now, despite his recoil, and, sitting down on a hard stool, gathered all the tattered threads of her emotions together and said quietly, 'Blane, what can we do? Is there no way of proving that you're innocent of this crime you are accused of?'

He shrugged sulkily. 'Oh, I killed him all right. It was a kind of war, after all. And anyway, prove, *mon Dieu*? What would be the purpose? They are determined that someone will hang, and I am a foreigner and therefore expendable.'

'*Hang?*' Only common criminals were hanged. According to the dreadful protocol of retribution, men of nobler blood were granted the nobler death of the axe.

Blane glanced at her impatiently. 'The degradation? What should it matter? It seems my fine French breeding is not fine enough for the headsman. And an axe may slip as easily as a rope may break. I have no great wish to be made into mincemeat before I die.'

She closed her eyes, wishing for and yet dreading the end of this terrible day. Through the dragging weight of exhaustion, she managed to ask, 'What happened, Blane? You must tell me because – because it is I who will have to tell your mother and Columba.' Her voice broke suddenly. 'How will they bear it? How will they bear it!'

'Adam will tell them.'

'Adam? How will he know what to say? Where *is* he? If he were here he might do something!'

'Such as get me out? Not out of this place. And I don't know where he is anyway. Somewhere safe, with plenty of witnesses.'

'What happened? Tell me what happened.'

He sat down with a thud on one of the other stools and, elbows on his knees, leaned forward and began picking compulsively at dirty fingernails.

'Adam and Robert Graham were to persuade Alexander of the Isles to muster an army, but they knew it would take time. So, since there was trouble already in Ardnamurchan, they left me to help it along. Any stick to beat the king and Gavin Cameron with . . . It didn't matter my being French. Robert Graham vouched for me, and that was good enough for MacRuairi. I did well, better than Adam could have done.'

He was proud of himself. 'I fitted in, you see. I was one of them, whereas Adam is one with no one but himself.

'Adam said I wasn't to come to Inverness with MacRuairi, but we're friends now, and I think a man should stand by his friends. So I came . . .'

'And Adam? And Sir Robert?'

'Oh, once they'd persuaded Alexander to move, they vanished. Sir Robert said it was Alexander's right to see the thing through on his own. And Adam said the whole point about being an *éminence grise* was that one stayed in the background and lived to plot another day.'

Ninian rose, and went to him, and dropped to her knees before him.

And then his jaunty composure broke. He had always been thick-skinned, and frequently thick-headed, plunging with his friends into situations fraught with danger, thinking – if he thought at all – that death's perennial ambush had been set for others, not for him. No more than any other human being was he ready to die, and he was pitifully ill-equipped to wait under the advancing shadow until the dawn came. And then the dark.

Ninian, who had escaped the shadow, knew something of how he felt, and she pillowed his sobbing head on her shoulder, and felt the bruising force of his fingers on her arms, and continued to kneel on the cold, uneven stone floor murmuring his name and thinking of Columba and Sévèrine, until the man-at-arms came and told her she could stay no longer.

9

THEY hanged him next morning, in the courtyard of the castle, in the shade cast by the three thatched towers.

Harry, knowing nothing of what had happened the day before, had said grudgingly that Ninian should stay in her chamber and he would attend instead. But, sleepless, confused, racked with guilt, she couldn't leave Blane to die alone, with no one of his own to reach out to.

The king was merciful. At the queen's urging, it was announced, he had decided to overlook M. de Verne's involvement in the unlawful assembly, which might well have been construed as treason. So the young man would be hanged, no more. He wouldn't be cut down, and disembowelled, and quartered, nor would his severed head be displayed on a pike as a warning to others.

The Lady Ninian dropped her deepest curtsey to the king, and thanked him.

Blane's gaze clung to hers with a desperate blankness during the final moments on the scaffold, as if his mind had stopped working. Ninian hoped that it had. But he held his head high, as a knight should do.

And then the rope tightened, and his eyes started from their sockets, and the chant of prayers became louder and a single sigh rose from the throats of all the onlookers, and the stupid, exuberant, good-looking young man who had been Blane de Verne was transformed into something that wasn't even remotely human any more. Into a doll, loose-limbed and grotesque, blessedly unfamiliar – a dangling, unrelated assemblage of head and trunk, arms and legs, kicking and capering its way through the inexorable measures of the last, long, lonely, infinitely dreadful dance of death.

In the moment before she fainted, Ninian remembered that, in another three weeks, he would have been twenty-one years old.

PART FOUR

1428–1429

CHAPTER ONE

I

COLUMBA could remember the very night Blane had been conceived. Sévèrine had been eighteen or nineteen at the time, and he not much over twenty. It had been Christmas, and they had not seen each other for almost four years, not since 1403 when they had first met and fallen in love. Pierre de Verne had accepted Adam, the son born nine months after that first meeting, as his own, for he had been a good man, and a kind one, and he understood that a green girl could not be expected to love a husband who was twice her age. All he had asked of her was affection, and an appearance of faithfulness, and she had given him those.

Columba had been back in Scotland by the time Adam was born, but three years later he had been accepted as a student in the faculty of theology at Paris – an honour accorded only to advanced scholars whose ability was thought to be outstanding. Bursting with pride, he had accepted Pierre de Verne's invitation to spend the twelve days of Christmas at Villeneuve, convincing himself that it would be useful if he could consult some of the rare theological volumes in the abandoned papal library across the river.

He had been bursting, too, with virtuous intentions in the little matter of sins of the flesh. But those hadn't survived his first sight of Sévèrine. All she had done was look at him with that half-forgotten, familiar, derisive little quirk at the corner of her mouth, with eyes heavy, warm, and unreadable, and all his good resolutions had flown from his head like pigeons startled from a dovecote. It had been that night that Blane had been conceived. He had always been sure of it.

And now . . . Hanged like any common thief in a wet, cold, windy little town in a God-forgotten country on the furthermost margins of the map.

There were two letters before him. Ninian, thinking to spare him, wrote only of 'execution'. But Adam wanted his father to share what had happened, and his bitterness rose gusting from the page, so that the rank, malodorous, after-scent of it lingered still in Columba's nostrils.

Neither of them told him how Blane had become involved, nor even in what; only that he had trodden on the king's, and Cameron's, toes. Restlessly, Columba wished he knew what was going on, but Adam's letters, couched in the oblique, allusive language they were always forced to use, never told him quite enough.

Séverine had said he should not give Adam a free hand, that his judgement was not to be trusted, but she hadn't had any alternative to suggest, except that Columba should simply resign himself to the situation. And that he would not do.

Between them, he had thought – he in Rome, Adam in Scotland – they must be able to bring Gavin Cameron down from his pinnacle, destroy his pretensions, ruin his prospects, send him back incontinent to the wild Highland glen from which he had come, never to be heard of again. Then they would all be safe.

There was a hint, in this letter, that Adam's enmity was not now for Cameron alone; he seemed to blame the king, too, for Blane's death. And that was worrying, because Séverine was right and Adam was apt, sometimes, to overdo things. But there was no harm in him, Columba knew, only an excess of vitality.

'Our interests,' Adam had written, 'march ever more closely with Sir R's. Between us, we will achieve what must be achieved.

'I would have come to you, instead of writing, but time is precious. And you know how I feel for you, *mon père qui j'aime plus que tous les gens du monde*. Be strong, and when you break the news to *madame ma mère*, tell her I will be both sons to her now.'

Columba had wept at that.

Ninian, forgetting the inquisitive eyes that might read her letter on its journey, had told him both less and more.

She told him, among other things, what Gavin Cameron had said about sacrificing Blane so as not to alienate the clan chiefs, and Columba, if he had been looking at the matter coldly, could have seen the sense in it and even, perhaps, approved. But it was his son – *his* son – who had been the sacrifice. Whether or not Adam was right in holding the king guilty of uneven-handed justice, it seemed humanly impossible to Columba that Gavin Cameron's thinking should not have been coloured by the knowledge that Blane de Verne was a young man very dear to Columba himself.

Until now, only Columba's brain and his instinct for self-preservation had been involved in his war with Cameron. But, reading and re-reading the letters, he found that to dislike and distrust were gradually being added a deeper emotion, born of the fierceness of his attachment to those he loved. It came very close to hatred, and there was a trace of fear in it, too. Because if Cameron had chosen to extend his battle front, then Adam, and even Ninian, might be in danger.

In much more danger, at this moment, than Columba – because just over a month ago, after silver, and more silver, had changed hands, the pope had called Columba to him and told him that he was to be restored to the archdeaconry of Teviotdale. Regretful sincerity in every hard, dark line of his face, His Holiness had said that, in the opinion of his advisers, John Bowmaker had proved to be a man unworthy of his high position.

The bells, the bells. And the incense, and the mists off the Tiber. The pilgrims and the praying and the shouting. The sanctity and the silver. Eternal Rome.

Martin had also said that it would give him much personal pleasure if Archdeacon Crozier were to remain at the curia for the time being, where his knowledge and experience would be of inestimable value.

So in Rome, at least, Columba had emerged victorious, and for the time being he would be listened to. He already knew what he was going to do and, sitting quietly in the October dusk, he went over it once more in his mind, searching for flaws. He could find none.

And then the bells began to ring for evening Mass, and he rose to his feet with an effort, feeling cramped, and chilled, and old. He had no idea how he was going to tell Séverine about Blane, their son, the child of that beautiful, loving, carefree night, at Christmas, just twenty-one years ago.

NINIAN swung the lure high, and the falcon dived and trapped the bait superbly in mid-flight, then dropped rustling to the ground with it only a few yards from where she stood. She gave him a moment or two and then, when he paused in his pulling and tearing at it, bent and took it from him and offered him instead a piece of meat laid on her gauntletted fingers. He hopped on to her wrist without complaint, and while he was still occupied, wings spread and body arched, she was able to slip the jesses through the swivel and secure them.

Why, she wondered, should she have become so engrossed in this bird, who thought of her only as the source of his food supply? Why should she have been almost tearfully pleased when she went into the mews, after six weeks away, and he recognized her with his special, low-pitched cry of greeting? A substitute for the child she had lost? She didn't think so, for it was like no human relationship she had ever known, this combination, in him, of dependence and independence, and in her the pleasure of paying tribute to something that was a perfect incarnation of beauty and pride and swift, heart-stopping efficiency. And of arrogance, too, for he had an insolent certainty that nothing he did could ever go wrong, simply because it was he who did it.

Rather like Adam, who was due to arrive at Dess in an hour or two. The trouble was that, with the tiercel she had named Greensire, things very seldom did go wrong, whereas with Adam they did.

The brilliant, yellow-ringed eyes stared into hers and the bird made a noise high in his throat that sounded more like an enquiring kitten than a prince of the skies. Ninian smiled and chirruped back at him, and stroked his feet gently, and then, picking up his hood by the tuft of feathers that served for a handle, slipped it over his head.

Tucking the lure back into her satchel, and calling the dogs to heel, she began walking back over the moor to the castle. She had a good deal to say to Adam, who hadn't been near her in the two months since Blane had died.

But she was not to be given the opportunity, because it was not just Adam and a handful of followers who rode into sight round the tubby little fleece-crowned hill three hours later, but a company of well over two hundred, with the Earl of Atholl at its head and Alexander, Lord of the Isles, its closely guarded prisoner.

Atholl didn't skimp on money where his retinue was concerned. It was well-mounted, well-dressed, and very well armed.

'G'day tae you,' said his lordship, who seemed to be wearing every scrap of armour he had been able to lay his hands on, including, on his head, an iron basinet fetchingly framed in rib-knit magenta. The helmet came off, after a struggle, and he plucked the lining out of it and crammed it back over his wild white locks, the saffron pompom battered and bruised.

'My nephew's put Alexander in my charge,' he explained, 'and God save us if he gets away. The king says "all his misdeeds and loose morals are attributable to the bad influence of his advisers" and he's tae spend a wee whilie wi' me so's he can learn decent manners an' polite behaviour.'

The pale eyes stared at Ninian expressionlessly, defying her to laugh, and all she could think of to say, weakly, was, 'Oh.'

'Ye'll no' mind us staying here the night, will ye? The horses need a rest. We're on our way to join the court at Edinburgh.'

In two more weeks, Ninian also had to return to court. The queen, granting her leave, had said she would like to see her back, fully recovered from the late sad events, by the end of October.

She said all that was proper to her unexpected guest, and made apologies for her husband's absence. He was out on the moors somewhere, because they hadn't been anticipating such distinguished company.

Then Atholl let out a yelp of 'Hey, young Sawny! C'me here and meet the Lady Ninian,' and the Lord of the Isles, not at all put out by this unceremonious form of address, sauntered across the courtyard towards them, grinning cheerfully. He was of rather less than middle height, and had a slight roll in his walk as if he spent much of his time at sea, which Ninian supposed he must, since he was chief of a whole swarm of islands as well as vast stretches of Scotland's western coastline, most of it inaccessible by land. And she had heard, of course, that the Lordship had always had close ties with Ireland.

It seemed that the *Magister* was sorely in need of instruction in courtly forms of address, for he wasted no time on beating about the bush. What he said, straight out, was '*Dia!* It iss a ferry great pleasure, so it iss, to be meeting such a good-looking lass as yourself. If all the other lasses at the court iss as fine and fair as you, it iss the time of my life I will be haffing!'

She didn't feel in the least embarrassed, because it was so unblushingly flirtatious, as if they were both grown-ups and knew how much value to place on a personable young man's compliments to an equally personable young woman. It was simply one way of saying, 'I like the looks of you', and she chuckled back at him responsively, rather as she had done to Greensire a few hours earlier.

Short though he was, Alexander was every inch a Highlander, with a noteworthy head of red hair, wide grey eyes, a pale, freckled skin, sturdy limbs and, despite the very engaging smile, an unmistakable air of hauteur. His dress consisted of a loosely pleated, wide-sleeved saffron linen tunic, stitched at its many seams with thick red and green threads, and reaching halfway down his thighs. Below this, a pair of short, tight-fitting, heather-purple trews went no further than the knee, leaving the rest of his rather hairy legs bare. He had deerskin slippers on his feet. Only a 'wild Hieland man', Ninian thought, could possibly look well, or even at ease, in such an outfit; it wasn't surprising that foreigners, seeing a fully armed specimen of the breed for the first time, didn't have to search far for an epithet. 'Savage', they said with one accord.

Alexander looked as if he could be formidable enough if he chose, even though he had been relieved of the dirks and swords and axes with which he would otherwise have been garlanded, but he appeared to be both perfectly at ease and perfectly philosophical about his immediate fate.

Atholl dug an elbow into Ninian's ribs. 'Ye'll huv tae be careful o' Sawny. He's got a way wi' wimmin. There was a lassie he took tae live wi' him in '25, and her da was sae wild aboot it he said he'd huv the law on him. An' the law said the wumman hud tae leave Sawny and go back and live modestly under her da's roof, but wud she? Not her!'

Alexander said plaintively, 'But she did! She did! Though not chust at once – only when her sight began troubling her. It wass failing badly. Ferry sad, it wass.'

Ninian, about to make some suitably sympathetic remark, bit it off suspiciously, and Alexander went on, his full-lipped, mobile mouth stretching into the most disarming of grins, 'She said her eyes wass chust not able to keep up with mine any more – or not when we wass in a room full of pretty lasses.'

It was then, when they were all laughing, that Adam joined them, and Atholl, cut off in the midst of a cackle, said, 'Och, an' here's Honeypot! Are ye no' going to give the wumman a wee kiss?'

Adam, ignoring the nickname, bent and saluted Ninian on the cheek. She wondered why Atholl took such pleasure in baiting him, and why Adam put up with it. It was quite unlike him.

But the absence of laughter in Adam's eyes had nothing to do with Atholl, and Ninian hoped, almost vindictively, that it meant Blane's death was on his conscience. And then she hoped it didn't. It was too much of a burden for him to bear alone. If only she could find out exactly what had happened; and if only she knew what he and Robert Graham were up to now – because, although she hadn't said as much in her letter to Columba, she was becoming increasingly frightened.

Atholl, a proprietorial hand still on the Lord of the Isles' shoulder, said to Ninian, 'Me and your cousin have a fine wee arrangement. I'm having Archdeacon Crozier's tithes collected, tae save your cousin the bother, and in return he's saving me the bother of looking after Sawny here. For a' the time Sawny's in my charge, Mishure de Verne's going to stick closer to him than a brother.'

It was a tactless and a cruel thing to say, and Ninian, looking at the old man, saw that he had meant it to be.

She smiled calmly, and looked around. 'How satisfactory for you. But I imagine you must all be in need of refreshment? Will you have it here, since it is such a pleasant evening, or up in the High Hall?'

3

COLUMBA's messenger arrived at Villeneuve only two hours before he did. It was so unlike him not to give proper warning that Séverine had all her emotions collected and confined before he even rode into the courtyard – before she saw his face and knew that her instincts had been right, and that something appalling had happened. There were tears on his cheeks. She could see that he had been scourging himself, all along the way, with the thought of what he had to tell her.

It was Ninian's name she murmured as he embraced her, because she had feared for Ninian, naïve and vulnerable, ever since she had ridden away from Villeneuve just over two years ago. But Columba shook his head and, the tears falling openly now, said, 'No. *Our* child. Blane.'

It wasn't a surprise. Death was never a surprise. Sévèrine had known always that, some day, someone would come and tell her that her sons were dead. She had never feared it, or not unbearably. What she had feared was the manner of their dying.

She sat, dry-eyed, and listened to what Columba had to tell her. She had lost the knack of weeping, years ago, and was filled, instead, with a sadness for which there was no release, an exhaustion that weighed down all her limbs so that to rise, or stand, or walk was unthinkable.

She was grateful to have Columba's arm around her, but his presence could not ease the pain because, although he had a clever and a subtle mind, his heart was like a child's. He had loved Blane unthinkingly and unreservedly while he was alive, and mourned his death in the same way. It was the whole sum and substance of his grief that their son had died, and at a rope's end.

He was remembering, aloud, little things from Blane's childhood, so that it was with seeming irrelevance that she said, 'It is why we all love you so much — because you love us so much, without complication or qualification. À vrai dire, we would be inhuman if we did not respond.'

The arm round her shoulder tightened convulsively, but she didn't, as another woman might have done, turn and bury her face in the rich velvet of his robe and find comfort in his closeness. Instead, the fine-drawn brows high over her heavy-lidded eyes, she said, 'If one were sure he had done no wrong, it might be less hard to bear.'

'Wrong? Less hard?' Columba, his voice uncertain, replied, 'If he did wrong, it cannot have been more than a boy's tricks. No. They hanged him because of me.'

'Did they?' She was distantly surprised. 'How could that be? They did not know in Scotland — did they? — that he was your son?'

'Cameron knew he was close to me.'

Slowly, Sévèrine shook her head. She had always been able to assess people from even the briefest meeting, and no more than once or twice in her life had her assessments proved to be wrong. Gavin Cameron had seemed to her an intelligent man, and a man of integrity — not one who would use the innocent as a weapon against the guilty. She wished she knew more about this folly that had taken Columba in its grip, this campaign he was engaged on. He and Adam. Hearing only Columba's side of it, she could not judge. But she could suspect.

She said, 'No. Not a boy's tricks. Some bêtise of Adam's, for which Blane has paid the price. I know my sons too well.'

242

Turning her eyes on him, she said, 'You have won, now, at Rome. If I were to beg it of you, would you cry truce in this war against Gavin Cameron?' She hesitated for a moment, but there seemed to be no compelling reason why she should leave the rest of it unsaid. 'Would you cry truce – before Adam also dies?'

It was useless. The noble lines of his face disintegrating and the tears standing in his eyes again, Columba said, 'I cannot. You must see that I cannot. It takes two sides to make a truce. I will never be safe – *we* will never be safe – until Gavin Cameron is brought down. Adam will be all right, I will see to that. And Cameron has Blane's death to answer for, now. Oh, my dearest love, don't beg something of me that I cannot grant!'

So she turned her eyes away from him again, and dropped them to her loosely clasped hands. But she had to swallow hard before she was able to say, 'Very well. I will not ask, if you do not wish it.'

4

IN THE first few weeks after Ninian's return to court it was like some mad game of chess, with the bishop chasing the queen's pawn all over the board.

Bishop Gavin seemed to have developed a sudden, intense interest in what Lady Ninian was up to. At first, she thought it was only coincidence that he so often happened to join any group of which she was a member, but after a week or two she began to find herself waiting for it. It didn't happen invariably. If she were surrounded by frivolous young knights and squires, or playing at riddles with the queen's ladies, or engrossed – as she so often was – in some nonsensical sparring match with Alexander of the Isles, he left her alone. But if she were talking to someone serious, like Bishop Wardlaw, or the Earl of March, or Master Laurence of Lindores, she could be absolutely sure that, sooner rather than later, the tall, austere figure of the chancellor would materialize at her side. It was tiresome, because although she wanted nothing whatever to do with him, both pride and an irrational determination to pretend that nothing had happened between them forced her to stay where she was, instead of moving away, as she would have preferred.

Gavin himself would have been hard pressed to identify his motives during those weeks, although he satisfied himself with the very cogent argument that, if he had not, during their encounter at Inverness, succeeded in diverting Lady Ninian's mind from his own virtual confession of heresy, he might still be able to salvage something from the wreckage if he were there in person when she innocently asked the Grand Inquisitor about it.

Even the thought sent icy shivers down his spine, and he wasted a good deal of time trying to construct an acceptable theological case for free will as a component of predestination. But he couldn't quite make it cohere and he could visualize only too clearly the expression on Master Laurence's pale, big-boned face as, with contemptuous ease, he took it apart again.

Gavin couldn't, of course, invigilate over more than a small proportion of Ninian's conversations, but, wary and watchful, he continued to study the looks in the eyes of all the men who might be dangerous – his fellow bishops, the leading nobles and, of course, Master Laurence – and eventually came to the conclusion that he was safe. Or as safe as he would ever be; that single blunder would haunt him for the rest of his life. Why should Ninian Drummond, of all people, have succeeded in slipping under his guard?

And then, having decided he could relax, he made the extraordinary discovery that he didn't want to. Because the Lady Ninian, in sensible company, turned out to be a quite intelligent young woman who understood most of what was said and, when she didn't, was sufficiently interested to ask to have it explained. It began to annoy him that she should spend so much time flirting with vacant-minded young men, and especially with the far from vacant-minded Alexander. Which she undoubtedly was.

And that, Gavin, supposed, was largely his fault for trying to persuade the king that he ought to economize.

The king, remembering how his former jailer, Henry V of England, had dealt with the need to curb royal expenditure, had said, 'Right! Anyone who hasn't an official reason for being at court can pay for their own food and lodging when they're here. And their horses'. And we can limit the number of attendants for folk who *are* entitled to be here. Archie Douglas never brings less than a hundred men with him, and I don't see why I should have to feed them all. He'll just have to make do with fifty. Will that do? It ought to make a substantial saving!'

It wasn't the kind of economy Gavin had had in mind, but he

supposed it would have to suffice for the time being, and one un-doubted advantage was that the number of superfluous males clutter-ing the place up had diminished spectacularly, most of them being constitutionally opposed to paying out money for something they expected to be given free.

Harry Graham had vanished with the rest, leaving his wife with no one to keep an eye on her. It was surprising, because Graham was undoubtedly a jealous young man, and Gavin had caught Moragh – two-faced minx that she was – encouraging him on more than one occasion, with sly remarks about Lady Ninian's extraordinary popularity with everyone.

Now, his eyes strayed to where Ninian was sitting on a window seat, with the Lord of the Isles beside her. Alexander was trying to teach her the Gaelic, which was presumably why he was reaching his pursed fingers towards her lips, making as if to pull them outwards to help her master the characteristically deep-throated 'oh' sound.

Gavin was abruptly reminded of the feeling of those same lips against his.

Lust, no more. He preferred not to think about it. Turning away, he began discussing with Tom Myrton some of the minor details of Tom's forthcoming diplomatic mission to London.

5

NINIAN wasn't sure whom she despised more, Gavin Cameron or herself. For his callousness about Blane she had almost convinced herself that she hated him, until, thinking about it less emotionally, she had recognized that, with death so much a part of life, no man – not even Columba, who was her yardstick for everything – spared time to mourn the death of another, unless he was close. Death came when it came; when God ordained it. She had frowned over that whole problem for a while, because it seemed to her that for anyone who believed in free will, it must be an encouragement to *do* things instead of submitting tamely to events – and that meant that Gavin Cameron did not have other men's excuse for shrugging off the responsibility for Blane's execution.

Resentfully, she recalled his evasion. 'Predestination can encompass free will', he had said, fobbing her off as if she were an unlettered child.

Well, *perhaps* it was true; though she couldn't see how, and she had known at once that he himself didn't believe it.

She shuddered suddenly, for she had no doubt at all that it was heresy he had been talking, and she couldn't help remembering what she had always been told about heretics, all the disgusting tales of human sacrifice, incest, blasphemy, obscene commerce with the devil. But it was impossible to think of such things in connection with Gavin Cameron.

She tucked it all away for future consideration; she didn't even know whether she had the kind of mind that was capable of thinking in the concentrated, logical and yet abstract terms that were a precondition of any study of theology. That much, at least, she had learned from Columba.

About Gavin's heresy, she was prepared to keep a doubting, though open mind. But every time she thought about the way he had treated *her*, she was reduced to speechless fury.

Her pride, her resolve, her concern for Blane – all had gone down before the wild surge of hope that had possessed her when he kissed her, and it had been a kiss with a greater, deeper, more perfect meaning than any she had known in her whole life before. Was it like this to die, she had wondered, to drown in the soft, compelling seas of night and come to shore in the arms of the sunrise? One thing she had felt, above all – that, whether by God's will or her own, this was the fulfilment of her destiny.

Then he had stepped back and said with insulting courtesy, 'We should not suit.'

Her heart mightn't have broken if he had really meant it, but she knew that, whatever he chose to say, he *had* recognized that there was some alchemy between them. It had made his rejection so unexpected, so cruel, so shocking, that she couldn't at first absorb it, living through all the guilt-clouded misery of the execution and its aftermath in a daze of unbelief. Only when she was back at Dess, solitary on the moors without even Greensire for company, had she been able to make any kind of sense of what had happened. And that was when she had come to despise him. Because, by pretending that what was between them had been no more than something physical, and not even very strong, he had proved that he neither understood her, nor trusted her, nor wanted to.

For herself she felt a sick contempt; contempt for the ease with which she had fallen, and the naïvety that had led her to believe, however briefly, that her world could again become the Paradise Garden of her childhood. Now, she had been left with nothing. She couldn't even weep over the graves of her roses.

By the time she returned to court, she no longer found it necessary to avoid Gavin Cameron, although she preferred to. It didn't dawn on her at first why he was haunting her, because she didn't flatter herself it was from any particular desire for her company. And then, incredulously, she realized that he must be afraid she might repeat to someone, intentionally or unintentionally, what he had said to her about free will. So he thought her a fool, as well as a cheat and a whore! Or did they all go together? It was then that her careful dislike gave way to a healthy flush of anger.

She sensed him watching her with Alexander of the Isles, so she smiled more vividly, and teasingly made as if to bite the young man's fingers, and thought that some day soon it would give her the greatest pleasure to teach Gavin Cameron a lesson he would not forget.

6

FOR almost two weeks, Adam succeeded in avoiding the *tête-à-tête* Ninian was determined on, and when she finally cornered him was at first superior, and then artificially amused, at the change in the submissive little cousin who had dared to cross him only once in her life before.

'I have grown up,' she said with some asperity. 'And I think it is more than time that you told me what has been going on. Also about the plans you have for the future. I love Columba as much as you do. I know him as well as you do. You must convince me that what you are doing for him is something of which he would approve.'

Blane's death had changed him. Once, he would have been honestly entertained by her presumption, but there was no laughter in him now, except on the surface, and that only from habit. She thought at first that he was going to lose his temper with her, but then the glitter in his eyes faded a little, and he condescended to give her the explanation she wanted, although his voice was brittle and imperfectly controlled.

Everything had happened much as Blane had said. Robert Graham had insisted that it be left to the Highlanders to carry through the plan they had hatched between them. 'If it is to cause real trouble,' Graham had said, 'it must appear to be spontaneous. Let anyone else's involvement become known, and the whole affair will be attributed to agitators and cease to be taken seriously.'

'It appeared to me that he talked good sense,' Adam went on, 'nor has it ever been my ambition to offer myself up as a sacrifice. But Blane thought it cowardly. He would not yield, and in the end I let him be. I thought he would run no danger beyond the ordinary.'

'No danger!' Ninian exclaimed. 'But he walked straight into a trap!'

Adam was standing with his back to her, his hands clasped behind him, and she saw the knuckles whiten for a moment before he whirled round. 'Do you think I should have foreseen the trap? Don't be stupid! If I could have foreseen it, I would have foreseen also that the whole affair was doomed to disaster.'

He stared at her pale, strained face. 'Do you not recognize that James and Cameron knew all about everything in advance? Do you not recognize that someone must have given them warning?'

His gaze was so intent that, for a moment, she wondered whether he thought she was to blame, but he said contemptuously, 'No. I am aware that you knew nothing. But you will know nothing, either, of what we plan next. When the fiery cross goes round again, it will carry with it a warning of silence or death. This time we will not fail.'

She had never seen him so implacable. The fiery cross – again? She could have wept. What next, what next! She had the unexpected thought that, if only she could contrive a private meeting with Sir Robert Graham, he might be prepared to tell her. But she had no idea where he was, though Harry might know, if she could extract the information from him without rousing his suspicion. He seemed to be so suspicious of everything she did or said nowadays that she almost wished he would come back to court and see for himself that there was no reason for it.

And then, a week later, Bishop Wardlaw of St Andrews came to her, a smile on his lined face, to tell her that he had received a letter from Rome instructing him to make public throughout the length and breadth of Scotland the news that His Holiness had seen fit to reinstate his dear son, William Columba Crozier, in the archdeaconry of Teviotdale. 'We are happy for your uncle, Lady Ninian,' he said, his own smile deepening at the gratitude in her face. 'Let us hope that these sad misunderstandings are now over.'

She could scarcely wait to find Adam and tell him, but his first reaction had a reserve in it that puzzled her. He was pleased – of course

– not only for Columba's sake, but because his father would no longer need every penny of his tithes at Rome.

'It has not occurred to you, I am sure, that during these last months I have had to depend on Atholl even for my bread.' Which at least explained his extraordinary submissiveness towards the old man. It had been mystifying Ninian for months.

But when, out of the immensity of her relief, she went on, 'No more plotting, Adam! Oh, thank God!' he stared at her as if she had taken leave of her senses.

He was clad in scarlet as always, and on his head he wore the dashing, turban-draped hood she remembered from her wedding day in Villeneuve, a lifetime ago. His hair curled long and black and luxuriant as it had done then, and his shoulders were as wide and his hips as narrow as they had always been. Only his eyes had changed.

'But we have scarcely begun,' he said. 'This might be no more than a temporary victory. Something of the sort has happened before, if you recall! No, Columba will never be wholly safe until Cameron is brought down. Have you forgotten the barratry laws? They have not been enforced yet, but Columba's restoration could anger Cameron into changing that. Columba could still be banished. They could prevent me – or try to prevent me – from collecting and sending his tithes to him. Where would Columba be then? Or Sévèrine? Or I myself? Oh, no. The danger is far from over.

'And even if you have forgotten all that . . .' He paused, as he always did when he wanted to emphasize his next words. ' . . . you cannot have forgotten that Blane's life is still to be paid for.'

CHAPTER TWO

I

GAVIN was fully occupied during the last months of 1428 and the early ones of 1429, because all James's foreign policies were coming home to roost. The English were very sour indeed about Scotland's laxity in the matter of ransom payments, about the endless skirmishing on the Borders and, above all, about her dealings with France.

None of this would have troubled the king in the least, had not the queen's uncle, Cardinal Beaufort, been involved. But it was Beaufort who had been mainly responsible for the terms of James's release five years before, and now, recently back from Rome, he had a strong personal interest in seeing them fulfilled. He was anxious to raise forces in England for a crusade against the heretics of Bohemia, and had been told in no uncertain terms that, unless Scotland's neutrality could be guaranteed, England would not spare him a single soldier.

Where cardinals and kings were involved, nothing was ever simple. There was no question of Her Majesty's uncle arriving on a private visit, hoping for a quiet word in James's ear. It meant emissaries and safe-conducts, letters patent and licences to treat, dates and locations, hundred-horse escorts, and sumpter ponies to carry the feather beds.

The preliminary negotiations were entrusted to Tom Myrton, and when he arrived back from London in December, soaked, stiff, and weary, it transpired that he had been active in other directions as well.

Plumping down gratefully on the edge of Gavin's bed and dripping all over it, he said, 'I've news from Rome. About yourself. There's one of Beaufort's wee secretary laddies who's got an awful good memory for gossip and an awful weak head for wine. And it seems friend Crozier isn't satisfied with having Teviotdale back. He's out for your blood, my boy, and I mean that very seriously. This isn't just some ordinary dispute over a benefice. From what I hear, Crozier's turned it into a full-scale vendetta!'

Gavin handed him a cup of hippocras. 'You don't surprise me.'

The surprise had worn off now, though it had been appreciable when, not too long ago, he had taken time to piece together all he knew about the more disruptive events of the last eighteen months, and had noticed how often the name of Verne had cropped up. There had been nothing altogether specific, except in the case of the younger brother, but the elder . . .

Gavin had remembered his first, instinctive suspicions of Adam de Verne on that day when he himself had gone head first down the winding stone staircase at Perth. Although he had chosen to let it appear an accident, he had subsequently made such enquiries as he could, without result. But Verne had been nearby before the accident, and could have overheard enough of Gavin's exchange with the king to know where he was going; setting up the accident would have been the work of a moment.

After that, there had been the business over Lady Elinor, whose murderer had never been found. There were several witnesses to prove that Adam de Verne had been elsewhere at the time – but he had been the last outsider to see her alive, and no one, apparently, had taken the trouble to count the number of his escort when he had arrived, or to match it against the number when he left.

And the gathering at Strath Conon. Gavin had heard one or two whispers about that, about two men who were not of the clans but had been busy among them for weeks beforehand. One of the men was said always to wear fine armour, and always to keep his visor down. About the other man, no one said anything at all.

Even Ninian Drummond's approaches to him at Inverness, Gavin had concluded, might be open to more complex interpretations than he had originally thought.

None of it was provable, but he had no real doubts. And if Adam de Verne was involved, then it made no sense at all unless Columba Crozier was behind it.

He said to Tom, 'Tell me.'

'Well, as far as I can make out,' Tom took a reviving gulp of the warm, spicy wine, 'His Holiness had heard about our barratry laws but wasn't taking a blind bit of notice until Crozier and his friends started making a fuss. You'll note I say "and his friends"? Seems he's enrolled Poggio Bracciolini – the humanist, you know? – and Gabriel Condulmer as well. I don't doubt Condulmer hopes to succeed Martin some day, so he'll have what you might call a personal interest in the state of the papal treasury!

'The story has it that, by the time they were done, they'd convinced His Holiness that Scotland was trying to rally all the nations of Christendom to a crusade against the papacy, and that if he let Scotland get away with forbidding her churchmen to spend money at Rome, everyone else would soon be at the same game, until His Holiness didn't have a penny to bless himself with. And so on, and so on.

'Anyway, His Holiness got a wee bit hot under the pallium about it. You know how he feels about folk flouting his authority! Left to himself, he'd probably just have sent a rude letter to James. But Crozier and friends pointed out that it's better strategy to attack the servant than the master, and that in this case it was all the servant's idea, anyway. So . . .' Absently, Tom began casting off surplus garments.

'Well, get on with it.'

'So they've raked up a terrible collection of charges against you. Not just being responsible for parliamentary statutes "against ecclesiastical liberty and the rights of the Roman church", but simony in the collation of benefices. And before you were consecrated, they claim you'd committed "such crimes as to have forfeited all right to elevation."'

Wagging his head mournfully, Tom said, 'Gavin, Gavin! You've been keeping things from me.'

'Don't be a fool,' exclaimed his irritated bishop. 'What are they doing about it?'

'The case has been referred to two of the cardinals for investigation. If they find against you, you could be in serious trouble. I mean it, Gavin!'

The wintry grey eyes were far away as Gavin said, almost to himself, 'It's an impossible world, isn't it? I believe in God, I fear God, as all men do, but I'm not cut out to have thousands of souls in my charge. I haven't the patience for it, or the right kind of faith. But to be chancellor, to do what I'm competent at, to work for people's physical and mental wellbeing, I have no choice.

'I knew from the beginning I was going to have a conflict of loyalties. You can't reconcile the stability and common sense of everyday government with the dictates of an unpredictable, unknowable God.

'But I *have* to be a priest. If it weren't for that, being deprived wouldn't worry me at all. The people of the diocese might even find themselves, for once, with a bishop wholly and exclusively devoted to their spiritual welfare.'

'*Might!*' Tom said witheringly. 'Your trouble is, you're an idealist. When did you ever hear of a bishop wholly and exclusively devoted to anything but the welfare of his own pocket?'

'And your trouble is, you're a cynic. Well, we'll just have to wait and see what happens next. But I tell you, Tom, at this moment I'm considerably more interested in what Crozier's son is up to here, than what Crozier himself is up to at Rome. Because I suspect Adam de Verne of being out for a good deal more than my blood. I wish I knew what! It's been a relief to have him here at court under my eye for these last weeks.'

And then he struck his forehead suddenly and violently with the heel of his palm and jumped to his feet. His voice fizzing with exasperation, his fists raised heavenward, he exclaimed, 'What Atholl thinks he's up to putting Verne in charge of Alexander, I can't imagine. But when James said he thought a captain-at-arms would be a better idea, Atholl told him the young men were two of a kind, and "Mishure de Verne" would be far quicker to spot any move to escape than some clod of a soldier.'

He sat down again, with a thud. 'Misbegotten old fool!'

It was a very mild outburst, but it surprised Tom, as always. He smiled to himself. It was too easy to forget that Gavin was a Highlander born, with just as much passion under his thick crust of self-control as any of them.

2

'AYE, it wud fair rile Cameron,' chortled the misbegotten old fool a few weeks later. 'Whit's mair, it's time Sawny did something useful 'stead o' fornicating aboot the court here like the Whore of Babylon.'

Adam grinned. It had done wonders for his temper when Atholl, inspired by Alexander's colouring, had begun referring to him as the Scarlet Wumman. By comparison, Honeypot sounded like a compliment.

Ninian said sweetly, 'So we can rely on you, then, my lord?'

'Oh, aye. Ye can rely on me for anything, lassie.' He rubbed his hands together and Ninian curtsied hastily and began to back towards the door. 'We will leave you, then. And thank you.'

They could still hear him cackling from halfway down the corridor. Ninian turned just in time to fix Alexander's mischievous eye and say, 'Don't you dare!' whereupon he carried his own hovering hand upwards and smoothed it innocently over his chin.

His chuckle was as infectious as his smile. 'It iss a clever lass you are,' he said. 'And if we can be relying on his lordship, and if all the timing goes right, it iss for ever I will be loving you, I swear!'

Three days before, the king had left for Coldingham, an English monastery on Scots soil, to meet Cardinal Beaufort. He had taken neither his queen nor his chancellor with him, a decision heartily approved by all the conspirators except Alexander, who had no particular interest in the discrediting of Gavin Cameron and wanted only to shake the dust of Edinburgh from his feet and get back to his beloved Isles again.

Gavin was deep in conference with a rather touchy French envoy some hours later when his door opened a dozen inches to admit the all too familiar toorie with the manic white eyebrows beneath.

'I'm away, then! I'm off!' said Atholl's voice briskly. 'I huv tae get back to Blair – the barmkin's on fire. I'm taking Mishure de Verne with me, so ye'll huv tae keep an eye on Sawny yerself.'

Gavin's long legs carried him to the door just in time to stop his lordship from vanishing into thin air like some disreputable cacodemon.

'Since the message must have taken at least a day to reach you,' he said, 'I imagine the fire will be out by now. Would your lordship not be advised to wait until morning? You will travel faster then, and it would give me time to make arrangements for guarding Alexander as the king wishes him guarded.'

'Naw, naw! There's a fine moon to aid us. Sawny'll no' give ye any bother. I've left him in the Great Hall, blethering his head off tae Lady Moragh.' He turned, bellowing, 'Verne!' and Adam materialized with the captain of Atholl's escort, both of them well wrapped up against

254

the cold. Most of Scotland lay under a blanket of wet March snow, and Gavin didn't envy them the journey.

As they disappeared towards the main gate, he caught a glimpse of another figure entering, tossing off a sodden cloak. It looked remarkably like Harry Graham, but Gavin didn't have time to wonder about it as he finished giving his usher hasty instructions to find John Cragy or Tom Culbyn. 'Send them to the Great Hall, to the Lord of the Isles. I'll be there myself as soon as I can manage.'

But the French envoy was already offended at having their talk so unceremoniously interrupted, and, as if to repay Gavin, insisted on going into every tiniest detail of the previous month's unfortunate affray outside Orléans that had resulted in the deaths of several of the Scots in the Dauphin's service, most notably John Stewart of Darnley. The envoy was quietly satisfied to note that Bishop Gavin was paying him very little attention, so little that he didn't even raise the question of compensation, which was a relief.

Eventually, the envoy rose and took his farewell in a flurry of the scent that had kept his host on the edge of sneezing for the better part of two hours, and Gavin was able to lock all his documents away and stride off towards the Great Hall.

There was no sign of Alexander, nor of Tom Culbyn, but he found John Cragy conscientiously working his way round the room, examining every alcove and sidling into every group of people as if he expected to find Alexander quietly curled up somewhere in the middle.

With a long-suffering sigh, the chancellor said, 'If Alexander were here, you'd see him easily enough. I hope Tom Culbyn's with him, but just in case, get as many men as the captain of the guard will spare you, and start searching. Try not to make too much fuss about it. And, John! The gateway first, and then work inwards from the curtain wall.'

The young man nodded his head and turned away. 'And *hurry*!' muttered his master with such venom that the startled John abandoned his dignity and took to his heels.

'Moragh?' She had been talking to Walter of Lithgow, one of Ninian Drummond's more sedate admirers, and turned, eyebrows raised at the crispness in his voice. 'You were with Alexander an hour ago. Where did he go?'

'I haff no idea.'

'When, then?'

'Not long. The length of a Miserere, perhaps.'

'No more?'

'No. What iss the matter, Gaffin?'

'You're sure? He was still with you after Atholl left?'

'Long after.' Then, with dawning laughter, 'Gaffin! Has Sandy slipped through your fingers?'

'I hope not,' he said grimly, and nodded to her, and made for the door.

3

THE moon was like a great pearl, ringed round first in sapphire, and then aquamarine, and then chrysoprase; set in a frothy, silver-grey filigree of cloud; and hung against a sky of sheerest black velvet.

The effect, astonishing and uncanny, faded within a minute, but Ninian continued to stand there, willing it to return, trying to remember what it meant to see a ring around the moon.

She was brought back to earth by a furious hiss from Alexander, who at the prospect of action had become quite another person from the cheerful philanderer she knew. The easy smile, the leisurely charm had gone, and he was a Highland chieftain again, the Lord of the Isles on his way back to his people.

They were out in the open, just the two of them, Ninian in full view of any passerby, Alexander flat against the curtain wall in the deep shadows by the Wellhouse Tower. There was a good deal of coming and going within the castle precinct, most of it at the further end, but it was still a nuisance, because the steps up to the parapet walk were in full view of anyone who cared to look. To reach his first objective, Alexander was going to have to inch his way up thirty feet of wall that, to Ninian's uninstructed eye, scarcely offered enough footholds for a fly. But Alexander had laughed. 'That iss the easy bit! Your hands and your knife iss able to prepare the way for your feet. Climbing downwards iss not so much fun at all.'

It took him only three breath-stopping minutes to reach the top, moving crablike astride the angle of wall and tower, using the roughly masoned stones when they gave him purchase, and digging finger-grips out of the mortar when they didn't.

Ninian, heavily cloaked and hooded, trying to look like some serving woman waiting for an assignation, heard his voice, a little breathless, floating down to her. 'Iss there anyone?'

The next moments were the most dangerous, he had said, because to climb down the outside of the wall was beyond even him, when there was nothing but a vertical rock face below it. So he had to tie a rope round one of the teeth of the battlements to carry him down to the crag on which the castle stood. Even to look at the crag had been enough to give Ninian vertigo, but it held no fears for him. 'When you haff been used to climbing the Cuillins to giff you an appetite for your dinner, it iss nothing to worry about at all.' He had been much more concerned by the quality of the only rope they could find, for he didn't trust hemp and would much have preferred a good, reliable length of twisted heather roots.

Ninian stared around her, eyes trying to pierce every shadow, ears tuned to every whisper of sound. To anchor the rope, Alexander was going to have to emerge into the lesser darkness, and although the rope was looped and ready, passing it round the huge tooth of the battlement wasn't going to be the work of a moment. However, because the king had taken so many men with him to Coldingham, there were no more than two soldiers patrolling the parapet on this north side of the wall, and they were far away and showing no inclination to hurry back.

She could sense no other presence closer than David's Tower, and the people there wouldn't be in line of vision, so she turned her face up, and said, half-aloud, 'All's clear.'

Alexander's short, uncluttered Highland dress was now proving its worth, not only in the scaling of unscalable heights, but in minimizing all sound of movement. Although Ninian was aware of swift, disciplined activity above her, there was no identifiable noise, no murmur of robes or flutter of sleeves, no rustle of broidered cloth, no scuffle of soles.

Then she heard him say, 'It iss done. And now, *slàn leat. Théid sinn dhachaidh.*'

And now, goodbye. We are going home.

There was a slither of movement, and then silence.

She felt her eyes prick with tears as she turned and began to stroll towards the parapet steps, and then mount them as if her only purpose was to while away a few minutes admiring the snow-blanched, rolling fields and, beyond them, the river and the port of Leith. But she had a knife tucked in her girdle, and when she heard the harsh, false cry of a peewit below, she leaned forward and hacked at the rope until it parted and disappeared over the wall.

257

Then she straightened up again, hands clasping the cloak tightly around her against the wind. The clouds were moving up fast from the south-east now, covering the moon, and the land had become ill-defined as a blurred woodcut. But the moon still shone on the distant water.

A cold voice behind her said, 'Are you expecting someone, Lady Ninian?'

4

WHEN her heart began beating again, she said, '*Grand dieu!* How quietly you move. You startled me.' And the evidence of it, if he had known, was her lapse into French, a luxury she had long forbidden herself.

As if she had not spoken, he repeated, 'Are you expecting someone?'

His eyes were scanning the shadows along the parapet walk, flickering over the gaps in the battlements, gazing down into the blackness by the Wellhouse Tower, and then he moved, deliberately, so that he was between Ninian and the curtain wall. She found herself having to turn towards him, conscious that her face was lit now by all the light there was, the dim reflection from the moonlit river.

'Should I be expecting someone?' She kept her voice low, faintly amused, and very faintly seductive.

It was what she was here for – to distract any man who might interfere with Alexander's escape, especially if that man happened to be Gavin John Cameron. She owed him something, and this time it was she who would be in control. She had no conscience about it at all.

She could see his face as little more than a blur, but she sensed some kind of change in his expression. And when he said, 'Your husband, perhaps?' it was on a descending note, as if he were filling in an unwanted silence rather than asking a question.

The natural thing to do would have been to smile, and say, 'Alas, no! He is at Dess,' and move over to the gap in the battlements, and make some perceptive remark about the beauty of the landscape in winter.

But she couldn't, because a hundred feet or so beneath them, Alexander would still be visible negotiating his way down the rock face, fingers sunk in a fissure, toes resting on some tuft of roots, moving with care but always in danger of loosening the little fall of pebbles that would give him away to anyone who was there to hear. Ninian thought of Adam, down at the bottom with the horses, waiting; swearing under his breath in his anxiety to mount and be away.

'Alas, no,' she said and, slipping out from between Gavin Cameron and the wall, began walking towards the stairs, treading warily as if she were nervous of obstacles she might not see in the dark, and glancing back once or twice with a smile that spoke both of tension and a breathless, almost frightened invitation.

Not since Inverness had they been alone together. Let him think – let him think! – that those few spellbound moments when they had kissed were with her still. Let him think she wanted only to be in his arms again. Let him think anything he chose, as long as he moved away from the place where he might still look down and discover the king's escaping prisoner, spread-eagled on the hillside for all to see, like a piece of stitchery on a stretching board.

She thought, for a moment, that he wouldn't follow her, and then the tall, immobile, dark-robed figure stirred, and he did. He couldn't know, yet, that Alexander had gone, otherwise the hue and cry would have begun.

She would lead him on, down the steps to the courtyard, across to David's Tower, and in through the private side entrance at the foot of the stairs to the royal apartments. There would be no one in the waiting chamber on the ground floor. She would allow him, then, to take her in his arms if he wanted to; and he would, because she knew with absolute certainty that he had felt that kiss as she had, regardless of what had come after. And then, when she judged the time was right, she would break free, and perhaps give him a full-blooded, resounding, satisfying slap on that handsome, impassive face of his, and cut his arrogance down to size by telling him exactly what she thought of him. She was looking forward to it inordinately.

But long before any of that could happen, before they had even left the parapet, she felt his hand settle on her arm like a vice, and he swung her round and drew her with him into a patch of shadow.

With one arm round her, and his body brushing hers, he unlaced the ties of her cloak and pushed it aside. The cold air rushed in, chilling her in her low-cut court gown, whisking round her neck like a wind off the eternal snows. She could see the satiric gleam in his eyes, so close to hers, as, wordlessly and with exaggerated precision, he began to remove the pins from her hair, one by one, until the coiled locks fell like a heavy curtain about her shoulders. And then, with equal care, he laid the pins in a neat pile on the wall.

She didn't struggle, didn't move. As the terrible, beautiful, bone-melting excitement welled up inside her, she told herself that this was what she had intended. Nothing had changed.

Nor had it changed when his lips dropped to hers, and he kissed her.

It was the same. The same thrill, the same unstable joy, the same perfection and the knowledge of rightness. Except that now there was more. His long, capable fingers were smoothing themselves over her bare skin, and his lips were hardening, and she knew that, in a moment, she would have forgotten what she meant to do. Because she wanted him to go on. Dear God, she wanted him to go on.

But if she didn't stop him now, she never would.

And then, even as she braced herself, he raised his lips from hers and murmured, 'Perhaps you will tell me, when we have done, why you were so anxious to flirt with me.'

It didn't hurt, because she had been expecting something of the sort.

He gave her no opportunity to answer either the words or the mockery in his voice, and this time, as his mouth raked hers, she could feel the active stirring of his body where it held her own ruthlessly imprisoned against the wall. It was like some dream on the frontiers of waking, the cushioning cloak behind her and the weight of his robes between them muffling the raw desire that had taken both of them in its grip, lending it a kind of decency that was wholly spurious. And then his hands began easing back the shoulders of her gown, and as she stood there, shaking, the pale ghost of her resolve struggling to fight free of the emotional shambles of love and hate, stiff-necked pride and appalling physical pleasure that possessed her, he sank his face between her breasts and murmured, 'And you flirt most exquisitely. Do you find it works with everyone?'

Dear God, what did it take to break down the barriers he had erected against her? But it gave her the strength to do what she had intended. With a furious jerk of her body, she was away from him, and as he staggered, off balance, she brought her hand up and struck him with every last ounce of force she possessed. It wasn't a cold, calculated blow, as it would have been if everything had gone as she planned it, but one that carried with it all the flaring misery and anger that were in her.

'I flirt with *you*, and it works,' she gasped. 'Any whore in the stews could flirt with you, and it would work!'

There was a disastrous silence.

Gavin had suspected that, if Alexander had any idea of escaping, Ninian Drummond must be involved. When he had seen her standing alone on the ramparts, he had been sure of it, and surer still when she had tried to entice him away. It had angered him, as it had angered him at Inverness, that she thought she had only to flutter those spectacular eyelashes at him, and he would fall. That it happened to be true made no difference. He had decided to avail himself of her offer, briefly, to teach her a lesson, persuading himself that, while they were so engaged, she could scarcely be helping Alexander to escape. It had been a mistake, and his anger with himself was even greater than hers.

He said icily, 'I came in search of Alexander of the Isles, and I know that your only purpose in this last ten minutes has been to prevent me from finding him. I thought he might have some mad scheme of climbing out of the castle by way of the battlements, though it would need more than a single girl, however seductive, to help him accomplish that. But you know where he is.' He took her again, hard, by the arm. 'Where is he? *Tell me.*'

He would be down, and safe now, she was sure.

So she said, 'He has gone,' and, with bitter pleasure, led Gavin Cameron back to the gap in the ramparts. Because she knew what to look for, she saw them at once and, raising her hand, pointed to the two mounted figures, already in the middle distance, riding fast in the glimmering moonlight for the north and freedom.

'*Do you know what you have done?*' he said.

It was then, much too late, that a score of royal soldiers, routed out of their beds, fanned out into the courtyard to begin their search for the Lord of the Isles, who was said to be missing, and good luck to him.

5

GAVIN CAMERON had been savagely angry with her, allowing her not a word of argument, justification, or explanation. Yet even at his most fluent, he had kept his voice low and, when he had finished, he had pushed her roughly into the concealing dark beside the Wellhouse Tower and told her to remain there until she could return to her chamber without being seen. Then he had left her.

She saw no one on her way back but Lady Moragh, who favoured her with the calculating look Ninian remembered from the early days of their acquaintance, and then smiled and said, 'You iss looking ruffled.'

'Am I? I went out for a breath of fresh air and it turned out to be much fresher than I expected!' She was shivering, convincingly enough, and she hoped it accounted for the tremor in her voice, the tremor that betrayed the tears waiting in ambush for her when she was alone, and safe.

But there were more than tears waiting, for when she shot the bolt on her door and turned, with a sob of relief, she found Harry standing there, his face like a thundercloud.

It cost her most of her remaining control to say, 'Harry, my dear!' in tones of something resembling pleased surprise. 'I didn't expect you.'

'Didn't you? You sent for me.'

And then she remembered. She had hoped to wheedle out of him the whereabouts of Sir Robert Graham, so that she could find out what Adam and he were planning. And she still needed to know. She was obsessed, tonight, by the macabre feeling that in her own hands lay the threads of many lives.

'So soon, I meant. I didn't expect you so soon.'

'I can see that.'

She knew that her face was flushed, and her lips felt swollen, although she thought it mightn't show; but under the hooded cloak she was wildly dishevelled. An ill-timed giggle rose inside her and was immediately suppressed as she remembered the neat little pile of hairpins sitting outside forgotten on the ramparts.

There was a screen in the corner of the room. She went towards Harry, and kissed him lightly, and said, 'I will just make myself respectable. I have been out for some fresh air.'

But before she could reach her refuge, he stopped her. 'Fresh air — and what else?' He pulled off her cloak.

The unpinned hair she might have explained. But the new bruises on her arm she could not, nor the long, red graze just above the neckline of her gown, where the amethyst ring that symbolized Gavin Cameron's lordly celibacy had scraped across her skin as she tore herself from his grasp.

The rancour and contempt in her husband's eyes as he stood there, her cloak still in his hands, made her feel sick.

He threw the cloak down and moved behind her, but even as she turned, nervously, his hands came round, pressing into her stomach, searching, kneading, probing vindictively into its soft curves and valleys until she doubled over, choking. 'What are you doing?' she gasped.

He took his hands away. 'Nothing there?' he said sarcastically. 'When you have had almost six months to do as you pleased? How many men?' His fingers sank into her shoulders and he pulled her round to face him. '*How many?*' She had no real idea how this jealousy of his had started, or why.

Her eyes closed suddenly under the weight of exhaustion and disgust, and he shook her violently. 'Look at me! Dear cousin Adam, of course. And Alexander of the Isles. And who else? *Who else?*'

'Oh, Harry,' she said, her voice breaking. 'Neither of them – and no one else. I swear to you. Perhaps one or two men have tried to kiss me. What else can you expect at court? But no more than that, and it means nothing.'

He placed his fingers over the bruises on the soft flesh of her upper arm and squeezed them deliberately. 'This means nothing?'

She knew as clearly as if he had said so that he had spent these last few months of separation torturing himself, sure that he was missing something, feeling left out, and, because his imagination was too limited to think in any other terms, his jealousy had burgeoned until he had convinced himself that his wife was regularly unfaithful to him. On any other day, at any other hour, she might have persuaded him that it was not so.

But, although she understood, understanding was too frail a vessel to carry all the burdens life was placing on it tonight.

The cruel, numbing ache lancing up the whole length of her arm was the last straw. Tears leapt to her eyes, and to her heart a childish, spiteful need to retaliate, and she lashed out hard with her foot, catching him full on the shin with the toe of the wooden patten. It sounded like a whip cracking and he let out a grunt of shock and stood on one foot, hopping ridiculously, as the pain swelled, spread, and then slowly began to recede.

But it wasn't that that roused him to madness. It was what she said, unforgivably, afterwards. 'If only you would think with your head sometimes, instead of what you call your guts, you might realize that bruises are more likely to be a sign of resistance than acquiescence.'

He was in the wrong, of course. But she was a million times more so.

She knew it, and that she had never been to him what any man had a right to expect in a wife; that although she had not, in truth, sinned with her body, in her mind and heart she had played him false all the days of their life together. She condemned herself utterly.

And that was why she didn't fight when he snatched his knife from his belt, and slit her gown from neck to hem, and took her as coarsely and brutally as if she had been some girl from the stews.

As she lay there in her dark, deadly night of the spirit, her flesh bleeding where the knife had ripped it, her whole body flinching as her husband hammered himself into her, again and again and again, she knew with a fearful, superstitious certainty that tonight he would be potent, and tonight she would conceive.

CHAPTER THREE

I

SUMMER came early that year. After a week of alternating sun and rain, the trees had greened up in a single day. The primroses in the ditches around Edinburgh were a mass of pale, sweet yellow, and the wild cherries had scarcely shed their blossom before the apples and the barberries came into bloom. There was even a posy of briar rosebuds in the royal bedchamber.

It jumped six inches into the air as the king slammed his fist down on the table. 'I hold you personally responsible!'

There was nothing for Gavin to say. He had said it all before, just over two months ago when James had returned from Coldingham to discover that the Lord of the Isles had escaped.

And now, Alexander had celebrated his freedom by giving Inverness to the flames. Everything had gone except the castle, and Alexander was comfortably encamped outside it with two thousand men, waiting for it to surrender.

If you had done this . . . not done that . . . moved more swiftly to do the next thing . . . James went through it all over again. There was no room for other people's mistakes in his philosophy.

It was the first serious mistake Gavin had ever made, and he took the onus of it entirely on himself. He had said nothing of his belief that Atholl had been party to the whole thing; nothing of the French

265

envoy's intransigence; nothing of young Culbyn's incompetence; and nothing, above all, of Ninian Drummond. He had wondered, more than once, whether the queen had had her suspicions, because on the very next day the Lady Ninian had been granted several weeks' leave of absence from court, at her own most earnest request. It was unusual, because the queen was possessive about her ladies, and disliked them being away.

Something else Gavin had not said – that Alexander would have done precisely the same thing if he had simply been released instead of escaping. The king had intended to set him free at Easter.

At last, when he had roared himself out, James pushed the pudding-basin hat back from his forehead, leaving a dark red ring on the already flushed skin, and announced, 'I want every baron and knight in the kingdom to be at Urquhart castle by the tenth of next month. I'll take the field against Alexander myself. I want to know how many of his wild Hielandmen he's likely to be able to collect in that time, and I'll expect the barons and knights to bring enough followers to give me an army not less than half the size of his. I'm going to teach Alexander a lesson he'll never forget.'

Two weeks to send messengers all over the country; to persuade the barons to stir themselves; to give them time to gather their men together and march them all the way to Urquhart castle, fifteen miles south-west of Inverness. In the case of the Border lairds, that meant a six- or seven-day journey for the foot men, and five, perhaps four, for the horse.

'It's tight,' Gavin said.

'I don't care whether it's tight,' James bellowed, the veins springing to prominence again on his forehead. 'I want it done! And *you* can do it! And then you can come back here and look after the women and children while I sort out the trouble you've caused.'

Every last vestige of colour drained from his face, Gavin said, 'As you wish, sire.'

2

MANY of the barons could be trusted to obey the king's command without pressure having to be brought on them; especially when there was a fight in prospect. But the Lordship of the Isles had long been part of the intricate web of alliances that had made the Douglasses, the Hamiltons and the Lindsays the most independent of all James's nobles, and Gavin knew that only he himself could be sure of enlisting their active support against Alexander. Not because of the fluency of his arguments but because, having been secretary to Douglas in the past, his memory was stuffed full of the materials of blackmail. And in his present mood he wouldn't hesitate to use them.

Atholl was a different proposition, only too likely to refuse the king's demands because he didn't like the man who delivered them. But if James didn't choose to appeal to Atholl personally, his chancellor had no other choice; because, *enfant terrible* or not, Atholl was equally capable of taking offence if he felt he wasn't being accorded the respect that was his due. However, Gavin had the feeling that he would be able to swing the balance by judicious reference to the circumstances of Alexander's escape and an extravagant interest in seeing the damage caused by that very convenient 'fire'. While the king didn't want to upset his uncle, Atholl didn't dare alienate his nephew. The last royal relatives who had done so had found their heads on the block, and Gavin wouldn't hesitate to remind Atholl of it if he had to.

It was in this ruthless frame of mind that he set out on ten hard-riding days that began with the hundred-and-twenty miles from the Lindsays in the east, by way of the Douglasses in the south, to the Hamiltons in the west. After that came another hundred miles north to Blair Atholl; a side trip of eighty miles to Lochaber, accompanied not even by his body servant, for a conference he didn't mention to anyone; back across Rannoch Moor to pick up his escort again; and then to Edinburgh.

Everything went better than he had dared to hope, so that, when he found himself only two miles from Dess on his way back to Edinburgh, it seemed sensible to call in and make sure that Harry Graham was going to have his men ready in time. Gavin had no doubt at all that Robert Graham had been a prime mover in the Highland troubles of both last year and this, although it was impossible to prove – Gavin had tried – which meant that Harry Graham would be hoping to slide out of his obligations to the king. It was going to give Gavin, his temper in no way improved by ten days in the saddle in a Mediterranean heatwave, great personal pleasure to squash any such notion.

But Sir Harry, it seemed, was somewhere in the hills looking for a strayed heifer; the steward would send a message for him at once. In the meantime, the Lady Ninian could be fetched from the mews, if His Lordship would care to enter and be seated.

Repelled by the prospect, His Lordship said he had no time to sit down, nor was there any need to take Lady Ninian away from whatever task she was engaged on. Then he followed the steward across the yard to the castle's ramshackle-looking hawking establishment.

3

NINIAN didn't hear them at first. She was standing in a big, airy room with her gloved left hand extended, laughing up at a peregrine tiercel in whose huge marigold eyes was the frustrated expression of every half-moulted hawk since the Creation. He was flapping about just under the roof, staring hungrily down at the bait on her gauntlet as if he had no faith at all in his own ability to take it.

She called, 'Greensire!' and then again, 'Greensire! Come on, boy. Come on then!' and the hawk, visibly annoyed at being hurried, went into one unsuccessful stoop, and then a second, and then a third which brought him, wobbling precariously, to her wrist.

Amused in spite of himself, Gavin exclaimed, 'Bravo!' whereupon the tiercel, as surprised as his mistress, overbalanced completely and fell off in an affronted flurry of claws and wings and feathers.

She was careful, Gavin noticed approvingly, to see that the bird was back on his block, with jesses linked to the swivel and his leash fixed to the pin, before she turned, the echo of laughter still on her face, to discover who it was who had been responsible for upsetting Greensire's dignity.

Then all expression died and, as it did, Gavin felt his own face close. No more than he, it seemed, had she forgotten the terms on which they had parted on the battlements at Edinburgh. And yet, although Alexander's latest exploit had revived all Gavin's anger with her, as it had revived James's with him, he felt a sudden stab of regret at the disappearance of the warm, pretty, unaffected girl who had been there for an instant and then had gone, to be replaced by a cool young woman who looked strained and not very well. It didn't occur to him that she might be possessed neither by the dislike nor the resentment which he was half-reconciled to deserving, but by a far more complex mixture of emotions.

He was the last person she had expected to see. She had thought he would never forgive her, and yet there he was, standing before her with his eyes, for the briefest of moments, dancing, and the long, stern mouth curling in the smile she had dreamed of but never yet seen, a brilliant, infectious smile of the kind that sprang straight from the depths of the heart.

She had almost forgotten, after all this time of seeing him only in sober episcopal garb, what a striking figure he had made in the black leather brigandine tunic and trunk hose he had worn on that first day at Villeneuve. His dress was the same today, except that he had a white shirt carelessly open at the neck, and neither cloak, nor head covering, nor any sign of a tonsure.

Though he was dusty and visibly tired, the impression of animal and spiritual vitality was so strong that, in spite of all the cares that possessed her, she was almost overcome by her desire to laugh back at him, and hold her hands out, and say, simply, 'I love you.'

But nothing was simple, now. Nothing could ever be simple between them again.

And so they stared at each other, stiffly, until Ninian remembered herself and welcomed him to Dess, and Gavin said crisply that he was here only to ensure that Sir Harry was going to be able to muster the two hundred men required of him, and that they would be at Urquhart castle, a couple of days' march away, on the appointed date.

Lady Ninian should have been able to reassure him at once, but after she had floundered around for five minutes without giving him anything remotely resembling an answer, he decided it was as well he had come, after all. He hoped Sir Harry wouldn't be long.

He did make a concession, of sorts, to what he imagined her feelings to be. As they walked back across the courtyard, she thanked him – rather stiltedly – for not reporting to the king that she had been involved in Alexander's escape, and he said, 'The error was mine. Whether it was you or a whole troop of men-at-arms who helped him over the wall, the result was the same. If it is of any satisfaction to you, I am paying for it now.'

'Satisfaction!' she exclaimed – as if it had not been her sole object to make him pay for his contempt of her, his enmity towards Columba, his callousness about Blane, the whole aura of power and authority that surrounded him and still half fascinated and half repelled her.

Glancing at the hard, effective profile, she wondered why he should choose to say something so revealing to her, and because she was beginning to learn what it was to be herself, and alone, and accountable to no one – least of all Harry – for what she thought or felt, she said, 'The king?'

He hadn't expected her to take him up, but, to his surprise, found himself answering, 'Of course. The king has no patience with incompetence. Nor have I. And neither apology nor excuse can have any meaning when incompetence brings even one man's death in its train.'

'But if it's *competence* that brings one man's death in its train, that's all right?'

He turned sharply towards her, but all he could see in the intensely blue eyes was a frown of almost abstract interest, although the expression lines at the corners of her mouth were very pronounced.

'Your cousin?' he asked. It was not a subject he had any desire to pursue. He didn't want to find himself in the same trap again, talking of decision and responsibility and, by implication, free will. He still had nightmares about that, and wished he could be sure she had forgotten.

So he refrained from answering directly. 'Do you believe the church is more important than its individual members?'

'Yes.' It was what Columba had always maintained, even when he had first been deprived of his benefices.

'Then you should understand, too, that there are times when the good of the country – the good of *all* the people – must be more important than the fate of one, or two, or three of its individual members.'

She sighed, and began to walk on again. 'I suppose so. But I wish I understood more about so many things. I almost feel as if, having helped Alexander to escape, I am personally responsible for having plunged half the country into a state of war.'

If she had hoped for reassurance, she was disappointed. Inhuman though Gavin Cameron usually appeared, his mind was as susceptible as his body to normal human impulses. 'Oh, you are,' he said outrageously, in a tone she had never heard before but which Tom Myrton would have recognized.

'I . . . You . . . *Am I?*' She stopped again, looking as if she didn't know whether to laugh or cry. Surprisingly, it was the laughter that won.

And then she turned away and said seriously, 'I do assure you that I had no idea at all that Alexander would do what he has done. He swore to me that all he wanted was to be home again, among his own people, and in the landscape he loves.' She paused, and added wistfully, 'He made the Isles, and the whole of the western Highlands, sound very beautiful.'

'They are.' He said nothing more for some time, because there was only one thing he wanted – could even think of – to say. It was, 'I will take you there some day, to Kinveil.'

Long ago he had persuaded himself that, if ever he were to fall in love, he would have the strength of character to withstand it, not because of his vows but because in any continuing liaison between a priest and a woman it was the woman on whom Holy Church laid the major burden of sin. For a man, a lover, to collude in that had always seemed to Gavin contrary to the very nature of love.

He had been fortunate until now, perfectly reconciled to a life of transient affaires, closely guarded – except on one unforgettable occasion – and giving release to his body while touching his emotions not at all. He had never met a woman who had attracted him more than briefly; certainly none with whom, even if circumstances had permitted, he would have chosen to share his life.

But now . . . He didn't believe it. It was a hallucination, brought on by this sudden hour's respite after the physical stress of these last ten days.

He said, 'Yes, the western Highlands are very beautiful.'

And then Ninian pointed and said, 'There's my husband. Oh, he's found the heifer! Shall we go and meet him?'

Bishop Gavin spoke to Sir Harry briskly and to the point. There were penalties for disobeying even the king's lightest command, he said, and this was no light command. It would be well for a young man whose family did not stand well with the crown to take care not to offend his sovereign lord, particularly in a situation such as this. No excuses would be acceptable.

And thank you, but no. The bishop had neither the time nor the desire for refreshment.

Then he was gone.

4

SEVERAL hours later, in the June dusk that, as far north as Dess, never quite achieved the status of darkness, the little heifer that had found her way up into the hills again paused in her methodical chewing to listen to a sound strange among the night sounds of Ben Vrackie. After a while, as she watched, the rustling and scrambling resolved themselves into two strangers on Highland ponies appearing over the brow of the hill from the west. Soon after, two other people, whom the heifer knew well, arrived on foot from the south-east. Inquisitive as all her kind, she began to drift over towards them until she was breathing damply and amorously down Harry Graham's neck.

Impatiently, he pushed her away. 'Of course I'm getting my men together! After that kind of threat, what else can I do? And why are we meeting here secretly anyway? Why couldn't you just come to the house? There's no law against it!'

'I prefer not to advertise my activities,' his uncle said calmly. 'And what you can do is take your time about getting to the rendezvous. You won't be the only one. I have visited most of James's less ardent supporters in the last few days and given them the same message. If you judge it well, we should have reduced the royal army to a rabble before you even get there.'

'Are you sure?' Harry asked.

It was a source of regret to Sir Robert that his nephew had so little stomach for a fight. 'If God wills,' he said.

He sounded very sure that God *would* will. Ninian, able to distinguish his features only as a dark cross in the pallor of his face, envied him his certainty that he was engaged on the work of God. She would rather have put it down to the devil. Or perhaps to the vainglory of man.

Harry was still looking doubtful, and Adam said, 'My dear Harry, God can scarcely do other than will, after all the effort we have expended. Everything has been most carefully arranged, and it has involved calculations of the most intricate!'

'Calculations?' Ninian asked. She wasn't sure why she had come, except that she had thought Adam might have news of Columba.

Sir Robert didn't dismiss her question as if she were just a woman

272

and therefore stupid. He said, 'We have allowed it to be known that Alexander can muster six thousand men. James will probably decide to satisfy himself with only half as many. It is the right odds for him, because he will be fielding a modern army of knights, archers, and men-at-arms, many of them mounted and most of them well equipped, against an undisciplined mob of Highlanders with only the most rudimentary weapons.

'If James were to find himself with *more* than three thousand men, a victory over such opponents would earn him little credit, and he might not even trouble to take the field himself. But with too many fewer, he could back out altogether, without loss of face. And we do not want that. So it has been my object to ensure that precisely three thousand men turn up at Urquhart castle on the due date.'

Adam laughed. 'Both Bishop Gavin and the king should be grateful to Sir Robert, do you not think?'

He was standing with his arm carelessly round Ninian's shoulders, but Harry didn't even notice.

For the first few weeks after their return from Edinburgh, Harry had scarcely even spoken to her, and then only as if she were a servant who was out of favour. It was one of the accepted ways of dealing with erring wives, and less harsh than some, but that didn't make it any easier. So Ninian had tried to learn all over again what she had forgotten – what she had wanted to forget – how to be a good and thoughtful helpmeet. But before long, knowing more of human nature than she had done before, she had come to realize that Harry derived a kind of pleasure out of feeling wronged. It was as if he was never happy unless he was miserable.

He wasn't the kind of person to help set things right, and after a while she herself had stopped trying. She had gone out on the moors one day, quite alone, to think. She didn't like the moors – sometimes she almost hated them – but there was something there that stripped away convention and self-delusion, the things that fogged one's mind and spirit. She had looked at herself, and looked at Harry, and thought that it was time for her to stop taking everything on her own shoulders. It wasn't possible to build a marriage, or anything else, on abasement and apology.

With a little of her self-respect restored to her, she had gone back to the castle prepared to make concessions within reason, but no more, and she and Harry had been living for the last month in a state of arm's-length, just bearable truce. But there was something she had to say to him before he rode away to the rendezvous at Urquhart, something she ought to say to him tonight, that might change everything. Or might not.

He said now, his jaw hanging loose, 'But – but if Alexander hasn't far more than twice as many men as James, the king'll be able to make collops of you!'

Despite everything, Ninian was embarrassed for him. 'I think Sir Robert is telling us that Alexander will really have a much greater army.'

'Well, why can't he say so!'

Sir Robert bent his head and carefully began tightening his pony's girthstraps. 'It will be instructive to see what kind of soldier James turns out to be.'

The tone, more than the words, set Ninian's spine prickling. 'To *see*?' she exclaimed. 'Do you mean to be there, at the battle? To commit yourself openly? But surely . . .'

Sir Robert straightened up. 'This time, yes. This time I myself intend to measure swords with James.'

She turned to Adam and his white teeth flashed in a grin. 'And I! How can I stand aside when victory is assured?'

'But if you are there openly, and recognized, and something should go wrong! Adam, you would have to leave Scotland, and how could you help Columba then?'

Even as she said it, she wondered what had possessed her. Because he seemed to bring Scotland nothing but trouble, trouble on an alarming scale, and all because he thought he *was* helping Columba. If only he would go – go anywhere – the world might return to sanity. She had the illogical feeling that Robert Graham, alone, would be far less dangerous.

Adam's teeth flashed again. 'Ah! Would you miss me, *mignonne*?'

And then, as Harry took her by the elbow and pulled her roughly out of Adam's grasp, she snapped, 'Life would certainly be more peaceful!'

But however much he might anger her, he was still the idol of her childhood, and still Columba's son – his only son now. She couldn't bear the thought that anything might happen to him. 'Oh, Adam, Adam! Why should you want to be involved? Why rush into danger? It isn't even your country! You've declared war on Gavin Cameron – and war now on the king! – all for Columba's sake. If you were to be killed, it would a thousand times outweigh any good you might have done. If you were killed, it would kill Columba, too!'

Adam threw back his head and laughed. 'What a fuss! But have no fear, little one. Even the Highlanders have never seen my face. Trite though it may be, I keep my visor down always. They call me the Red Lord, and believe that it is no man inside my mail, but the ghost of the Wolf of Badenoch! It is quite amusing, in fact. And as for being killed, or even wounded – show me the clod of a Scots archer or man-at-arms who could penetrate my good French armour!'

'What you mean is, you enjoy it! Battle and bloodshed and death! It's exciting, it's spectacular, it's what a man should do. But it isn't, Adam! *Grand dieu*, what would Columba say!'

'You will be able to ask him soon. That was why I came with Graham tonight, to tell you that Columba is in England even now, and on his way here on some commission for His Holiness.' She had offended him, and it was said with a kind of jealous triumph. 'And this battle will be my welcome for him! *Now* he will see what his son can accomplish!'

Even through the sudden, overwhelming relief, she became aware of an extra stillness in Sir Robert Graham, less of surprise at the open avowal of Adam's relationship to Columba, she thought, than of an abstract interest in having his suspicions confirmed. She managed a wry smile at him, as if it wasn't really a matter of any great importance, and in the already lightening sky she saw his mouth twist in response.

It was time for them to be gone. Harry had already turned away, pushing the errant heifer before him, when Ninian reached up and kissed Adam's cheek – in forgiveness, affection, she didn't know what. 'Be careful,' she murmured.

And that was all, even though a vision of Blane dancing on the rope's end stayed with her all the way back to the castle.

5

IT was one of the hardest things she had ever had to do, but she could postpone it no longer. As soon as she and Harry were back in the privacy of their bedchamber, she busied herself, falsely, rummaging for a fresh shift in the clothing chest, while Harry as usual dropped all his clothes on the floor and climbed straight into bed.

She said, 'Harry, I have something to say to you.'

'At this hour of the night? Leave it. I need my sleep.'

And then she turned and faced him. She had been trying for days to decide how to phrase it, to rob him in advance of all the cruel words that would spring to his tongue, but she hadn't found an answer. The best she could manage was a quiet, 'Don't you want to know that I am carrying another son for you? And that this time I will be sure he comes to birth?'

There was an interminable moment of breath-held quiet, and then he sat up abruptly. 'Another son for *me*? Don't you mean for Adam? Or Alexander? How can you tell?' His fair skin was flushed and the strong muscles of his neck stood out like cords.

'I can tell very easily. I have lain with no man but you.'

She watched the doubts and the questions chase themselves over his face, and the hopes, and their rejection. He wanted a son so much.

So she put every ounce of truth and conviction into her voice when she went on, 'Oh, Harry! Can you not believe me? Can you not take my word against that of the gossips? Have you ever known me – and I mean *known* me – to do anything a good wife shouldn't do?'

It was a mistake, because she could see from his face that he was remembering, as she was, the state she had been in on that last night at Edinburgh – the night when this seed had been sown in her womb. By Harry, not by anyone else.

She hurried on, 'Can you not believe me *now*? Must you wait until he is born, so that you can see for yourself how like you he is?' As she prayed to God that he would be.

Prayed to God, but not to Harry. She knew that he was waiting for her to weep, and beg, and persuade, and she might have brought herself to do even that if she had thought it would serve any useful purpose. But all it would do, she thought, would be to feed his carefully tended superiority. It might even make things worse. So she stood with her head high, and her face white and strained, and waited while he lay down again, and turned his back on her, and said, 'Then, I might believe it. Now, I need my sleep.'

After a moment, she took her shift and robe, and went to one of the small guest chambers to live through another night of fear – the fear that would stay with her until the child was born, and perhaps beyond.

GAVIN, sometimes at Edinburgh, sometimes at Glasgow, was furiously busy during the next two weeks, interrupted daily by messengers from James bearing instructions, complaints, and news of his progress.

The rebel army had chosen not to sit tamely waiting for James at Inverness, but to lead him a merry dance up and down the mountains. James had thought, to begin with, that Alexander was running away, but his followers had stayed with him, so it couldn't be that. The other possibility was that he was trying to even the odds by wearing James's levies out before the battle, because the heavily armed royal troops were by no means as nimble as the lightly equipped Highlanders, nor as used to the terrain.

'God save us, but they're clumsy!' James wrote. 'This very day, when I wanted to send a ballista across the water to lay siege to the Lordship's castle of Brochel, there was an accident which enraged me beyond bearing.'

Gavin could guess what was coming next, because James wouldn't have turned a hair if it had just been an accident to the men, whereas the ballista was one of his most expensive playthings, an immense, windlass-operated crossbow of unheard-of accuracy. As a siege weapon, it was invaluable – once it had been got into position. Getting it there was the problem.

James went on, 'You may know Brochel – set on the strangest rock I have ever seen, purple-brown in colour and studded with small black nodes, as if some cookboy had scattered it with raisins of Corinth! But although it is unscaleable and said to be impregnable, I believe it could not withstand the kind of weapons we have nowadays. So I instructed the serjeant to land the ballista on the green slopes to the south, and all went well until, just as the men were heaving it across the plank from boat to shore, some great, screaming birds appeared – shags, or gannets, or some such, I could not see from where I was on the mainland – and began to dive at them. Whereat our fine, courageous soldiers dropped the ballista so that they could protect their own heads. The shaft of the machine is quite wrecked and must be replaced. Oblige me by ordering a new one next time you are sending to Flanders.'

A day or two later, there were more complaints of the men's unhandiness. 'This night we camp at a place with the uncouth name of Dalchreichart where the glen opens out into a wide, narrow plain. I had some targets set up to test the longbow men, but soon had to retire to my tent. It is five years now since I forbade men to play golf and football under pain of fine, so that they might practise at the butts instead! Five years! And not one man in three could hit what he aimed at. It is as well that the Highlanders have but shortbows. When this campaign is over, something must be done.'

It seemed to Gavin that James, distracted by ballistae and target practice and all the other immediate harassments of the pursuit, was missing a vital point. Alexander might, indeed, be trying to wear James out, but that was by no means his only reason for leading him such a dance.

Though it wasn't a chancellor's – and certainly not a bishop's – place to comment on military matters, Gavin couldn't ignore it. He knew that, even if James had made an effort to find out the real size of Alexander's force, the best answer he would be likely to get from any eye-witness in the glens would be, 'Och, a great host, a great host. As many as would cover aal the side of Ben Loyne – inteet, yess!'

He worded his message carefully. 'My own personal knowledge of the Highlands leads me to suspect that Alexander may be collecting reinforcements from the clans through whose territory he is passing. If that is so, then you may find yourself facing, not five or six thousand men, but ten thousand or more. I have no doubt that you will defeat them, but it is well to be forewarned.'

No more than anyone else did Gavin know the quality of James's leadership in the field. He had never been tested before. But at least he had been in France with Henry V, however reluctantly, and must surely have learned something about tactics. If he hadn't, if he lost, the results didn't bear contemplating.

Gavin shrugged his shoulders and went back to the problem of next month's truce negotiations on the Borders. The question occupying him at the moment was whether England's recent defeats at the hands of the extraordinary French girl known to her allies as Joan the Maid, and to her enemies as the Witch of Domrémy, would make his talks easier, or more difficult.

7

IT was June 23, and a fine, sunny, blowy day under the looming presence of Ben Nevis. It was also that hour of the morning when, in a civilized country, a man would be coming in from his early ride, his appetite sharp for pottage and leche meats and a cup of good wine.

But although the thought passed fleetingly across Adam's mind, for once it was untinged with regret. His stomach might be clapping against his ribs with hunger, the landscape might be one of blacks and purples and virulent greens instead of the white and sand colours of his beloved south, and the company such as he would never willingly have chosen, but excitement was the breath of life to him and he was intoxicated by the prospect that lay ahead.

He knew that his feelings must be visible, audible, almost tangible, and glanced obliquely at the immobile Robert Graham, sitting his horse a yard away, looking just like the statue of Marcus Aurelius on the Capitol hill, even to the pointing arm. Although the horse didn't have a barbarian under its foot – yet.

Without expression, Sir Robert said, 'There's Harry with his men. James must have sent back to Urquhart to round up the latecomers. A pity. I have no great desire to cross swords with my own kin.'

Adam's eyes followed his. 'Oh, yes,' he said pensively, identifying the quarterings of Harry's surcoat amid the furious kaleidoscope of yellows, whites, red, blues and blacks that made up the knightly division of James's army. 'Then perhaps you had better keep to the other side of the field.'

'I spoke metaphorically. I intend to cross swords only with James, or anyone who blocks my path to him.'

'You will be busy.'

The panorama spread out below the ridge on which they sat was like nothing Adam had ever seen before, although to Robert Graham it was familiar. As a fifteen-year-old squire he had been at Harlaw – on the regent's side – when Alexander's father had clashed with a royal army under the leadership of the Earl of Mar.

This would be Alexander's first pitched battle, as it was the king's, but warfare was in his blood and he had needed little in the way of advice from Sir Robert when he was planning his tactics. All the way from Inverness he had known precisely where he intended to make his stand – in a valley not far from his own Inverlochy castle, where the foothills of Ben Nevis opened out into a plain covered with grass and scrub and slashed through the middle by a narrow river running shallow over its bed of flat stones. The ground was marshy, he said, fine for his light-footed Highlanders, fatal for heavy cavalry.

He had been ready before dawn, with his ten thousand men marshalled in their traditional, crescent-shaped battle line, even if the numbers were so great that the crescent was more theoretical than real. To the uninstructed eye, the wild-haired, saffron-shirted men seemed to swarm like red ants all over the eastern half of the valley, their backs to Ben Nevis and the rising sun, their faces to the river, where Alexander's bard was fulfilling his hallowed duty of reciting all three hundred lines of praise, invocation and genealogy that constituted the battle song of the Lords of the Isles. 'Sons of Conn remember, fearlessness in time of strife . . .'

After the first twenty or so everyone had stopped listening, because James and his army had begun lumbering into sight on the other side of the river to form up according to the pattern that had become orthodox since Edward III of England first used it at the battle of Crécy, more than eighty years ago. There were three main bodies, with the knights in the centre and, somewhat forward of them to right and left, a division of dismounted men-at-arms with bowmen on their flanks.

So far, save that the marsh had dried out after the long weeks of hot, dry weather, everything was exactly as Alexander had foreseen, for it had been one of his main objects to ensure that James's knights would be seriously hampered – possibly neutralized – by having the river to ford and the sun full in their eyes.

Neither Adam nor Sir Robert Graham would have denied that the principle was admirable. It was just that the practice seemed to be going wrong, because James was refusing to cooperate.

According to all the traditions of war, his cavalry should have initiated the battle as soon as everyone was in position by charging straight towards the lightly armed ranks of its opponents with the aim of sinking a huge metal wedge into the crescent and splitting it in two for the archers and men-at-arms to deal with.

Alexander's theory had been that the river crossing would reduce the momentum of the charge, and that the knights would be hot and bad-tempered in their cumbersome armour and scarcely able to see with the sun full in their visor slits. All it needed, he had said, was for the Highlanders to wait until the cavalry was almost upon them, and then a few hundred men, crouching low out of the knights' visored line of vision, could stop them in their tracks by slipping in and hamstringing the horses. When a fully armed knight landed incontinent on the ground, it took him a very long time to struggle to his feet again. Today, Alexander had said, none would live to make the attempt.

But three hours had passed, and there was no sign of any charge or even of preparation for it. The knights had not yet troubled to mount, and James, a vision of red-on-gold lions rampant over black plate armour, had set up his standard on the rising ground behind his central division and appeared to be sharing a cheerful repast with his entourage.

Adam said, 'You'll never get to him. He's too closely surrounded, and he doesn't look as if he intends to do any fighting himself.'

There was scorn in his voice, but Sir Robert said judiciously, 'Don't underestimate him. It's not cowardice, I think, but because he has no son to succeed him. He believes the country cannot afford to have him die. Even so, it is my intention to try what may be achieved.'

And then, without any perceptible change of tone, he added, 'The clansmen are becoming impatient.'

It was the kind of thing one could scarcely fail to notice, ten thousand men fidgeting, every one bearing an axe, a knife, and a circular oxhide shield, and wearing no more than a saffron shirt knotted between his legs to give him ease of movement. But where the movement had at first been inchoate, a matter of vague swirls and eddies across the whole surface of the crescent, it had suddenly become purposeful at the far end.

Adam said, 'Trouble!' as Alexander, in quilted war coat and high, conical helmet, spurred his tough little black pony towards it. There was an interval of talk and gesticulation between Alexander and a handful of the chiefs, their men standing stiff around them and the atmosphere of rancour drifting towards those who were watching like smoke on the wind.

'What the devil?' Adam exclaimed, and Sir Robert made a silencing gesture as if nothing must disturb the intensity of his concentration. His eyes were like a thin jet line in the unremarkable contours of his face.

Alexander had his hand on his sword, but the chiefs were shaking their heads. And then they signed to those behind them and, unbelievably, something like two thousand men began to move forward, shambling towards the river and across it. That their purpose was in no way belligerent was obvious to everyone.

Before James's men-at-arms had even moved forward to lead the chiefs towards the royal standard, the other eight thousand of Alexander's Highlanders had erupted into such frenzy that Alexander could no longer have held them back, even had he wanted to.

As they surged madly forward, all idea of tactics lost in fury against the deserters, Adam said briefly, 'Who?'

And Sir Robert Graham, his eyes opening wide, replied, 'Can you not guess? The Camerons.' Then he laid spurs to his horse and went hurtling down the hillside to join the clans.

Adam waited only a moment, and followed.

If they had known, James had been as surprised as anyone at the defection of the Camerons. He had been holding back from action not because he was waiting for deserters, but for quite other reasons. As soon as he had seen the field of battle, he had decided that his only hope of victory lay in enticing Alexander into taking the offensive.

So, when the frenzied Highlanders rushed into action, he was ready for them. His longbow men, however inadequate at the butts, could scarcely miss when there were eight thousand men, unable to retaliate, scrambling over the rough ground and through the water towards them, and they fitted, and drew, and sighted their arrows like veterans, and the twang of the bowstrings and purr of grey goose-feathers through the air was sweet in James's ears. The steel points fell glittering like rain on the enemy, and the sheaves of arrows vanished so swiftly that there were scarcely enough lads to fetch replacements from the arrow wagons. Less than half the Highlanders even succeeded in crossing the river.

Then the archers gave the lads their bows for safe keeping, and drew the axes and swords from their belts, and joined the men-at-arms and the knights, unmounted and virtually unassailable, in fighting hand-to-hand.

Adam, a magnificent athlete trained in the jousting field, fought for a while, and hard. Only once did he raise his visor, and there was a grin on his sweating face as he looked down at the sprawled body of a stalwartly built, fair-complexioned young knight in old-fashioned armour, the great artery of his thigh severed by a sword cut that had bypassed the leg plate. There was a lot of blood, but most of it was soaking away quickly into ground thirsty after six weeks of drought.

Adam wiped the rest of it from his blade, and then, turning the body over with a careless foot, took the ring from Harry's finger.

The time came soon when there was no longer any doubt about which way the battle would go. Alexander would not leave, but Adam and Sir Robert Graham, who had fought like a demon without progressing nearer to James by a single inch, met again on the ridge, as if by prior appointment, and rode off as fast as their weary horses would carry them, towards the east and safety.

There was blood on both of them, but none of it was theirs.

CHAPTER FOUR

NOT for years had Columba enjoyed a journey so much. The treasury had been uncommonly generous in the matter of funds, and the respect accorded everywhere to a papal envoy warmed his soul most pleasantly. Nor was there any need for haste, for he had no urgent desire to reach his destination. There was too much joy in anticipation.

Unhurriedly, he progressed from Rome to Parma, Pavia to Besançon, Rheims to Peronne, and finally to Bruges. It was a sadness that so little of his route lay through France, but the years had done nothing to diminish his instinct for self-preservation, and France – more of a battle ground than it had ever been – was not a place to linger in these days, a place of blackened ruins, uncultivated fields, roads vanished forever in a wilderness of brambles and weeds.

When he reached London, he found that it, too, was humming with war fever. In the fourteen years since Agincourt, the English had thought it only a matter of time until the whole of France was in their keeping, and their sudden defeats on the Loire – and at the hands of a peasant girl – were now being used as ammunition by the great nobles battling for supremacy at home during the minority of England's boy king. As Columba made his rounds with the various confidential messages entrusted to him by the curia, he kept his eyes and ears open for all the tiny details that might some day, alone or together, give

Rome a lever in the manoeuvrings that were inseparable from the exercise of power. It was the kind of thing he was very good at.

And then, as June drew to its sun-drenched close, he sent a messenger off to the curia as fast as the man's purse and brains would carry him, and was free to set out on the final stage of his journey, which would take him to Scotland and the encounter he had been savouring in his imagination ever since he had left Rome three months before.

Since he had talked to all the right people, he knew exactly where he would find Gavin Cameron, and that it should be in Teviotdale was an irony he greatly relished.

On July 12, as he and his little cavalcade emerged from the Cheviot Hills just above Yetholm, he could see, even from five miles away, the wide flat field of the Hawdenstank, right on the bank of the river Tweed, right on the boundary between Scotland and England, and the most favoured meeting place when the two countries had sensitive business to discuss. For most of the year, the Hawdenstank was featureless, flat and untenanted; too open, and much too close to the Border for anyone but a passing reiver. But today – depending on the eye of the beholder – it looked either like an armed camp or a cheerful little fairground, alive with people and horses, and covered with straight-walled, conically-roofed tents, with pennants flying from their bright summits.

It was early evening when Columba rode into the camp, and began searching for the tent of the Scottish chancellor. He could have asked, but it was more interesting, more instructive, to look for himself. As he quartered the field with its separate clusters of tents, some tidy, some not, he noted that the most pristine of the English ones belonged to the Earl of Salisbury, who had been Richard Neville until his father-in-law had obligingly had himself killed at Orléans, a mere two months ago. And next to Salisbury's tents were those of the Earl of Northumberland. Columba had no need to refer to the liveries or escutcheons; the earl himself was lounging outside, the man who had once been Harry Percy and was still as wiry, still as silver-fair of hair as he had always been, though very much harder of eye.

Beyond Percy's tents was a pavilion, the neutral territory on which the commissioners presumably met to argue their cases. The English would be complaining that James hadn't paid his ransom – but not too loudly, in case James stopped merely dickering with the French and entered into a properly signed and sealed alliance. And the Scots would be making a fuss about England subsidizing the Scots rebels who had fled to Ireland after Albany's execution – but not too much of a fuss, in case England refused to agree to another exchange of hostages. Columba's mouth twitched. He would have been prepared to wager that all the two sides would agree on would be better policing of the cattle reivers on the Borders.

Then his breath caught in his throat, because he had come to the Scots tents and there, outside one of them, was Gavin Cameron himself, deep in conversation with Bishop Alexander of Galloway.

Cameron looked up, half turning, and the sun cast the bones of his face into high relief against the black of his hair and the grey, shining fall of the tent flap. There were deep shadows at the outer corners of his eyes, almost as if he were amused.

But that was impossible.

Columba dismounted, and bowed, and Cameron said, 'Welcome back to your benefice, Archdeacon,' just as if these last two years had never happened.

Columba smiled, releasing his reins to a groom, and began carefully to shake out his robes. Dust rose from them, thick as smoke, and there was a strong smell of horse. By the time he had finished, Cameron had expertly disposed of Bishop Alexander, blue-eyed, cherubic, and bursting with curiosity, and was standing with one long, flexible hand raised, ushering Columba into his tent.

It was pleasant to sit down on something that didn't rattle one's guts around, pleasant to be relatively cool and to be given a cup of unexpectedly good wine to wash the grit from one's throat. Pleasantest of all to postpone the purpose of one's errand by making meaningless small talk.

Even so, he didn't succeed in forcing Cameron to ask why he was here. The bishop, nodding politely and contributing an occasional remark, peaceably occupied himself tidying away all his rolls of parchment, his note blocks, his pens, and seemed likely to go on doing so forever unless Columba stopped him.

As at last he did.

His satisfaction threatening to choke him, but his eyes hooded and his lips as luxuriantly soft as those of some Greek Apollo, Columba presented Cameron with the citation he had carried for three months next to his heart. And then he waited.

He had not expected shock, anger, or dismay, or not visibly, although he had had a curious dream in which Cameron had pleaded for his help and understanding, as a woman might plead with her lover. But that, he thought, was because they were tied together by some strange, mystic bond of hatred and dependence.

He hadn't expected anything obvious, but knowing humanity as he did, he had certainly expected to glimpse something of what the man felt. Yet he sat, every nerve alive for Cameron's response, and there was nothing at all.

The chancellor read the citation aloud, faintly bored. '". . . crimes before consecration . . . statutes against ecclesiastical liberty and the rights of the Roman church . . . simony in the collation of benefices . . . so guilty as to deserve deprivation. . . ." Mmmm. And I am to appear in Rome in person to answer the charges.'

He laid the document down, and his grey eyes gave away no more than his voice as he went on, 'But I fear, archdeacon, that when – or indeed whether – I obey this papal summons is a matter not for me, but for the king.'

Columba was disappointed, but unsurprised. He had known that Cameron would be bound to say something of the sort. His most charming smile deepening the chasms that ran from nostrils to mouth, he replied, 'Then let us go to him together.'

It was then that he discovered just how much Cameron knew, because the chancellor, with a smile scarcely less charming and far more ingenuous, said, 'If you wish. But I should warn you that His Majesty is in Inverness. You may not know that only about two weeks ago he put down a dangerous rebellion in the Highlands . . .'

The sun must be getting low, Columba thought, feeling a chill on his back. He could hear the crackling of dry grass as someone passed outside, and there was a raucous English voice in the distance, shouting something he couldn't make out.

'. . . and is still engaged on rounding up the last of the rebels. There is one he is particularly anxious to find – a man known only as the Red Lord, from the clothing he wears. Curious how one's mind works, don't you think? There was one name that came immediately into my head. But it could not be M. de Verne, could it, despite his penchant for red? What interest could he possibly have in the affairs of the Highlands?'

Moving forward, Gavin took the empty cup from Columba's hand and turned away to put it on the table. 'I have not, of course, mentioned this to His Majesty, since I would not wish to have him suspect an innocent man.'

It was a threat, scarcely disguised. But it told Columba that, even if the rising had failed, Adam had escaped. It told him, too, by its very lack of subtlety, that Cameron was far from being impervious to the citation – or to the man who had brought it.

2

IT was a long, tedious, largely silent ride, during which the two men learned nothing about each other at all. It would have been difficult to talk, even if they had wanted to, in the lacklustre company of Gavin's two fellow commissioners, William Fowlis and fussy old John Forrester.

Columba's irritation over Adam's flamboyant courting of danger was far outweighed by his worry about the boy. Where was he now, and in what frame of mind? That Cameron, who had already been responsible for Blane's death, should now threaten Adam as well, filled Columba with an intensity of loathing beyond anything of which he would have thought himself capable. If his opposition to Cameron had begun, almost imperceptibly, to fade in the glow of his own triumph over the citation, it was now restored to its fullest power.

Gavin, however, though he could hardly fail to sense the hostility of the man riding beside him, gave little thought either to the archdeacon or his troublesome family, because, to his surprise, the summons to appear at Rome had brought him face to face not only with his conscience but with his faith. It was disconcerting to find himself shocked by his own attitude to the summons from the Holy See, which he thought of as little more than an irritating irrelevance.

All his life he had been in the same, intolerable quandary of being possessed too much by reason and too little by personal knowledge of the faith that begins where reason ends.

In his boyhood, he had assumed, as everyone did, that God and His church were inseparable, and had concluded from the church's cruelty and selfseeking that the idea of a benevolent God was a contradiction in terms. But he had been too dedicated to his own private ambitions to be much troubled.

In the years since then, nothing had happened to improve his view of the church, even though his idea of God had slowly begun to change. He had found himself very much attracted to William of Ockham's view – which was also that of Wyclif and the Lollards – that every

288

individual, without interference from the church, should interpret the laws of the Bible for himself, and was aware, too, of a growing desire to discover how the God he knew could be reconciled with that Son of God who was also the loving, forgiving brother of Everyman.

And in that thought alone, he reflected, there were at least three major heresies.

But ever and always, he returned to the question that mattered most deeply to him. Were the laws of the church indeed the laws of God?

All through the ride north, he worried at the problem without coming any nearer to a solution, until, just beyond Dunkeld, Archdeacon Crozier suggested that they should seek hospitality that night at the home of his niece, the Lady Ninian Drummond, whose tower house of Dess was not far away.

Since that had been Gavin's intention all along, he nodded and pulled his horse's head round to the east.

3

WHEN Ninian, surrounded by deeds and documents and all the lesser impedimenta of a dead man's past, heard the watchman's trumpet and glanced out of the window of the Speak-a-Word room to see the black-and-silver liveries and streaming pennants that proclaimed the approach of the Bishop of Glasgow, she was struck first by a nervous surprise and then by a blessed sensation of deliverance. Because, riding with him – riding *with* him – was Columba.

Not even pausing to wonder why they should be together, she ran straight from the Speak-a-Word room on to the outer staircase, and all the time she stood there waiting, the words 'Columba! Oh, Columba!' were ringing like an anthem in her heart.

She greeted Gavin Cameron politely, of course, noticing that his forbidding manner had returned in full force, but her whole attention was on Columba. Freed from the restraint of Harry's jealousy, she threw her arms round him, trying not to weep, but her heart was in the eyes she raised to his. Columba's own eyes were wet, and she thought that probably neither he nor Gavin Cameron had known of Harry's death until they had seen her standing on the staircase, black-clad and alone, and guessed.

She wouldn't let them talk of Harry at first. The speech tumbling from her lips was all questions, questions first about Columba, and about Sévèrine, and then, as her excitement calmed a little, about his journey.

'And when you were in France, did you hear anything about Joan the Maid? What's happened?'

His mobile mouth turned down in self-mockery. 'I heard a good deal of superstitious gossip about some peasant girl who claimed she could save France for the Dauphin. And that, I thought, would be a miracle.'

'Which it was!'

'Don't remind me. I have lost all faith in my own judgement. I reached Bruges to find the streets buzzing with the news that she had just forced the English to raise the siege of Orléans.'

'What were they saying in London?'

'You can imagine. But your royal mistress's uncle, Cardinal Beaufort, is not going to be popular with His Holiness. When I arrived, his crusade against the heretics of Bohemia was said to be ready to set out at last, but by the time I left, all the talk was of persuading him to take his three thousand spearmen and archers to France instead.'

And that was very interesting. Gavin said, 'Is it likely to happen?'

'It's possible. The English have nothing personally against the Hussites of Bohemia, but they have a very great deal against the Maid of Orléans.'

Gavin watched the pair of them as they sat there talking, and envied them their relationship, which was of a kind he had never known. And as he watched, he acknowledged to himself at last what he had been fighting against ever since that day at Inverness, almost a year ago.

Seeing, now, a side of her he had never seen, the warmth and the tenderness, he saw, too, that he was in love with her.

There was nothing he could, or would, do about it. He was a prelate, and she a woman surrounded by people whose sole aim seemed to be to destroy what he and the king were trying to build. In love! So much for the quality of his faith!

After a time, with no very good grace, he realized he should leave them to say all the things they must want to say in private. Neither of them pressed him to stay, and so he went to his chamber and sat there for much of the night, staring blindly out of the window at the summer dusk, and listening to all the low, erratic murmurings of the empty places.

4

THERE was so much to talk of, after more than two years. But Columba's first words, after Gavin Cameron had gone, were, 'What news of Adam?'

'Very little. He wasn't hurt in the battle, except in his pride.' She gave a shaky laugh. 'He was so anxious to have a grand victory to welcome you. He wanted to show you what your son could accomplish!'

And then her expression changed, and she leaned forward and grasped him hard by the wrist. 'Thousands of men died because of him! You *must* see him when you are here, and talk to him. Because I don't think he means to let things lie, and whatever he does will mean more killing. You must stop him. Whatever the purpose, it *can't* be right!'

'I will see him,' Columba said placatingly, but it wasn't enough.

'It's such a waste!' she cried. 'Such a waste! Why must men kill each other? Why?'

She had asked Adam the same thing, on the day he had come to tell her about Harry. He said Harry had died in his arms, and it had been quick because of the nature of his wound, and his last thoughts had been of her. With his dying breath, he had begged Adam to bring this ring to his dearest Ninian, as a token of remembrance, and of the love that would not die with his body.

Even the chaos of her emotions had not prevented Ninian from noticing several improbabilities in this touching story. Adam, she had thought, was colouring the truth to save her pain, and she was both grateful and resentful – grateful for the kindness, resentful that he should think she could be so taken in. Was she a fool, to believe that there had been no blood and no horrors, that a man dying in pain and fear should have wasted his last agonized breaths on romantic babblings about a love that had never been?

She had said, 'I don't believe a word of that, Adam. What happened – truthfully?'

He had looked at her oddly for a moment, and then shrugged. 'He was dead, but I thought you would like to have the ring.'

It had been that – the offhand indifference of it – that had upset her more than anything, and it was then that she had burst out about the stupidity and wastefulness of war. But when she had cried, 'Why kill?' Adam had replied, his lip curling, 'It's the way of the world, *p'tite*. Men are made to kill.'

'They are not!' she had exclaimed passionately. 'Was Harry made to kill? Does Columba kill? Even Bishop Gavin – does *he* kill?'

'Of course he does. It's merely that he gets the public executioner to do it for him.'

Columba, now, didn't answer her question because he took it to be rhetorical. Killing was an aspect of God's will, and therefore not open to challenge. So, soothingly, he patted the hand clutching his wrist, and said, 'It's Harry, isn't it? That's what's upsetting you. Tell me.'

Even he, it seemed, didn't think her capable of looking beyond her own private troubles.

But because the last months of Harry's life and the manner of his death had distressed her more than she would yet admit, even to herself, and because she had had no one at all whom she could talk to, Columba's question offered her a release that she needed. She hadn't intended to burden him with her own woes, but once she began to talk it became impossible to stop.

'Yes, it's Harry,' she said. 'But not entirely. I've wept a good deal these last three weeks, more out of regret than anything else.' Regret for the Paradise Garden she had once thought the world; regret for lost innocence; regret for the love and kindness that had shone bright as the sun over the landscape of her youth. 'No, that's not true. Out of regret *and* out of guilt.'

Her eyes were dark and unreadable in the candlelight, and Columba, disturbed, said, 'You have no reason to feel guilt. I know you too well to believe that of you.'

The familiar little smile quirked the corners of her lips, but slow tears were rising and beginning to bead her lashes. 'Should I not feel guilt when I remember the pleasure and relief I felt, watching Harry ride away over the hill to his death?'

He frowned. 'You didn't know he was going to his death, and it is no sin, only a sadness, that you should have been happy to be without his company for a while. If you had quarrelled, the quarrel could not have been of your making alone.' He couldn't imagine his sunny-tempered, loving Ninian in the wrong about anything.

'Perhaps not. Perhaps we were both responsible.'

She sighed and, rising to her feet, began to roam aimlessly about the small, sparsely furnished Laird's Hall, the private room that Harry had spent no money on because outsiders rarely saw it.

'It began on the night I helped Alexander of the Isles escape from Edinburgh castle. Harry misunderstood something, and we had a dreadful, a hideous scene. Someone had told him I was being unfaithful to him, he said, and he wouldn't believe me when I told him it wasn't true.'

Columba was overcome by the un-Christian thought that he couldn't altogether regret Harry Graham's death.

'It was an impossible situation, though it improved, after a while. We kept each other at a distance, but it was bearable. I suppose, before, we had always been strangers trying to live as if we weren't; now, we lived as if we were.

'And then, about six weeks ago, I realized I was pregnant.'

She flung round. 'No, don't look happy for me! Why do men always think that having a child is the answer to everything? It isn't. It's only more heartbreak. I know exactly when this child was conceived, and I don't believe it can possibly be a – can possibly be a . . .'

Abruptly, her face crumpled and tears began to flow, not slowly but in a cataract. She didn't turn away, or bury her face in her hands. She just stood there, looking at him, racked by sobs, weeping with a terrible despair, hopelessly and helplessly.

But when he took her in his arms she rested her head against his shoulder only for a moment and then drew back. 'No. Don't comfort me. I need it too much, and it will drain me of what little strength I have.'

'What I am trying to say is that, however much I want a child – and I do! – no child conceived under such circumstances can possibly be a good or loving child.'

Harsh with his dread for her, he exclaimed, 'Don't be foolish. You know very well that God does not punish a child for its parents' sins. Its destiny is written, and nothing can change that, however it was conceived!'

She was silent for a moment. There were some things she could not say, not to Columba, not now. Already, she had held back one thing that mattered – the key to the whole, sad story of a marriage fated before it had even begun. To him, of all people, she could not speak of Gavin Cameron. And now, it seemed as if she could not speak to him of God, either, because she had thought, and thought, and thought, and she couldn't believe in predestination any more. As Gavin Cameron had said, it was too easy.

The knowledge that she was keeping so much from Columba, that she had opened up the first deep fissures in the perfect trust that had always been between them, chilled her to the bone.

She shook her head, shivering, and said, 'Yes. Yes, of course. Well, when I discovered, all I could think of was how frightened I was. I couldn't – I can't – forget the last time. Yes, I know. No one hates me now. No one is trying to poison me. All sense and reason tell me that this time it will be different, but sense and reason have nothing to do with it. When I was recovering from the miscarriage, I thought I should never be afraid of pain again, and I'm not, really. It's nothing as precise as that. I'm just terrified all the way through.'

He said nothing, because he had enough experience of human nature to know that instinct wasn't amenable to reason. What she needed was faith, and it seemed that she had none. Where had it gone? Yet he felt hesitant about trying to comfort her with talk of God, as if it would drive her further from him. And he knew, however she tried to hide it, that she had gone too far from him already.

She had begun roaming the room again, and her voice floated back to him in gusts, as he sat with his heart breaking for her.

'When I told Harry, he was like all husbands who imagine they have been betrayed. He wouldn't believe the child was his. But it was, Columba. It is.' She knew she had no need to say so, but she went on. 'I have slept with no other man than my husband.'

He knew her too well. He knew that she had wanted to.

'It was too much for me, in the end. For the last few days before Harry went, I could scarcely bear to be in the same room as him. That was why I was happy to see him go.'

Unexpectedly, she dropped to her knees before Columba and, staring up into his face, as if she were afraid he mightn't believe her, said, 'I didn't think he was in any danger, you know! Robert and Adam said that, as long as he didn't hurry, he wouldn't even be involved in the fighting. And even when Adam came to tell me he was dead, I had no premonition at all.'

Columba laid his hands on her shoulders, and shook her gently. Then, his long upper lip widening in the way it had when he was at his most earnest, he said, 'You have nothing, *nothing*, to reproach yourself with. Harry was a difficult young man, with no lightness of spirit, and you did everything you could have been expected to do to make your marriage work. I can think of no reason why you should feel guilty.'

He badly wanted her to tell him about the other man, the man he had guessed at, the man who might be the answer to her future. She would have to marry again; all widows did.

Instead, her eyes dropped and she said, 'You can't purge my guilt about Harry by telling me I oughtn't to feel it. Or the other, greater guilt. Because, you see, I feel that by helping Alexander to escape I was responsible for setting in train everything that has happened since. Not only Harry's death, but all those other deaths at the battle in Lochaber. They were all my fault. *My* fault!'

He couldn't believe what he was hearing. 'Your fault? How could such a thing be? This has all been by God's ordinance. It is God's will!'

'Is it? Did my own will have nothing to do with Alexander's escape? Did Adam's will have nothing to do with precipitating the battle?'

'*Ninian!* You mustn't say such things, nor even think them! Oh, my dearest child . . .'

There was panic in his voice, and she had the feeling that, even as he spoke, there was another voice in his head frantically saying prayers for her.

'It's no use, Columba. I don't understand why the idea of free will is so dreadful. You are a theologian – tell me!'

He said heavily, 'It's because I am a theologian that I can't tell you. It would be a sin in me to burden you with arguments that even the most sainted philosophers can scarcely construe. But I will say one thing – if ever you find yourself questioning something simply because you can't understand it, you must remember that the mind of man is, of its very nature, incapable of encompassing the workings of the divine. And you *must* believe me when I tell you that those who preach free will are guilty of the heresy of trying to subvert God's grace. They are wrong – and doomed to eternal damnation. I beg of you, never speak or think in such terms again. You must put such sinful thoughts right out of your mind!'

He was seriously upset, so she kissed him and said, 'You are a good man, and I love you so very much. What will happen now that you have Teviotdale back? And why – you haven't told me yet! – are you going to Inverness with Bishop Gavin?'

The sun was almost up before they separated, Columba to lie down for an hour or two before another long day's ride, Ninian to sit gazing blindly out over the landscape, just as Gavin had done, until it was time to go down to the gate and bid them farewell.

With the new, ironical humour that had begun – still timidly, and sometimes inappropriately – to manifest itself, she remembered herself saying to Adam a few months ago, when they heard that the pope had restored Teviotdale to Columba, that it was the end of all their troubles. She could smile now at her own naïvety, for it had been, instead, a new beginning.

Columba's personal campaign against Cameron had now, it seemed, taken on the flavour of a crusade, because he had persuaded the pope that Cameron's deliberate purpose was to seek independence for the church in Scotland, by breaking the curia's hold over it. The statutes against barratry were only a first step towards banning the annates, and services, and tithes, which were Rome's legitimate due. Of all this, Columba had convinced not only the pope, but himself.

And to him, he said proudly, had been delegated the responsibility of bringing the Scots kirk back, tamed, into the Roman fold. Which would, of course, be impossible for so long as Cameron remained chancellor.

Curious, Ninian thought, what changes a mere three years could bring about. All through her childhood and adolescence, she had looked on the world from Columba's viewpoint, as if he were the centre of it, but now she had begun to look for herself, and even if she wasn't always sure what to make of it, the perspective was hers and hers alone.

Tonight, loving him no less than she had ever done, she had seen him clearly for the first time. And to find herself, who had adored him uncritically all the days of her life, assessing his thoughts and his motives as she might have done those of a stranger, was at once heartbreaking and amazingly exhilarating.

He was, she supposed, two men. The private man – the one she had always known – who was good, kind, loving, and sincere in his detestation of violence and bloodshed. And the other man, the one whom she had just discovered but thought Adam must always have known about; a true man of his time, hard and single-minded, who, believing that his ends were God's ends, believed also that any means were justified in the pursuit of them.

Bloodshed wouldn't be his first choice, she knew; he had too subtle a mind for that. But it would be Adam's, for so long as the cause of the father he worshipped coincided with his own consuming desire for excitement and intrigue.

She couldn't stop either of them, and she knew there would be nothing but violence until they achieved their object and Gavin Cameron was brought down.

And so she sat by her window and watched the sun awakening the lurid greens and budding purples of the moors, and thought perhaps it would be best if Gavin Cameron did conform with the citation, and did go to Rome. Best if he were found guilty, and deprived of all his benefices and all his power. It would put an end to everything.

5

THE king was so exuberant, so bursting with good humour and self-satisfaction, that Gavin saw the archdeacon wince a little, as if such vitality were an offence against sensibilities better attuned to the stately gravity of Rome.

'Bishop Gavin!' James bellowed, bounding across the room to throw a pair of muscular arms round Gavin's shoulders. 'You are forgiven everything! I cannot tell you how grateful I was to have the Camerons bow out of the battle, and the Macintoshes with them. Your doing, I was told! How dare you arrange such things behind your sovereign's back?'

Gavin returned his sovereign's glare for a moment, counting the cost of the riotous new topaz velvet and the matching ring on the royal finger, and then grinned, so that James, his protruberant eyes popping with amazement, embraced him for a second time and with even greater vigour.

But James could change his moods as fast as he could his hats, and even as his hand went out for the citation his eyes were shifting from Bishop Gavin to Archdeacon Crozier and back again, calculating, estimating, anticipating. He read the document as swiftly as any scholar could have done, and then returned to the beginning and went through it again, more slowly.

He looked up. 'Crimes, Bishop Gavin?'

Gavin shook his head, smiling faintly.

'Simony in the collation of benefices?'

297

'Only, I think, on one occasion. In the matter of Your Majesty's nephew, James Kennedy. You may recall.'

'Oh.' It was clear that His Majesty did recall. His sister Mariota was a strong-minded woman who gave no one any peace until she got what she wanted. She had wanted one or two nice little benefices for young Jamie, the clever son of her second marriage.

'Ummm,' he said, and sat staring into infinity for a while, his fingers drumming on the table top.

Then, 'Can't be done!' he erupted, transferring a fully focused gaze to Archdeacon Crozier. 'I'm sure His Holiness will understand. I rely very heavily on my chancellor, and I can't spare him at the moment. How long would it take – a year, near enough, with the travelling and the case itself? No! No! Can't be done. What I'll do, though, is give you a letter to take to His Holiness, and then we'll appoint some special envoys to go to Rome and argue Bishop Gavin's case on his behalf. That ought to satisfy everyone. What do you think, archdeacon?'

The archdeacon thought otherwise, and said so courteously, intricately, and at length in his rich, warm voice, although both the courtesy and the warmth began to fray after a time in the face of James's pale-eyed obduracy.

'Yes, well,' said James at last, visibly bored. 'Let's try it just the same. Now, archdeacon, I have things to discuss with Bishop Gavin. Have a safe journey back to Rome.'

When the archdeacon had bowed himself out, James glowered at his chancellor and said, 'I'll thank you in future not to sit there with that disapproving look in your eye. Don't think I don't know what it means by now.'

Gavin allowed the smile to come out. But although the king might be able to tell when he was suppressing an unsuitable amusement, it would have been impolitic to let him know that his chancellor's present mood was due as much to relief as anything else. Gavin hadn't been at all sure of his welcome, or of how James was going to take the summons from Rome. Even if you were Gavin Cameron and the only man in the kingdom to whom the king was prepared to delegate an atom of his power, he could still be a chancy devil, and Gavin had the uneasy feeling that, almost imperceptibly, he was becoming more so. It was over five years now since he had ascended his throne, and during those years he had accomplished more than most people would have thought possible, and far more than the barons approved of. But it was still only a drop in the ocean of what he wanted to do, and in many of the important things – widening the base of parliament, rationalizing the law, protecting his people against the exactions of nobles and priests – he was being frustrated on all sides. And he was not learning patience with the years.

Drily, Gavin said, 'I was admiring your handling of the archdeacon. Quite masterly!'

'It was, wasn't it?' A jaunty beam split the mahogany-red beard. 'And I'll charge him for his bed and board if he's not gone by tomorrow, too! Anyway, you'd better start thinking who to send to Rome to speak for you. Alexander Lauder, perhaps? And John Crannoch – he knows his way around. Take your time preparing your case; it's too important to scamp on it.'

And that was certainly true.

James tossed the citation across the table to him. 'Now! You can tell me later what happened at Hawdenstank. At this moment, we've more immediate things to attend to. That impudent young ruffian Alexander tried to make terms with me after the battle, if you can believe it! Said that though half his men lay dead, he could raise as many more again, just by clicking his fingers. I told him not to be so sure. He might find the Camerons and the Macintoshes aren't the only clans that hesitate to wage war when they see the royal standard and realize they're facing the king in person.

'Anyway, the long and the short of it was that he surrendered unconditionally. I've got him cooling his heels in the dungeon here. And the question is – what are we going to do about him?'

6

THE weather had broken and it was as if all the elements were trying to make up for three idle months of heatwave and drought. There was a wild north-easterly blowing, churning up the Firth of Forth, thrashing the trees, filling the air with uproar, a wind that carried rain not in drops, nor in sheets, but in cascades as thick and solid as if they had been sluiced directly out of the tidal flow of the river.

The roof of the Chapel Royal at Holyrood shuddered under the assault, the noise reverberating round the rib-and-panel vaulting, and the lancet windows of the clerestory shaking and quivering under the battering of the rain. A trickle of moisture showed here and there on the lime-washed walls, sometimes fanning out into a rivulet. The yellow, green and brown floor tiles were puddled with wet mud. And the bas-relief heads of kings, prelates and courtiers on the arcading had drips on the ends of their noses.

The living king stood with his back to the high altar, dressed in bright yellow, the colour of hostility, and surrounded by the officials and nobles of his court, or as many as could squeeze in among the carved and painted oak screens, the grave slabs, and the brass and marble tombs. The queen and her ladies, Ninian Drummond among them, sat and shivered on the stone benches that lined the northern aisle.

James was in a mood to match the weather, his air intemperate and his eyes moist with royal rage, as he stared down at the kneeling figure before him — Alexander of the Isles, in saffron shirt and short, heather-purple trews, holding his naked sword by the tip as he offered its hilt to the king in token of submission. It was over four feet long, and not at all easy to balance, especially when one was understandably reluctant to take a good, firm grip on the business end.

Alexander had kept his stiff neck bent for a long time, as James worked his way with growing enthusiasm through every unflattering epithet he could decently use when there were ladies present. Rascal, scoundrel, rapscallion . . . Savage, brute, barbarian . . . Viper, snake, scorpion . . . Traitor, knave . . .

'Varlet,' Gavin murmured helpfully under his breath, and James, whose hearing was acute, scowled at him.

The light was dim, despite the huge stand of candles beside the retable, and the atmosphere chill, because the gale that always found its way in through the great portal divided itself into several smaller draughts that whistled and bounded and side-slipped their way up the full length of the nave before they reconvened with mutual and baleful rejoicing in the sanctuary. The rain rattled against the windows with undiminished force. There was a faint, bubbling snore from his lordship of Atholl, perched nodding on the tomb of Malcolm IV. One of the queen's ladies sneezed.

'So!' the king said at last, impatience gaining the upper hand. 'Since that you, Alexander MacDonald of the Isles, have been taken in undoubted rebellion against your true and lawful sovereign, and since that despite our own beneficent attempts in times past to lead you away from the paths of malfaisance, you have shown no desire to abjure your evil ways, it is my judgement that for the good of the kingdom, and likewise for the good of your soul in the sight of the

Lord, you shall be subjected to the most extreme and awful penalties our human law can command.'

He paused for breath, and there was a general shifting about and some muttering among the barons, and a rustle of shocked dismay from the queen's ladies. Alexander had made himself very popular when he was at court.

James raised his voice again and the murmuring died. 'You have our permission to address us, Alexander MacDonald, if that there be any good reason why this our judgement should not be fulfilled, but we warn you that we are not of a mind to alter our decision.'

Alexander, in no position to avail himself of this grudging invitation, glared up at his sovereign, but James showed no disposition to relieve him of his sword. So, with a neat twist of the wrist, he flipped the hilt back into his own grasp, rising to his feet at the same moment in a single, enviably lithe movement.

Despite bare feet, muddied knees and blood-streaked palms, he looked remarkably impressive standing there, with the candlelight bringing a gleam of gold to the flaming hair, and his hands resting on the quillons of the great blade which he held with its point to the floor between his feet. He also looked wholly impenitent.

Prudently, Gavin moved forward and removed the sword from his grasp.

Alexander cast a haughty and comprehensive glance around the company before his eyes returned to meet those of the king. Then, clear and only faintly sibilant, his voice rang out. 'Is it that you expect me to beg?' His chin tilted a little. 'I will not.'

There was a faint sigh throughout the Chapel Royal. It was only too obvious that the boy was about to make a speech, and most of those present could have reeled it off themselves with scarcely a moment's hesitation. It would be sons-of-Somerled first; it always was.

Alexander, pride in every fibre of him, announced, 'I do not beg. I, who am of the sons of Somerled, descendant of kings, ruler of all the western sea, kin to the Vikings, heir to a tradition inviolable for a thousand years and more – I do not beg! I, who am the son also of my people, a people fierce and upright, a people of sea-splendid galleys and island strongholds that span the sounds from Lewis to Kintyre, a people whose proud spirits have kept them independent across all the centuries and against every foe – I do not beg!'

Gavin, listening absently, reflected that it would all sound much better in the Gaelic. This wasn't an oration for a damp and cynical audience with its mind on dry clothes and the midday meal, but one that should have been shouted from some heather-clad hilltop where the air was fresh and salt, the landscape wild and free. It was an oration to appeal to the converted, to rouse fire in the clans; one that might equally be flung, with useless but satisfying defiance, in the teeth of the cloud-riding Valkyries as they ranged the sky in their nightmare hunt for the dead.

But the barons bore singularly little resemblance either to clansmen or Valkyries, and Gavin's own unexpected twinge of sentiment was submerged almost at once in annoyance, because Alexander hadn't enough sense to leave well alone.

Spreading his feet wide and planting his fists on his hips, he went on in a changed tone, 'And if I did beg – if I *did* – I would not beg of a man whose family were no more than stewards – *lackeys* – until they were knighted by the Bruce. Nor would I beg of a man who sits on the throne of a country whose so-called kings had no entitlement either to coronation or unction until a mere one hundred years ago.'

James's face was a study, and even Gavin was taken aback. For it was perfectly true. Not until June 1329 had the pope issued a bull entitling Scotland's king to these privileges – and on the centenary of that important date James had been so busy chasing Alexander round the Highlands that he had forgotten all about it. Gavin folded his lips and looked disapproving.

It was clear that James couldn't decide which insult to react to first. It would have been more dignified to ignore them altogether, of course, but dignity to James was something for special occasions and he liked to work up to it in advance. Today, he was in a squabbling mood.

'Coronation or not,' he snapped, 'the records show that I, James Stewart, am the one-hundred-and-first king of Scotland in line from Fergus!'

Alexander looked down his handsome nose. 'In *direct* line?'

James snorted. 'More direct than yours is between Conn of the Hundred Battles and your precious Somerled, let me tell you!'

Gently, Gavin cleared his throat, and James remembered himself. Given half a chance, Alexander would be off on the famous three hundred lines of bardic genealogy, which no one, least of all James, had the slightest interest in hearing. Crisply, he said, 'You may resume your plea.'

Concealing his frustration, Alexander went back to putting the king in his place. His voice held none of the soft sibilance he adopted when flirtation was in his mind. When it came to business, his Scots was quite as good as his Gaelic, and his Latin, Gavin knew, on a par with both. Unlike his father, he hadn't attended the university of Oxford, but his education most certainly had not been neglected.

'Until a hundred years ago,' Alexander said, 'my predecessors were as great as yours. And when I was installed in the Lordship, I was installed with ceremonies more ancient than yours. I placed my foot in the print on the great Stone. I received the White Rod, and with it the power to rule. I received the ancestral sword with which to protect my people. I, too, have my council, and my judges, my keeper of the records, my bard and my harper, as befit a great prince. And the Lordship's revenues,' he paused provocatively, 'are greater by far than those of the Crown of Scotland.'

James was purple in the face, and Gavin cleared his throat a little more loudly. It was Alexander, this time, who took note.

Smoothly, he went on, 'Three hundred years since, my ancestor Somerled swore friendship to the king who then ruled Scotland – friendship in all but one thing. For he said that, as long as he breathed, he would not resign any of his rights to any man, that he was resolved to lose all, or keep all.

'And so it is with me. For although none can deny my right to inherit the earldom of Ross, you, James Stewart, have kept it from me, so that I have been forced to try and take it for myself.

'This is why I have done battle with you. You know as well as I that my cause is just. You know that I am no traitor. But I will not beg, for the reasons I have told you.'

Then his voice dropped to a lower register, and although it was no less intense there was something in it that brought a faint unease to the hearts of several of those present, as if it were touching some forgotten chord.

'You say I must die. So be it. I have no fear. When my time comes, whether it be days from now, or years, my earthly body will be taken to Iona, and there will be a wake held for eight days and eight nights before it is laid in the grave of my forefathers. And my soul will be carried in the White Barge as it speeds like a bird, needing nor wind nor sail nor oars, across the western waves to where the sun sets, to Tir-nan-Og, the isles of the blessed, the land of the ever young. No. There will be no pain to me in dying, for I will go to join the elect.'

In the chapel, there was no other soul but Gavin who knew the meaning of the dream, no other man who knew the lure of the west and

303

its islands, whose blood ran salt in his veins, or whose spirit had its homing among the wild, majestic hills, and the seas that raged around their lone and lovely shores.

For an instant, he was lost to time and place, carried back on a current of purest paganism to the Kinveil of his childhood, which he had abandoned with scarcely a thought, his eyes set on the wider seas around which history was made. He knew the worth of those seas now, and the value of the history being made around them. But there was no going back. It was too late, too late to recapture the mystical landscape of his youth and of his heart – and it would not now, in any case, be the same. For his eyes had changed.

The Earl of Mar, the old reprobate who had fought against Alexander's father at Harlaw – a battle that both sides claimed to have won – broke the spell by saying loudly, 'Going to join the elect, eh? Well, the sooner the better, in my view.'

It was enough to start everyone else off. Next to him, the Earl of Douglas, his slender, cultured presence belying the ruthless man within, said, 'Come, now, Mar. The boy has some right on his side.'

'Right? What's right got to do with it?' Poking Douglas in his expensively-tailored ribs, the king's Justiciar of the North said, 'He's nothing but trouble, yon one. Dod! You should know. You've had enough to do with him.'

Douglas ignored James's suspicious glare and, his bland eyes on Gavin, replied, 'Only from a distance, my friend. Those of us who have had the benefit of a formal education like to keep in touch.'

Meanwhile, the Earl of Atholl, who had been awakened by the general change in the atmosphere, sat up, stretched, scratched himself vulgarly, and demanded, 'Whit's happening? Huv ye done? Can we get our dinner yet?'

'I have just,' James said repressively, 'condemned Alexander to death. You're all supposed to be here to confirm the sentence, as representing the Estates.'

'Oh?' said Atholl, surprised. 'Och, well, he's a pest. I'll confirm that, any day.'

The Earls of Angus, Crawford, and Huntly, followed by Alan of Caithness, Fraser of Lovat, and Seton of Gordon, all gave the king their unqualified approval. James knew as well as Gavin did that it was their acquisitive instincts, not their sense of justice, speaking. With Alexander out of the way, one of their most immediate priorities was going to be a brisk land-grabbing expedition.

None of it came as any surprise to Alexander, who knew his enemies, even if he were disappointed at the lack of conviction in the voices of his friends.

What did surprise him, and everyone else in the chapel, was when one of the queen's ladies came forward in a rustle of grey silk skirts, and begged leave to address His Majesty.

It was Ninian Drummond, and she was shaking from head to foot, as much from nerves as from cold. Gavin, who had only seen her once, from a distance, since her recent return to court, felt a tightening in his chest at the drawn look on her face, and then, as she took up her position before the altar, he saw how awkwardly she was moving and realized, with shock and an irrational disbelief, that she must be several months pregnant.

He scarcely heard what she was saying at first.

'. . . too much killing. How many men have died? How many women have been widowed? How many children are fatherless? Your Majesty, the world is full enough of death, without the sword. Plague and the sweating sickness, starvation, tainted food, bad water, accidents, drowning, childbirth . . .'

Her voice wasn't going to last, Gavin thought, and her tears had begun to fall. But although every nerve in her was quivering, she would not stop. If he had had any doubt of his love for her, it vanished in that moment.

'Fear of death lies over everything like a cloud, blotting out the sun, darkening men's spirits so that they abandon all hope of making a better future, because they believe there is no future for them. Your Majesty, there is nothing man can do about plague or disease, accident or misfortune, but it must be possible to try, at least, to put a stop to death by the sword!

'Men – some men – enjoy killing, I know. But if you, now, were to allow Alexander of the Isles to live, if you were to make it known that even one more death would bring the tally too high, you would set an example to all – to your barons here present, and to their followers, and to all who heard of what you had done. I beg of you, Your Majesty, for this reason if for no other, to spare Alexander's life.'

Then, curtseying, she backed away and, her eyes on the ground, went unsteadily to rejoin the queen's ladies.

They stared at her, astonished, and the men laughed under their breaths. It was as if they hadn't understood what she was saying. Even Alexander had his eyebrows quizzically raised.

But James's eyes met Gavin's, and he said heavily, 'I believe the Lady Ninian speaks from the heart, and though it is not her place to speak at all, I have taken note of what she has said.' And then his eyes shifted, and Gavin saw a trace of relief in them. 'Ah!' said the king. 'It seems that Her Majesty also wishes to make her opinion known.'

There was no emotion at all on Queen Joan's face as she advanced to the high altar, nor in her voice as she begged leave to address her husband.

When he had signified his gracious consent, she bowed her head and said truthlessly, 'I have no wish, sire, to intervene in matters of which I am ignorant, but from what I understand, the Lord of the Isles, who comes of a proud people, was moved to do what he did because he believed that he was being deprived of something that was his. Of the rights and wrongs of his case, I know nothing. But young men of spirit will always choose action rather than words, especially when they believe they will win. And when they lose, if they are clever enough, they learn.

'Alexander has lost, and from what I know of him, he has learned. By executing him, sire, you could throw all the Highlands into turmoil, whereas by sparing him, you will show the clans that neither malice nor hatred has a place in your heart. Temper justice with mercy, I beseech Your Majesty, as you of all men know how to do. That is all I wish to say.'

The king, with the courtesy and gentleness he showed only to her, took her by the hand and led her back to her place. Then he raised his voice and demanded, 'Is there anyone else who wants to speak? No? That's as well. I'm beginning to think it's only the women's opinions that're worth having.

'So!' He fixed Alexander with a forbidding eye. 'You may thank the personal intervention of Her Majesty. We have decided to spare your life. No Tir-nan-og for you just yet, my lad, not unless you give me any more trouble. What I want is peace in the Highlands and islands. Though you're not going back there, not for a while, anyway, because the Earl of Angus has a nice, secure wee castle at Tantallon, and I'm putting you in his sternest custody until further notice.'

'Oh, Christ!' said the Earl of Angus.

7

GAVIN was last to leave the chapel, but he walked swiftly and by the time he entered the corridor leading to the King's Lodging he could hear voices ahead of him, women's voices, and saw a flurry of skirts as the queen's ladies disappeared round the bend. There was a solitary figure in grey trailing some yards behind the others.

He hesitated in his stride and then, because he would not be able to avoid her for ever, walked on at the same brisk pace.

She was startled when he overtook her, and stepped aside as if to let him pass, but he said, 'You will allow me to walk with you?' It gave her no choice, and he fell into step at her side.

He could see that, if there was to be any conversation, he would have to make it, so he asked, lightly enough, 'You are still uneasy? Even though Alexander has been granted his life?'

The blue eyes rose swiftly to his. 'But in such a way! No one there cared at all whether he lived or died. Was it weak-minded of me, to feel sick listening to their lordships? I found I preferred his enemies to his friends.'

'There's nothing unusual in that! But never mind. They served their purpose.'

She took two more steps, and then stopped, frowning. 'Served their purpose? What do you mean?'

He should have known – her passionate little speech should have told him – that she hadn't sensed the farce it had all been, although somehow he had expected her to. But no one else had, not even men who had attended many such occasions before. He shrugged, and smiled as if he had meant nothing, and signalled that they should walk on.

But she said again, 'Served their purpose? *What do you mean?*' and grasped him by the arm so hard that he had no choice but to stop.

If she had been in a state to notice, his face was less guarded than she had ever seen it, and there was something very close to pity in his eyes. He hoped she wasn't going to be upset.

He said, 'It would have been a bad tactical error to execute Alexander, but everyone would have taken any lesser sentence as a sign of weakness. So what you have just been watching, I'm afraid, was a charade of a kind that takes place more often than you might think. The barons are perfectly satisfied that the king genuinely intended to do what was proper, and that is what matters.'

He smiled. 'Though I may say it is a total mystery to me why, when most of them will scarcely even give their own wives the time of day, they think not a pennyweight less of His Majesty for abandoning his intention merely because the queen asked it of him.'

But he wasn't allowed to shrug it off.

'*A charade?* Who knew?'

'The king, the queen, myself. No one else.'

Not even Alexander. She thought of him standing there, head high, saying there would be no pain for him in dying. And of herself, sick and grieving, possessed by a furious anger over the idiocy of men. No pain in a traitor's death? To be hanged, and cut down alive from the gallows, and disembowelled? Some men had lived even through that, lived until their agony was ended by the severing of their heads. No pain in dying? It wasn't bravery. It was stupidity, futility, madness.

Because of that, she had forced herself, in an anguish of misery, to beg the king for Alexander's life. And there had been no need. The barons had laughed aloud at what she had said, and she knew now that the king, and Gavin Cameron, and the queen, must also have been laughing at her privately.

Her voice rasping in her throat, she exclaimed, 'It must be splendid to be so superior, the puppet-master with everyone dancing on your strings. It's just the same as it was at Inverness, when you had Blane de Verne hanged. Just the same, except that this time it was more convenient to have a man live than die. Feelings don't matter to you, people don't matter, lives don't matter. It's all a game to you, making the world turn as you want it to. It's . . .'

Almost as distressed as she, he tried to lay a hand on her arm but she shook it off and cried passionately, 'No, don't touch me. Don't dare to touch me. It's time *you* suffered. It's time *you* learned how it feels to have others manipulating you. It's time *you* were brought down to the level of ordinary people who have no say in their own destiny.'

There was so much he could have explained, so much he wanted to explain. In some ways, he knew she was right, but in other ways she was impossibly wrong.

And then, although she was scarcely aware of it herself, the channel of her thoughts diverged, and she said, 'It will happen. It *must* happen.

There will be no peace for anyone as long as you are chancellor of this kingdom!'

It wasn't, perhaps, surprising that he should have misunderstood what was behind her words. But he saw rise up between them the substantial ghost of the man whose blind self-interest was at the root of most of the troubles that had beset Scotland for these last two years.

Coldly, he said, 'I would advise you to remember, Lady Ninian, that Archdeacon Crozier is not God. Nor does his will inevitably come about. I wonder if you really know how much damage he has done? I hope not. But I tell you now that, whereas in the past I have done no more than defend myself, and Scotland, against him, that is no longer true. From now on, he will have to look to himself, because I will give no quarter.'

PART FIVE

1430–1431

CHAPTER ONE

I

NINIAN'S baby was born in the first, icy days of January, and came into the world feet first.

Somehow, during the last months of her pregnancy, Ninian had succeeded in bringing her fears under control. She had done all the right, the sensible things, dosing herself with wormwood against the possibility of miscarriage, eating properly, resting when she felt tired. She had made sure there was a tisane of rue ready to ease the pains of the birth, and another of feverfew in case her labour was difficult. And for days before the child was due, she had been deliberately calming both mind and body with a brew of valerian, which worked well, however disgusting the taste.

When the time came, she was grateful that she had taken precautions, because a breech birth was always difficult, the midwife said, and if she had been tense, it might have killed her. The woman didn't say that it was against the order of nature, but Ninian knew, and there was one dreadful moment when all her fears surged up in her again as she sat in the delivery chair, with the child inside her almost fighting to be born, as if it couldn't wait to see the dull grey light of the winter's day.

But it wasn't a monster, after all. It was just an ordinary little girl, with excellent lungs, who didn't like being bathed, and, when the midwife tucked some warmed rushes into her tiny fists against the chill of the air, took a grip on them like a vice.

'A fighter, my lady,' the midwife said, laughing. And so it seemed appropriate that, although the baby was named, unavoidably, for the queen, she should privately be called not Joan, but Jehane – after the Maid of Orléans.

2

TO Columba's annoyance, the cardinals before whom Cameron's spokesmen were required to present themselves in the spring of 1430 did not include Gabriel Condulmer, because the pope had sent him to Bologna to discourage its inhabitants, by whatever means, from pursuing the innovations on which their hearts appeared to be set.

'And as we all know,' Poggio Bracciolini said cheerfully, stuffing yet another Frati fritter into his mouth, '"innovations" means they want to be independent of the Papal States, and "any means" equals mass executions. How pleasant it is to be just a lowly secular scribe, with nothing to do but write apostolic letters, eat, drink, make jokes and make love. Did I tell you that I have just become papa to my twelfth little bastard? A dear, sweet child.'

Appreciatively, he inhaled the bouquet of his *vernaccia* before pouring the whole cup decisively down his throat. 'My mind is made up. It is fifty years ago this year since I was born, and it is time I was married.'

'Congratulations,' Columbia said ironically.

He had been looking forward with deep interest to how Cameron intended to try and refute the irrefutable – if somewhat exaggerated – charges Columba had initiated against him, but unfortunately, everything was now in the hands of men greater than he. He found it peculiarly frustrating to be called in to the Rota only occasionally, to verify some point or other for the judges at the big round table, and to have to rely on gossip to fill in all the gaps.

To begin with, he was not at all happy about the way things were going. The king's resident representative at Rome had somehow managed to rake up two hundred florins to pay off another instalment of Cameron's long-overdue annates, which had inclined the judges to think that the bishop's soul was not quite lost beyond redemption.

And when the case began, Crannoch and Lauder made a good deal of capital not only out of Cameron's care for his diocese, but out of the king's munificence in all matters relating to the church in Scotland.

Bishop Gavin, it seemed, was a model prelate, looking after his cathedral admirably, increasing the number of prebends, making new statutes for its government, and enriching it with books and vestments. And the king had founded the Charterhouse at Perth, erected Corstorphine into a collegiate church, confirmed grants and gifts to Lincluden and Brechin and Cambuskenneth and a number of other livings, and in all ways shown himself a devoted son of the church. None of it had much to do with the points at issue, but it sounded impressive.

What troubled Columba was that James seemed to be backing Cameron to the hilt, despite all Adam's efforts to discredit him, and that meant that His Holiness couldn't condemn Cameron without offending the king, which he had no desire to do. Everything depended on the judges, and how seriously they chose to regard the anti-barratry laws.

Even Poggio, the most tolerant of men, soon began to tire of hearing about Cameron, and confided to the luscious Vittoria that he feared Columba was becoming quite obsessed with this tiresome Scotsman. Vittoria said that she had already discovered the truth of this for herself, and had been forced to ban Columba from her company until he was able, once again, to think of something other to talk about. Or do.

It was just when the judges were ready to delve into the details of the anti-barratry legislation, and when Columba was beginning to feel rather more sanguine, that he himself was summoned to appear before a different court and answer charges brought against him by a certain Laurence Piot.

Totally mystified, he did as he was instructed, and discovered that Master Piot, acting on behalf of King James I of Scotland and his chancellor, had delivered to the papal court a royal document citing Archdeacon Columba Crozier for violation of the laws of Scotland.

Bishop Gavin had not been a lawyer for nothing. Even the papal notaries were confused.

They had Bishop Gavin himself, in one ecclesiastical court, being charged by proxy with instituting laws against the export of currency that Archdeacon Crozier, in another ecclesiastical court, was being charged with violating.

If the laws were essentially secular, as Crannoch and Lauder claimed, then Bishop Gavin was not guilty, but Archdeacon Crozier was. If, however, they weren't, then Bishop Gavin *was* guilty – and so, still, was Archdeacon Crozier.

The judges were all Italians and inclined to lose their ecclesiastical tempers, so that, in the end, the casting vote was left to His Holiness.

And His Holiness chose to cut the Gordian knot. He had no wish to alienate James because, with the ecumenical Council of Basle due to convene in a few months, he needed allies more than he needed enemies. There was a move afoot to arrest the increasing absolutism of the Holy See and make the pope responsible, as he had been formerly, to his council, and Martin didn't relish the idea at all.

As a result, the allegations against Columba were withdrawn – though he was rapped over the knuckles by the Rota for exaggerating – and the case against Bishop Gavin, whom Crannoch and Lauder cynically promised would 'behave laudably in future and help to obtain the repeal of the barratry statutes', was dismissed as not proven.

And, as Columba furiously pointed out to a tactically deaf Poggio, 'That means, "Not guilty, but don't do it again."'

Then, scornfully rejecting Poggio's invitation to go with him to the horse races, he withdrew to his lodging, and embarked on a long and intricate letter to Adam.

3

NINIAN drew a breath of purest pleasure, feeling the wind fresh on her cheek and smelling the strange mixture of smells that were the moors in spring – damp earth with the merest whisper of warmth on it, the rancid sweetness of winter's decay, and the sharp tang of fresh growth that her eyes told her must be there even if her nose couldn't quite detect it.

The silence was profound under the white-stippled blue sky, because she was flying the peregrine today – only to the lure, but the other birds couldn't be expected to know that. As soon as she had taken his hood off, there had been a frantic twittering among the little ones, and a corncrake had begun creaking like a rusty gate, and the peewits had sprung up, circling and shrieking neurotically to distract the enemy from the vicinity of their nest, until they remembered that it wasn't only the nest that was at risk and had hurriedly made themselves scarce.

It was astonishing that even quite large birds could vanish so completely on moors that offered little cover at this time of year, even if they were not as bleak and barren as Ninian had always thought. Now, in early May, they formed a subtle honey-and-umber tapestry, framed in the low black ridges of the mountains and stitched with acid fronds of new bracken, and fine, thin, scattered blades of grass, and a prickling of dark green round the gnarled brown stems of the heather. The lichens on the leeward side of the tumbled grey rocks were a most beautiful silvery olive.

Ninian remembered with a kind of detached surprise that this time last year, after Harry had brought her back from court, she had found nothing to admire in the landscape at all. Nor any spring before that. It was attitude of mind that made the difference.

During these last twelve months Harry had died, and little Jehane had been born. And Ninian herself had reached the age of twenty-one and was learning how to manage Dess and its lands and its people as Harry had done; perhaps a little better. It was interesting – engrossing, even – although it meant that when the queen spared her to come to Dess for a few weeks, she had to work from dawn until long past sundown, except when she gave Greensire his exercise.

Poor Greensire! He had to rely on old Wat, nowadays, to take him hunting properly, as he had been born to do, because she couldn't bear to watch the terrible efficiency of his kill.

She took off his swivel and leash. The white down on his front looked like snow-satin in the sun, and he ruffled his grey-dark neck feathers impatiently, and fidgeted. 'Ready?' she said, and raised her arm high, the muscles aching under the weight of him, and gave a twist of her wrist and he was off, powerful wings flapping, lumbering a little until he caught the wind currents, and then sure of himself, and surer with every gain in height until he was up in the heavens and in his true element.

Taking the lure from the leather satchel on her hip, she began swinging it on its three-foot cord, round and round, smoothly and insistently, keeping his attention so that he wouldn't get bored and stop circling, and make off on his own.

Then, smiling to herself, she whistled piercingly three times, and swung the lure high and sideways, watching the bird snap back his wings and go into his stoop, ripping through the air like some impossibly elegant stone. At the last possible moment, she twitched the cord so that the lure was behind her back and out of his sight, but this was a game and he had expected it. With perfect control he tore on past and up again, a flash of white-and-dark movement in an echo of windrush and silver bells.

'Good boy,' she called, and began swinging the cord again. 'Good boy. Now, once more.'

She remembered her first winter here, the isolation, the boredom, the miserable disappointment with husband, home, and life itself. How adolescent she had been! And then the next winter and spring, when she had been so near death, and her loneliness had been of a different kind; a compound of pain, and self-pity, and the knowledge that those who cared for and comforted her did so out of duty, not love. But last year had been the worst, when she had lost even the faintest trace of contact with Harry, and had felt more alone than ever in her life before.

She had always thought that she hadn't been born to be solitary, but the last months had changed all that. She still needed human company, still yearned for the warmth of loving and being loved, but she had found a new need to be alone. There had been too much of emotion in these last four years.

Everyone to whom she had been close had vanished from her life. Blane and Harry were dead, Columba was in Rome, and she had no idea where Adam was. Alexander was imprisoned at Tantallon, and Malise and Patrick Graham were still hostages in London. Only Robert Graham sometimes came to see her for an hour or two, always late at night, as if he were an outlaw. He wasn't – no one had connected him with the risings in the Highlands, or not officially – but he seemed to feel as if he was.

And Gavin Cameron, to whom she wasn't close, was so busy with parliament, and the exchequer audit, and truce negotiations, and the plan to marry little Princess Mary to King Henry VI of England, that she seldom saw him. Which was as well.

But she had friendship, of a kind, with Lady Moragh, though it wasn't close. They never opened their hearts to each other. Ninian had promised to take Moragh's eleven-year-old daughter into her household next year, to teach her the duties of a young lady. It was the custom; sons and daughters at that age were always sent to other families to be trained, just as babies were sent away to wet-nurses for the first three years of life. It was one way to avoid becoming too attached to one's babies, which was sensible when children died so easily.

But Ninian hadn't been able to bring herself to send Jehane away – the child who was miraculously whole and impossibly healthy, with a fuzz of light brown hair and an intensely serious look in her blue eyes. She was four months old now, and bursting with personality. Her wet-nurse, whom Ninian had brought to live at Dess with her own baby and her husband, a carpenter and a good man, said she had never fostered such a determined little mite.

Ninian summoned the tiercel back to her, and this time gave him the lure. She smiled again, ironically. Greensire. The Green Knight. Sir Gawain and the Green Knight. It was only a few weeks ago that she had recognized the association of ideas and realized that, when she had named him, somewhere in the hidden recesses of her mind there must have been the thought of another Gawain, another hawk, a man as effective as this bird of hers – and, within himself, as far from her.

She stroked Greensire's claws and he mewed at her in protest as she dropped the hood over his head, and turned back towards the castle. It was the end of freedom for today, but at least her freedom now was real, which it had never been before, and she knew its worth.

She hadn't made any conscious decision to try whether life would be more tolerable if she taught herself to let her head rule her heart, as other people did, but she was at least learning to stop, and use her mind, and to value her own company. Was all that a sign of maturity? She didn't know. But she hoped it was.

4

AUTUMN was wet that year. Ninian, torn between exasperation and a slightly overwrought mirth, battled her way on in the teeth of a gale that was whipping so violently in from the west that the rain it carried seemed to be falling horizontally rather than vertically. Physically, she was a good deal less uncomfortable than she might have been, because she was quite improperly dressed in one of Harry's doublets, a pair of his long leather trews, and a tight-fitting hood with a shoulder cape attached. What Robert Graham was going to think, she couldn't imagine, and didn't care very much. If he insisted on summoning her out to meet him at the dead of a wild September night, he could scarcely complain at lack of conventionality in dress.

It was typical of him, she reflected, that although he was prepared to entrust a messenger with a note of assignation that, if it fell into the wrong hands, would completely ruin her reputation, he wasn't prepared to make do, in return, with a letter containing all the scraps of political information that everyone who wasn't banned from court already knew.

She would have been much happier putting at least one of those pieces of information in writing, because she knew exactly what his response was going to be when she told him.

He was already there when she arrived, in a shallow pocket on the hillside that only the most dedicated optimist would have dignified with the name of cave, and had even built a little cairn of stones and managed to get a peat fire smouldering in it, more for the faint red glow it gave than for its heat. The eye-stinging smoke, drawn outwards, was whipped invisibly away on the wind.

Dripping, breathless, and blinking, Ninian collapsed on the cloak he had laid out for her and surveyed what she could see of him, as thin and morose as ever, his face satanic in the red underglow.

'Double, double, toil and trouble,' she said. 'Where's the cauldron? I can't think what Master Laurence would make of *this*!'

Seriously, he asked, 'Do I seem like a warlock to you?' and because she was slightly uneasy with him when they were alone together, she gave a hiccup of laughter and said, 'Only when you summon me out on the moors at the time of the equinox.' Which wasn't true at all.

It was one of the great mysteries of human relationships that one could quite like a man and yet be terrified by the thought of what he might do. She knew that Robert Graham had developed a surprising respect for her, and that he was prepared to talk to her and even listen to her on almost any subject that might arise – except the one by which he was obsessed, the subject on which she might as well be dumb, or he deaf. Nothing would turn him from his hatred of the king which was, by now, so much a part of him that to comment on it would have been as silly as commenting on the colour of his eyes.

And now another blow had been struck at the Grahams, or what Robert would see as one, and he was undoubtedly going to blame the king for it.

She had the foresight to ask for his news first, so that she would at least be sure of hearing it. 'Let me get my breath back,' she said, 'and afterwards I can tell you what has been happening at the glorious court from which you are so sadly banned.'

He smiled a little, and then leaned back on one elbow and produced a cavernous yawn. 'I would not say that I have been doing anything worthy of remark, other than journeying from clan to clan, talking. After the Lochaber debacle, I have been thinking, too. I have never favoured your cousin's expansive way of going about things. If we are to achieve our objectives, I believe we need to approach the matter in a less speculative fashion, and with much more precision. It will take time, but the likelihood of striking our targets will increase in proportion.'

Ninian closed her eyes. It meant a respite of sorts, during which some miracle might happen. Though if there were no miracle . . . She didn't underestimate Robert Graham simply because he had chosen, until now, to give Adam his head.

'And what about Adam?'

'You have not heard from him? I suppose not. He was in Wales for a time, where there are many refugees from James's persecution, but he should be back at Blair Atholl by now.'

Her eyes snapped open. 'Again? What *is* this unholy alliance with Atholl? When I ask Adam, all he tells me is that it's convenient, a matter of give and take. Atholl collects Columba's tithes for him and smuggles them out of the country, and Adam does what the earl asks of him in return. Such as,' she went on with asperity, 'carrying out tasks that seem to me might as easily be carried out by the lowliest messenger boy. It isn't like Adam!'

In the glimmer of the peats, she could just see Sir Robert's shoulders shrug. 'After Blane's involvement at Inverness, and the foolishness of playing the "anonymous" Red Lord at Lochaber, Adam would be suspect at court if it were not for Atholl's patronage.'

She was very tired of being underestimated. 'I had already worked that out for myself, but since Adam has shown his face at court only two or three times in the last year it still doesn't explain things. The truth is that if anything happens to James, Atholl is still first in line for the throne, and you both hope to make profit from it. That *is* the truth, isn't it! And what I would very much like to know is – does Atholl himself have any idea at all of what you and Adam are up to?'

Perhaps the wind direction had changed, or the rain had washed some obstruction out of a crack between the rocks, but the whole cave was filled with a soughing, whining noise that made the atmosphere suddenly feel much colder. Robert Graham leaned forward and moved one of the peats so that the red brightened and a myriad of tiny sparks sprang up.

He said, 'I have never made any secret of my attitude towards the king, and Atholl also knows, I believe, how Adam feels about Cameron, and why. He himself is strongly opposed to the chancellor. I am quite certain, however, that Adam has told him nothing of our involvement in recent events.'

And that was quite unsatisfactory.

Ninian said, 'Yes. Well, I didn't exactly visualize Adam saying he was late for supper because he'd been trying to start a civil war!'

Robert Graham grinned and, rising, went to where his saddlebag lay in the shadows. He handed her the leather bottle of usquebaugh and said, 'Take a good mouthful. It will warm you. If you have not heard from Adam, you may not know that he now feels quite as strongly about James as he does about Cameron.'

Ninian, still gasping after the excruciating shudder the drink had induced in her, could do no more than shake her head.

'It seems that lately, at Rome, it has become clear that James is throwing all his weight behind Cameron, so Adam now feels committed to war on both. I am sorry, by the way, that Archdeacon Crozier's case failed. It would have been convenient for all of us if Cameron had been deprived of his offices.'

'Yes.' She handed the bottle back. 'No, thank you, no more. Now or ever.'

'It warms, and gives courage when necessary.' He raised it to his own lips. 'Now, what is it that you have been putting off telling me?'

She had to raise her voice against the whine of the wind, so that her careless tone wasn't as convincing as it might have been. 'Putting off? What are you talking about? There's nothing very much to report. I am commanded back to court for the queen's lying in next month. Her physician believes she may be carrying twins this time, but only the king has any hope of sons after so many daughters.'

'And the other thing?'

She gave an irritable tug at the boots that were far too big for her, and resigned herself. 'Your brother William, Lord of Graham. Patrick's father, you know?'

Kindly, he said, 'Yes, I know who he is.'

'Well, he has decided that, although Patrick is his eldest son and legitimate heir, he is to be passed over. Now that the Lord of Graham's present wife has at last borne him a son, he has chosen to make the new baby heir to his title and lands.'

As she had known he would, he exclaimed, '*He* has chosen? His wife has chosen, you mean! Dear Mariota, the king's sister. And I imagine the king sanctioned the arrangement without a quibble?'

'I have no idea. About the quibble, I mean. He must have sanctioned it, or it wouldn't be legal. I do feel sorry for Patrick. Perhaps if he had been at home, instead of a hostage in London, he might have persuaded his father to change his mind.'

'It's James's doing. James and Cameron. It's the old story – anything to enrich the royal treasury, and damn the means and the morality of it. They are calculating that when my saintly brother dies, the crown will have control over the Graham inheritance throughout the child's minority.'

'Oh, Robert!' she exclaimed, forgetting the niceties in her annoyance with him. 'You can't seriously think the king would meddle in an affair like this merely for the sake of a highly debatable future profit!'

'Would he not! Profit is the only thing he thinks of, debatable or not. Do you have any idea of the rental value of the lands he has stolen from their rightful owners in these last six years? Including my own!'

Her eyebrows rose. 'You mean those lands of yours that belonged to the crown in the first place, until Albany gave them to you – illegally?'

He wasn't accustomed to opposition, but after a moment the glare was replaced by a grimace. '*Touché!*' he said.

It was irrationally important to her that he should not believe himself to have yet another grievance against the king. Because, however often he claimed that his opposition to James was a matter entirely of principle, there was no question in Ninian's mind that, every time James trod on the Grahams' toes, Sir Robert's opposition became sharper and more embittered. After three years at court, the king still frightened her, but only personally, not politically. In a wider sense, Sir Robert Graham frightened her a great deal more. She knew that it was like reaching for the moon, to hope to turn the edge of his enmity, but she had to try.

She said, 'You know your brother better than I do, but from all I have heard he seems to be a most rigid moralist. Patrick's – er – Patrick's sins against nature . . .'

'His sodomy, you mean.'

'Whatever you choose to call it! It seems to me that the Lord of

Graham must disapprove most strongly. And goodness knows, *you* ought to be on your brother's side, because if Patrick inherits, and will not or cannot father children, when he dies the title and estates could quite legitimately be annexed by the crown, instead of just administered for a few years!'

'An expert in Scots law, Ninian?' But he was hesitant. And then he said, 'No. It will not do. There are other arrangements that could have been made. This whole thing is James, James, James, all the way. James and Cameron. Adam is right. It is impossible to separate one from the other.' Then his face changed in the glow from the peats, and he said, 'But tell me. Are you well? And little Jehane?'

Insofar as it was possible to flounce in sodden leather boots and trews, Ninian flounced. As Robert Graham also rose, she said caustically, 'Exceedingly well, thank you. I find it does wonders for one's health to be so closely related to revolutionaries and rabble-rousers. Nothing like an alert mind and a good tramp across the moors to keep one in trim. Good night to you, Sir Robert.'

5

ON October 16, in the Royal Lodging at the abbey of Holyrood, the queen gave birth to twin sons. The king, for what was certainly the first time in his life, was speechless.

For the next two weeks, no one in the royal household had any sleep at all, because His Majesty had decreed that the little princes should be baptised at the earliest possible moment and in the greatest possible style. And that involved not only all eleven of Scotland's bishops, but the Master of the Household, the Chamberlain, the Treasurer, the Comptroller, the Marshal of the Hall, the Clerk of the Kitchen, the Keeper of the Horse, the Serjeant of the Tents, the Master of the Revels, the Keeper of the Privy Seal, and every single one of the clerks in the king's chancery, whose first task it was to write to all the monarchs of Europe informing them of the happy event.

Tom Myrton, who had recently had the role of treasurer foisted on him in addition to everything else, for once permitted himself the luxury of disagreeing with his economical bishop. 'Och, Gavin, Gavin!' he said. 'Of course it's costing a lot. But, well . . . Just pray that those poor, sickly bairns live long enough to see their baptism. That's why the rush. James means to be sure their souls are saved, at least. And all the display's just his way of persuading himself that the worst isn't going to happen.'

Gavin nodded soberly, and Tom had to smother his astonishment. What were things coming to, that Gavin Cameron should be showing tolerance of other folks' weaknesses? He would have liked to go into it, but he didn't have time.

On the night before the great day, the inhabitants of the four hundred low wooden houses that comprised the king's loyal city of Edinburgh were kept awake all night by the hammering, but even their cynical souls lifted a little when they saw the transformation that had been wrought. As the king and his retinue, who, on the previous evening, had ridden unobtrusively from Holyrood up to the castle, set out to ride back again in very different style, all those citizens who weren't involved in the special displays or the trades procession turned out to cheer with a very fair semblance of conviction.

Gavin, waiting in his ceremonial vestments outside the chapel at Holyrood, where he was to celebrate High Mass, reflected that they were probably scrambling for the largesse with even more conviction. It wasn't often that James threw money away.

In his mind's eye, he watched the procession wending its way down the long hill that led directly from the castle to Holyrood. He felt as if he knew every brush stroke and every stitch that had gone into the decorations, because although it wasn't his business he seemed to have spent much of the last two weeks arbitrating between the Serjeant of the Tents and the Master of the Revels. They had been bursting with ideas, most of them impractical and none of them original.

He had had to put his foot down firmly on one that had involved living representations of Father, Son, and Holy Spirit perched at some second-storey gates of Paradise, from which angels would descend – on wires – to place a crown on James's head as he passed underneath. 'But it was done with great success,' the Master had argued sniffily, 'when Queen Isabella entered Paris in 1389!'

Gavin, with nightmare visions of broken wires, broken necks and bolting horses, had said, 'Indeed? However, I suspect a fountain running with spiced wine might perhaps be more popular and less dangerous. At the mouth of the Canons' Gait, do you think?'

The Master had been so displeased that Gavin had given in to the other set piece outside St Giles. Here, the Serjeant of the Tents had been inspired to erect an ingenious scaffolding across the full width of the street, with a great canopy over it painted to represent a starry sky and emblazoned with the sun, the moon, and the most fearsome lion rampant anyone had ever seen. Not to be outdone, the Master of the Revels had installed under the canopy a beardless youth dressed to represent Our Lady, holding a naked and shivering babe in his inexpert arms, and surrounded by a number of small children dressed as angels and rigorously schooled in their chosen songs. Gavin hoped to God that Tom wasn't right in thinking they'd start screaming their infant heads off at their first close sight of all that royal majesty.

It was a relief when the procession came in view and nothing appalling seemed to have happened.

After Mass and baptism, the king knighted the two baby princes and seven deserving young noblemen, and then the babies were displayed from the open gallery above the portal of the chapel, and there was more cheering. The courtyard was full of Edinburgh's tradesmen by this time; the fishmongers had excelled themselves by bringing along four horses each bearing a silver model of a salmon as big as a fisherman's dream. The king smiled, and waved, and dispensed more largesse, while the queen, with every evidence of gratitude, accepted from the burgesses of the city two little silver-gilt cups for the princes.

And then it was time to dress for the banquet.

6

THE queen had dismissed her ladies, saying she would manage very well by herself for a little, and that she would ring when she needed them.

But she did not, and in the end it was Ninian who went in and found her face down on the royal bed weeping, repeating over and over two lines from the poem the king had written at the end of his captivity in England, when his release and their marriage were at last in sight.

'"That to my freedom I am come again, to bliss with her that is my sovereign". Such high hopes we had then! And there has been nothing but difficulty and danger for him, and no reward.'

All the queen's ladies knew that, under her calm exterior, Her Majesty was possessed of considerable determination and a strong sense of moral rectitude, but she had always kept her inner emotions so firmly under guard that it was generally whispered that she had none.

Certainly, she had never confided anything even remotely personal to those who attended her, unless, perhaps, to Lady Egidia, to whom all gossip was anathema.

Ninian, not at all sure what protocol had to say about soothing distraught sovereigns, chose her words with care. 'But Your Majesty, the king needs no more reward than your love for him.' And it was true, in a way. His feeling for her was more than touching; it was almost beautiful. 'And now, as well as four lovely daughters, you have given him two handsome sons. That, surely, is reward enough.' She put a faint, coaxing smile in her voice as she added, 'Even for a king!'

The queen was silent. And then, her voice still muffled by the pillows, she said, 'Do you believe that? Can you look at my babies and think they will live?'

It was an impossible question. Alexander, the first-born, had gained almost nothing in weight since he emerged from the womb, and James, the younger, had the fire mark on his face, huge and purple and disfiguring. Neither had any of the natural liveliness of a healthy infant.

Ninian knew that the queen would scorn her if she gave a falsely soothing answer, but she had to find something to say that might help. There was a vial of rosewater on the chest, and she damped a piece of linen with it and took it back to the bed. As the queen, unresisting, offered her face, Ninian said simply, 'How many babies even survive the process of birth? Those that do must have an extra strength in them to face the process of living.'

But the queen would not be comforted. 'Alexander will die. And Jamie is so small, so vulnerable. If anything were to happen to the king, his uncle Atholl would become regent, and regents have great opportunities to mould things to their own desires . . .'

Chilled, Ninian said helplessly, 'Madame, your labour was a hard one, and many women suffer from depression afterwards. Today has been a great strain for you. It will all seem quite different when you begin to feel stronger again. Now, will you let me help you dress for the banquet?'

IN another room in the royal lodging, the Earl of Atholl was washing his hands of the future.

It was almost seven years since James had married the Lady Joan Beaufort, and every daughter born of the marriage had made Atholl's eventual succession to the throne more likely. Or if not his – for he was an old man, after all – his son's. But now there were two infant princes between the Atholls and the throne.

Atholl said he didn't care. He said he never had cared. 'Whit wud I be doing with the throne?'

Blandly, Adam remarked that there were advantages.

'Och, I couldny be bothered with a' that negotiating and tax-raising and law-making kings huv tae do! Naw, naw.' He pointed. 'Seize a haud o' yon breastplate there; that'll dae fine for the banquet.'

Adam handed him the breastplate and even buckled the straps for him. 'But the Master of Atholl will be disappointed when he hears. And what does young Rob have to say to it?'

'Och, he's as bad as you. Nothing but ifs and buts, and will I be king some day or won't I. He's cultivating that fine perjink manner of his, just in case. "Oh, grandfather this, and oh, grandfather that." I tell you, I've had enough. Maybe if the English were tae free my son . . . Maybe when my grandson comes of age, if he is my grandson and no' a bastard . . . And maybe a bastard grandson's better than none. It's a' maybe, maybe, maybe. I want to hear nae mair o' it.'

'Not even if something were to happen to James, so that you would become regent?'

Atholl glowered at him, and jammed the toorie on his head. 'Regent? Yon's a right dirty word. D'ye remember whit happened tae the last regent?'

Adam smiled. 'He was short-sighted enough to let the king grow to manhood.'

The old man sniffed noisily. 'Aye, he never had as much sense as ye could stuff in a flea's balls. But ye can save your breath to cool your pottage, Mishure de Verne. My nephew's got two fine wee sons to come after him, and we're both gaun off to drink their health. As far as the succession's concerned, I've got no further interest in the proceedings. C'mon. I want my dinner.'

Adam, following him down the stairs, reflected, 'But if someone were to clear the path to the throne for you, and no questions asked, you'd mew on a very different note, you shaggy old buzzard!'

8

THERE was a certain forced gaiety about the banquet, because there hadn't been time for anyone to come from a distance, not even from France, and everyone present knew everyone else too well and saw enough of them in everyday life to feel ecstatic over being stuck beside them, yet again, for hours on end. Especially when the Master of the Revels had been busy here, too, so that the servers – including the ceremonial ones like the Earl of Douglas, who got quite uppish about it – could scarcely move for the great wooden castle on wheels that filled most of the space between the tables. It was full of exuberant young squires pretending to be Trojans, while other young squires who were pretending to be Greeks were accommodated in a wheeled wooden assault tower whose navigator wasn't perfectly in control. He missed the royal table by a hair's breadth and crashed, instead, into the one full of minor earls and knights, who were disgruntled enough already.

After three of the ladies had fainted, and Atholl had farted twice – explaining loudly that a' this stramash was giving him indigestion – and after a window had had to be broken to let in some air, the Master of the Revels sulkily removed his Greeks and Trojans, leaving the castle and assault tower behind as mute witnesses to the philistinism of all Scots. He was Irish, himself.

It was a relief to retire from the Great Hall to the private chamber for wine and spices and relatively civilized conversation but, even so, the atmosphere was abominably stuffy. It was at times like these that Gavin remembered his youth, and the scented silence of Kinveil, with no sounds but those of nature and the sea. There came to him, suddenly, a memory of November nights with clear dark skies and the firmament inconceivably full of stars, sparkling in the frosty air. Nights of a beauty he had never seen again, because he had never taken time to look. He had given up hoping to see the future written there.

If Ninian Drummond had still been present, he would have stayed –

at a distance. But the queen had retired early and all her ladies with her.

Gavin had seen very little of Ninian in this last year; he had been away so much, and she had been spending a good deal of time at Dess. Nor had he wanted to see her, because he loved her and to spend time in her company would have been unwise. It was just that sometimes he thought he would go mad, not knowing if this nagging, low-key torture was his alone. Two years ago at Inverness, she had said that she felt for him as no woman should feel for a priest, and he hadn't dared to believe her. Now, he was obsessed with the need to know whether it was still true – whether it had ever, really, been true. Only to know; not more than that. But to ask was impossible, even though they had now reached the stage of being able to talk together, like two ordinary, adult human beings who had no feeling for each other at all.

Were the stars still there? No one noticed as he left the chamber and made his way quietly down and out into the Common Court, the abbey kirk on his right, the gatehouse on his left and the wall all around. There was not a soul in sight as he walked out past the gatehouse and into the wide spaces of the park, and turned his feet towards the high ground, where there would be solitude, to the hill that some called Arthur's Seat and others *Ard-na-Saigheid*, 'the height of an arrow's flight'. The crisp air rinsed his eyes and forehead like ice-water on a hot day, and vigour surged back into his limbs again.

There was a faint, frosty crunch to the turf as he began the easy climb to the summit from which he would be able to see, spread out before him under the cloud-veiled moon, the whole panorama of Edinburgh and the Pentland Hills and the Firth of Forth.

Still lingering in the air, trapped between earth and sky, was the faint, elusive tang of last night's bonfires. It had been All Hallows, traditionally the end of the old year and the beginning of the new, the night when the barriers between this world and the next were down, when the dead returned from the grave, and strangers from the underworld briefly walked the earth. It was paganism, far from pure, and not at all simple, which the church had been incapable of wiping out. Even the queen, a model Christian, had hesitated about having the infant princes christened at such a time, but the king had said, 'When better? When the past has gone, and there is a new beginning!'

The blood singing in his veins, his head empty of all except exhilaration, Gavin reached the summit to find that he was not, after all, alone. There was another night owl sitting there on the grass, her hood thrown back from unbound hair and her eyes dark in the finely structured face. She was tossing a small white pebble in her hand, and smiling faintly.

'Congratulations,' she said. 'Breathing quite unhurried, no signs of stress, and wide awake despite the hour.'

He smiled back, in the sudden, startled knowledge that for the first time in his life he wanted to share his solitude.

He took the tone of the conversation from her. 'In answer to your first two points, when one is used to playing tennis with the king and discussing business with him at the same time, all other forms of physical exertion pale by comparison. And as to the third, I was born just before midnight and have been twelve hours behind or ahead of other people ever since.'

She moved over, to make space on the turf beside her. 'Were you? I was, too, but I'd never thought of it like that before. How nice to have an explanation to give all those people who are so offensively bright in the mornings and think you should be, too!'

The beauty of the night invited silence, which was as well, because the only things they wanted to say were things that could not be said. Certainly not now, when there was a frail, new thread of something that was almost friendship between them.

The strain began to tell on Gavin first, perhaps because he had not lived with it for so long. His eyes on the white pebble, he said at last, 'Your Hallow-fire stone? What did it tell you?' It was the custom for everyone to lay a marked stone at the edge of the bonfire, and if one's stone was still there next day, whole and undamaged, the omens were good; if it were cracked, its owner would not live to see the next All Hallows fire.

Absently, she said, 'It's still whole, but it wasn't where I put it, and there was a footprint nearby. That means death, doesn't it? But not mine.'

'It means that someone kicked it by mistake when he went to look for his own stone!'

Her face turned to his, alight with laughter, and it was only with an effort that he kept his hands clasped round his folded knees. 'Bishop Gavin! Is it possible that you don't believe in omens from on high?'

Unaccountably cheerful, he replied, 'Oh, but I do! I spent the better part of a day last week averting them.' And then, because she was looking amused and enquiring, he told her about the Trinity, the gates of heaven, and the descending angels, and she saw exactly what he meant. It reminded her of something of the sort that had been done at Villeneuve once, with disastrous consequences, and then of a banquet at Avignon when one of the cardinals had been entertaining Benedict, the last of the anti-popes.

'The Clerk of the Kitchen had heard of a Florentine idea of serving a pasty full of live birds, but unfortunately, he didn't know the trick of it. He told the cooks to bake a huge pie-case, and then tip in a cageful of birds and hold them down while they put the lid on. It was pure madness, of course! The kitchen was a shambles by the time they'd finished, and when the pastry was cut at table and the birds flew out their distress was – how shall I put it? – only too evident. The cardinal finished up almost bankrupt, because all his guests demanded new finery to replace what had been ruined, and His Holiness even demanded a new golden tiara!'

Gavin threw back his head and laughed. 'From what I've heard of Benedict, it was probably all his idea in the first place. An astute man, and an interesting one.'

She almost made the mistake of saying how Columba had revered him, but stopped herself in time. She didn't want to break this new sympathy between Gavin Cameron and herself.

Especially when she was about to betray Columba to him.

She had thought and thought, and had come to see that Gavin Cameron was right, and that the realm – which meant all the people – might sometimes matter more than one or two individuals. It must be wrong to risk thousands of lives to satisfy the ambitions of one man, even if that one man believed his ambitions to be synonymous with God's. Perhaps they were, but perhaps they were not. How could one judge the truth of someone else's revelation?

She feared Columba's reaction to Gavin Cameron's success at Rome. Even more, she feared what Adam might be planning. Robert Graham had mentioned Wales to her, and it was the only real clue she had. She hoped that, somehow, she could warn the chancellor without resorting to the final treachery of naming names.

He said, 'And what, by the way, *is* the trick to baking a pie full of live birds?'

'Quite simple, really, when you know how. You bake a hollow pie case, complete with lid, and then cut a hole out of the bottom and feed the birds in, one at a time, by hand. Then the bit you cut out goes back in place again, and that's all there is to it.'

They went on talking, lightly, for a few minutes longer, until she began to rise, saying, 'It's chilly. I must go back.' He didn't help her to her feet, and as they walked together down the hill, pausing only to look at the half-built chapel perched on one of the spurs and ultimately to be dedicated to St Anthony, he neither came close to her nor touched her even by mistake.

They were down on the flat before she managed, without being too obvious about it, to bring the conversation round to her own ignorance about the landscape of Scotland, the differences between north and south, between Scotland as a whole and England. And Wales. Was Wales like Scotland?

If he was mystified, he didn't show it.

At last, just as they were approaching the gatehouse, she stopped. 'Are there many Scots exiles in Wales?'

He looked at her, his face momentarily still, and then looked away again. She could have wept with gratitude, because she could see that he had understood not only what she had said, but something of what it had cost her to say it.

His 'Ah!' was almost like a sigh. 'Yes, there are a number. All Highlanders, and all anxious to come home as soon as possible. Perhaps next summer, which is always the time for migrations.'

'So I have been told.'

The Common Court was still empty and quite silent. All the torches but one had gone out. Ninian knew that, in the quire stalls of the abbey kirk, the canons would be at service, but no sound filtered out through the portal. The royal lodging was dark and quiet, too, except for a glimmer of firelight from the windows of the Great Hall, where all the servants and squires would be bedded down on the floor for the night, with their cloaks for coverlets.

Suddenly realizing that this miraculous interlude was nearing its end, she began casting round desperately in her mind for some way, any way, of prolonging it. But all she could think of was a shame-faced confession. 'I don't even know where Wales is.'

'Would you understand a rough map, if I lent it to you?'

'I don't know.'

'Wait, then. I have one in my room.'

His room opened directly on to the Common Court, and as the last torch guttered and went out, she followed him almost aimlessly, drifting over to the door without even recognizing the temptation that had her in its grip, the temptation to see a place that was distinctively his and might tell her a little of what she did not know about him.

333

The room was austere, as she would have expected, the walls lime-washed, the flagged floor swept and garnished. There were two vestment chests made from some silken old wood, and a smaller document chest with a travelling shrine on it and a handsome whalebone casket, bound and strapped in bronze, and secured with a double-hasped lock. A simple wooden honeycomb structure on the wall held a number of rolled parchments, one to each cell, and on the table, with its pricket candlesticks and the stool before it, there were books and pens and inkpots and a few more documents. There was only one luxury in the room, a glowing charcoal brazier, and only one other piece of furniture, a fourposter bed with a white tester over it and an unusual and beautiful coverlet of bleached linen, woven and embroidered with one of the intricately interlaced designs that Ninian knew were traditional to the Highlands. There were no curtains round the bed, and the room looked more spacious for it.

And then he turned from his rummaging at the table and saw her standing there doubtfully, her eyes huge and dark in the candlelight, and the fall of red-gold hair gleaming like shuttered sunshine. The deep night silence was around them, and there was no movement except their own. No perfume except the crisp night air, touched with woodsmoke. No light beyond the circled radiance of the candles.

He said, 'God help me. I love you so much.'

9

SHE was dreaming, of course, although it surprised her that the dream should take such a form tonight, when all her senses were focused on the liking, sweet and strange, that had so unexpectedly blossomed between them. The liking, not the loving. And when all her mind was on the warning she had given him, and on her own treachery in betraying the only other men she loved on earth.

For an eternity she stared at him, his face underlit by the candles so that it was a study in contrast, golden light and charcoal dark. Yet there was nothing harsh, nothing even of the familiar sternness in his straightset, unwavering eyes or the strong, sharply arched brows, now drawn together in the faintest of frowns; in the thick, black hair or fine-boned authoritative nose; in the long, flexible mouth whose curling corners were tight and deep-shadowed . . .

When she understood, at last, that this was reality, her own lips parted a little, and a smile of the most profound joy and thankfulness came to her face. There was such beauty and serenity in it that all Gavin's doubts, all conscience, all hard-held control, slipped from his grasp.

His eyes wide on hers, he took the three paces that brought him to her. Then he drew her into the room, and closed the door, and slid the bolt home.

They stood motionless for a while, deceptively tranquil, two dark figures profiled against the light of the candles, the only contact between them his long fingers lightly spanning her waist. It was as if all time was theirs to conjure with, now that the waiting and the dreaming were over, now that all happiness was there in their hands.

But despite everything, they knew of each other only what they had seen, what they could sense, and what love told them. And so Gavin, in the end, broke the silence by asking the question that, two years ago, it would not have occurred to him to ask, and, two years later, he would not have needed to. For him he knew, and for her he hoped, that the feeling between them would last for life and beyond, but because they were two mature, intelligent human beings it seemed to him important that their minds should first concede what their passions so urgently demanded.

Because tonight would be their once and only loving.

The Gaelic lilt unfamiliarly strong in his voice, he said, 'Woman of my heart, will you lie with me? On this single night that will be all our lives together?'

It was not, perhaps, very lucid. Perhaps he had not wanted it to be.

But all questions, for her, had been asked and answered in that moment when he had looked up from the table and said, 'God help me. I love you so much.' That knowledge was all that mattered to her, and now she heard only what she wanted to hear. So she took one short step forward, and raised her lips, and said huskily, 'Kiss me now, or I think I will die.'

His hands had released her as she moved, and he held them, taut on the empty air, for a last brief moment of indecision. And then he pulled her to him and his mouth came down on hers and all else was forgotten in their aching need for each other.

Twice before they had kissed, and the beauty of it now was the same and greater, but tonight they could see beyond the kiss and there was in them the urgency of all lovers since the beginning of time. Yet even as he drew the gown and the shift from her shoulders to fall rustling and soft to the floor, even as her chilled, hasty fingers struggled with the laces of his shirt and hose, their lips clung together as if all life was in the contact.

There was no part of her that did not respond to him, no inch of her that did not quiver at the swift caresses of his lips and hands, just as his own hard flesh vibrated at her lightest touch. But there was a furious impatience in them for the moment when their two bodies should be joined, and when that moment would no longer be deferred he took her in his arms and laid her on the bed. She smiled up at him, the lovely serenity lit by new fires within, and raised her hands, feather light, to stroke them down the sensitive skin at the sides of his waist and hips, so that he gave a deep, shuddering intake of breath, and laughed unsteadily, and bent to kiss her again. Then he swung his tall, limber body over hers, and her hips arched to receive him, and all the splendour of the world was theirs.

Because their passion was more than physical, and because it had been held at bay for so long, this was the true moment of its culmination. Before, they had been separate beings, and afterwards – when they had travelled together along the road that lay before them – they would be separated again by the rough, destructive radiance at its end. But now, for a time no scale could measure, they lay mouth to mouth, heart to heart, body to body, silent and still, no muscle moving except those that, warm, throbbing, unimaginably sensual, locked them together as if they were a single being.

And then, at last, he began to move inside her, gently at first but soon demandingly, and she opened dazed and smiling eyes on his and responded as he asked her to. Their bodies might have been specially fashioned for each other, or perhaps love was enough to make them so, but both pace and rhythm were perfectly matched as he swept her along the magical path. All the way, braced above her and resting his weight on his hands, he kept his gaze on hers, reading every subtle change in her, every cadence, every inflection, as, sometimes imperative, sometimes tender, he ravished her senses until she cried out for release from the long, ecstatic torment of it. And then, in the end, the craving became too great for both of them, and the joy too infinite to be borne.

Afterwards, their bodies still lightly joined, they lay for a while with her head cradled on his arm and his lips buried in the shining tangle of her hair. When he raised his head to look down at her, she was not quite asleep but lost in some drowsy limbo, and he allowed his hand to drift at will over the fine-grained skin and the gentle curves, learning about her, loving her, willing himself to accept that this first time was also the last time, that for her own sake and his he should be teaching himself not how to remember, but how to forget.

Puzzled, frowning, he traced a light finger over the knife-thin, almost invisible line of a scar that ran from between her breasts down over her stomach, to break and resume again on the soft flesh of her inner thigh, and as he did so she stirred, and murmured, and tried to turn in his arms.

And then, forgetting everything else, he laughed softly, because her movement had been enough to rouse him again, and she opened her eyes, aware of it, and laughed back at him, and this time they celebrated their love with a gentler passion and a leisured delight, and a coming together that was slow and exquisitely sweet.

He was leaning over her when she awoke, his face serious despite the hint of amusement in the low, flexible voice.

> *Douce dame jolie,*
> *Pour Dieu ne pensés mie*
> *Que nulle ait signourie*
> *Seur moy fors vous seulement.*

'Sweet lady fair, 'Fore God I swear, That none but thee, Do govern me.'

She chuckled at him. 'Don't let the king hear you say so!'

Then, struggling up to a sitting position, and tucking herself in voluptuously against his side, she went on, 'And why should you know the songs of Machaut? I remember wondering, the very first day we met in Villeneuve, where you had learned your French. I decided Paris, but you never studied there, did you?'

'I wish I had! No, I was too poor for that. Twice, when I was at St Andrews, I had to go before the bishop and beg to be excused the fees, because I couldn't afford them. A salutary experience! But perhaps it was no bad thing, because it meant I had to excel in my studies. Several of my teachers had degrees from Paris . . .' Including Columba Crozier, but he could not, would not, say so. 'And I learned everything I could from them.'

She pressed a kiss into the hollow of his shoulder. 'Did you ever think, when you were poor and hungry, that you might rise some day to be Bishop of Glasgow and Chancellor of the Realm?'

'Oh, yes! I always meant to.'

'You *what*!'

He grinned down into her startled eyes. 'I did, I did! Why are your eyes such a beautiful colour?' Fleetingly, he kissed the lids. 'I was about nine years old, I think, when I decided to reform the world, and since I hadn't been born rich or royal, there was only one path open to me. The church.'

His expression had been changing even while he spoke and had become almost sombre. 'I wonder, would I still have taken it, if I had been able to look ahead?'

She waited.

'I couldn't have foreseen – you. Until these last months, I have managed my life quite comfortably, you know. I always believed love was something people thought themselves into, and I had no intention of doing anything so foolish.'

The breath stumbling in her lungs, she asked, 'And now?'

He didn't answer at first, and then, surprisingly, said, 'How do you think of God?'

'How?'

'Do you think of Him as a just God, a benevolent God – what?'

'Have I a choice?' She was uneasy about this sudden access of gravity, and took refuge in mischief. 'Does my free will extend to choosing between the aspects of God?' It was blasphemy, near enough. Columba would have had a fit if he had heard her.

'You're a wicked woman! Have you any idea how fearful I was that you would expose me?' He bent his head and kissed her again, deeply, intensely, like a man still starved. Like a man who expected to go on being starved for the rest of his life.

He said, 'Never risk saying that kind of thing to anyone but me.'

'I know. It's heresy. But it was you who made me think about free will, and I believe in it now. Will you explain all about it to me, some day, and why it's so wrong?'

'Perhaps. Now answer my question.'

She couldn't escape it after all, it seemed. 'A just God? Yes, I suppose so. But a benevolent God – no.'

'An avenging God?'

'Yes.'

Just then, beyond the heavy door, they heard the handbells ringing for Prime. Though it was only six o'clock and still black dark, the day had begun.

338

They dressed quickly, Ninian grateful that she had changed from her banquet gown into day clothes for her walk on the hill. She had gone out because she had wanted to breathe and be alone, and that simple desire had brought her the greatest happiness she had ever known, greater – because it was real – than anything she had ever dreamed of.

Before he opened the door to see whether the way was clear, he held her in his arms once more and then, as he draped the cloak hood gently over her hair, he said, 'I, too, believe in an avenging God. What we have done tonight may be forgiven us, but . . .' It was hard to go on. 'But, for the future, the burden of sin would be too great. We can't be together again. We shouldn't allow ourselves even to be private again. Do you understand?'

It wasn't shock or pain that flooded through her, but the sheerest exasperation. Those silly church laws about lust being forgiven a priest, but never love!

She said, 'Yes, but . . .', and then he closed her lips with a kiss, and opened the door, and found the way was clear. She had no choice but to go.

Shaking her head over the idiocy of men, even the best of them, she slipped out into the Common Court, and by devious routes back to her room. Clearly, it was going to be necessary to have a very serious talk with Bishop Gavin in the near future. Next time they made love, perhaps.

10

BUT that was not to be soon.

That she was accustomed to living without him made it not easier, as she would have expected, but harder to bear – even though she had something to treasure now, something she could take out from her heart, as from a private strongbox, in the darkest hours of the night. Something to look at from every angle, and remember with enchantment, and live through again when she had to, when the sense of privation became too great.

And then the king summoned her.

She was still irrationally nervous of him, and was grateful that he treated her, in general, as he treated all the queen's women except the

Lady Egidia, very much as if she were part of the furniture. But she didn't delude herself into thinking he had forgotten her part in the Lady Elinor affair, or her relationship to the young man he had hanged at Inverness, or her intervention in the trial of Alexander of the Isles. If it had not been for the queen, she knew she would have been banished from court long ago.

As she hurried along the corridors at Perth in response to the unexpected summons, she wondered whether he could possibly have found out what had happened at Holyrood on the night after All Hallows. But it was impossible – wasn't it?

So she was shaking as she knelt before her sovereign, even though he was looking at her quite kindly.

He waved his hand impatiently at her, as he always did, telling her to rise, and came to the point with characteristic lack of ceremony.

'We are told that you have been widowed now for eighteen months, Lady Ninian?'

She nodded, bewildered.

'It is enough. Scotland needs strong sons, and it is our wish that you should marry again. We have an excellent husband in mind for you, and it will be fitting that you should be wed within the year.'

CHAPTER TWO

I

IN the bitter, plague-ridden winter that followed, not only Scotland but all Europe was caught up in a furious surge of activity.

To Ninian, it felt sometimes as if she were the only person in the whole wide world who wasn't involved, as she sat at Edinburgh or Perth or Dess with her hands metaphorically folded in her lap, attending the queen, or listening politely to Walter of Lithgow, the downright, middle-aged widower the king had decreed she should marry, or carefully rehearsing in her mind all that she meant to say to Gavin Cameron, on that subject and others – if ever he stopped long enough to listen.

He was as busy as a tick in a sheep shed. First, there were the arrangements for the forthcoming negotiations with England, and then an unfortunate incident of Scots piracy that came home to roost, necessitating letters of marque that James was exceedingly reluctant to sign, and then he had to go and attend to some unexpected and urgent cathedral business in Glasgow.

And no sooner was he back than the English ambassadors arrived. They wanted to talk, not about a truce, but about the unpaid ransom, which came very low on Scotland's list of priorities. As a result, the talks were both evasive and exceedingly protracted, and the only way the ambassadors could be got rid of was by James promising to send

341

Bishop Gavin and a Scots embassy to London as soon after Christmas as was feasible. What with that and the imminent session of parliament, Bishop Gavin found himself working twenty-five hours a day, eight days a week.

And when he arrived back from London with the truce in his pocket, it was to discover that James had thrown into jail one of the most powerful nobles in the land. The Earl of Douglas, it seemed, had been indulging in private negotiations with the English, with the object of having his wife's brother, Malise Graham, released from the Tower.

'Well, it was treason, near enough!' James yelped, when Gavin raised an eyebrow. 'I won't have the barons – Douglasses or anyone! – acting like a law unto themselves. What worries me is what he was offering in exchange for the dratted boy. Have you thought about that, eh? The help of the Douglasses when England next decides to invade us? It's been done before, often enough, and I'm not having it done again.'

'Quite,' Gavin said. 'But putting him in jail seems unlikely to make him any more loyal.'

'Oh, you think not?' There was a pause, and then the royal tone changed. 'No-o-o-o. He's not going to turn enemy to me just because I locked him up in Lochleven for a few weeks, is he?'

'Ah,' said Gavin, smothering a weary grin. 'Only for a few weeks?'

'Oh, yes!' The smile wreathing the royal beard could scarcely have been more innocent. 'Just until the end of the month, I thought.'

'Well, that's all right, then.'

Across the Channel, things of even wider moment were taking place.

The English had succeeded in laying hands on the Maid of Orléans, and on 21 February she had been put on trial for her life before a court of the Inquisition, charged with heresy and sorcery.

And even more far-reaching, from Scotland's point of view, was what had happened in Rome just the day before. Pope Martin V, in the sixty-third year of his age, and in the fourteenth year and third month of his pontificate, had died of an apoplexy.

2

THE funeral rites, consisting mainly of Masses and absolutions, went on for nine interminable days, but most of the general weeping and wailing around the brass tomb was left to the ordinary people of

Rome. Everyone else was much too busy intriguing over who was going to sit next on the throne of St Peter.

The conclave was relatively quick about reaching a decision, but, even so, it seemed a long time to Columba, especially when he felt an irrational compulsion just to stand, and go on standing – in company with half the officials of the curia – outside the enclosed, heavily guarded building, waiting for something to happen.

It was foolishness, of course. There wasn't even any gossip worth hearing, because from the moment the unimpressive wicket door closed behind the eighteen cardinals, all contact between them and the outside world ceased. There wasn't much contact inside, either, because each cardinal had his own private chamber, and wasn't allowed to meet his fellows except in the privy, the chapel, or the election hall.

The third day, however, was frequently the day of decision in papal elections, and so it proved this time. Doubtless, it was pure coincidence that the third day also happened to be the last on which, according to the regulations governing such affairs, the cardinals were permitted a square meal. After that, until they reached agreement, it was bread and wine only, no matter how long it took.

It occurred to Columba, as he stood there waiting, that there might after all be advantages to being a Lollard, because he would very much have liked to be able to convey his views to God directly. 'Oh, Lord,' he would have said, with every ounce of charm he could muster, 'I beg of Thee most earnestly – *most* earnestly – that Thou leadest them to choose the cardinal whose election would best advance Thy interests. And mine. That is to say, Cardinal Condulmer.'

Poggio thought that either Orsini or Comitum had a better chance. Indeed, as far as Condulmer was concerned, he was prepared to offer Columba odds of nine to five against.

But miracles could happen, and they did. When the traditional announcement, '*Habemus Papam*' – 'We have a pope' – was made, the name that was dropped into the waiting silence was, indeed, that of Gabriel Condulmer, who had chosen to be known henceforth as Pope Eugenius IV.

Columba followed in his train to St Peter's, and stood quietly to one side as, at the altar of St Gregory, the new pope was robed for Mass and afterwards crowned – by the dean of the College of Cardinals, who looked as if he had voted for someone else – with the triple tiara, symbolizing power in temporal things, fatherhood in matters spiritual, and pre-eminence in all to do with heaven.

He was still in the papal entourage as His Holiness, expensively mounted, rode through Rome to the Lateran church of St John. Most of Rome was in the streets and a dozen times it was necessary to toss handfuls of small coins down to divert the people's attention and clear the way.

And then, at the Lateran, before he was entitled to mount the throne, the pope had to seat himself on another, special chair, spreading his white robes wide; a chair of porphyry, pierced in the seat, so that one of the younger cardinals could crawl underneath and verify His Holiness' manhood. Ever since Pope Joan, whom Columba didn't entirely believe in, there had been a certain sensitivity in such matters. There wasn't even a flicker of expression on the grave, bird-like features of the man who had formerly been Gabriel Condulmer.

And then, to the *Te Deum*, Eugenius IV was borne to the high altar and was pope indeed.

3

COLUMBA was too old a campaigner to rush things, but the first few weeks of Eugenius's rule were sufficiently inauspicious to persuade him that neither would it be wise to loiter. At Eugenius's first consistory, the floors collapsed and the Bishop of Sinigaglia was trampled to death in the panic. And although that was the kind of augury that impressed only the credulous, the next one looked as if it might be more far-reaching. His Holiness, persuaded that his acquisitive predecessor had left a great treasure hidden somewhere, set about finding it by methods so ruthless and so single-minded that he alienated every last one of Martin's relatives, dependants, and adherents. Since it wasn't wise for a mere Venetian, however elevated, to annoy the Colonnas, there was clearly trouble ahead, and of a probably murderous kind.

However, there were advantages. Eugenius began to lean very heavily on old friends, and in no time at all was prepared to do almost anything they asked. As a result, just two months from the day of his enthronement, His Holiness took Archdeacon Columba Crozier –

very officially indeed and with a great deal of publicity – under his own personal protection.

Columba celebrated, that night, with another old friend, someone whom he knew would understand and enter with him into his triumph. Understanding was one of the most agreeable of Vittoria's many agreeable talents.

She was overflowing with it, this night. When he knocked lightly on the secluded door of the house near the S. Maria in Capitolio, she opened it to him herself, naked as a statue of Aphrodite and a thousand times more desirable. Until then, he hadn't even been aware of the hunger in him, and he stood there in his expensive velvet robes, a man inclining to stateliness, with a head like a Roman emperor and a finely cultivated air of distinction, and gaped at her, quite unable to move or speak, as if all the life essence in him had flowed together to concentrate itself in the single raging tumult in his loins.

'Welcome, my dove!' she said. 'All honour to His Holiness's new acolyte and emissary! Will you enter?'

'Oh, yes,' he said. 'Oh, yes.'

Afterwards, the servants brought a light meal to the high, richly hung bed. Columba was surprised at its comparative sparsity, for Vittoria enjoyed her food, and so did he, but its quality was excellent, and he said nothing. He had the most delightful feeling of satiety, with a faint undercurrent of regret that, nowadays, he couldn't manage more than once in a night – although it was a while since he'd tried, and it hadn't been with Vittoria. Perhaps, perhaps . . . She had been careful not to tire him, and it had been unusually pleasant to take the passive role for a change. His figure wasn't up to athletics any more, but there was nothing at all wrong with Vittoria's muscle control and her riding skills were unmatchable. It was a very long time since he'd had such an exciting climax.

'So,' she said. 'The Archdeacon of Tee . . . Tee-vee . . .'

'Teviotdale.'

'. . . is now also the Archdeacon of Lottiano . . .'

'Lothian.'

'. . . and an accredited papal acolyte, and emissary, and what else?'

'And he has been exempted from the jurisdiction of all ordinaries. That is to say that the decision of the Glasgow chapter that gave me so much trouble just four years ago has been overturned. The Bishop of Glasgow no longer has any control over me.'

'Our young and intolerant hawk?'

345

'The same.'

'And what else? There is still something more, is there not? I smell triumph of a nature almost sublime.'

'Not sublime.' He laughed. 'Sinfully human.' He picked up the wine bottle, an unusual one made of marbled red and green glass and shaped rather like a pestle. 'Persian?'

She nodded.

Removing the stopper, he refilled their beakers. 'His Holiness has despatched an order to King James and his chancellor, requiring them to permit all my tithes and revenues in Scotland to be collected and . . .'

It had always intrigued Vittoria that, even in bed, Columba remained dignified. But now the high-nosed features were lit by the kind of gleeful, gutter-brat grin she had never seen except on the face of a Roman *ragazzo*. With something that was more a giggle than a chuckle, he said, 'I should think James may well have a seizure, and Cameron, too, with luck. Because His Holiness has demanded that my revenues be collected and sent to me – here, *in ready money*.'

She was just a little puzzled. 'And this is funny?'

'Oh, yes! The particular piquancy of it is that His Holiness, in all innocence, has offered James and Cameron a far more exquisite insult than even I could have devised after much deliberation. Because the spending of Scots gold at Rome is what most of our own private war has been about.'

He stretched luxuriously, and then turned against the heaped satin pillows and looked at her. 'I think that today has been the most perfect, the most satisfying day of my whole life. It is I who have the upper hand, now. Nothing anyone can do can harm me.'

Then, as he surveyed the rich, perfumed flesh, his expression began to change, and after a moment he raised a hand and cupped it thoughtfully under her breast.

She smiled, cat-like. He was ready, after all. So she said, 'Then there is certainly something to be celebrated. I have a new plaything in my house. Come and let me show you. No, there is no need to dress.'

It was a small room with large windows looking on to the inner courtyard, a courtyard filled with tubs of scented trees and herbs, and lit with half-shaded lanterns; since the night was mild, the windows were open.

The room itself was the plaything. Instead of a floor it had a most elegant sunken pool filled with warm, scented water.

Vittoria said, 'Many public woman-houses have baths now, but theirs are only tubs to sit and caress in. Mine is one where we may do more.'

It was like being young again, and thin and agile. Columba felt weightless, and so, too, was Vittoria, sliding and gliding in and out of his arms like some well-fleshed water nymph. Under her voluptuous tutelage, he performed prodigies he had never dreamed of. He was inexhaustible, and so was she, and they laughed, and made love, and, finding that even the most impossible angles had become possible, laughed again and tried another way.

'In the Grand Seraglio,' said Vittoria, spluttering slightly after an unexpected submersion, 'they know of only eleven positions, but in Cathay they are said to be familiar with forty. Think shame on yourself that you have not been counting!'

Columba, who had always enjoyed physical love without being obsessed by it, said, 'Nine, so far,' and reached out again.

When, at last, both strength and invention failed, dawn was breaking and it was time to leave, although he was uncertain whether his legs would carry him. She said, 'And what will you do now? About your war against the hawk? Surely you must be satisfied?'

He hadn't thought about it but, in his present mood, it seemed to him that in victory one could afford to be magnanimous. 'You are right,' he said. 'I will send a letter to my son. There is, after all, no longer any need for him to demean himself, to waste his energy, on destroying a mere provincial bishop. Let Gavin Cameron find his own way to the eternal fire!'

4

IF Columba's messenger had found Adam in time, many things would afterwards have been different. But while the man was politely enquiring for M. de Verne, first at Dess and later at Blair Atholl, Adam himself was admiring the view of Loch Linnhe from the prow of a galley bound for the invasion of Scotland.

He was still no convert to Highland scenery, but after these last months in Wales he observed it with a less critical eye. It had been unconscionably wet until they were almost out of the Firth of Lorne, but now at last the sun had deigned to shine, that unreliable Highland sun that functioned on a different time scale from the sun elsewhere. Here, a sunny day meant a sunny morning, or a sunny afternoon – seldom both.

But now, it was casting its characteristic blue light on the great vista of mountains that lay ahead, and the narrowing channel into which the galleys were bound. The decks of all six of them were threatening to give way under the feet of the returning exiles, most of whom, chattering away in their own outlandish tongue, were almost dancing with impatience at sight of their native shores. Adam had the feeling that they were all going to fall on their faces and kiss the ground when they landed.

The little fleet was bound for Loch Sunart, where Donald Balloch, cousin to Alexander of the Isles, was waiting for them with his own army and all the latest news. Adam had resisted the choice of Loch Sunart as a rallying point, not for any tactical reason, but from superstition, because it lapped the shores of Ardnamurchan – and that reminded him of Blane. It was James and Cameron, between them, who had killed Blane, but if Adam had never sent the boy to Ardnamurchan, he might be alive today. It made him feel uncomfortable.

He shrugged the feeling away as he waded ashore. God be praised, Robert Graham was there, sinewy as ever, the red hair gleaming above the dark crucifix of his features, and his thin nose twisted in distaste. And it was true that the crowded galleys were sending their own pungent message before them on the inshore wind.

'Well, what do you expect, after two weeks at sea?' Adam demanded irritably, his feet still wet and his balance unreliable as they climbed together up the hillside.

Sir Robert shrugged. 'How many men in all?'

'A thousand.'

'Donald Balloch has another twelve hundred. And every day we stay here, more are coming in from the glens.'

'Is there any news of James?'

The dark eyes stared at him expressionlessly. 'That depends on how you look at things. It is my belief that we have been betrayed again.'

It wasn't possible. Adam stared back. He could feel his face darkening, becoming congested with rage, and it was as if his chest would burst open under the pressure and spray all his heart's blood over this damned, this double-damned heather. 'What do you mean?'

Sir Robert, peaceably chewing on a stalk of grass, said, 'Sit down, man. There is no call for all this Gallic temperament. Spring was late this year, and the passes remained closed until early in May, but as soon as they were open, the Earl of Mar marched into Lochaber with a royal army at his back. The Earls of Huntly and Caithness are with him, and Fraser of Lovat, and some others. The Macintoshes and the Mackays – and the Camerons – are also with him. They are camped by Inverlochy.'

Adam's '*What?*' was almost a screech.

Robert Graham knew what he was thinking, and his slack-muscled mouth broke into one of his rare and oddly predatory grins. 'No, not quite the same battlefield as last time.' He scratched the red stubble on his chin. 'I spoke of betrayal, but I do not think the traitor is to be found among the clans, because the men have always known too much rather than too little. I think whoever warned James knew only that there was something in the wind, and no more than that. Otherwise, James would be here himself.'

'Have you been in Perth? What is the gossip there?'

Sir Robert grinned again. 'Give the devil his due; James has been clever. Or perhaps it was Cameron. All the talk is that the troubles in the Highlands are ended. It is an illusion that must be maintained, you see – because if James's victory over Alexander failed to accomplish that, then it accomplished nothing. So, as far as Perth knows, Mar's army consists of no more than a few hundred archers and men-at-arms, whose ostensible objects are to appropriate some of the more fertile land for the crown, and – this will amuse you! – to discover whether it might be profitable to set up a customs port in Loch Linnhe to deal with the Irish and the Bristol trade.'

'*Grand Dieu!*' said Adam devoutly. 'That an Irishman or a Bristol man should pay customs?'

'Or a Highlander. However, the essential point is that Mar's army is far more substantial than rumour says.'

'Then what, in Satan's name, are you grinning about? How substantial?'

'Two thousand, at least, and well armed. And I am grinning because you will be quite charmed when you see it. It is sprawled all over the place. There is no discipline, no training, nothing. The men play cards all day, except when they are playing football. After eight uneventful weeks, Mar no longer believes – if he ever did – that any real threat exists.'

'You mean they have no idea that we are so close?'

349

'None at all. And they will not, until we are ready. This time it will be no set-piece battle, my dear Adam. This time, we will come on them suddenly, from the hills.'

5

JAMES never wasted energy on tantrums when things were really serious.

The Earl of Caithness had been killed, and one of the Lovats. The Earl of Mar, Justiciar of the North, had fled the field with an arrow through his thigh. A thousand men had died, and another thousand or so were scattered among the hills. And the Earl of Huntly, having quarrelled with Mar, had withdrawn his men and stood spitefully by and allowed it all to happen.

The news had spread through the glens like wildfire.

By the time the details reached Perth almost the whole of Scotland west and north of the Highland line was in ferment, and there was nothing the king could do about it, except try, with little hope of success, to raise another army.

'What will they do next?' he asked Gavin. 'Stay where they are? Come reiving and plundering into the Lowlands? Or mount a proper invasion, and try to set Alexander on my throne? You're the Highlander. Read their minds for me!'

The spectre of civil war was there before them, and Gavin knew that, whether it ended in victory or defeat, the very outbreak of such a war would be the greatest defeat James had ever known, or could know.

When he had returned to Scotland to take up his throne, his whole desire had been to give peace and stability to the country whose dim memory had been burnished bright for him by eighteen years of exile. Hard-headed in most things, in this he was deeply sentimental. But when he had come home, he had found the crown all but bankrupt, its revenues plundered, its estates given away; the church laid waste, and the nobles at war. He had said, then, 'If God grant me but the life of a dog, I will make the key keep the castle, and the bracken bush the cow.'

Yet now, seven years later, a lock on the door offered little more protection than it had ever done, and to tether a cow to a bush meant only that the thieves took the rope as well as the cow. It wasn't that

350

James – and Gavin – hadn't tried and weren't still trying. The trouble was that almost no one, from the barons down, was prepared to cooperate.

Gavin said slowly, 'If it were only a matter of Donald Balloch and the clansmen, I think we would have a few weeks of fire and slaughter and cattle reiving, and then everything would die down again. It would be the same story as always. The men are willing enough to fight in the summer, but as soon as it's time for the harvest, they vanish in the direction of home without so much as a by-your-leave. Donald Balloch is only a boy, no more than eighteen, and he wouldn't be able to stop them. From what I know of him, I doubt if he would want to. He's loud, he's insolent, he's a bully. To him, this whole episode, I think, is no more than a rude gesture in the face of royal authority.'

'I see. So we might have a respite from, say, next month until the spring?' There was no lightening of James's tone. All he was doing was mentally ticking off the possibilities, one by one. 'And if it were *not* only a matter of Donald Balloch and the clansmen?'

It was a bitter moment for Gavin, and also, he knew, a dangerous one. Because if it were not Donald Balloch, it had to be someone else. Gavin had no doubt that Robert Graham was involved, but it couldn't be Robert Graham alone, because he hadn't vanished from his usual haunts for long enough to do all the things that must have been done to bring this crisis about.

His mind working furiously, Gavin had been trying to think how to avoid putting a name to the 'Red Lord'. James would remember him from the battle two years ago. He had harped on the mystery for quite a while, suspecting the Douglasses, and then had seemed to forget the whole thing. Seemed to.

Once Gavin mentioned the Red Lord, there would be no going back. Because unless he said who, there would be no point in saying anything. And when he had said who, he would have to say why.

He had no choice at all in the matter, because Scotland's whole future was at stake. But with every word he uttered, he would be saying that most of the crises of these last four years had arisen because Gavin Cameron was Bishop of Glasgow and chancellor of the realm. He would be saying, too, that Ninian Drummond was cousin to a traitor. What penalty James might try to exact from her he did not know, but prayed that the queen's favour would protect her.

'If it were not Donald Balloch,' he said from his position at the window, 'then we would still have the respite, but no more. At winter's end, I think we would have war.'

'And who would declare it?'

Gavin took a deep, invisible breath. 'You will remember the Red Lord, I imagine?'

There was an arrested silence. Then, 'Yes?' James said.

'He is behind all this.'

'Is he, indeed? So? If you know that, then you must know who he is.'

'Yes.'

For a moment more, Gavin continued to stare out of the window of the royal chamber. Over to the right, in lively, smelly, bustling little Perth, the usual medley of bells was ringing out; among them the end-of-work bell which brought freedom to everyone except the tanners, who laboured on until midnight, when Matins was rung. One of the gate bells was jangling, too, announcing that the gate was closed, long before time, and anyone who wished to leave the city would have to use some other exit; there would be trouble about that. And also – a constant, familiar sound in this mortal world – the mournful tolling of a passing bell, bidding the healthy to pray for someone who was dying.

Ahead, across the water meadows and the marshes, every single trading ship in the river seemed to be rocking under the returning weight of its stout merchant owner and his clerks, the day's negotiating over, the evening's calculating of profit and loss not yet begun.

And to the left, only the hills.

'The spectacular young man we know as Adam de Verne,' Gavin said, and turned. 'Who is, as it happens, the bastard son of Archdeacon Columba Crozier.'

James would have made a good merchant, if only he had been of an economical habit. There was a silence during which Gavin could see his mind click-clicking like a smartly-handled abacus.

The king said, 'Does his bastardy have anything to do with it? Bastards are common enough, even in the church.' He was playing absently with his silver drinking cup, his eyebrows raised a little.

'Not directly. But everything he does is for his father. And I understand that the relationship between Archdeacon Crozier and M. de Verne's mother is of very long standing.'

James's face changed. Though a profoundly uxorious man, and despite his differences with Rome, he was always zealous of the honour of the church. 'Indeed,' he said. 'Not, then, a forgivable lapse from his vows?'

'No.' Gavin's eyelids felt peculiarly heavy. A lapse, indeed, and the only thing Columba Crozier had ever done that he could sympathize with.

'So?' James said coolly. 'Go on. How long have you known Verne to be this so-called Red Lord?'

'Not long. Until recently, it was no more than suspicion.'

'Which was why you kept it so carefully to yourself? What happened to confirm it?'

'I deduced it from the – the source of my information about the Welsh venture.'

James was relentless. 'And that source was?'

Oh, Ninian, Ninian! 'I can't reveal it.'

Not even to your king? Deep inside himself, James sighed. Was Gavin Cameron to be another tool that turned in his hand? The only man to whom he had been prepared to delegate power; the man he would have thought of as a friend, if he had not been a king and Cameron a commoner. The man he had relied on, and trusted. Who now defied him. Why? A brother? A cousin? A woman?

He didn't insist, but said again, 'Go on.'

'I am reduced to guessing, but I have come to the conclusion that everything stems from Crozier's unfounded belief that I want to destroy him.' It *had* been unfounded, to begin with. 'He and his son have been doing their not inconsiderable best to forestall me – to destroy me first. They have already tried and failed more than once.'

He stopped, and then found he wasn't prepared to go into all the sordid details. Perhaps James might guess, perhaps not; and perhaps it didn't matter very much. Crozier had won, at Rome, for the time being at least. And his son had won, in Scotland. It remained to be seen whether he, Gavin Cameron, was going to be allowed the opportunity to fight back, to bring those successes down in ruins about their ears. He went on, 'And now, because Adam de Verne is the kind of man he is, they have become more ambitious.'

James said, 'But it is *my* kingdom they are attacking, not yours.'

To his own surprise, Gavin laughed. 'Indeed, sire. But it is my reputation that suffers. I think, sometimes, that chancellors were invented for the sole purpose of taking the blame for everything that goes wrong.'

'I see.' There was a very long silence, and then James resumed,

'What you are saying is that, if I dismiss you, the whole threat would vanish, and the country would be safe?'

It was brutal, but it was probably true. Gavin wasn't sure how far Robert Graham would go on his own. '*Might* be safe. Yes.'

He rose from the hard wooden stool that was all the seating the royal chamber afforded besides the canopied chair. 'I will go now, if you wish me to.'

Everyone expected that a servant should be loyal to his king. But a king loyal to his servant?

In this, as in so much else, James was surprising. There was no outburst of anger, although neither was there any great display of cordiality. Thoughtfully, he said, 'No, sit down. Sit down.' And then, 'I'm not prepared to have chaos brought to the nation just to satisfy some young man's private whim. We must do something serious about Crozier, too, but that can wait. What do you think the next move is likely to be?'

It was extraordinarily difficult to sit down again, calmly, and answer as if nothing of importance had happened. 'He will try to hold us to ransom.'

'In other words, offer us peace in exchange for – what?'

'My dismissal, perhaps.'

James snorted, beginning to become more himself again. 'More than perhaps, I should think. But would that be all?'

Gavin looked at his short, broad-chested sovereign in the expensive topaz velvet. At the heavily ringed hands with their spatulate fingers. At the pouched Stewart eyes and the chestnut-red beard. Nothing there to suggest the poet's tongue, the musician's ear, the idealist's heart. He was a remarkable man, and could be a great one, if the odds weren't in the end too heavy, if the mind didn't break under the impossible strain.

Gavin said, 'No. I think as you appear to do that, given a taste of power, Adam de Verne will want more. The dismissal of a royal servant, even of a chancellor and bishop of the church, would scarcely advertise his triumph to the outside world. He will want something more spectacular. Something for himself. And I think that, very soon, he will tell us what it is.'

CHAPTER THREE

I

EVEN through the blindfold, Gavin knew he had been right. Adam de Verne had made his first mistake.

It was October before the message came. October, by which time the Highlanders must have evaporated back to their glens and Donald Balloch would be wondering whether to linger on, or take himself and his plunder off to Ireland, the final refuge of all Scots dissidents, to wed some black Irish beauty and see out the rest of his life in bibulous idleness.

By that time, James had raised half an army, but it wasn't enough and it wasn't reliable.

The message said, condescendingly, that the Red Lord was prepared to talk to the royal chancellor; no one else. And only under the conditions laid down.

These were at once precise and extremely nebulous. Bishop Gavin would be wasting his time unless he came with full powers to treat, because he would be given no opportunity of referring back to the king. He was to present himself at a particular spot – the confluence of two small rivers some twenty miles north of Perth – this coming Friday at moonrise. He might bring an armed escort of not more than six men, but he was not to be armed himself. The Red Lord would choose where the talks were to take place, once he had satisfied himself that

355

everything was in order. Bishop Gavin should, of course, bring with him proof of his authority in this matter, and also the Great Seal, to attest the validity of the agreement they would reach.

The king had jibbed at almost everything, from the insolence of the demands to the implication that his chancellor's word wasn't good enough without the warranty of the seal. He had then gone on to say that Gavin could make any agreement he wanted to, because he, James, had no intention of honouring it.

What the chancellor was to come back with was the Red Lord's head on a platter. Or else.

Gavin had little time in which to make his dispositions, especially as they entailed some very intricate thinking and some even more intricate organization. Sir Robert Graham, he knew, was in Perth, and Gavin was most anxious that no rumour of any out-of-the-way activity should reach his ears.

It was a pleasant ride to the place where the Allt Menach flowed into the river Ardle, through hills covered in the washed-out golds and vivid ambers of the dying year. The rowan trees were towers of rusty fire, with fieldfares and redwings squabbling and scuffling in the branches, neatly and methodically stripping all the bright berries before they rose as one and flocked chattering on, over the hill. Above them in the darkening sky, chevrons of greylag geese swept past, honking, making for home among the heather moors of the west.

Once or twice, during the latter stages of the ride, Gavin was conscious of being under unobtrusive surveillance. He caught a flash of saffron from the brow of a hillock ahead and, turning sharply, more than a flash from a fall of rocks by the roadside behind. He was sorely tempted to sing out, 'Have no fear! I have no secret army at my back.' Unfortunately.

There were about fifty men waiting for him at the rendezvous, armed to the teeth, several of them on the shady side of sobriety. As they relieved his men-at-arms of their weapons, there was a certain amount of horseplay, but since the men-at-arms, appearances notwithstanding, were the pick of the royal guard, they took it with commendable good humour.

Gavin himself, summoning up every ounce of episcopal dignity, opened his over-robe to show that he wore no sword, and was gratified to find that that was good enough for the Highlanders – despite the fact that neither pacifism nor probity was among the more manifest attributes of their own Bishops of Orkney and the Sudreys.

It came as no surprise when they signed that he should dismount and, with vague Gaelic apologies that they clearly didn't expect him to understand, tied a thickly-folded kerchief round his eyes. Then, with more apologies, someone took him by the shoulders and spun him round like a top. It might have caused him to lose his sense of direction if he hadn't been listening carefully to other sounds; but no one had thought of moving the horses, and when he remounted, he knew that his courser was still facing in the same direction as before.

The next two hours were alternately tedious and farcical as the little party ambled up hill, down dale, and – twice – made a complete circle that brought it back to its starting point again. About half an hour after that, by which time both Gavin and his courser, which disliked being led, were beginning to lose patience, an argument developed among the Highlanders about the most direct route to their objective.

Gavin could have told them.

He had known from the start that the meeting point on the river Ardle made an expedition to the west unlikely. It was unlikely for other reasons, too, because if there were no great concourse of clansmen within sight when the chancellor of Scotland arrived to treat with the victorious Red Lord, it would be a plain advertisement that the Highland army had, indeed, melted away.

And if it were not one of the Lord of the Isles' castles in the west, but something within reasonable range of the meeting point, then Gavin had been able to think of only three possibilities.

Throughout the ride, he had been paying the closest possible attention to the information that his four available senses were able to provide, and he knew that the terrain hadn't been steep enough to make it Blair Atholl, which, in any case, had been bottom of his list. Nor were there any of the smells of human habitation that would have told of Dunkeld, where Columba Crozier had a canonry. So it had to be Dess.

Half of him had prayed that it would not be; the other half had been sure that it must. And the regular, shallow ascent, the absence of tree sounds, the steadiness of wind that meant featureless landscape – all these confirmed it. Which was as well, because he had staked everything on it.

'NO, you will not!' Ninian said furiously. 'You will take your damned men and your equally damned horses and leave here this instant!'

Adam stood, legs astride, hands on his hips, and grinned at her, his embroidered scarlet coat-armour swinging over the polished black breastplate and fauld, the sword with its ball-shaped pommel hanging naked at his side. 'Such language, *p'tite!*' he said.

She knew she was wasting her breath. When he was in this mood, laughing down at the common herd from the bright cloud of his own self-esteem, Adam was oblivious of what anyone might say. Only Sévèrine had ever been able to bring him back to earth, and only sometimes. Briskly, Ninian began raking through her vocabulary for words that Sévèrine might have used.

'Appropriate language, however,' she replied. 'Since you have this fancy to behave like Satan incarnate!'

'Not Satan,' he remonstrated. 'I have no ambition at all to tempt others into following my example. How very dull life would be if everyone else was as reprehensible as I. Lucifer, perhaps – you remember the king of Babylon whose boast it was that he would ascend to the heavens and make himself the equal of God?'

Ninian stared at him for a moment, and then said coldly, 'Perhaps you have forgotten the sequel. "How art thou fallen from Heaven, O Lucifer, son of the morning!" Adam, how can you say such things? You must know how shocked Columba would be!'

His blinding smile flashed out again. It made him look very like his father; not the smile itself, because Columba's was less brilliant and very much warmer, but the way it narrowed his eyes, emphasizing the overhang of the straight, dark brows, and tightened the skin over the bones of his nose, so that the hook became very pronounced.

He began to remove his armour. 'We have no wish – have we? – to look as if we expect anything but total victory. Without a fight.'

Forgetting her temporary concern for his soul, she said again, '*Not here!* Adam, I will not have it. You must leave, and leave now.'

'But it will be dark in an hour,' he pointed out reasonably. 'Would you have my poor Highlanders condemned to spend a cold October night on the moors?'

'Why not?' she enquired tartly. 'Goodness knows, they must be used to it!'

Unexpectedly, his hands fell hard on her shoulders.

'I like it,' he said expansively. 'The colour in your cheeks, the flashing eyes. This new fire in you, it is a great improvement. You have always been so soulful, so spineless, so weak-mindedly anxious to be liked. And now you do not care what anyone thinks. I wonder why?'

In one respect, he was as wrong as it was possible to be. The reason she was so angry, the reason she was so determined to send Adam away, was that it was of supreme importance what one man thought of her.

She jerked out from under his hands. 'Does it matter? For the last time, Adam, you cannot stay.'

He sighed over her persistence. 'Why not?'

There were several reasons, of which the most important was the one she could not mention. Séverine's voice echoed in her head so that, her own voice taking on even the intonation of it, she said, 'My dear Adam, if you were not blind to everything except your own adolescent desire to be the largest fish in this small and exceedingly dull Scottish pond, you would not need to ask. I am already out of favour with the king for many reasons, not least my unwillingness to marry again. For me to permit you to make free of my house, so that you can hold the entire kingdom to ransom, would bring the direst retribution down on my head. And not only my head but, more important, my child's. *No*, Adam.'

But it was not enough, just to sound like Séverine. The only effect it had was to bring the approving gleam back to his eye.

'And that is all? But what a fuss about nothing! Cameron and his escort will be blindfolded, coming and going. I have instructed my men to follow a roundabout route, to make sure they are not being followed. I will deal with Cameron in the Speak-a-Word room, which I imagine he has never seen, and will take care the light is so dim that, even if he had, he would not recognize it. And my own servants will do everything that needs to be done. You have nothing to fear, *p'tite*. No one will know anything about it, neither the king, nor even the so boring Sir Walter of Lithgow.'

He was facing her again, much more closely than she liked, and as she made to step back, his hands once more clamped down on her shoulders. 'And even if none of that were true,' he went on, his eyes glinting down into hers, 'it would be of no importance. Because I have the upper hand from now on – in everything.'

Her eyes, her face, her whole being fighting him, she said with extreme precision, 'Have a care, Adam. You are too sure of yourself.'

He misunderstood. 'A threat? Does the Lady Ninian think she is going to put a spoke in my wheel?' His head went back and he laughed, a joyous, agreeable, light-hearted sound. '*Oh, yes!* I like this new little cousin very much.'

And then he had her in a grip that prisoned her whole body to his, so that she could feel him hard and avid against her as her mouth fought the arrogant lips and she struggled grimly to free herself.

But it was only a brief outburst, however intense. He put an end to the embrace as suddenly and decisively as he had begun it, withdrawing his lips from hers, though not at once his body. 'Not now,' he said gaily, though his breath was coming fast. 'Business first, and then we will have leisure. But just in case you should have the idea of taking independent action of any kind, I fear, *p'tite*, that I shall be compelled to lock you up.'

<hr>

3

THEY led Gavin up the outside staircase and into a room smelling of ink and parchment, and out again into a draughty corridor. It was then that a pair of clean-smelling hands removed the blindfold from his eyes, and a moderately cultured voice enquired whether the bishop would wish to visit the garderobe before the meeting with his Lordship. Amused, the bishop said he would. M. de Verne, it seemed, brigand or not, had tonight adopted the trappings of civilization.

The owner of the hands, a steward whom he had never seen before, waited to escort him back into the ink-smelling room, and then left him.

There was a single, flickering candle whose light was sufficient only to show that the tall, immobile figure of the man who stood there was dressed wholly in red, without jewel or ornament, and that his face was covered by a scarlet mask. Vaguely irritated that M. de Verne should think him a child to be impressed by such tricks, Gavin went and filled a cup of wine for himself and drank it slowly and with appreciation, watching the other man over the rim. Did he hope to disguise that slight accent of his, too?

After a time, Gavin said politely, 'Are we waiting for the minor demons?'

He could feel a sudden radiation of anger, but then the other man's stillness erupted into a wide, expansive flourish of arms and hands, and there was laughter in his voice, muffled though it was by the mask. 'And they will come widdershins, my Lord Bishop! For tonight I am Lucifer. Sit, and let me tell you what Hell I have in store for you!'

His demands were very simple. If the king would invest him with a title and give him a free hand beyond the Highland line, then he would engage that James would no longer be troubled by the clans. 'I speak of James only, you notice. Because it is, of course, a condition that you yourself, my dear Bishop Gavin, should be deprived of all your secular and ecclesiastical offices.'

Gavin, his mind elsewhere, sipped again at his wine and said, 'You are very sure of yourself, that you should dictate to the king.'

'I, dictate? No, no. My army dictates.'

'But your army has taken itself home to the glens for the winter.'

'You think so?' The man in red walked to the window and threw open the shutter. Below, the torchlit walls of the tower and barmkin were surrounded by men, half of them asleep, half wakeful. Gavin, swiftly estimating, made the number about a hundred and fifty. Which was what he had wanted to know.

'And there are many times that number beyond range of the light,' said the scarlet figure. But he couldn't prove it, and Gavin didn't believe it. There would have been campfires, if it had been true.

Restfully, he said, 'His Majesty has an army, too.'

'And we both know what it is worth. Reluctant soldiers, unpaid, unaccustomed to the terrain, terrified of wild men with dirks and axes. No, no, Bishop Gavin. I can wreck the kingdom if my demands are not met.'

'And what then?'

M. de Verne was taken aback. It was, after all, a moderately silly question. He said, 'What then? Then, chaos is come again. Scotland will be strewn with the dead and dying, and there will be a new king on the throne.'

'Who?'

But the other man only shrugged. 'To me, it is of no importance. Whoever it may be, he will be bound to recognize my authority.'

Gavin studied the dregs of wine in his cup and said, carefully, 'Why should you think I can be influenced by any of this? If I accede, on the king's behalf, to your demands, you insist that I should personally lose everything. And even if you did not insist, I imagine the king would be angry enough to strip me of his own accord. Whereas, if I refuse, at least I have a chance of saving what I have fought all my adult life to gain.'

He wondered, with the portion of his mind that was not concentrated on the moment when Aquarius would drop below the western horizon, whether Verne had anticipated that he might react in such a way.

It seemed that he had. Drily, he replied, 'Vengeance is mine. I will repay.' It was a blasphemy, Gavin thought, which Archdeacon Crozier would not have relished.

'I will repay,' Verne went on, 'a thousandfold. But I would not like that you think me so crude as to threaten your life directly. If you refuse my demands, you will continue to live – until some other death overtakes you.

'No, if you do not agree what I ask, I promise you that every man, woman and child named Cameron, wherever in the Highlands they be, will die. There will be a massacre. It is as simple as that, and I can arrange it.'

It was a threat Gavin had not foreseen, although perhaps he should have done. He felt his heart turn inside him. These were his folk Verne was talking about, even though he had no knowledge of most of them. His people, though he had exchanged words with scarcely a dozen of them. His family, who had no family except an ancient uncle who lived at Kinveil.

He could see the eyes glinting behind the scarlet mask, and suddenly the charade ceased to be tolerable. 'My dear M. de Verne,' he said, 'if I have no care for my king, why should you think I have any care for my clan?'

The guttering candle sent up a thin, pungent column of smoke, and its erratic light brought a blue-black sheen to Adam de Verne's curling locks. His hands were flat on the table before him, hard, bony, relaxed. 'Because blood matters,' he said. 'What I do, I do for my father. What you will do, you will do for your kin. You have no choice.' And then he pulled the mask from his face. He was smiling. 'I was not sure whether you knew.'

'I knew.'

362

'Then you should have known that nothing could stop me.'

He was sure of himself, thank God.

Leaning heavily on the table, like a man suddenly old and tired, Gavin rose to his feet. And then he tossed back his over-robe, as if the weight were too much for him, and said, 'But Archdeacon Crozier has won, anyway, now that Eugenius has taken him under his protection. Was there any need for you to do what you have done, when all that you wanted had already been accomplished?'

The dark eyes flashed at him. 'But I enjoy it,' said Adam de Verne. 'What is life without challenge, and what greater challenge can there be than the pursuit of total victory?'

And then came the sound Gavin had been waiting for. The first cry of a sleepy guard as Aquarius dropped below the horizon and five hundred carefully picked royal soldiers rose up from the empty moor, where they had been lying prone since the dark hour before moonrise, and charged down upon the unsuspecting Highlanders scattered round the foot of the tower.

The two-foot arming sword that had lain all evening in the special scabbard across Gavin's back was in his hand at once, pointing at Adam de Verne's heart, and in his other hand the short, triangular, stabbing dagger that had been hidden in his belt.

He said, 'There will be no total victory for you. Give up. You want too much, and you cannot be allowed to win.'

But he shouldn't have wasted time, talking, as if his opponent were a man of sense and honour. He should have struck first, in the brief moment while he had the advantage. But he hadn't the stomach for cold-blooded murder, and even before his words were out the other man was on his feet, his face stark with fury, his own longsword in his hand.

They were exactly of a height, and of the same reach, and all the advantage was Verne's, his blade a foot longer and most of his life devoted to the skills of chivalry. Gavin had learned swordplay once, and had fought now and then with his sovereign, for amusement, their points muffled. But he knew he was no match for an opponent like this, whose wrist was like sprung steel, whose arm seemed to have a strength more than human, as if it were reinforced by some other power – by thoughts of his father, perhaps, or of his dead brother.

And yet Gavin, too, had more than mere technique to match against him. He had his own, new hatred of Columba Crozier, who for so long had tried to block his path at every turn, and who had also come,

363

insensibly, to symbolize all that stood in the way of his love for Ninian Drummond. It lent assurance to his dagger as he deflected the long, murderous blade, just as the memory of wild childhood scrimmages with Donny Mackenzie came back to him, to add guile to his movements and tricks to his armoury, tricks that at first confused an opponent whose point knew none but the formal rules of the joust.

Though only at first. Because after a pile of documents had become airborne, after a dagger-flicked inkpot had flung its contents in his eye, Adam de Verne recognized that this was no tourney and settled swiftly into the new mode. There was blood on his forearm by then, because the room was not large and even a two-foot sword was hard to avoid, but it was no more than a scratch.

Back and forth and round about they swirled, like leaves on the wind, relying on memory as much as sight to help them avoid obstacles that were scarcely visible in the erratic light of the candle, its flame shifting and veering wildly in the draught of their passing. And their blades were hampered no less than their feet, because neither dared risk flinging his arm wide or back to give him the full length and impetus it took to deliver the blow that would end the whole thing.

The corner of a wall shelf caught Verne full between the shoulders as he skipped backwards, graceful as a dancer, but before Gavin could take advantage the long diamond-sectioned blade was presented, rock-steady again, to his attacking point. And then it was his turn to find himself in trouble, trapped between table and cupboard, so that he had to slip sideways and down, slashing at the candle as he went and plunging the room into darkness. Crouched low in the gloom, motionless, re-tuning his eyes and ears, he heard the point of Verne's blade bury itself uselessly in wood, and then the sound of it being jerked free, and then a pause, and a shuffling, and a thin, steady, whining sound.

It took him a moment to recognize that the other man was swinging savagely round in a circle, sweeping the air at shoulder height, relying on the length of his sword to do damage even where he couldn't see. The risk of ducking under the scything blade was too great, so Gavin, his sight beginning to adjust, half rose and kicked a stool, and Verne, turning sharply, tripped and lost his balance, and saved himself from falling only by dropping his blade.

It clanked against the worn flagstones, and there was a momentary tremor of metal as the tip slipped into a crack between them and was trapped, shiveringly upright. But even as Gavin lunged Verne had freed it and was erect again, the effort and the fury almost palpable.

Both men were tiring now, both streaked with blood from superficial cuts, but Gavin's breathing was under better control and his temper ice-cold. Verne, unused to opposition, was beginning to strike out viciously, almost blindly, much of the science gone but the sword's edge no less butchering nor the point less lethal because of it.

He was unpredictable, now, and it was nearly the end of Gavin. Suddenly, expecting a wild, horizontal slice, he caught a fugitive glimmer of moonlight on the edge of Verne's sword and saw that it was raised high and beginning to slash down in a great head-cleaving arc that would have ended everything there and then. With no time to look, no time to think, Gavin leapt back out of its path and caught his own foot in a trailing fold of the over-robe he had discarded.

Stumbling violently, he tried to throw himself aside from the following blade, but only partially succeeded. It was his shoulder that took the blow, the half cutting, half mangling blow that, after the first moment of paralysis, he willed himself to ignore. He had no time for pain, not now. But as he felt the blood pulse out and begin to flow, thick and wet and heavy, soaking his sleeve, slowing his reactions, a furious urgency possessed him.

Verne had begun driving hard at him, careless of defence, his purpose not to wound or even kill, but to claw the hilt of Gavin's sword out of his failing hand. If he could succeed in that, he could have the pleasure of disposing of him at leisure. It seemed to Gavin, his ears still alive to all the sounds outdoors, that Verne had forgotten everything except the enemy before him.

And then Gavin found himself backed up against the wall in a corner, with Verne whirling round to catch him from an angle where it was impossible for him to parry, his sword still in his right hand and the dirk in his left. There had been no time, and there was no time now, to change hands, but he had to try, and as he did so he stuck out his foot in the almost forgotten, toe-curling hook of half a hundred juvenile skirmishes.

Adam de Verne went crashing to the floor.

But he took Gavin with him, and somehow, as they fell, their swords clashed together and the points, as one, became wedged in a crevice between the flags, where they stayed upright, vibrating wildly, almost singing, until the stress was too much, and there was a crack, and the hilts, with a kind of insane logic, sprang straight to their owners' hands, while the broken blades subsided, naked and useless, to the floor.

Where weapons were concerned, the two men were equal now, for Gavin's dirk had gone skidding off in the fall under a chest. There was no longer any suggestion of civilized adults engaged in a civilized, swordsmanlike duel. They fought instead, in a panting, impenetrable tangle of arms and legs, of tearing hands and bloodied knuckles, pitting against each other elbows, feet, knees and teeth, stabbing at each other with the jagged remnants of the broken blades. Over and over they rolled, jabbing and gouging and, unbelievably, missing, and missing, and missing again.

But Gavin's right arm was beginning to lose all sensation and he could feel the waves of unconsciousness rolling nearer. Inexorably, Adam de Verne had worked his way round so that he was on top, and now he had his hand raised to the full tug of his muscles, ready to plunge the six rough inches of steel into Gavin's heart.

In spite of everything, he was too sure of himself, still. Because in that moment he paused, his eyes glittering, gloating, before he struck down with the final blow.

All the tensions of his being were concentrated in the gesture that would satisfy four long years of hatred and rancour, so that when Gavin's upward thrust caught him between the ribs, just to the right of his heart, his muscles held him together for a harsh-breathing eternity before his grin of triumph set into a rictus and the wide-shouldered, narrow-hipped body slowly crumpled and collapsed.

As Gavin lost consciousness there was a picture in his mind of another man, long ago, impaling himself like some great bird on the dagger of a boy who hadn't really meant to kill him.

4

'MY lord, my lord!'

He had no desire at all to return to the world, but the voice was urgent. So he opened his eyes to find his captain's anxious face a few inches above his own, macabre in the flickering candlelight. The smell of tallow was suffocating.

There was no enjoyment in sitting up, especially with Wilkie's unhandy assistance, but Gavin's spinning head stabilized with unpleasant speed.

'Where is he?' he demanded.

'Who, my Lord?'

'*Christ!* You don't think I reduced this room to a shambles all by myself!'

'No, my lord.'

Gavin took a deep breath and said laboriously, 'The man in red. We fought, and I killed him. I *think* I killed him. Not long after you attacked from the moor. So, where is he? Have you moved the body? Or has someone else? I want every inch of this place searched. And the moors, too, if need be.'

Somehow, he rose to his feet and stood swaying slightly and feeling extremely sick. But he managed to say, 'I take it that the attack succeeded?'

'Yes, my lord. There was very little resistance. The Highlanders don't like falling victim to the kind of tactics they specialize in themselves.'

'True. What have you done with them?'

'We've piled up the dead, and the men are guarding the others.'

'Good. You've done very well, Wilkie. I will see that you and the men are rewarded.'

'Thank you, sir. Oh, and sir . . .'

'Yes?'

'We found the castle servants locked up in the mews, with the hawks.'

Gavin gave a sudden gasp of laughter. 'And I suppose the hawks were all having a fit?'

'Yes, sir.' Wilkie grinned. 'And the lasses, too.'

'The Lady Ninian?'

'No signs, sir.'

'Have you searched the castle for her?'

'No, my Lord.'

'Then get on with it. And send Geddes to me. I can't bind this arm up by myself.'

5

THEY found no trace at all of Adam de Verne, nor of the man with the clean-smelling hands who was presumably his steward or body servant.

But locked in the gallery at the very top of the tower they did find an overwrought Lady Ninian, with her screaming small daughter and an irritable wet nurse in attendance.

She demanded an immediate interview with Bishop Gavin, but he was too busy to see her at the present moment. And what, she thought bitterly, was new about that! The relief of knowing that he was not only alive but behaving precisely as he always did was enough to exacerbate a temper already frayed from eight hours' incarceration with neither food nor drink nor any idea of what was going on. And in her own castle, too!

The first glimmer of dawn was in the sky when the captain came to say that Bishop Gavin was in the Laird's Hall and would be grateful for a word with her.

The Laird's Hall, of all places! The chamber above the Great Hall that had been both private reception room and bedchamber when Harry was alive. She had scarcely been inside it since he died, because when she had been set free to choose, she had taken another smaller room entirely for her own.

Her heart turned over when she saw him, his face haggard with pain and exhaustion, his right sleeve cut away, and his shoulder bound up with strips of bloodsoaked linen. Every part of him that she could see seemed to be covered with cuts and bruises.

But there was something in his face that stopped her going to him. Not hostility, but a coolness and a reserve that she thought had gone from their relationship forever. Her anger of these last hours, and the other thing that had troubled her these last months, were both submerged in a wave of discouragement that forced her to curl her lips tightly over her teeth so that she should not weep.

He smiled faintly. 'I'm sorry, do I look dramatic? It is mostly superficial, I assure you. Although your cousin tried hard. I have to ask you – do you know where he is?'

She shook her head, thanking God that Adam, too, must still be alive. 'I still don't know anything at all of what has been happening, except that your men are all over the place, and the Highlanders under lock and key.'

He frowned wearily. 'We fought. I imagine you must know why. And – I'm sorry, my darling! – but he is either dead, or near it.' Then his voice was level again, as if the two words that had so magically healed her heart had never been spoken.

She found another voice, her own, lamenting inside her head. *Oh,*

Adam. Not you, too? How can I break it to Columba and Séverine?
That both the sons of their love are gone?

Gavin said, 'I lost consciousness, and when I recovered, he had disappeared. But alive or dead, he didn't vanish without help. Do you swear to me you had no hand in it, and know nothing of where he is?'

She had to tell the truth. 'I didn't help, and I know nothing. But I would have helped, if I had known, and if I had been able.'

He nodded, as if he had expected it, and she went on, 'It must have been his steward – unless you have found him?'

He shook his head. 'My men have already searched the castle and are going out now to search the moors. I must ask you, is there any hiding place you know of, that an uninformed search might miss?'

It was only the moors he was asking about, she told herself. And on the moors there was nothing but the cave she thought of as Robert Graham's lair. There was no possibility that a wounded man could have travelled so far and, besides, the searchers would find it for themselves, if they looked properly.

'No,' she said.

He gazed into her eyes a moment longer. 'Very well,' he said. 'But it is a mystery that must be solved.'

'Yes.'

They stood and stared at each other as if there were nothing more to be said, until Ninian, at last, murmured, 'Have you had something to eat?' It was commonplace enough, but it was something that mattered. Hunger could be very lowering, and very distracting.

'Thank you, yes.'

'I will get some fresh linen and put a new bandage on your shoulder.'

His left hand came out and he said, 'No!' as if it had been forced out of him.

'Why not? That one is soaked already!'

'Yes, but . . .' His own stomach had revolted at sight of the damage. It wasn't a clean cut, because the sharp edge of the blade had been followed by the thick, blunt weight of the rest of it, and the result was a mangled, bloody mess. The kind of wound a man could die of, if it turned rancid.

'Yes, but what?'

'It will make you ill.'

'Mother of God!' she exploded. 'Men!'

There was linen in the bedding chest, and she marched over to it, and dragged out two of the fine pillow covers she had brought from France,

369

and a sheet. Harry's belt knife was still there, and there was water in the ewer.

She ripped the linen into strips with considerably more vigour than was strictly necessary, talking all the time. 'Does it never occur to you that women know far more about pain and distress than men do? Oh, yes, you go riding out to display your pretty armour in stupid, unnecessary battles, and amuse yourselves with idiotic swordfights, and sometimes you get hurt. And that comes as a surprise, doesn't it? You don't expect to be hurt. If you did, you might find some more civilized way of settling your quarrels.

'Hold your arm up, so that I can unwind these stained bandages! Yes, I know it's painful!

'Whereas every woman who doesn't retire to a nunnery knows that she's fated to be hurt every year of her adult life. Have you any conception of what it's like to suffer a miscarriage, or to go through all the pangs of labour, and have something go wrong, so that the child is born dead and you can feel all your life's blood draining away? And the other kind of pain, when the child survives its birth, but dies before it's old enough to walk or talk? So that all the physical pain was for nothing and the mental pain stays with you for the rest of your life?

'But – oh, no! – you don't want me to rebandage your arm in case it upsets me!

'There, that's off. Oh.' She took a breath, and began talking again, this time to distract herself as much as him. She had helped Séverine bind up Adam and Blane in her childhood, often enough, but it hadn't been like this.

'I won't wash it, I think. I'll just put some of this salve on the bandage. Don't look so doubtful. I can assure you, there's no powdered earthworm or horn of toad in it. Just garlic, rosemary, juniper and thyme. I brought it from Avignon. Hold still!

'Yes, well, I was saying . . . I've been lucky, myself. I've only had one miscarriage, and borne one child. But my luck may have run out, don't you think? After all, I can't rely on Sir Walter being as infertile as Harry, can I? *Be careful!*'

Regardless of the half-wound bandage, he had torn his arm free and was grasping her by the shoulders, his face a mask of strain and incomprehension. 'What are you saying? What are you talking about? *What do you mean?*'

She had been weeping, deep inside, for all these months, because she thought he had known, and had chosen to say and do nothing to comfort her.

Limply, she said, 'Didn't you know? The king says I have to marry again. Walter of Lithgow. I have argued, but His Majesty won't listen.'

With a groan, he sank his head in his hands. 'I should have foreseen it. No well-bred woman is ever allowed to remain a widow for long, unless she has sons; sometimes not even then. Don't blame James for it. It's common practice everywhere.'

'Not in Avignon.'

He looked up, and there was a dry spark of amusement in his voice. 'No? But then Avignon is a more civilized place, isn't it? They don't go out, there, in their pretty armour, and fight, do they?'

'Well . . .'

She went back to winding the bandage. 'What am I going to do?'

He didn't answer for a long time. Only when she was tying the last knot did he say in a flat voice, 'Sir Walter is a good man, with an honest heart. You could do worse.'

6

AFTER a long moment, she said in a voice as flat as his, 'Don't you understand? You are my life. How *can* I marry? I loved you even when I was married to Harry, but that was before . . . That was before . . .'

She couldn't go on looking at him, and dropped her eyes, her lips tight against the tension in her throat. There were traces of blood, she saw, on her hands, and began to wipe them off with a piece of linen.

'Before we made love. But we agreed, then, that it must never happen again.'

'We *agreed*?' Suddenly, her voice rose almost an octave and her eyes were brilliant with anger. 'You mean – you told me! And gave me no time to argue. And have taken care never to see me alone since, for fear I might ignore your decree! *I love you.* Can you not understand that? There is nothing else that matters in the world.'

For all this last year, he had thought that she had accepted his edict of separation with a meek compliance that he found surprisingly hard to bear. And she, he suddenly realized, had thought that he was unfeelingly prepared to accept her forthcoming marriage, without even discussing it with her. So, because they had both misunderstood, neither had been prepared to swallow their pride and take the crucial step that would bring them together again. To talk, of course. Only to talk.

Irrational with relief, and weakness, and weariness, Gavin took Ninian's long-thumbed, artist's hands into his own, and drew her to her feet, and gathered her into his one good arm and kissed her.

It was all he had meant to do. He thought, if he thought at all, that the effects of these last hours would have been more than enough to compensate for any deficiencies in his strength of character. But it didn't turn out like that.

Even as they kissed, and he felt the wild flooding of desire all through him, he told himself that it was only relief from tension. Two battered survivors clinging together to the wreckage. Death, cheated of its prey, taking revenge in this furious urge to create new life.

He tried, then, to push himself back from her, but it was impossible. For she, too, had suffered this night, though not physically, and there was still anger in her at the stupidity of it all.

So she smiled, her eyes alight, and took matters into her own hands, and after a moment he groaned, 'You're a witch. A vile, wicked woman. How I love you!' And then their lips were locked again, and all thought, all feeling had fled, except their need for each other.

At some stage during the next frenetic minutes, Gavin heard himself say, a choke of laughter in his voice, 'Oh, God, I can't bend!' But it didn't matter, because the bed was there, and high, and she lay down in just the right way, so that he could stand, and look at her – loving her and making love to her – the smile in his own eyes answering the mischief in hers until their focus changed, and she began to moan, and then to cry out, and he knew that it was time.

Afterwards, he succeeded in joining her on the bed, rejecting her help with a disdain that covered – he thought – all sign of what it cost him. So she teased him, and caressed his marked body with thistle-down fingers, and they kissed again, long and sweetly, and laughed at each other like familiar lovers.

He fell asleep at last, and all the laughter vanished from her face and she wept for him, and for herself, and for Adam, and Columba. Then she rose and dressed, and drew the coverlet over him and went to look for Captain Wilkie.

He was almost asleep on his feet and so were his men. They had found nothing, it seemed.

She went to the kitchen, next, to make sure everyone was being fed, and to make with her own hand a special herb posset that was to be kept warm for Bishop Gavin when he awoke.

And then she went to the secret dungeon.

7

ADAM was there, as she had known he must be. And he was alive, and conscious.

His steward had gone prowling for food, relying on his respectable appearance to save him if he should meet anyone.

'He put a cloak round me and dragged me down the outside stair,' Adam said, the breath bubbling in his lungs. 'Cameron's captain was busy rounding up the Highlanders. So Hamilton dumped me against the wall while he went to prospect.'

It was several moments before he could gather enough strength to go on. 'The captain had told his men to pile the bodies up neatly in a corner, and they took me for the foundation stone. When I came to, there were a dozen corpses on top of me.'

A laugh rasped from his throat, and Ninian thought there was a trace of madness in it. 'It seemed as if I had wakened to Hell. But when the men went out on the moors, Hamilton got me out and brought me here. Is Cameron alive?'

She stood there looking at him, and could feel her eyes beginning to blur. It seemed then as if all her life in Scotland had been a nightmare, and one that would never end. Without expression, she said, 'Yes. He is alive, too. Are your wounds bad?' Hamilton had stripped him to the waist and bound him up almost to his neck in what looked like strips of his own shirt.

'Not good. But I'll heal. I always do. Have you some of *maman's* salve?'

'Yes.'

This was Adam, the glorious, invincible cousin whom she had once adored, lying now in a filthy dungeon, on the bare floor, in the half dark, and likely so to die. Or on the executioner's block. She couldn't allow it.

She said, 'Everything has gone too far. Too many men have died, too many women been widowed. I will help you, Adam, because you are

373

Adam. But you must leave the country as soon as you are fit to travel. You must go to France and never come here again. Unless you promise that, I will go now to Bishop Gavin and tell him where you are. I mean it, Adam. *Nothing* is worth this. Will you promise?' There was no pity in her voice, nothing except an implacable determination.

Suddenly, he held out a hand to her and, seeing the pain etched sharp on his face, she reached her own hand out.

His grip had astonishing strength. 'My little cousin,' he said. 'How – how you have changed. I can't – I can't leave you. I need you. I want you.' His voice was thick, almost liquid. 'I can't leave you.'

She saw with horror that he was trying to raise the other hand, too. In a moment, he would have a grip on her skirts. It was as if, knowing that he had finally lost her, he couldn't let her go.

She tore herself free, and backed away, overcome by a terrible revulsion. And as she moved, he began trying to drag himself towards her across the floor, his face stiff with pain and concentration and something that might as easily have been hatred as love.

Choking, she stood there and said, 'Adam, no!' and then she turned and opened the door, and fled.

8

WHEN Gavin awoke, he had a fever, as she had known he would. Stubbornly, he refused to admit it. When he had dressed himself with Geddes's aid, and sent the man away, he said, 'I must get back to Perth. The king will be anxious to know the outcome.'

She snapped at him, childishly. 'You intend to tell him with your dying breath, do you? Because you cannot possibly think you are fit to ride!'

'Don't,' he said, his head swimming. 'Please, my dearest love. Don't let us part so.'

'You would prefer to remember me, smiling, on your death bed? Smiling, as you tell me – again! – that our love is impossible?'

He sat down heavily. 'You know what the church says.'

'I don't care what the church says! What does it matter?' She sank on her knees before him, pleading. 'Let me live with you as your mistress. Perhaps the church won't understand, but surely God will?' But it was like pleading with a stone. 'Look at Columba and Sévèrine,' she said desperately. 'She has been his mistress for thirty years, and no thunder-bolt has struck her down!'

He shook his head. 'God's justice isn't a matter of thunderbolts. If Harry had still been alive, could you have done as Sévèrine has done? Could you have lived with him, and let him appear to father your children, when all the time your love was for someone else? If you are forced to marry Sir Walter, could you treat him so?'

She was silenced, and he went on, 'When I met Sévèrine, she seemed to me a woman of sense, a realist, one who had made a cool, deliberate choice. But you are different. There's – too much warmth in you, too much passion. I think that if we can't be together all the time, we shouldn't be together at all. We're not made for it. To be my mistress, in secret, would kill you. I think it might also kill how we feel for each other.'

Once, she would have thought he was right. Once, she had thought that to be a man's mistress must be the least satisfactory of all human situations. Now, she said, 'We could find some place where no one knows us, and I could live there, and you could come to me when it was possible.' The tears started to her eyes. 'I've thought about it, about everything. I ask you – of my own free will. I've thought about that, too.'

Gently, he took her hand in both of his. His tired mind knew all the arguments, for he, too, had been through them more times than he could count. 'Have you thought of what it means? If we are pre-destined to Heaven or Hell, whatever we do, it isn't too difficult to confront the future with stoicism. But free will means the choice is ours, and that is much harder. We choose, and we pay. And on earth, at least, you – because you are a woman, a daughter of Eve – are made to pay much more heavily than I.

'I can be fined for having a mistress; I suppose I could even be deprived of my see. But those are things of the world. They don't touch my soul. Whereas you . . . If you were my mistress, you wouldn't be received in any church to the kiss of peace at Mass, nor to the benefit of blessed water. You would not be accepted at confession. And if you died in my house, you would be refused Christian burial.

'All these things are laid down. But even if they weren't – could you live with the knowledge that every moment of joy must, in the end, be repaid a hundredfold to a vengeful God?'

She had a memory, suddenly, of all the paintings she had ever seen of the tortures of Hell, of the damned hanging by their tongues from trees of flame, or burning in furnaces, or suffocating in thick, foul smoke. Of sinking in the terrible black waters of an abyss peopled by serpents and man-devouring demons. Of being left naked, nameless and forgotten in the eternal fires, with no hope, ever, of release.

After a moment, she said, 'I don't know.' Then, 'Yes, I could.'

His eyes, already glittering with fever, became brighter, and she saw that there were tears filming them. It was wrong of her, she knew, to force such a confrontation now, when he was ill, and scarcely master of himself. But she could see no hope for herself at all if she waited until he was strong again.

It made no difference, in the end, because he said, 'I, too, could face the certainty of Hell – for myself. But not for you. Because it seems to me contrary to the very nature of love that I should consent to laying on you such a burden of sin.'

He lifted her hand slowly to his lips and she could feel them hot and dry, burning her skin. His voice was barely audible as he said, 'It is over, woman of my heart. It must be over.'

CHAPTER FOUR

I

WHEN Gavin rode away, he left Captain Wilkie and a hundred men behind, surrounding the castle and fanned out over the moors to keep watch for any sign of Adam de Verne. He gave Wilkie instructions to stay for ten days, and to go over both buildings and land, not once but several times, with the utmost thoroughness.

'And Wilkie,' he said, 'I want you to pay a few surprise visits to the castle at inconvenient hours. There may possibly be some secret dungeon that is impossible to find without knowing the key to it, but a rat has to emerge from its hole some time. You might just possibly take Verne unawares. Remember, however, that the Lady Ninian is one of the queen's gentlewomen, and watch your step. Despite her relationship to Verne, I think her innocent in all this.'

It was almost true. She had told him that she had not been responsible for spiriting her cousin, alive or dead, away from the Speak-a-Word room, and that she did not know where he was. Gavin had believed her. But something held him back from repeating his questions just before he left, as he had meant to do; some superstitious dread of making her feel as if he were trying to force her into choosing between him and Verne.

Or was it a dread that, this time, she might be lying? Which would place him in a quandary he was quite incapable of dealing with.

377

No, it was impossible. He was almost sure that Adam de Verne must still be alive, even if only just, because if he were dead, his servant could have had no purpose in hiding his body. And if he were alive, he must have escaped in the general confusion when the prisoners were being rounded up. He could not be at Dess. Gavin convinced himself of it so successfully that the instructions he gave to Wilkie were designed, not to capture Verne, but to demonstrate to everyone in the clearest possible way that Lady Ninian was guiltless.

He hadn't expected sympathy from the king, which was as well, since, when he finally caught up with His Majesty in the great oak wood of Falkland, the best – and best-preserved – place in the country for the chase, he found that James was out of sympathy with everyone.

His temper was not improved by the news Gavin brought. 'Wounded and gone to ground?' he exploded. 'It isn't good enough, even if you do think it will have put an end to the conspiracy. What else have you done to find him besides leaving men at Dess?'

'I've split the other four hundred into eight search parties and distributed them round the perimeter of a ten-mile circle with Dess as the centre. If they work carefully back in towards it, they ought to stand a good chance of catching the man.'

Grudgingly, James said, 'More chance, certainly, than if you'd set them to work outwards, but will they find him in that rough country? I doubt it. It's all of a piece! *Nothing* is going right these days.'

The other source of royal discontent seemed to be that James's desire to raise a general 'subscription' towards the expenses of the army that had been defeated at Inverlochy had met with stubborn resistance in parliament. He had succeeded in pushing the measure through, he said, but if more than a few pennies ended up in the auditors' coffers he would be much surprised.

Spitefully, he added that he had also forced a statute through that would teach some of the earls, barons and freeholders a lesson. Those who hadn't contributed to the replacement army he'd needed after the Inverlochy debacle were going to be liable to the death penalty if they couldn't come up with a good excuse!

Gavin could feel the feverish colour draining from his face. It seemed, at times, as if James's whole ambition was to set all his people against him. But he managed to say, with fair composure, 'I trust they were suitably downcast?'

James snorted. 'They didn't like it, if that's what you mean. They don't like anything that reminds them they have duties as well as privileges. Mary Mother! How I regret those eighteen years of mine in England! They had things all their own way for far too long. What's that damned horn supposed to signify? Have the hounds caught the trail, or not?'

It was true that the Albany regents, father and son, had been too comfortable on James's throne to do anything to offend any of the other great lords, who might tip them off it. But it was slowly being borne in on Gavin that James – with Gavin's own connivance – had been trying to do too much, too quickly. It was a bitter irony that now, when he had began to recognize the need to try and control his headstrong sovereign, he should be losing the royal confidence that would have made it possible. Because although the king knew, in one part of his mind, that it was Columba Crozier who had been directly responsible for so many of Scotland's troubles in these last years, Gavin could sense that, in another, he had come to feel that his chancellor was not entirely guiltless. No smoke without fire. It was a perfectly normal human reaction, and Gavin told himself that there was nothing to be gained by brooding over the injustice of it.

'I hope your wound isn't going to incapacitate you,' James said unfeelingly, finger-combing his beard. 'Because you've come back just in time to draft the charter for Finlay Duff, and I want you on the committee to frame the statutes for St Andrews university.

'*What* is that damned huntsman doing?'

2

THREE weeks later, one hundred and seven members of the Clan Cameron, men, women and children, gathered for Mass in a little church in the hills east of Mamore.

The church had peat walls and a heather roof, and it burned well – and slowly – when their former allies, the Macintoshes, surrounded it and set it alight. None of the Camerons survived.

ONLY Gavin knew what it meant, and by the time he heard about it he knew also that Adam de Verne was back in France and beyond his reach.

In his capacity as chancellor, he had received a formal little note from the Lady Ninian Drummond, saying she had heard from M. de Verne's mother that M. de Verne had returned to Villeneuve, suffering severely from his wound, and that it would be many months before it healed. The Lady Ninian hoped this information would be of value to His Majesty and Bishop Gavin.

'In France?' James said. 'How do we make sure he stays there?'

It was to be months, too, before Gavin's shoulder healed, but heal it did. The French salve, perhaps, and the fact that the thick flap of flesh and muscle hadn't been quite severed. But the muscles continued to pain him, and he would never lose the scar, any more than he would lose the scars on his heart.

He closed his mind to both, blocked out his bitter hatred of Adam de Verne, silenced the jealous voice speculating on how much the woman he loved had known of it all, and devoted himself to the new exchange of hostages that was afoot. It included neither the Master of Atholl nor Malise Graham.

There were also letters of privy seal to be framed, their purpose to improve the enforcement of justice. Settling the wording of those to James's satisfaction — without, at the same time, spelling out to the barons just how deeply their traditional jurisdiction was being encroached on — was a task that Socrates might have enjoyed, but Gavin didn't, particularly when he was also trying to catch up with a considerable backlog at Glasgow, including a new code of statutes for the cathedral, some long overdue inventories, and a catalogue of the library.

And then, of course, there was the problem of Rome. Martin had called a general council of the church just before he died, to be held at Basle, but on the official opening date not a single bishop from all western Christendom had put in an appearance. If Eugenius, who disliked committees and especially committees with large ambitions, had acted swiftly, he might have saved himself, and Europe, a good deal of trouble, but by the time he issued a bull announcing the phantom Council's dissolution, he was too late. Because the Council had ceased to be a phantom. And since, in theory, it derived its authority directly from Christ, it wasn't prepared to stand for any nonsense about papal infallibility.

Whatever His Holiness chose to say, the Council of Basle refused to be dissolved.

All of which placed the monarchs of Europe in something of a quandary. Finally, France, Bohemia, and the Holy Roman emperor decided to support the Council against the pope, and James thought perhaps he might do the same. Bishop Gavin could go to Basle as his representative, and take the Abbot of Arbroath with him.

But then Eugenius, with so much trouble on his hands that he hadn't time to be subtle, began showering grants and recognitions and plenary remissions on any Scotsman who cared to ask. James's determination wavered. Perhaps it might be better to send Fogo, Lauder, and Ogilvy to Basle, he thought, while Bishop Gavin went to Rome. It was always best to have a foot in both camps.

Resignedly, Gavin waited for the next volte-face. But it seemed that, wherever he went, he would be going *some*where, and for quite some time. The Council of Constance had lasted for four years. And at least, whether he were at Rome or Basle, he would be free from the ache of knowing that Ninian Drummond was only a day's forbidden ride away.

4

NINIAN was gathering all her courage together to present herself at Edinburgh for the Christmas season when the message came.

It told her that, because of her close ties with the notorious rebel and traitor Adam de Verne, the self-styled Red Lord, the Lady Ninian Drummond would no longer be welcome at court. But if she were to receive any news whatsoever concerning this renegade, whose person, alive or dead, had so far escaped His Majesty's justice, she would fail at her peril to convey the aforesaid news to the royal chancellor.

It was no surprise. After Gavin had ridden away, Captain Wilkie and his men had been in and out of Dess with nerve-racking frequency for ten days, and in the five weeks that had followed they had returned silently, by night, on three further occasions. It had made it very difficult for Robert Graham to get Adam away.

If Captain Wilkie's men had found the secret dungeon, Ninian's punishment would have been heavier by far than mere exile from court, but they hadn't, because the flagstone that hid the entrance looked and sounded exactly the same as all the other flagstones covering the ground floor of the tower, and could only be moved by a lever that operated from an innocent-looking pothook at the back of the cooking hearth.

They did, however, find Robert Graham's lair in the hills, with its evidences of occupation, and leapt to the conclusion that that was where Adam had been hidden, although Gavin, Ninian reflected, must have had doubts when he heard its precise location, because he knew the disabling extent of Adam's wounds.

She didn't see how he could *not* know that she had kept Adam hidden from him. Yet he had said nothing to the king, it seemed, which must mean that now at last he trusted her. Trusted her to ensure that Adam, if he were still alive, could do no more harm. And she had, indeed, made Adam swear that he would go straight from Dess to France, and never set foot in Scotland again.

Scarcely a week after the message from court, she received another message, written in a clerkly hand that did not belong to the man whose seal it bore. The essence of it was that Sir Walter of Lithgow no longer felt himself able to contemplate matrimony with a lady whose reputation was so seriously tarnished by association, and must therefore, with regret, release her from their engagement. She wrote back at once, overflowing with goodwill, to say she hoped he would find another lady soon, and one who was truly worthy of him.

The relief over that was considerable, but royal coldness had other and less convenient results.

In November, Lady Moragh's daughter Fiona had arrived with her maid and two or three servants to learn, in Ninian's household, all the gentle, ladylike arts. She resembled her mother a good deal, but Ninian found it difficult to like her, for whereas Moragh's air of calculation was offset by smiling good humour, Fiona's was emphasized by an excessive self-assurance that sat ill on twelve-year-old shoulders. Within days, Ninian discovered that she was sly. She was also impertinent and unpleasantly inquisitive.

If it had not been for Jehane, Ninian might have sent the girl straight back to her mother. But the children took to each other on sight.

Jehane was almost two, now, fair and sturdily built like Harry, much too full of herself, and brimming with an energy for which she had no real outlet. She was too young to be allowed to play with the servants' children, and her nurse had neither the figure nor the inclination for the kind of rough-and-tumble Jehane revelled in. Ninian wondered, sometimes, if she could possibly be a changeling.

Fiona, however, had six brothers and sisters, and in no time at all was treating Jehane exactly as she wanted to be treated, like an irrepressible small boy.

Amused despite herself, Ninian felt it necessary to remonstrate when she came on the two of them one day, out on the moors accompanied only by a fast-asleep servant, playing tournaments. Fiona, careless of her third-best gown, was flat on her back, having been brought crashing to the ground by a well-aimed blow from Jehane's rowan-branch lance, and the child was now bouncing gleefully up and down on her victim's stomach.

Ninian plucked her daughter off, to an accompaniment of furious kicking and screaming, and said, 'Fiona, my dear, you are here to learn to be a lady! This is not the way.'

Scarlet and sulky, the girl rose and began to brush herself down. Without looking at Ninian, she said, 'Even ladies don't have to be ladylike all the time. They'd never get themselves with child if they were.' And then, seeing Ninian's frown of distaste, she added, 'Anyway, I like Jehane – I *love* Jehane – and she loves me.'

She held out her arms, and Jehane at once stretched out in response, struggling so hard that, in the end, Ninian had to let her go.

And so it was partly with regret and partly with relief that she received her third message of rejection in as many weeks. Lady Moragh wrote – or her clerk did – that she was sure Ninian would understand when she said that she thought Fiona ought to pursue her education elsewhere.

So the weeks passed, and the months, and Ninian felt sometimes as if the world had died and no one had told her.

PART SIX

1432—1433

CHAPTER ONE

I

'FIONA's coming! Fiona's coming!'

It was extraordinary, Ninian thought, and rather sad, that whenever she was with Jehane she seemed to do nothing but stop the child from doing whatever it was that she wanted to do – which, at this moment, happened to be pummelling her mother's thigh with all the strength of a pair of sturdy three-year-old fists. It was painful, and Ninian bruised easily, so she turned from the table and imprisoned the fists in both her own, saying firmly, 'No, darling.'

'But Fiona's coming! Fiona's coming!'

'Yes.' Lady Moragh's message had said simply that Fiona was travelling from Haddington to Drum Castle, near Aberdeen, and would be most grateful for a night's lodging. There was nothing surprising in this except that Moragh should have taken the trouble to write. One of the pleasures – or penances – of living in an isolated place was that one's home was treated as an unofficial hostelry by every traveller on the road, although since Harry's death Ninian had been wary of giving shelter to strangers.

'Will she be here soon, *maman*?'

'Yes, I should think so. You'll have to keep your eyes open for her, because the watchman has a sore throat today and he can't blow his trumpet.'

Ninian glanced out of the window. They were in the Speak-a-Word room, restored now to respectability but still scarred by the battle that had been fought there almost exactly a year ago. There was one deep cut near the edge of the table that Ninian always kept covered up with books and rent rolls because it made her shudder whenever she caught sight of it.

It was chilly outdoors. There had been a fall of wet snow a day or two earlier that still lay streaking the umber of the moors, and the sky sat heavily over everything in separate layers of grey. The fluffy coronet that ringed the tubby mountain was a dirty shade of yellow.

Ninian said, 'Go to your nurse, *p'tite*, and she will put a nice, warm wrap round you so that you can run out and meet Fiona when she comes.'

'Oh, *yes*!'

And she had gone, helter-skelter as always. Ninian turned back to her abacus. There were the tithes to pay, and since more than half the animals had died during last year's bitter winter she wasn't sure how she was going to manage.

Lost in her calculations, she didn't hear the little cavalcade until Jehane ambushed it, noisily, about fifty yards away.

By the time Ninian looked up, Fiona had dismounted and lifted the child into her arms, returning her hugs and kisses with a fervour equal to Jehane's own. The girl had filled out in the last year, Ninian observed, but she didn't look well.

Then, even from upstairs, Ninian heard Jehane shriek, 'Surprise!' and saw her produce from under the ample folds of her cloak the toy lance the carpenter had made for her. Groaning, Ninian willed the child's nurse to stir herself and put a stop to it. But Mistress Marjorie stayed where she was, in the comfortable lee of the barmkin, and like Fiona's maid and the four men-at-arms stood and watched with a kind of patient impatience while Jehane embarked on a game of tournaments which ended, according to ritual, with Fiona collapsing artistically to the ground, and Jehane jumping on her.

'Children!' Ninian thought despairingly as, drawing her own cloak around her, she made her way down the outside staircase. It didn't seem as if Fiona were any nearer to becoming a lady than she had been when she left.

Ninian's eyes were still on the stairs when she heard a harsh choking sound. She couldn't, for a moment, think where it was coming from; it sounded almost like a rook that had something wrong with it.

And then she realized that it was Fiona.

The girl was struggling to sit up, one hand at her throat and the other pressed tightly to her breast. She looked as if she couldn't breathe, and even as Ninian stood, momentarily frozen, the choking sound came again and then changed to something that was a ghastly combination of cough and whimper. The cough tore at the girl's thin body, and then she made a retching noise and, abruptly, like a squeezed pustule, a spurt of thin, yellow-grey mucous burst from between her lips. Yellow-grey – and streaked with blood.

Ninian's first thought was that, somehow, Jehane had hurt the girl, and she was just picking up her skirts to run towards them when she stopped, as suddenly and sharply as if some invisible obstacle had dropped down to block her path. Because Fiona's maid, still mounted, also had a hand at her throat, and her chest, too, was heaving.

In the terrible moment that followed, Ninian heard her own cry of, 'Jehane! Jehane!' ringing on the moorland air like the dirge of a dying phoenix.

'Jehane! Do as I say! Step back from Fiona and go and stand over there by the tower wall. Don't go near anyone else. Do as I say! Just for once, *do as I say!*'

But the child stubbornly went on standing where she was, ignoring her mother and staring at her friend with doubt on her face.

And then the nurse, who, like Ninian, had seen the plague before, said, 'Oh, no, my lady! Oh, no! *It can't be!*'

2

PLAGUE, the chastisement of heaven. There were two kinds, one that showed itself in terrible swellings and great black blisters. That was the kind Ninian's mother had died from, in Villeneuve, eleven years before, but some people had been known to recover from it.

It was the other kind that came in winter to northern Europe. The kind you caught just by breathing the same air as someone who had it. The kind that choked your lungs and turned your face the colour of slate, that robbed you of all control over your limbs, and suffocated the life out of you in three days or less. The kind no one ever recovered from.

Ninian stared at the little party fifty yards away, her brain still numbed by that first jolt of sickening horror.

There were eighty people in the castle behind her – and all of them doomed to die if Fiona came even one step nearer. Doomed, perhaps, even without that. Because if it were truly the volatile pestilence, death must already be floating on the air.

And Jehane had been in Fiona's arms.

La cavalcade de mort.

Ninian wanted to scream, 'Go away! Go away!' but she couldn't. There were six pairs of eyes fastened on her, clinging like leeches, trying to draw strength from her. She remembered Columba saying once that the end of the world could not be far off, because charity had begun to congeal in people's hearts, a proof that the human soul was ageing and that the flame of love that once had warmed it was sinking low.

She couldn't turn them away.

After a moment, she succeeded in fighting down the panic, and her mind began racing. She would have known what to do, if it had been the other plague. But this one . . . This one that lived in the air . . . How was it possible to control the air people breathed, today, tomorrow, or next week? Because the infection could hang about for months after an epidemic, trapped in the very moisture on the walls.

Holy Mother of God! What were the things she ought to do, the things she *could* do to save her people? Not the people she was staring at now with such intensity, for they were not her people and they were doomed and dead already, save for the agony of dying, but the others, the servants and their families who depended on her. Who weren't doomed – yet.

Air. Air. Air. Breathing. Air.

Slowly, swiftly, reason began to fight its way out of chaos.

Air. The wind was blowing *from* the castle to where Fiona and her servants stood. So that meant it must be carrying contamination away from the castle, not towards it. That was something.

Avoid the contamination. Cut off the air. Set up some barrier. She stood there, concentrating as she had never concentrated before, and gradually a kind of febrile order asserted itself in her brain. It seemed to take an eternity but she realized afterwards that it couldn't have been more than a minute or two. Because they were still there, motionless, watching her, waiting for her to tell them what to do.

She was accustomed to being obeyed. It was something she had never thought about until now; until now, when it mattered so desperately. If she couldn't impose her authority, make them do what she believed to be necessary, everyone at Dess would die.

Speaking loudly and clearly, she said, 'You must know that the Lady Fiona is ill and may have a dangerous fever. I am not going to be so unkind as to send you away, but you must do exactly as I tell you. Do you understand?'

Fiona was sitting on the ground, temporarily silent and exhausted, but her servants said obediently, 'Yes, my lady.'

And then at last Jehane, who had never seen her mother look so stern, went of her own accord to stand where she had been told.

Ninian, a voice inside her keening, 'Too late, too late,' turned coolly to the wet-nurse, who had not been nearer than thirty paces to the newcomers, and said, 'Mistress Marjorie, go indoors and find some linen and tapes to make masks for our noses and mouths, and put every woman in the castle to work. I want nine masks within the hour, and enough for everyone else as soon as it can be managed. No one is to come near any of us without a mask. One of the first nine is for you. Wear it when you come out again. I will need you.'

Then she unclipped the ring of keys that hung from her girdle and selected one. 'This is the key to my spice chest. We must burn spices to purify the air. Ask Master Lindsay to find every brazier we have. And we will need vinegar and rosewater, too, to rinse out our mouths and noses, and a good deal more of it to sprinkle on the floors. No, wait. There's more.'

Fiona, her face already suffused, had suddenly begun talking to herself in a ceaseless gabble. It was a moment before Ninian could make out the words.

'*Educes di tubulacio me animam meam . . . Et perdes omnes qui tubulant animam meam . . .*' The prayer against the plague. The girl had been well taught.

Ninian went on, 'And, Mistress Marjorie, tell Master Lindsay to clear out the buildings along this side of the barmkin, and stop up all the doors and windows and every gap in the walls so that no air can escape.'

Fiona, and her maid, and the men too, and – Jehane – would have to be isolated in buildings that could be burned down afterwards. Ninian didn't know whether burning them down would be enough, but it was the only way of destroying the pestilence that she had ever heard of.

'And when that has been done,' she said, 'he is to send away everyone – *everyone* – who has a place to go to. The others must camp out on the moors. There will still be heavy work to be done here. Master Lindsay will know. But tell him I would prefer those who do it to do it voluntarily, not by order. Now, go.'

The nurse half-turned towards Jehane, but Ninian shook her head and said, with difficulty, 'She must stay here.'

While they waited, Ninian filled in the time and tried to close all their minds to the nightmare by calling questions across the space that separated them. It was like calling from bank to bank across the river Styx, the river that divided life from death.

Fiona, panting and choking, said yes, there had been the pestilence in Haddington. No, she didn't think she had been in contact with it, but how could one tell? She had only begun to feel the pain this morning. For all she knew, the friends she had been staying with, who had been perfectly hale when she left them, might be dead by now, every one. She began to weep hysterically, then, and it brought on the coughing again. Ninian, her own face taut, had to fight down her instinct to go and comfort the girl.

Instead, her heart pounding in her breast, she turned to the men-at-arms. There were four of them, fanned out in a wary semi-circle round their mistress. Their horses were shifting nervously, and Ninian suddenly knew that they were on the very edge of turning and running. If they did, they could spread the plague across half the countryside, passing the infection on to everyone they met, everyone they went to for food, or help, or shelter. In their own fear, they wouldn't even think of the damage they were doing.

She said, calmly, 'You look like sensible men. Have you met or spoken to anyone at all since your mistress began coughing? No? Good. Well, I'm sure you know the dangers, but you will be safer here than anywhere else for the next few days.'

One of them said, after a moment, 'Locked up to die?'

'Locked away from catching the fever, if you don't already have it,' she replied sharply, although it would be a miracle if they weren't infected.

Their horses were still restive, and the men's eyes shifty. They were avoiding looking at each other. Ninian knew she hadn't convinced them, but then she had an inspiration. 'I know these next days will be hard to bear but, if you like, I will see that you have enough ale to drink yourselves insensible, if you wish, until the danger is past.'

The one who had spoken before said, 'Thank you, my lady.'

She half-smiled, with the aristocratic graciousness they would expect of her, and then turned to the maid. 'Tell me what happened.'

'We left Haddington three days ago,' the girl stammered. 'My mistress only began to feel sick this morning, and then she began coughing. Just an ordinary fever, she thought it was, though her head wasn't hot. But she said it was like having hammers inside it. And then . . .' She gulped, in rising hysteria. She wasn't more than sixteen.

'And then this afternoon, I began to get the pain, too. She's given it to me! She must have! The first thing she's ever given me in her life, and now I'm going to die, too! It isn't right, it isn't right!

'I hate her, I hate her, *I hate her!*'

3

FOR the next three nights and two days, Ninian sat in the courtyard and listened to Fiona die, and then her maid, and then three of the men-at-arms.

And for a day and a night after that, it was Jehane.

The thin wooden walls scarcely muffled the sounds as they fought for air against the agonizing, relentless closing up of all the channels that gave them breath. Fiona wept and prayed ceaselessly between attacks, and her maid squalled, a glutinous, indescribably awful sound. Two of the men swore and screamed to be let out in voices that thickened as the hours passed until their words had no more meaning than the grunting of pigs; in the early stages the strongest one of them nearly succeeded in breaking the door down. The third man drank himself into a stupor almost at once.

Towards the end, the choking and the coughing were all that were to be heard, except for the quiet, monotonous voice of the almoner, the domestic chaplain, intoning his prayers.

He was a truly devout man, and stupid. He wanted to open the nailed-up door and go in to Fiona to administer extreme unction, and Ninian had to call Master Lindsay and the Clerk of the Kitchen to stop him by force, because he couldn't, or wouldn't, understand that if he himself became infected there would be no one to give unction to the others when they needed it.

He said, 'The Lord will watch over me,' and Ninian replied coldly,

'Will He? Why should He make an exception of you, when He allows priests to die in droves every time there is an outbreak?'

The almoner said, 'Then if I die, it will be because He has ordained it.'

It was a long moment before she answered him. 'But if you go in, I cannot allow you to come out again. Which means that, if you go in, you will go in inviting death, and that would be the same as suicide – which is against God's law.'

Her argument was full of flaws, but he wasn't clever enough to see them. So she won. She saved his life.

It meant he was still there to pray for Jehane when the time came, to draw the sign of the Cross in consecrated oil on the door of the wooden hut in which her life was ending almost before it had begun.

Ninian and the wet-nurse had made sure that the child had all her toys with her – the little clay animals, the wooden sword, the carved figure of a knight that she was convinced was a picture of her father – and all the foods she liked best, and two big jugs of milk, which she didn't like. But she was difficult at first. She screamed, and shouted and kicked against the door, and couldn't understand why making a fuss didn't work now, when it had always worked before. And then, when no one came to soothe her and hug her, and make the nasty dream go away, she took refuge in sobbing pathetically until she could sob no more.

Ninian talked to her cheerfully through the door for a while, pretending it was all a game, telling her stories and saying that, if she was good, she might go to a beautiful place called Paradise, where the rivers flowed over jewelled rocks and silver sands, and she would have a splendid palace to live in, with columns of crystal and jasper.

But it only seemed to make things worse. 'Don't like you,' Jehane shrieked. 'I don't like you. You're not nice to me.'

She was very small, and all of her short life had been spent in the clean, unsullied air of Dess, so she had no resistance at all. She began complaining about the pains in her chest and side scarcely forty-eight hours after she had thrown her sturdy little arms round Fiona's neck, and the choking began that same night.

Ninian, unsleeping, chilled to the bone, blinded by a headache of stupefying proportions, sent the almoner away and sat alone outside her daughter's hut until the dawn was beginning to break, and Master Lindsay came out, as he had done these last three mornings, to ask what he could do.

He had been awake and watching all night, from under the over-hang of the stairs. And this morning he knew what she wanted before she could bring herself to speak.

Six years ago, when she had come to Dess as Sir Harry's bride, she had been pretty, spoilt and selfish, so that instead of making her husband pleasanter and more cheerful, she had had the opposite effect on him. The servants hadn't liked her; they hadn't realized, at first, how unsure of herself she was, or how unhappy. It was only when she had come home from court, after the poisoning and the miscarriage, that things had begun to change a little, and by the time Sir Harry was killed, their loyalty had been more for her than for him.

Master Lindsay had thought he knew her well by now, but he had been wrong. Not until Monday had he discovered what she was prepared to sacrifice for the people who depended on her.

The light of the brazier was no more than a faint, grey-dusted glow that, under the lowering sky, lent no comfort to the bleak and empty courtyard, bounded on one side by its tall, forbidding stone tower, and on the other three by the poor wooden structures that Sir Harry had never had the money to improve.

There was the silence of death from five of the huts; a faint, drunken snoring from the sixth; and from the seventh the choking, racking whimpering of a child.

The Lady Ninian cleared her throat carefully, and then said, 'Master Lindsay, are you – I should know after all these years, shouldn't I? – are you . . . Have you . . . a steady eye and hand? Could you . . .' She stopped, and started again. 'Could you . . .'

Her lids closed and he watched as she fought to bring the muscles of jaw and throat under control, noting the heavy black-purple rings under her eyes, and how the lines that ran from her nostrils to the corners of her mouth, framing the rounded, colourless cheeks, were as dark and deeply incised as a carving on a choir stall.

He discovered that he couldn't, in the end, allow her to put into words what she was trying to say, although he was a servant and hadn't the right to speak first.

When she opened her eyes again, he was already shaking his head.

He said, 'In full light and with space to move, I might put an arrow or a knife in the middle of my target. But through a slit in the door, into a dark interior – no, my lady. And there is no one in the castle that could do better.'

Every single nerve in her face and body was quivering, as if she were about to disintegrate, and the first tears were standing in her eyes.

Her voice was husky and unreal, but only a little unsteady. 'Thank you. I wanted to know if it was possible. That was all. I wasn't going to ask you to do it.'

'I would have done it. I *would* do it – but only if I could be sure.'

'Would you?' She said it politely, interestedly, as if this were quite a reasonable conversation. 'No. It is for me to do. I almost went in, earlier. With this.'

He followed her eyes, and for the first time saw that she had Sir Harry's dirk in her lap.

'But I couldn't decide. I still can't decide. I would be infected if I went in, so I would have to kill myself, too – one way or the other – and that would be sinful.'

She was stating things very clearly and simply, talking to him as if he were a child, but he didn't try to stop her, and showed no sign of his own concern.

After a moment, she went on, 'Does it seem strange to you – when the priest talks of God's mercy, I mean? Do *you* see any signs of mercy in any of the – alternatives?'

And then, 'No, don't answer me! Why should I put your soul in jeopardy?

'But what I can't be sure of, Master Lindsay, is – if I died, what would happen to all of you? What if something were to go wrong that I might have prevented? Would you know what to do, and be sure that it was done? Could I trust you, absolutely? To destroy everything that might possibly keep the plague alive – not to miss anything at all?'

She didn't pause for an answer, but went on as if she had to pour everything out now because it would be the only opportunity. 'The other problem is that I don't know what will happen to you all if – when – I go. The king would probably confiscate Dess, because there isn't a direct heir, and then you might all be turned out of the only home you have. I can't make up my mind what's for the best.'

She had sat there for much of the night with a voice crying in her head, 'Columba! Columba! Tell me what to do!' It had come as automatically as saying her paternosters, because his wisdom and his love for her had always been her first resort in time of trouble. But though the words formulated themselves as of old, what she had been asking for was comfort and warmth of soul, not advice. She knew exactly what his advice would be, and it wasn't acceptable to the person she had become in these last three years.

He would have said, 'My child. This is God's will, and it must be done. You must let things take their course. Your daughter will go to God, the finer for her suffering. And your sorrow for her, though you may not believe it now, will in the end enrich your own soul beyond all reckoning.'

She had wondered, quite unexpectedly, what Gavin would say, and thought that he, too, would try to dissuade her, though his reasoning, she knew, would be different.

But it wasn't Columba's nor Gavin's daughter who was involved; not their child who cried out for mercy and release. Not their child who had been conceived in misery; who had known, with the instinct of babyhood, the imperfection of her mother's love; who was dying alone, and slowly, in a torment she didn't understand. That her mother could end for her.

Ninian said, 'I don't know what to do for the best, Master Lindsay, but I must decide soon.'

He went down on his knees before her, and lied as he had never lied before. He was a plain countryman, and not clever, and he knew nothing of the plague. He hadn't the strength or the courage to be responsible for the lives of eighty people. He begged her not to lay such a burden on him, lest he should fail her.

And all the time he was listening, desperately, for any change in the sound from the hut close by.

She still had the same concern and indecision in her eyes when she dismissed him to go about the affairs of the castle.

He took inordinate care to see that she wasn't left alone for a single moment during the hours that followed, and that there was always at least one of the strongest of the men servants within reach.

But it was the sheerest chance that he himself was beside her, trying to persuade her to swallow a posset, when the quality of Jehane's coughing changed. It became harsher, and more violent, the pain beyond bearing.

Master Lindsay took his mistress in an iron grip as she leapt to her feet. 'No, mistress. No, my lady. *No!*'

And even as she struggled against him, there was a rattling sound that both of them would remember all the rest of their days.

Then nothing.

CHAPTER TWO

IT snowed all winter, so that the moors were like a rolling white sea, empty save for the tower of Dess, a tall, gaunt, lonely ship with its wake churning behind it – the wake under which lay the ruins of what had once been the barmkin. The wind had changed just when the flames had taken hold of the death huts, so that the funeral pyre had turned into a holocaust and now there was nothing left at all under the fresh white blanket except sodden ashes and a scattering of bent and blackened scraps of iron.

Not even bones.

It had been a cruel task, sifting and sorting them, but it had to be done, because without them there could be no Christian burial. The dead still needed their bodies after death. How, otherwise, could they rise again on the Judgement Day?

Ninian had stared, for a long time, at the six neat, separate piles that represented the whole earthly legacy of six living, breathing human beings. *Memento mori*. It was better so, she thought. At least there would be no dust, no worms, no flesh lying putrefying in their graves.

But when all the ceremonies were over, she went up to the gallery at the top of the tower, and from a chest took out what had lain there untouched for six long years – her brushes and inkpots, her papers and parchments and colours, everything she needed for the painting she had forsworn. She would have left it all at Villeneuve, except that Sévèrine would have wondered.

How unreal, now, was the exquisite, enamelled world of Pol de Limbourg that she had once admired so much, with the bright colours and the burnished golds she had despaired of copying. There had been no power at all in her brush when she was younger – or so she now thought – because painting had been a matter of hand and eye, beauty and technique, not of feeling.

She wasn't even aware of how the technique still informed her brush when she sat down again and set it to parchment. The shapes came without thinking, and the proportions, and the subject.

Harry and she, on their journey from Villeneuve to Dess, had spent some weeks in Paris, and had gone, as everybody did, to visit the churchyard of the Holy Innocents, a place of public entertainment, a social rendezvous. The cemetery itself was so much used that it wasn't possible to bury anyone who had just died until someone else was dug up. Over the years, great numbers of skulls and bones had been heaped up in the charnel houses that surrounded the cloisters. It was a place where friars came to preach, where people sometimes held banquets, too. Death was everyone's familiar.

On the walls of the cloisters was a new and much-admired series of paintings illustrating the *danse macabre*, the dance of the dead, where a horrible, grinning, shambling corpse took by the hand and led away, one by one, men of every kind and condition, men in all their forty guises, from pope and emperor down to pilgrim and peasant. Death the leveller.

The grinning figure wasn't an abstract of death, but personal to every man who looked at it. It was himself, as in time he would become.

Ninian hadn't understood. She had shuddered, and begged Harry to take her away. Until now she thought she had forgotten it all.

Until now, when her brush fled winged over the paper.

There was no coherent order as the twinned images grew under its miniver point. The dead Harry leading the living. Ninian's mother, frail and irresolute, dragged in the wake of a bloated, blistered hag. Blane hanged; and Blane vital. Fiona a jangling puppet made of strung-together bones; and Fiona, the thirteen-year-old girl who had loved Jehane.

And Jehane herself. With infinite care, so that the tempering would hold, Ninian mixed the egg-white glair with *terre verte* and white and

399

began the underpainting for the warm flesh tones of the living child. It helped, now, to concentrate on the technicalities of it. She would need to add a touch of lampblack and a trace of brazil red to the yellow of *graines d'Avignon* for the hair, and it would take several layers of azurite to get the right depth of colour in her eyes. For the dress, the red one the child had been so fond of, she would mix some walnut-bark ink into vermilion, and perhaps add egg-yolk to the glair to give it lustre.

It was easy, once the living child was there on the parchment, to strip the sturdy little body down to its bones, to the black and white skeleton that had as much personality as Jehane herself – stockily built, positive, stamping its foot and tugging the stubborn little fleshed-out figure after it. As if the determined spirit was there still, and had not died.

For Ninian, it was an exorcism. And, as she put her brush down at last and gazed out at the first flurries of snow, laying their innocent blanket over the fire-blackened ruins that seemed to symbolize all the heartbreak of her adult years, she reflected that she had come back, in a strange, erratic circle, to her beginnings.

And yet, not quite. Because she had thought, at seventeen, that she would never be able to paint to her own satisfaction, and that she could never have the love of the man she wanted. Time had proved otherwise, though imperfectly. There was still a long way to go, and she had no idea how the journey would end. All she knew was that, now, she had the strength and the patience to see it through.

2

THE flames were roaring, giving off a fearsome heat in the July sun. Columba averted his face a little and tried not to breathe, hoping that the voice from the heart of the fire would fall silent soon. It always surprised him how long heretics took to burn.

He would have preferred not to be present, but it had been impossible to avoid, since he happened to be in Scotland and his old friend, Laurence of Lindores, had been most anxious that he should carry back to Rome a good account of his zeal. Columba could understand it. As inquisitors went, Laurence's record was less than impressive.

This was only the third heretic he had burned in twenty-six years. And two of those hadn't even been Scots.

This man was from Prague, and quite a distinguished academic, it seemed. But he had come to Scotland to preach the doctrines of the late John Huss which were not only heretical, but in Columba's view sadly unhygienic. The Hussites demanded that the laity, as well as the priesthood, should be permitted to touch their lips to the chalice at Mass, which everyone knew to be an infallible recipe for turning an isolated infection into a full-scale epidemic. Columba shook his head and reflected on the folly of men.

When the fire was no more than a shimmer on St Andrews' bright summer sand, Columba, Master Laurence, and the other civic and ecclesiastical dignitaries turned away towards St Mary's, leaving behind the febrile, chattering crowd of students and tradesmen who had flocked to the scene as to a fairground.

'A pity,' Columba said lightly to his old friend, 'that it should be necessary to incinerate a representative of the university that relies, I am told, more than any other in Europe on your own admirable scientific treatises! How sad that they pay you in no other currency than heretics.'

He should have known better. Master Laurence had never had any sense of humour.

The big-boned, doughy face stared at him for a moment, and the light-toned voice that issued so unexpectedly from his powerful chest said, 'Frivolous still? I would have thought that the trust His Holiness reposes in you might have cured you of that.' He succeeded well, but not well enough, in concealing the fact that he, too, had derived pleasure from the burning. Columba found it faintly distasteful.

'But now,' Master Laurence went on, 'you must tell me the outcome of your talks with the king, and the Bishop of Glasgow. And also how Adam de Verne is doing. A favourite of mine, that young man. We can talk during our meal.' He sniffed appreciatively. 'I smell roast pig.'

Columba's stomach turned over, for there was an on-shore breeze and it seemed to him that the smell was not coming from the kitchens.

NINIAN said, 'You have lost me along the way, Columba dear. His Holiness sent you to Scotland to summon Bishop Gavin to Rome to give an account of himself – for the anti-barratry laws of '27 and '28? But surely that was all settled three years ago, just after you were last here?'

She looked thin and insubstantial, astonishingly like her mother. He had never seen the resemblance before. But she also had a new elegance, because instead of the embroidered silks and tight waists and alarming necklines he knew, she had taken to the simple dress of the countryside, a long tunic made of white linen with a fine black stripe, tied just above the waist with a leather and silver belt, and brightened with sleeves of scarlet cloth. It suited her as perfectly as if it had been designed for her.

There was something else that was unfamiliar; an inner certainty, a calmness of spirit that he had not expected so soon after the child's death.

'Settled? No,' he said. 'It was only postponed. We have a new pope now, and he feels most strongly that the anti-barratry laws must be repealed. The mere fact that they were passed five or six years ago makes them no less offensive and no less of a threat to the papal finances.'

'Ah,' Ninian said. 'The shoe is pinching, is it? Even here I have heard rumours of the troubles – the expensive troubles! – in Rome and Basle. Is it true that the Colonnas have threatened to drive His Holiness out of the Eternal City by force?'

Ignoring the Colonnas, which was easier to do in Scotland than in Rome, Columba exclaimed, 'It is a matter of principle!'

'Oh, I see. And how did Bishop Gavin respond to the renewed citation?'

Columba's nostrils flared. 'He was, I fear, offensive. Arrogant, in fact. He marched me off to the king as if I were an erring schoolboy and he the dominie.'

'And?' She moved slightly, turning her face to the sun. They were sitting on the outside steps at Dess, and the faint warm breeze from the moors brought the gossiping of birds with it and a scent of juniper.

Ninian had learned a good deal about the small birds in these last few months, because they had multiplied greatly now that the hawks were gone – freed, as a precaution, just before she set fire to the buildings in the barmkin. They had escaped the inferno and, afterwards, had hung about for a while before they took off hunting for themselves, farther and farther afield. She wondered, sometimes, how Greensire was faring, but she could never have flown him again, because she couldn't even bear, now, to handle the lure.

'James chose to regard the citation – and, I fear, my delivery of it – as a deliberate insult to himself. He appears to hold me personally responsible for most of the disorders that have beset Scotland in these last years. Anyway, it seems he had been undecided whether to support His Holiness or the Council of Basle in their present unhappy dispute, and out of simple contrariness has now chosen the Council. He has announced publicly that he will send Cameron to Basle.'

It would be two years, soon, since she had seen him. She had no idea whether he even knew that Jehane had died. And now it seemed it would be longer still. The last ecumenical council had lasted for four years. But she could bear it; she could bear anything, now. Although it would be easier if she could see him, just once, before he went.

Columba said heavily, 'I fear for this country, Ninian, with James's intransigence and his unbridled temper – he is far worse than he was. Nothing good will come of it. With such a king, wholly estranged from Rome, I see nothing but misery. If he would only return to God, so that his soul might be saved!'

Ninian smiled inwardly. Was this really Columba, who used never to mention either God or men's souls except when he wanted to make an impression?

'Return to God, or return to Rome?' she murmured.

'They are the same,' he said.

Later, when she had told him the details of the tragedy he already knew of in outline, and when he had said – as she had known he would – that it had been God's will, and that Jehane had been spared all the miseries that were the inevitable lot of sinful humanity, they spoke of Adam.

'He is well enough,' Columba said, but she could see it was untrue and it took little probing to discover the reality.

'His wounds have mended, but the Inverlochy affair still preys on his mind. He has become too fond of the wine flask, and nothing his mother or I can say has any effect.'

Columba was sitting with his head tilted back against the wall and his eyes closed against the sun, but the tears came to them and spilled over into the deep channels that bracketed his nose and mouth. 'I can no longer trust him in anything where he needs to keep a close tongue in his head, and it means I cannot give him any employment at all. I can't even have him at Rome, because everyone knows that James has declared him a traitor. So he spends most of his time at Villeneuve. I suspect – though I can't be sure – that he has joined forces with the Routiers.' The marauding troops who had turned from legitimate war to private war against society, who terrorized large areas of France, whose life was always violent, never dull.

She said, 'It is the kind of occupation that would appeal to him.'

He opened his eyes. 'What am I to do, Ninian?'

She put an arm round his shoulders, shoulders that sagged a little where they had always been firm, and laid her forehead against his cheek. Then she said gently, 'He was born to trouble. He has no other resources if he is robbed of – of *doing*, and of feeling important. I think you must leave him to work out his own salvation.'

Hesitantly, he said, 'Have you ever thought of returning to France – for a visit, I mean? Séverine would be so happy to see you, and perhaps you might have some influence over my poor, misguided son. He is very attached to you, you know.'

Somehow, she suppressed a shiver.

'My poor, misguided son'. Was this what love could do, make one blind? And, of course, she knew that it could.

She herself, warmed by the glow of Columba's passion for all who were dear to him, had been wilfully blind, for a long time, to Columba's other side, and Adam's. If she hadn't refused to believe what she had heard, that day in 1427 when Adam and Robert Graham had their council of war at Dess, she might have been able to prevent at least some of the tragedies that had followed. How dangerous love without judgement could be.

She had been fortunate, because another love had given her perspective, so that she could see more clearly now, without loving the less. She wondered, briefly, whether she should say something of this to Columba, and then discovered she couldn't. Clarity of vision was something that had to come from inside.

With sadness, she remembered Adam dragging himself across the floor of the dungeon towards her, hand outstretched, and knew that she could never willingly see him again.

So she said carefully, 'Columba, my dear, when did Adam ever listen to a single word his little cousin said? You should know better than that.'

He sighed, 'I suppose so. But you are not a little cousin now, you are a woman, and a strong one.'

'I'll think about it, but . . .'

She had, in fact, already thought several times of paying a visit to Villeneuve, because she needed to be away from Dess for a while. But every time the idea came to her mind, she had remembered the law that said she needed permission from the chancellor to take even enough gold and silver abroad to cover her travelling expenses. It meant she would have to approach him directly, and she had a superstitious dread of forcing herself on his attention in any way. In the slow chess-game of their relationship, they both knew that the next move, if any, was his.

Or so she had thought. But if he were going to be away in Basle, for years, perhaps, she would have to think again.

By the time Columba left on his long return journey to Rome, he had been restored to himself. When he embraced her, smiling, it was the loving, enveloping smile that had first taught her what true happiness meant. She knew then that, whatever face he wore, however she judged him, he would never be less than deeply beloved to her, more dear, more like a father, than her own father had ever been.

4

GAVIN had forgotten how the sun went down at Kinveil.

Forgotten the thunderous coppers and purples, the wild reds, the sweetness of rose and amethyst, the smooth richness of burnished gold. The only gold in all the world's store that soothed those who looked on it.

But both memory and knowledge settled round him like a well-worn, comfortable cloak in the single moment when he rode over the crest and saw Loch an Vele for the first time in twenty-two years.

It wasn't one of Kinveil's finest sunsets, though it was spectacular enough in its way – not in the west, where the sky was dark and heavy and unremarkable around the flaming sun, but in the other quarters, where the low-slanting light transformed all the colours of the landscape. There was no purple of heather nor green of bracken, no saffron of changing leaves, no blue of water. Instead, the whole floor of the glen – loch, shore, trees, fields – was a flattened-out study in sepia, shading into deep violet-brown shadows, as if everything in nature had given up its own separate self to the dying sun.

And as the miles passed and the little cavalcade drew nearer to Kinveil, Gavin could see that nothing else had changed at all. He half expected to hear again the voices of his childhood, the voices of the people who had been his whole world during the first eleven years of his life.

But his mother had died long ago, within months of his leaving; she had never told him how sick she was, and he had been too young and too careless to see it. Father Duncan was dead, too, the man to whom Gavin owed more than he had ever properly acknowledged, and so was Donny Mackenzie, a good fighting man who had been killed at nineteen in some skirmish between the clans. Donny had been Moragh's first husband.

Gavin smiled faintly to himself. After Donny, Moragh had looked higher, and higher still, so that in the course of two – no, three – more marriages, she had become so very much the lady that it was difficult, now, to remember her at six years old in bare feet and ragged brown homespun.

One other voice, newly missing, was that of Gavin's only close relative in the world, his father's brother, who had looked after Kinveil for him. It was because Uncle Archie had died that Gavin was here now. The king, who had strong views about property and its maintenance, had given him permission to take the two weeks he needed to come here, and do what had to be done, before he left for Basle. 'Because only God and His Holiness,' he had said malevolently, 'know how long it will be before you have another opportunity.'

Gavin hadn't been able to say that he was more concerned over what would happen to the country in his absence, than to Kinveil. It had begun to seem, during these last two years, as if James lost all sense of proportion when there was no one there to steady him. Gavin never knew, when he was away, which of the great barons would have been arrested or dispossessed by the time he returned.

His horse stumbled, interrupting his train of thought, and he glanced down and saw that the track was hard and heavily pitted. Some things, indeed, never changed. He could remember how annoyed he had been about the state of the track on the day he had left Kinveil.

It was early September, now, which meant that the sheep must have been driven this way only a week or two before, brought back from their summer sojourn in the hills by the local women and girls, almost as many of them as sheep, because the *caoraich bheaga* were frail, perverse little beasts who spent most of their lives looking for an excuse to pine away and die. Three months was a long time for the women to be away from home, and the procession of yapping dogs, yammering goats, bleating sheep and shouting shepherdesses was welcomed enthusiastically back to the glen by men worn out from a summer of fishing and chastity. The population of the glen had always shown a sharp increase nine months later; before Gavin had learned the facts of life, he had thought that Holy Church decreed May as the month for new babies just as it decreed December for Christmas and March for Lent.

It was three-quarters dark by the time they reached the shore and Kinveil loomed there before them, small and tall and forbidding against the satin waters of the loch and the thread of afterglow that still rimmed the far-off hills of Skye. The boat, scarcely more than a raft, lay on the beach, with its own pole thrust in the sand as a hitching post.

Leaving his men to settle themselves on the shore, Gavin floated the raft and gently, easily, as if he had never been away, poled himself across the few yards of water to the little island tower where he had been born.

5

NOT since childhood had he known the luxury of being alone and free, however temporarily, from the burden of responsibility, and by now it had become a desperate need for him.

So it was a blessing that there was little that needed to be done at Kinveil. Uncle Archie had looked after it well enough, and the fabric was sound. Nor were there any troublesome refinements, no wall paintings that needed to be kept dry, no tapestries to be rolled up, no splendid silver salts to be wrapped away against tarnishing. It was a barren place.

Gavin had no idea whether he would ever live here, or even come here again, but he had felt the tug of it recently and thought that, if ever he were his own master, he could be happy at Kinveil. And so, as if the act of making it decently habitable was a step towards the private future he could not, even in his dreams, foresee, he decided to set a few simple improvements in train. The staircase his father had always talked of, but never built; shutters for the windows; stone flags on the ground floor in place of beaten mud; some kind of sewer.

There were people in the clachan who could manage it all, provided they weren't rushed. Highlanders preferred to do things in their own good time, for they were a slow, peaceable folk as a rule. Strange that there should be a spark of wildness in all of them, deep inside, ready to be fanned. Was it boredom, he sometimes wondered, that made them so quick to respond, and so violent, when the fiery cross went round?

The same spark was there in himself, he knew, although until it had flared up inside the bastions of his heart, he had always thought, smugly, that he had smothered it.

Reflecting on all the self-disciplined years of his dealing with good men and knaves, fools and bigots, envious allies and homicidal foes, he found himself wondering whether God was, after all, as unjust as he had always supposed. If there was indeed free will, then most of humanity's troubles must lie not with God but with the weak vessels he had created.

Did that mean not an unjust God, but one who reserved His vengeance for those who erred against His law? Before he knew it, Gavin found himself back at the same question again. Was His law indeed the same law as that laid down by the church – that amorphous institution led by men who were no more than human and, as William of Ockham had proved, entirely fallible?

It was a question he couldn't face, or not now, when Kinveil had begun to weave its spell of timeless peace. So weary was he that at the first hint of relaxation he found himself suddenly and completely drained, as if there was nothing there of him at all but an empty shell.

For three whole days, in a mental and emotional vacuum, he moved about Kinveil and talked intelligently with Wat of Dornie about how much timber would be needed for the shutters, and where it could be got, and how they should be fixed; and with Angus of Bundalloch about finding the right kind of slate-stone for the floor, and the problems of getting it across to the islet on the raft; and with Iain of Keppoch about whether local sandstone would do for the sewer channels or whether the Torridon kind would be better – if Iain's second-cousin-three-times-removed could be persuaded to bring it down in his boat. He had to hear all their confessions, too, because Father Duncan's successor not only had a heavy hand with penances but a tongue that wagged as busily as the tail of a suckling lamb.

And then there came another sunset.

It had been a mild day and the sun was going down in a calm, peach-gold glow against a sky of aquamarine, with a few low clouds of smoke and amethyst drifting lazily in the west. The delicate capping of new snow on the mountains of Skye was peach-gold, too, and the mountains themselves a deep, pure indigo, while the gilded path over the silken waters of Loch an Vele seemed to run right on and up to Kinveil itself, over the shore, warming the rocks to black rose and turning the white sands, still wet and yeasty from the tide, into a spilling of pale, gleaming amber beads.

Gavin sat in the hollow of the hills above the loch that had always been his private eyrie. He had been conscious of beauty in his childhood, he supposed, without giving it much thought, or even being very much touched by it, because it was so much part of the only world he knew. And when he had lost it, when he had made the astounding discovery that nowhere else was even remotely like Kinveil, his shock had soon given way before all the other excitements of his new life. He had seen beauty of landscape since, and recognized it, but he had never been moved by it. Indeed, he had come to suspect that obsession with beauty of any kind was the merest emotionalism. And, God knew, there was enough of that in the world already.

But now, ruefully, he sat on the hill and retracted everything, soaking up the beauty that lay before him as thirstily as a dried-up plant.

Or a dried-up lawyer. Why had he worked so hard for so many years to break himself of normal human weaknesses, normal human plea-sures? So that he might be strong, and incorruptible? So that he might achieve all the things he now knew were impossible to achieve – his own and everybody else's human nature being what it was? He had begun building his shell when he was too young to know better, and had paid a hard price for it; now, he was paying a harder one.

But he had committed himself to the church, and the church forbade him to flout its laws for the sake of a love that was human, not divine.

The laws of the church, or the laws of God? Always the same question. He kept his eyes open, but closed his mind.

And what came to him then, for the first time in all the thirty-three years of his life, was a sense of divine presence.

He saw no visions, heard no voices, felt no breath of God's passing. But there was something. And it was kindly.

After a while, he shook himself and tried to smile. Awe at the beauty of terrestrial things was very different from the awe that was a prerequisite of faith. And had it been God indeed – or Satan? Because it was Satan who had taken Christ up on the mountain to show him temptation, and for Gavin a loving God *was* temptation, the temptation to believe that He would understand and forgive even what the church forbade.

And then Gavin found himself laughing, remembering the blasphemous old tradition that when Satan led the Lord Jesus into a high mountain and showed him all the kingdoms of the earth and the glory thereof, he had been careful to keep his thumb over Scotland.

6

NINIAN had written to the chancellor for permission to take gold and silver out of the country, and it was the excuse Gavin needed for paying a visit to Dess. There were things he had to say.

She had all the warmth of summer on her skin and her eyes were clear and calm. When he remarked on it, she said, 'What else can the world do to me?' She didn't add that whereas, once, if he had died, she could not have lived, she thought now she might survive even that.

The extraordinary thing was that – although she had always believed, even while loving him, that he was not sensitive to grief – it was he, not Columba, who touched the chord that gave her at last the relief of tears over Jehane.

She had been speaking, without sentimentality, of the pain of knowing that the child of her body, so alive and vital, had been abandoned to the earth, to corruption and decay. 'I don't know why that, particularly, should matter so much, but it does.'

There was a moment's silence, then he said quietly, 'You must look further. Corruption, too, perishes in its turn, and flowers grow in its place.'

She stared at him for a long time, and then bent her head and put her fingertips to her lips, and he saw that she was weeping. He held her in his arms until it was over and, without knowing it, placed the final seal on her love. Because whatever he had given her before, he gave her now the warmth and comfort that, since childhood, she had always believed to be the essence of it.

Afterwards he said, still holding her, 'I can't stay, and I shouldn't.'

She had expected it and, indeed, had wanted no more than to see him. It was another change in her that, for the moment, seeing him was enough.

She nodded, smiling.

Then he went on, unexpectedly, 'You know that they burned Paul Crawar, for being a Hussite?'

'Yes. The Maid of Orléans, then my little Jehane, and now Paul Crawar. It seems, sometimes, as if flames are licking round all the margins of the world.'

There were other flames that Gavin was sure she knew nothing of, the slow, dull, leisurely flames that had consumed more than a hundred men, women and children of the Cameron clan in the little church east of Mamore almost two years ago. Because of them, Gavin had learned to hate Adam de Verne with a deep, implacable and very personal hatred.

He should have asked her – he had meant to ask her – about Verne, but he couldn't, because loving her had given him understanding and he could see that she might have felt justified in protecting her wounded cousin, whatever he had done. Gavin hoped she would never know what he had done after; never know about the innocent people who had died because she had been loyal to a man who didn't deserve even to live.

He smiled faintly, and said, 'What an uncomfortable thought. But I wanted to remind you always to guard your tongue, most stringently. Never do, or say, anything that isn't orthodox.'

She nodded. 'You, too. Your danger is so much greater than mine.'

He hesitated and then said, 'There's something else, and I don't know whether I should tell you. It has been settled that the Council of Basle is to discuss the whole question of clerical celibacy. There is a move to abandon it completely.'

Such a light came to her eyes that he regretted it at once, and hurried on, 'We mustn't build any hopes. It has been discussed before, by other councils of the church. I told you only because I think you have the right to know.'

It wasn't the possibility that they might be free to marry that had put the light in her eyes, although she couldn't say so. It was the fact that, by talking of it, he had shown her fully and finally that he too was committed. And if that were so, then somehow, somewhere, they would be together in the end. At Kinveil, perhaps – this place he spoke of with such intensity?

Uncharacteristically diffident, he told her what had happened, and finished, 'Was it some kind of revelation, do you think? I don't know. All I know is that my mind is in confusion.'

She laughed suddenly. 'What an irony! Here am I losing all faith in God's mercy while you gain a new faith in God's love. What *are* we to do?'

It was almost time for him to leave, and he kissed her, long and deeply. Then she said, 'Let me make myself respectable. I would prefer the servants not to see that I have been weeping all over the chancellor of the realm. And I will ask the kitchen to produce something for you to eat and drink before you go.'

7

SHE would take no denying, so he settled back to wait, his mind racing ahead to what he still had to do before he left for Basle in two weeks' time. The door opened sooner than he had expected, but instead of Ninian it was her steward.

Master Lindsay, stiff and yet obsequious, aware that her ladyship was engaged elsewhere for the moment, wondered whether it would be convenient for my Lord Bishop to hear his confession.

Gavin was used to it. There were many other priests in Scotland like the one at Kinveil, over-free with their penances and their tongues, and since the church enjoined confession only once a year it was not unusual for sinners to reserve their sins for the ears of someone who didn't know them.

Master Lindsay's sins seemed to be commonplace enough, hardly worthy of a bishop's ear. Improper thoughts about one of the sewing maids; undue anger with the second-youngest scullion; a fondness for ale.

And then he said, 'And I have – Holy Mother, save me! – a sin greater than those on my conscience. Her ladyship will have told you that Mistress Jehane was doomed to die in a torment too great for a little child to bear?

'So before we locked her away, I took it on my own soul to put poison in the milk, that her torment might be the sooner ended.'

And then, seeing the bishop staring at him with a blankness in his eyes, Master Lindsay unknowingly struck him the most frightening blow of his life. 'For I swear to you, my lord,' he went on, 'that if I had not, her ladyship would have killed the child with her own hand. And then herself.'

PART SEVEN

1434–1437

CHAPTER ONE

I

'LET us strive, then, to be good because God is good, to be just, because He is just, to be merciful because He is merciful. To turn all our endeavours towards Him because all His endeavours are turned towards us. To look towards Him alone, with all our attention, nor ever turn aside the eyes of our mind, because it is thus also that He enfolds us with His regard. Then we may behold, as in a mirror, the image of life eternal, which is itself none other than that divine gaze, directed ceaselessly and lovingly upon each one of us, even into the secret places of our soul . . .'

The only consolation to be derived from preaching to a gathering of churchmen was that most of them, over the course of the years, had learned to snore quietly.

Gavin raised his eyes from his notes and directed a basilisk glare at Columba Crozier, seated towards the back of the congregation and carrying on a conversation, penetratingly *sotto voce*, with the Bishop of Urbino. Crozier had arrived and been officially admitted to membership of the council on the very same day as Gavin himself.

Tom Myrton said it was just one of life's little jokes. 'Now that His Holiness has deigned to recognize the legitimacy of the council, he's bound to send representatives, and who better than his dear son the Archdeacon of Teviotdale and Lothian? His Holiness wants to be sure that the council doesn't try to thieve too many of his perquisites. Crozier's got his own axe to grind, too. He'll want to get the council on his side against you and James. It's natural enough.'

'Thank you very much,' Gavin said.

As things turned out, Crozier guarded his tongue for almost two months, while he ingratiated himself with everyone who mattered. Gavin, who would have preferred to give all his attention to the council's deliberations, was constantly being distracted by wondering what Crozier was saying to Nicholas of Cusa, or Cardinal Cesarini, or the Bishop of Hertogenbosch.

Crozier, of course, had seen something of the Council of Constance, so a massed array of ecclesiastics had no novelty for him. Gavin's own initial reaction, however, was one of bemusement, for despite his preconceptions, he had expected a certain distinction of thought and utterance. It was disillusioning, therefore, to find that Basle differed only from a Scots council-general in that blatant self-interest was wrapped up in the clean linen of philosophy. As the council shivered its way through the last weeks of winter on the Rhine, its debates moved with awesome inevitability from extremist speeches to compromise conclusions, and very little of what was said or decided in public reflected the commonsensical opinions expressed to Gavin in private by a good many of the delegates. If this was how the laws of the church were formulated, he reflected, he had good reason for thinking that they and the laws of God were not necessarily the same.

James had been insistent that, as soon as he had made his presence felt at Basle, Gavin was to absent himself on a mission to Charles VII of France, to assure him that Scotland's present truce negotiations with the English posed no threat to the French alliance. Gavin postponed the mission for as long as he could, waiting for Crozier to show his hand, but the archdeacon continued to chat peaceably, and smile politely, and look as if his sole interest was in renewing old acquaintances. In the end Gavin could wait no longer.

Two days after he left, Crozier rose to his feet in council and requested permission to speak.

Tom Myrton's report on what he had said caught up with Gavin just before Troyes. 'He woke everyone up, I'll give him that,' Tom wrote. 'And he had the sense to go for James more than you (you'll be blithe to know you've made quite an impression here). Anyway, the gist of the thing was that James "and his ministers" have been trying to take over functions that properly belong to Rome, and that they've been discri-

418

minating against anyone and everyone who adheres to the curia. It seems we've been putting folk to death right, left and centre. I can't say I remember it, but maybe that was the week I was on my holidays.

'It was a real tirade, I should add; none of the usual sweetness and light. The council wants to hear your side of it, so you've got that facing you when you get back. Don't forget to bring me some of those aniseed comfits from Dijon, if you're coming that way.'

But the council had to wait for Gavin's arguments, and Tom for his comfits, for almost a year. Because His Holiness Eugenius IV, having incurred the lethal displeasure not only of the Colonnas but a good many others, found it necessary, one July night, to disguise himself as a monk and flee from the Eternal City to the more hospitable surroundings of Florence. The news travelled considerably faster than he did, with the result that James sent a brisk message to Gavin saying that, if he too went to Florence, he might catch His Holiness in a weak moment and settle all their outstanding differences without more ado. Eugenius was known to be very persuadable, and since he must have been cut off by his flight from most of his advisers, Gavin ought to have a clear field.

James, of course, didn't have to make the journey himself, Gavin reflected sourly as he sat in an ox-drawn conveyance that looked like a threshing machine, and listened to his guides banging on drums to bring down any impending avalanches before he entered the St Gothard pass. 'No,' he said curtly, when they told him the pass was precipitous and asked whether he would feel happier with a blindfold.

Nor did James have to cool his heels in the admittedly dazzling city of Florence for weeks, while His Holiness mediated between its warring factions. It was coincidence, no doubt, that his arbitration favoured the banker Cosimo de Medici, which augured well for the papal finances, although Gavin didn't think it would make His Holiness look on Scotland's anti-barratry laws with any greater favour.

In that, Gavin slightly misread him, because Eugenius enjoyed careful and learned argument, which Gavin was good at, and was always favourably disposed towards churchmen who did well by their churches. On the administration and improvement of Glasgow cathedral, Gavin couldn't be faulted. Also, His Holiness had been temporarily cut off not only from his advisers but from his filing system, and his memory of what all the trouble was about was conveniently hazy.

By the spring, Eugenius was sufficiently convinced of Gavin's respectability and the unimportance of the anti-barratry legislation to bestow on him the appointments of papal assistant and referendary.

Gavin, ungratefully, retired to his white-washed chamber and laughed until the tears came to his eyes and his sides ached. Archdeacon Crozier was going to be very annoyed indeed.

But even though he had developed a reluctant respect for Eugenius, Gavin knew that his favour was a transient thing. As soon as he himself was out of sight, he would be out of mind, and Eugenius would be open to whatever other winds blew strongest. Gavin's hints that His Holiness might be persuaded to send a legate to Scotland, as James passionately desired, had borne no fruit, but at least he had achieved a temporary truce in the war between Scotland and the papacy, which was considerably more than he had dared to hope for.

What he had missed was the debate at Basle on the subject of clerical celibacy. He doubted whether, even if he had been there to speak, he could have swayed the decision. Because the council had decided against abandonment and, instead, had reiterated and strengthened the existing penalties.

Now, any erring priest who failed instantly to banish his mistress would be deprived of the income from his benefices. And, if he ignored a second warning, he was to be deprived of the benefices themselves.

In May 1435, Gavin left Florence to return – although he didn't quite say so to His Holiness – to Basle.

The route he took was extremely roundabout, however, because he went by way of Villeneuve-lès-Avignon.

2

WHEN Sévèrine received the courteous message from Gavin Cameron, asking if she would be prepared to see him, she felt her heart turn over inside her. How did he dare – this man who had hanged one of her sons, and sent the other back to her, wounded almost to death?

'Absolument pas!' she exclaimed, and then, almost before the words were out, changed her mind.

He had not come casually, that was certain. There was a reason, and she should find out what it was.

So she sent the messenger back to the Val de Bénédiction, and waited.

He came straight to the point. He wanted to know where Adam was, and what he was doing.

Coldly, she said, 'What right have you to ask? And why should I answer you?'

He had expected it, and since he had the impression, from their brief moments of acquaintance almost ten years ago, that she was not a woman to be bullied but one who might be prepared to listen to, and even understand something that was distasteful to her, he said, 'You have much to blame me for, I know, but I think you may have heard only one side of the story. Will you allow me to tell you the other?'

It was the right thing to say. For eight long years, she had wanted to know the other side of the story. So she made a gesture of acceptance, and they sat, and he told her everything. He told her even about Ninian's involvement, though without giving any hint of their feelings for each other.

'So I think,' he concluded, 'that Lady Ninian must have sheltered your son until he was strong enough to travel. I am sure she does not know that he then carried out the threat he had made to massacre my kinfolk.' He shook his head at the look on her face. 'Not with his own hand, I admit. He could not have had the strength for that. But he must have given the order. And more than a hundred innocent people died, as a result.'

'How can you be sure that my son had anything to do with it?'

He looked at her, and saw that she had no real doubt, whatever she said. 'Such a gesture as that – it was Adam de Verne through and through.'

She bowed her head, studying her long slender fingers with the delicate, pointed nails.

She was thinking that, when she had seen him first – how long ago? eight years? almost nine? – she had been unexpectedly attracted by him. She had thought him not unlike Columba, but without the innocence of heart. He had struck her not only as clever, but passionate with the cold passion of a man who cared deeply for the world but had no knowledge of ordinary human loving.

Now, looking at him and listening to him, she could see that he had changed. The strength and certainty were still there, but they had moderated. The passion was still there, too, but it had become more personal. He had become a man capable of love and hate, just like ordinary men. And he hated her son. She was afraid of him.

Aware of a great sadness that he and Columba, between them, should have helped wreak such destruction – for she would not accept that Columba and Adam were guilty, and Gavin Cameron wholly guiltless – she said, 'I understand. I understand much that has been hidden from me until now. So I will tell you what you want to know.

'My son is recovered in body, but the wounds to his spirit will never heal. He rides now with the Routiers, and there is enough violence in their lives to keep him occupied. I have tried, without success, to interest him in things less deadly . . .' She stopped suddenly. 'I had not thought before. Is every man he kills a substitute for you?' Then she shrugged. 'No, that is foolish. But no man had ever defeated him, or even hurt him, until you did.

'However, I do not believe he has any intention of returning to Scotland. There is no need, now that Columba is established in His Holiness's favour.'

Astonishingly, Gavin Cameron grinned. 'So, too, am I! Though not, I imagine, for long.'

A light of purest amusement came to her heavy-lidded eyes, and it occurred to him that she must often be entertained by the machinations of the Holy See. They would have amused him, too, if he had not been involved.

They were sitting in the Grand Tinel and his eyes strayed to the tapestry of the Virgin and the Unicorn, its threads dulled a little by the passing of the years and bleached along one edge where the light from the window caught it. With unexpected clarity, he remembered how he had congratulated himself on the evening before Ninian's wedding that a woman such as Madame de Verne had never come his way before.

What irony that all his love, since then, should have been committed to the girl who had grown up under her tutelage and who in many ways was very like her, though in others quite unlike. Sévèrine de Verne, he thought, must have known self-control almost from her cradle, so that the extravagant, unorthodox things she had done had always been done knowingly. He suspected that she was capable of loving very deeply, but thought that her love would have none of the overflowing, open-hearted warmth that was Ninian's.

He had to say, and knew even as he said it that, by its very inconsequence, he was giving himself away, 'Have you any news of Lady Ninian?'

Her face changed completely, and into the worldly eyes came a look of surprise and softness followed almost at once by a strange, rueful smile. Shaking her head she said, 'No. No. You and Ninian should not live as Columba and I have lived.'

Her swift perception deprived him both of breath and speech, and, rising, he walked over to the tapestry, staring at it and remembering its symbolism, that the wild unicorn could be tamed only by a virgin. The weavers had given their virgin a delicate, blue-eyed charm, and hair that was the very colour of Ninian's.

He said, with some reserve, 'No, we cannot be like you and Columba. For us, to have nothing at all is better than not to have everything.'

Sévèrine, her eyes on his uninformative back, reflected silently, 'But it is you, my friend, not Ninian, who will have it so.'

She should not have taken him up so quickly, she thought, but she still had a picture in her mind of Ninian at seventeen, innocent, easily hurt, terribly dependent on those she loved – a Ninian who could never live the divided life that suited Sévèrine herself so well. It was hard to remember that Ninian was twenty-six years old now, and had grown up. Columba had said so more than once. He was so happy, Columba, that she was becoming just the kind of woman he had always hoped she would be.

But even without that, Sévèrine would have known that she must have changed. She had been through too much. It might have made her a worse person but, instead, it seemed to have made her a better. And a very different one from the pretty, plump child of old. Perhaps, now, she might indeed be happy in a life that was hers alone – for some of the time at least.

'Nothing at all?' she repeated quizzically. '*Voyons!* What a cold, damp philosophy to match your cold, damp climate!'

He turned, a reluctant half-smile on his lips. 'Oh, no! It is the philosophy of Rome, madame. It is the church that forbids a priest to love.'

She smiled back, sardonically. 'But if Columba, who is devout, cares nothing for that, why should you? You who are of little faith, *n'est-ce pas?*'

'You wrong me.' But he didn't go into it. 'I should not ask, I know. But do you ever regret it?'

She did him the honour of not answering immediately, but sat for some little time with her elegant brows drawn into a frown. Then she said, 'I regret, *évidemment*, that it has never been possible for us to be open and honest, but no more than that, I think. For we have been happy, and how can one regret happiness?'

'Does your soul not trouble you? The sin, and what you will have to pay in the world to come?'

'A little, a very little. But I believe that God understands. It has been His will that we should love, and if we are to be punished for it, then that is His will also.'

Drily, he said, 'How comforting.'

'Oh, yes. But there is little other comfort in this world. Do you not think that Ninian, too, deserves some comfort after all the tragedies that have come her way? Can you not bend a little? She must love you very much, or she would not love you at all.'

There was a sudden catch in his throat, and he couldn't answer her.

Sévèrine was wise. She left it there. But after a moment, she said, 'And Adam?'

He shook his head. 'You must understand that, if ever he comes near Scotland again, I can show him no mercy. He has done too much harm. So you must prevent him from coming. Only you and Archdeacon Crozier can influence him.'

After a moment, her eyes on her hands, she said, 'I will try, but I do not know if I will succeed.'

Then she rose, her white-lined sleeves falling like great arum lilies against the velvet black of her gown, and said, 'I am glad you came. For we are wiser, now, I think? Both of us.'

And he said, 'Yes. I believe we are.'

3

NINIAN, who had in the end abandoned her idea of going to Villeneuve, not least because she couldn't afford it after rebuilding the barmkin, was summoned back to court just before Christmas 1435. The queen, distraught over the death of the elder of her twin sons, Alexander, had succeeded in persuading her husband that no one but the Lady Ninian, whose own little child had died so tragically, could give her the comfort she needed.

Ninian remembered the queen's forebodings on that day, five years ago, when the two little princes had been christened. The day that had been followed by the night when she and Gavin had come together at last. Five long years. And still no end in sight, although she was gradually becoming possessed by an instinctive, illogical certainty that everything must be resolved soon, even if in her mind she could not see how.

With unexpected reluctance, she shook the creases out of her silks and velvets and set her women furiously stitching, made all the arrangements necessary for Dess to run smoothly in her absence, and then, with no more than a single backward glance, rode off towards Edinburgh.

The court was strange to her now. The air still vibrated with dampness and familiar smells, but the people were different and so was the atmosphere. The courtiers, nervous and abject when James was present, gravitated into surly, secretive groups when he was absent, and fell silent as soon as anyone came within earshot.

There was a new chamberlain of the royal household, Sir Robert Stewart.

Rob Stewart, son of the Master of Atholl, who had died in the Tower the year before, still a hostage of the English.

He was a fair, upright, good-looking young man with perfect manners and an engaging personality, and Ninian disliked him on sight. Wryly, she remembered how she had offended his mother almost ten years ago in Villeneuve, by describing him as 'almost grown up' and wondering whether he mightn't like to be king some day.

Suddenly, she found herself having to hold back tears. Despite her youthful woes, it had all seemed so halcyon then. Now, all that it seemed was – so very long ago.

She couldn't help but remember, too, how his mother had tried to kill her, and had died herself instead, by whose hand no one had ever discovered. The beautiful Sir Rob had almost been declared a bastard, then, but Atholl had decided against it. So now, between him and the throne there stood only his seventy-three-year-old grandfather and a sickly, five-year-old prince. The young man behaved as if he were always, deprecatingly, aware of it.

Ninian began to feel her skin crawling every time he came within reach of her. There was nothing in his manner to justify it, but she became convinced that he knew everything that had happened in those days of his adolescence; and that he hated her because of it. The smile never left his face but, almost without thinking, Ninian began to take care what she ate and drank.

She had never given much thought, before, to the custom of sharing every dish at table with three other people, except to be repelled when a neighbour, disdaining knives and spoons, plunged dirty fingers straight into a dish from which she, too, had to eat. But, now, dirty fingers seemed a small price to pay for the knowledge that, if Lady Elinor's son were thinking of finishing the task his mother had begun, he would have to poison three other people as well.

She wasn't seriously worried, but she couldn't rid herself of the feeling that it would be all of a piece with the general atmosphere of the court, where people rarely laughed or smiled out of ordinary good humour, and everyone responded to even the smallest provocation with disproportionate virulence.

Rob Stewart, however, did have the knack of handling James, more forceful, more unpredictable than ever, who had recently angered — and frightened — all the barons in the land by dispossessing the Earl of March, one of the greatest of them. The earl's son had gone to England for help, and mounted a raid into Scotland substantial enough to count as an invasion. He had been defeated, but James's relations with the English were worse than they had ever been, and acrimonious messages travelled back and forth with such frequency that the pleasant, exhausted young man known as Dragance Herald remarked to Ninian that every sparrow and squirrel on the road between Edinburgh and London must be capable of recognizing his tabard by now.

Even so, Christmas was moderately cheerful, and Ninian found a real pleasure in it. It was so long since she had been in company, and because ambassadors from France were the guests of honour, every possible luxury had been provided for their delectation. However impoverished the throne, there was no question of letting it show at a time like this, because the little Princess Margaret was to sail away at last, to be married to the Dauphin. The French ambassadors were to escort her on the voyage.

But the departure of the eleven-year-old princess, to become a stranger in a strange land, was an extra burden on Her Majesty, no longer the calm, controlled great lady she had been but a tense, nervous creature who started at shadows. Margaret was her first child, conceived in the early, enchanted weeks when Joan, as a new bride, had waited with her husband at Brancepath to embark on the final stage of the greatest journey of his life, the return to Scotland where he would take up the challenge that was his destiny. And now, after almost twelve years of trouble and strife and disillusion, darkness hung all around them. Only a few months ago, James had thought it wise to extract from parliament an oath of fealty, not to himself but to his queen – an acknowledgement that he went always, now, in danger of his life.

Not in fear of it, or he would have listened to the promptings of common sense and the soft voice of his lady. He would have gone about reform more slowly. He would have made sure that, when he imprisoned or dispossessed one of the barons, his case was watertight. But it seemed that he worked increasingly by instinct, foreseeing trouble, and nipping it in the bud before it became a reality – before there was a sufficiency of facts to prove his case. If he waited for facts, he said, it would be too late. It was as if the whole political life of Scotland moved in a vicious and ever-decreasing circle.

Revealingly, the queen said to Ninian one day, 'How I wish Bishop Gavin were here still. Although the king says he has become too cautious, there is no one else in whom His Majesty has ever felt able to repose his trust. And he so badly needs at least one man he can rely on! Although Rob Stewart is being very good – almost like a brother to the king – he is too young yet to have learned wisdom.'

Her breath trapped somewhere in her throat, Ninian said, 'Might His Majesty decide to recall the bishop?'

'Soon, perhaps, but not quite yet. My husband is most anxious for His Holiness to send a legate to Scotland to study and advise on the state of the church. He has just sent Canon Methven and Sir Walter Ogilvy to Florence as orators to plead our case, and Bishop Gavin will be too much involved in the arrangements to be spared for the time being. But when that is settled, perhaps . . .'

It wasn't much, but it was something.

4

THE journey from Basle to Florence was not one for a middle-aged man of comfortable girth in the depth of winter. By the time Poggio's message had reached Columba, telling him that Gavin Cameron was at Florence, there had been nothing he could do about it.

But as soon as the passes were open, he had set out, and only discovered later that he and Cameron had passed each other, going in opposite directions, somewhere near Cremona. There was nothing to tell him that Cameron had been on his way to Villeneuve.

Eugenius, silvery and birdlike, decisive in war and indecisive in peace, enjoying the modern bustle of Florence where they treated him as God's vicegerent on earth ought to be treated – so unlike the Colonna-ridden decadence of Rome! – said that Bishop Gavin had seemed to him a most intelligent young man and of irreproachable character.

Columba soon put a stop to that.

Had the irreproachable Bishop Gavin told His Holiness that the Scots parliament had recently declared Archdeacon Crozier – the pope's most dedicated servant and acknowledged protégé – a traitor and an outlaw? And that it had deprived him of the fruits of his benefices, and forbidden any other Scot at Basle, Rome, or Florence to have dealings with him?

No?

And had the irreproachable Bishop Gavin conveyed that Scotland had withdrawn its allegiance from the Council of Basle, and was prepared to align itself with His Holiness? Was it Eugenius' impression that Bishop Gavin had left Florence to go directly back to Scotland?

It was? Then why had he gone back to Basle instead?

During the months that followed, a disappointed and enraged Eugenius brought all the pressure of the curia to bear on James, trying to force him to reinstate Archdeacon Crozier. But James had had more than enough of Archdeacon Crozier, and even the threat of excommunication failed to move him.

There were, of course, advantages to the length of time it took for messages to travel from Florence to Edinburgh, because they frequently crossed en route, lending an additional incoherence to a correspondence that was far from lucid to begin with. With a gap of four months between apostolic letter and royal reply, it was possible to ignore almost anything on the principle that it must have been superseded in the meantime.

His Holiness was not surprised, therefore, when two orators from the King of Scots turned up at Florence as blandly as if excommunication had never been mentioned. His Majesty was most anxious for His Holiness to appoint a papal legate to investigate the general state of the kirk there, and set to rights whatever might be wrong with it. The costs, His Majesty knew, would not be negligible, but the Bishop of

Glasgow had the matter well in hand, and indeed was in Bruges at this very moment, arranging the finance that would be needed.

His Holiness, stayed by a particularly good wine and the presence of his dear son, Archdeacon Crozier, at his elbow, did not mince matters. 'No,' he said.

But the archdeacon, his voice soft as always, intervened. 'As Your Holiness desires. I am told, however, that our good brothers have something else they wish to say on their own account.'

Sir Walter Ogilvy, formerly Master of the royal Household, and Canon John Methven, a devout-looking nonentity, were both careful men, otherwise James would not have sent them. So it was not immediately clear, even to Columba, what they were trying to say.

When he worked it out, however, it was extremely interesting. In return for papal cooperation on certain personal matters – the granting of benefices, what else? – they were prepared solemnly to promise, on their own account and on the account of certain other clerics on whose behalf they were empowered to speak, that they would either persuade the king to repeal the laws against barratry, or would overturn them by some other means. If His Holiness considered this a fair bargain, they would guarantee to return within the year to report that their part in it had been fulfilled.

By some other means? Columba bent his eyes on the two men, who didn't look as if they carried much weight of influence with them, and was irritated to find that he could read nothing in their plain, stolid faces.

But as bargains went, it sounded excellent to Eugenius.

When they had left, he turned his deceptively venerable gaze on Columba and said, 'By some other means? What other means?'

Columba, puzzled and vaguely disturbed, shook his head.

5

THE Firth of Clyde was grey and choppy and the hills lost in mist on the late March day when Princess Margaret joined the French fleet at Dumbarton. There were eleven ships riding at anchor, and on the quay the thousand splendidly-clad lords, knights, and gentlemen of her escort, with the Admiral of Scotland and the Bishop of Brechin at their head. It was the kind of scene Ninian would have tried very hard to paint, once. Now, she looked and distantly admired, because although she could paint far better now than she had ever done, her palette and her subjects were quite different.

The girl looked very small and lonely as she stood there taking a good-mannered leave of her parents. Curiously, it was only the king who gave way to emotion, flinging his arms round his daughter and holding her so tightly that the rich blue velvet strained over the back that had once been sturdy and now was stout. The queen, in a purple so dark that it might have been mourning, stood by like a statue.

'Poor child,' Ninian murmured to Lady Moragh, standing beside her. 'She's too young to face what lies ahead of her. I was seventeen when I came to a foreign land, and I had my husband to cling to. But it was very hard.'

Moragh, like everyone at court, had changed. Ninian had seen little of her and, indeed, had the impression that she had been avoiding her. 'She iss alive, at least,' Moragh said briefly. 'And even a difficult life iss worth more than no life at all.'

It wasn't a casual remark. Ninian had been wondering whether Moragh might be ill – she had the look of it, and there was a weariness about her, as if she cared nothing about anything any more. She never laughed now, and rarely smiled, and all the beautiful colour had gone from her cheeks, so that the amber skin appeared tired and sallow. But when Ninian had tried to ask, Moragh had brushed her question aside as if it were offensive.

The wind was whipping off the land as if it were being sucked by some great sea monster out into the estuary where it belonged; a sailing wind, and a chill one. Ninian shivered, and pulled the fur-lined cloak more closely about her shoulders. 'Scotland doesn't become warmer with the years,' she murmured.

And suddenly Moragh turned towards her with something in her eyes that Ninian didn't recognize at first. It was as if Ninian's casual remark had been the last drop that had caused some invisible dam to burst.

'You complain?' Moragh said softly. 'About a country from which you haff taken so much? Stolen so much?'

Ninian thought at first that she had misheard. It was such a peculiar – such a meaningless – thing to say.

'What on earth are you talking about?'

The pointed face stared back at her, tired and inimical. 'A country iss its people. When an incomer steals from one of us, she steals from all.'

With genuine concern, Ninian said, 'Moragh, are you all right? Scotland is my country, just as much as yours, for I was born here, too, and all the blood in me is Scots. And I can't imagine what you think I've stolen, or from whom.'

The other woman's lip curled, and with a kind of contempt she said, 'Can you not? Then I will tell you. You haff stolen Gaffin Cameron. From me.'

Ninian closed her eyes. She didn't believe this was happening. And what in heaven's name were the two of them doing, standing here whispering – hissing! – at each other in the midst of the clamour around them? The only rational thought in her head was that it was the stupidest time and place for such a conversation.

Opening her eyes, she said soothingly, 'We should talk about this, if we must, at some other time.'

'There will be no other time.' It was extraordinary that a voice could be at once so flat and so vindictive. 'You wanted him from the moment you saw him. I could tell, that ferry first day at court, not chust with the eyes in my head but with the eyes that are within me. For I haff the sight, you know! Do not smile. The second sight iss not a fantasy. *Dia*, but I wish Elinor's poison had killed you! I did my best. It wass I that gave her the idea. I that gave the herbs to her chamber page.'

The world rocked a little under Ninian's feet. She couldn't possibly be hearing what she thought she was hearing.

The Highland sibilance became stronger with every word Moragh spoke, though her voice remained toneless and weary, muffling the venom, making it all sound strange and distant and unreal.

Ninian said, 'But . . . But you must have hated Lady Elinor, too. More than me. Because she had shared his bed.'

'Yess. I knew it meant nothing, but the poisoning was a revenge on both of you, do you see? You would die, and she would be blamed. The anonymous message that saved you came from Robert Graham, did you know that? I haff neffer been sure whether he killed her, though.'

She made a movement that might have been a shrug. 'But you caught him in the end, Gaffin, *my* Gaffin! Jehane wass of his getting, wass she not? The night Alexander escaped from Edinburgh, when you wass both out on the ramparts. I saw you then, when you had come from him.'

She didn't even notice Ninian's instinctive denial. 'I sent Fiona to you, later, to watch you so that I could find out efferything and make up my mind what to do. It wass a nuisance when you wass banned from court, because I had to take her away again or it would haff looked ferry strange. And then you let her die, and sent her man-at-arms home to me with her bones in a casket.'

Once, Ninian might have tried to deny or explain, but not now, although she had to suppress a sudden acid desire to suggest that Moragh didn't place so much reliance on her second sight, which appeared to be remarkably astigmatic. Unexpectedly, she remembered Robert Graham's belief that God was not to be found in the haunts of men – or women – and thought that he was probably right. Not God, only the devil.

In a still, calm voice, she said, 'Why are you telling me this?'

'Why?' Moragh turned away again. 'I haff no idea. I thought at first you had captured Gaffin only with your cheap tricks, so that it would not last. But I haff the sight often these days, and I haff seen the two of you together in the place where he comes from. Where I come from. And do you know, it iss strange, but I do not care ferry much, except sometimes, when you anger me. For I haff seen my own death, and it will come soon.'

There was a terrible fatalism in her voice, and Ninian exclaimed, 'No!'

'Yess. There iss something within me. But I tell you this, so that even when I haff gone you will be remembering. Gaffin Cameron iss still mine, and he hass always been mine, all the days of our lives!'

6

NINIAN did a good deal of thinking during the months that followed. Once, she reflected, she would have been almost distracted with nerves and misery over what Moragh had said, but now she felt no more than queasy as she looked back over the years of their false friendship. She didn't believe that Moragh had ever been Gavin's mistress, and thought that, although she had wanted him, he had probably always treated her only as a childhood friend. She would ask him some day. Some day . . .

And it didn't matter, really. The past was unimportant. The future was what counted.

But she found herself taking her precautions against poisoning more seriously, and redoubled them whenever the Lady Moragh was away from court.

She was away in July 1436. And so, too, was the king, because the truce with England had run out and James couldn't resist trying to retake the Border town of Roxburgh, which had been in English hands for just over a hundred years. There was nothing like a good, rousing military success to restore the barons to humour.

More in optimism than expectation, James had summoned every layman in the kingdom between sixteen and sixty without distinction, except for shepherds, cowherds, and the servants of the upper clergy. There was talk of two hundred thousand horsemen and the same of foot, innumerable waggons full of arrows and cannonballs, and of course the siege engines brought at vast expense from Flanders – ballistae and towers and a mangonel.

The siege began at the Feast of St Peter's Chains, the first day of August, not with a bang, but with a slow, uneasy rumbling that accurately reflected the temper of the besieging army. No one who mattered was on speaking terms with anyone else, and most of the rank and file wanted only to go home. By the time ten days had passed in idle squandering of arrows and cannonballs, they had begun to do so.

Two days after that, the Lady Moragh returned to court and begged to be allowed to speak to the queen in private, which meant with not more than two of her women in attendance. By the purest chance, Her Majesty's eye lighted on the Lady Egidia and the Lady Ninian.

There was no question but that Moragh had only a short time to live. Yet even though it had been necessary for her to be lifted out of her travelling litter, she still had enough strength and enough command over herself to drop to her knees before the queen as if she had some great favour to ask.

'My lady,' she said with a kind of desperation in her voice. 'You know that I am Your Majesties' most devoted subject. You know, too, that I am of Highland blood. There iss some of us who have the second sight . . .'

Mentally, Ninian sighed.

'We who haff it do not speak of it, because folk who are not of the Highlands laugh it to scorn. But it iss true, Your Majesty. I swear to you by the Holy Rood that it iss true.'

She raised her eyes to the queen's face. 'You must believe me, my lady. Two nights ago I saw something that filled me with a great fear.'

The queen was uncomfortable, embarrassed, as if she were doing no more than humour a dying woman, but, somehow, the Lady Moragh succeeded in transmitting her own conviction to her.

The words came in a flood. 'It iss the king I fear for, Your Majesty. I haff seen a crown rolling in the dust, and blood, and a throne overturned. His Majesty iss in terrible danger, my lady, and it iss treachery that threatens him, not war!'

The Lady Egidia said uncompromisingly, 'Rubbish!' but the queen held up a hand to silence her.

She was pale as a ghost and yet suddenly, after all the months of nerves and hesitancy, in full control. She said, 'We do not know enough of God's design to know whether second sight is reality or imagination, but it seems to me possible that it may be a gift He has granted, so that those who have it may catch a glimpse of what He has ordained. Tell me, Lady Moragh, what more did you see?'

'I haff seen nothing else.'

'No faces? Nothing to give you an idea of when this might happen?'

Moragh shook her head. 'The sight iss not like that. Do you believe me, my lady? You must believe me! For the king must be warned, before it iss too late!'

No one said it might be too late already. What the queen said, slowly, was, 'I do not know whether I believe or not, but I dare not ignore what you have said. I will go myself to the king, because there is no one else he would listen to. I will leave within the hour.'

7

THE king, to whom Lady Moragh's mystical vision came as no more than a reinforcement of his own familiar nightmare, would have dismissed the whole thing if the queen hadn't known about it. He might still have dismissed it, if the siege had been going well. But in the course of a mere two weeks half his army had evaporated, and it was clear that, unless he withdrew what remained, he would be left sitting there in solitary splendour, with none but his siege engines for company.

He had wanted and needed a spectacular victory, and Roxburgh had brought him military and political disaster. In no time at all, it was obvious that the spell his powerful personality had cast over most of Scotland for the last twelve years had been broken.

It was necessary to patch up a truce with the English, and, during the autumn of 1436, that was done. It was necessary to renew trade with England, and that was done. It was necessary to replace the gold and silver that had been spent abroad on the siege engines, and new laws were introduced to make sure that was done, too.

It was also necessary to make clear to the barons that the king was still completely in command. So statutes were brought in at the next meeting of the council-general to restrict the privileges of the greatest of them.

As a result, Ninian found herself with not just two outlaws in the family, but three – Adam, Columba, and now Sir Robert Graham, who lost his temper, finally and fatally, with the king.

The king could no longer afford to overlook, as he had done once before, one of his nobles laying violent hands upon him. 'Lock him up!' he exclaimed, when Sir Robert had been overpowered. 'This time you will die a traitor's death!'

Ninian heard about it all from Atholl, who had changed very little during the years of her absence from court. The main difference was that all but two of his yellowing teeth had gone, and the magenta toorie was beginning to unravel round the edges. It *couldn't* be the same toorie, she thought, and had a sudden, amused vision of some woman servant furiously knitting up toorie after toorie, and then being commanded to sleep in them, and rub them in the mud, and then jump on them, to take away the gloss of newness.

'Och, aye,' Atholl yelped at her, the pitch of his voice higher and its volume greater to compensate for his increasing deafness; the stubble on his cheeks bristling happily round the wide-stretched grin. 'Graham fair riled my nephew this time! There they were, standing gobbling at each other wi' their faces the colour o' my toorie! I near laughed mysel' sick. It's as well Jamie won't let anyone intae the cooncil wearing a sword these days, or there'd huv been guts and gore a' ower the place. But I'm feart your Uncle Robert's hud his notice this time. He's locked up in Johnnie Eviot's castle until the cooncil's over, and then it'll be a case of aff with his heid.'

The old man drew the edge of his hand across his throat. 'Brrrrmph!' he chortled merrily.

BALHOUSIE castle was very new, but although there was still a good deal of building activity going on, the dungeon was indisputably complete. Robert Graham, casting a swift glance round, saw that all the bars were in place, and all the stonework immaculate. No blocks of masonry that looked as if they might be levered out, given time and patience. No crumbling patches of mortar to be picked out with the knife that still nestled down the side of his boot; they hadn't searched him very thoroughly, presumably because they thought that, if he'd had a knife, he would have used it on the king. No chute in the floor opening to some convenient sewer with external access for cleaning. Even so, Robert Graham smiled to himself.

But John Eviot's lady was flustered. Never before had she found herself with an unwanted guest on her hands and no husband to turn to. For Sir John, pointing out to the king that the royal guard knew much more about looking after important prisoners than he did, had been careful to distance himself from the whole business. State prisoners were kittle cattle, and he had no intention of taking the blame if anything went wrong. Besides which – he had said aloud – it was his clear duty to stay on for what remained of the council-general's deliberations.

He didn't know that, that very morning, one of the vessels arriving from the Continent had been laden with materials he had ordered for the roof of the barmkin. Or that his lady, anxious to tidy everything away out of the rain, had told the men to put them in the big stone dungeon that doubled as a store room. They would be dry there, she had thought, and since the chamber was at ground level, easily accessible for the builders.

The captain of the royal guard permitted himself the luxury of a groan when he saw not only the barrels of salt fish and brined pork, the sacks of dried beans and barley and the kists of oatmeal to be found on the ground floor of every towered keep from Berwick to the Isles, but the piles of jointing and framing boards, of wainscots and laths, the bags of oak pegs and iron ties and he didn't know what else besides. But he scanned what was visible of the floor and the walls and the roof, and was reassured. A few planks and nails weren't going to do the prisoner much good in a place like this. If he left four men on guard outside, where there was no chance of the prisoner braining them with a baulk of timber – or bribing them, come to that – it should be all right.

Sir Robert gave himself ten minutes to look round and make his plans, and then hammered on the door and asked for food and drink and privacy. After the events of the day, he said austerely, and considering what lay ahead of him, he had need to look to his soul. His guards, remembering that he was reputed to have the evil eye, hastened to accommodate him.

Half a fowl and a flagon of wine later, he rose softly and went to stand behind the door and listen. It was satisfactory. The guards, as he had expected, were comfortably settled with bread and ale and dice box, and would soon be fast asleep.

He worked all night, able even in the long hours of darkness to carry on by touch alone, so that when morning came, he was ready.

He waited, with the patience that was the everyday counterweight to his occasionally ungovernable temper, until he heard the bells and the expected sound of many feet within the castle. Then he set to work again with silent, perfectly coordinated speed. It was the one time of day when he could be sure that everyone in the household, from her ladyship down to the meanest carpenter's apprentice and stable dwarf, would be out of harm's way in the gallery at the very top of the house, attending morning Mass. He was no longer concerned about his guards, for he was out of their line of vision.

There was little left for him to do – only to whip some good, stout lengths of sack-cord round the crossjoints – and then instead of a bundle of loose struts of wood he had a tall, narrow, but perfectly stable scaffolding tower. Tall enough to reach the flagstone trap in the roof that, when the store room was in everyday use, gave ladder access to and from the Great Hall above.

Swinging himself up in an economical series of movements, he was soon directly under the trap. Was it weighted? It shouldn't be, unless her ladyship was less of a fool than he thought.

It moved. For the first time, he began to sweat slightly as he levered it up, taking the weight on braced shoulders, half prepared for the exclamation that would mean someone hadn't, after all, gone to Mass. But no sound came, and he inched the flagstone gradually off his back, sliding it along the floor until the space was clear. Then, with a lithe twist of his body he arched himself up and into the hall, taking care not to fetch the scaffolding a kick that would send it clattering down to the ground below and give the game away. For no more than a moment or two, he stood listening, and then he lifted the flagstone by its inset ring and moved it back into position.

Afterwards, without attempt at concealment but with his dagger ready in his sleeve, he walked to the door, down the outside stairs, and across to the stables, where he chose the best of a poor-looking lot of horses, mounted it bareback, and rode coolly away over the brow of the nearest hill.

Rob Stewart, who with six hired bravoes had been in hiding there since daybreak, was somewhat put out to discover that Sir Robert Graham had been perfectly capable of rescuing himself. And that he knew exactly where he was going, and what he was going to do.

CHAPTER TWO

I

NINIAN was at Dess when the message reached her, the impossible, beautiful message saying that Gavin was home, and would see her before many days had passed.

It was the first direct word she had had from him in three long years, although she had heard, as had everyone at court, of the progress of his negotiating, his bargaining, his diplomacy. Not long ago, distrusting his influence over the king and his fellow-bishops, the pope had expressly forbidden him to return to Scotland. It was one of the conditions on which His Holiness had agreed, at last, to send a legate.

The legate had arrived at Christmas, and now it seemed that, regardless of the papal prohibition, Gavin Cameron, Bishop of Glasgow, had landed at Leith only seven weeks later.

He had urgent matters to attend to in Edinburgh, he said, and then he must go on to Perth to report to the king. If he did not find Ninian at court, he would contrive somehow to escape to Dess.

So she would see him soon, perhaps today, perhaps tomorrow, perhaps next week. She was overcome by a mad, ridiculous impatience, like a green girl who had lain with her lover only yesterday and could scarcely bear to wait until tomorrow to lie with him again.

It was the end, it seemed, of the state of suspended animation in which she had lived for so long. The very fact of the message was a declaration in itself. She laughed excitedly. Even if, after the Council of Basle's decision, he had persuaded himself that there could be no future for them, even if he thought he was coming to say farewell forever, she knew with absolute certainty that she would win. That, even if she had to fight every inch of the way, even if she had to die for him – or with him – she would win in the end.

She ranged the castle like a prowling cat, unable to rest, unable to concentrate on anything except the days ahead. To stay at Dess, where they would have privacy, or make the journey to Perth, where she would see him sooner? He might be held up there, and she couldn't bear that.

She stared out from the narrow, ill-glazed window of the Speak-a-Word room. There had been a thaw, of sorts, and the ground was grey and slushy, but passable. If it froze again, or snowed, Dess might be cut off for weeks. It was enough to decide her. She sent for Master Lindsay, and for her gentlewomen, and told them to make the arrangements. She would be leaving the day after tomorrow for Perth.

And then, just as darkness fell, she heard the sound of horses. Not more than two, or perhaps three; not an episcopal cavalcade. But that didn't necessarily mean anything.

Master Lindsay came himself, pale and expressionless as she had always known him except during those few terrible days more than four years ago, when he and she together had saved Dess from the plague, at such cost.

He said, 'My lady, a gentleman has arrived. Much wrapped up against the cold. He claims to have a message for you.'

She was sitting by the fire in the High Hall, with a huge branch of candles beside her, her untouched stitchery in her hands and the spaniels strewn sleeping round her feet, boneless and limp as gutted herrings.

After considering Master Lindsay for a moment or two, she turned her head and said courteously, 'Mistress Isabella, I need some more of the dark blue thread. You will find it in the small chest in my own chamber, I think.'

Then, when the woman had gone, she turned back to Master Lindsay, and said, 'Who?'

'Monsieur de Verne.'

It wasn't possible. 'Are you sure?'

'Yes, my lady.'

She closed her eyes and, sighing, pressed her fingers over her lips. 'Oh, dear,' she said. 'Trouble.'

'Yes, my lady. The gentleman says there will also be another gentleman arriving soon.'

'*Another?*'

'So the gentleman says, my lady.'

She gave up. 'Oh, well. He had better come up, I suppose. And ask Mistress Isabella to occupy herself elsewhere, if you please.' She would have preferred to have someone with her, but knew that Adam would give the woman short shrift. 'And Master Lindsay . . .'

'Yes, my lady?'

'You may interrupt us as often as you feel inclined.'

With the ghost of a smile, he bowed and left.

Ninian stirred the dogs awake with her foot, and then bent to poke some life into the fire. When she turned again, Adam was there before her.

It was the Adam Columba had spoken of, not the Adam she knew. The wide-shouldered, narrow-hipped, athletic figure had thickened and become bloated; his eyes were puffy; his skin had coarsened and was patched with broken blood vessels; and although the thick, curling dark hair was the same, it had an uncared-for look.

But he sounded his old, arrogantly cheerful self as he threw an arm round her resistant shoulders, dropped a cousinly kiss on her unresponsive mouth, and announced that he and Robert Graham had things to discuss, and knew she wouldn't mind that they had chosen to do so here before they went on to Perth.

'Mind?' she exclaimed. 'Not in the least. What is one extra outlaw, more or less, among so many! Have you eaten?'

'Yes, but I haven't drunk. Is your ale still better than your wine, as it was in Harry's day?'

'You must ask Master Lindsay. I rarely drink ale myself.'

When his wants had been met and he was sprawled on the bench by the fire, she surveyed the eye-catching riches before her and said politely, 'You don't starve, I see.'

'There are more profitable occupations than collecting Columba's tithes, *p'tite!*' He drank deeply and nodded, 'Not bad. Yes, I and my friend Villandrando, the Routier captain – you remember the name, I see – took our men to the Auvergne last year, to exercise them in the arts of war. An innocuous enough pursuit, you might think, but the local nobles felt an urge to buy us off after a while. Three thousand gold crowns. No, I don't starve.'

'And what persuaded you to abandon this lucrative life for cold, damp, uncivilized Scotland?'

The eyes between their puffy lids were as brilliant as they had always been; more so, perhaps, as if there were a touch of fever in them. He waved a scarlet arm airily. 'Boredom, debts, who knows?'

Her hands plying the comforting needle, she said, 'Debts? With a share in three thousands crowns, you are in debt?'

'Not in France. I was thinking of – ah – my lord Atholl.'

He had been forced to rely on Atholl during most of his time in Scotland, but he had always seemed to do enough for the old man to repay any debt there might be there. And yet Ninian, remembering their odd relationship, could readily imagine Adam going to him now and tossing a handful of gold coins contemptuously in his face.

Even so, it didn't seem enough to warrant either the journey or the risk. 'And?'

He studied his cup. 'And Robert Graham and I owe each other something.'

Her sense of uneasiness increased. 'What?'

'He shipped me out of the country when I was in no state to go by myself. Or had you forgotten.'

'No. And in what coin do you propose to pay him? Or he you?'

Waggishly, he smiled. Waggishly, he shook his head. 'Can't tell you. It's a secret!'

She felt slightly ill. 'You do remember, I take it, that you are at the horn and can be taken and executed out of hand if you are recognized?'

The strong dark eyebrows rose, and for a moment it was the Adam she had once worshipped, grinning at her. His teeth were still flashing white and the extra weight made him look more like Columba than he had ever done. 'Am I so like the wicked Red Lord of Inverlochy? Would *you* recognize me if you knew me less well?'

'Possibly not,' she said tartly. 'But I would recommend you to cover up all that vulgar scarlet with a nice dark robe that won't blind every honest burgher in Perth. And why are you going there, in any case? I am beginning to think you have taken leave of your senses!'

It was clear that there was some kind of plot afoot, but she couldn't think what. It seemed unlikely that it was aimed at Gavin. They couldn't know he was back, she told herself reassuringly, and Adam had no urgent reason to hate him now, when Columba had achieved the position he wanted and Gavin no longer stood in his way. Deep down, though, she knew that it wasn't just a matter of Columba. Adam must still bear a massive personal grudge against the man who had ruined all his plans, and almost killed him. But if Adam had still wanted to harm him, there must have been many opportunities in these last years, when Gavin was always on the road and, like every other traveller, at the mercy of the Routiers, the 'free companions'.

If it wasn't Gavin, then it could only be the king. Ninian knew, chillingly, that with the country in its present mood, another rebellion would be almost bound to succeed. And Adam and Robert Graham were expert at manipulating rebellions.

Even so, the mention of Perth didn't fit until Adam said, 'Did you not know? Columba arrived there a few days ago, and I have not seen him for almost a year. I want my father's blessing!'

'Columba at Perth? But I don't understand! The outlawry – why is he here? How does he dare?'

'Do you think James would arrest an official adviser to the papal legate?'

'Ah!' But, gradually, the delight faded from her face as she recognized the complications of having Columba Crozier and Gavin Cameron, the two sworn enemies she loved most in the world, both in the same small city at the same time.

There was some activity outside, and then Sir Robert Graham arrived, as little changed by these last months in hiding as by anything else that had happened during the years that she had known him.

She left them, after a while, when it was clear she could learn nothing more of what they planned, and retired to her room, to become absorbed again in thoughts of Gavin, and what his message meant.

2

IT was a pretty room now, because once the barmkin had been rebuilt there had seemed no reason not to spend just a little money on herself, and her own comfort. Dess itself was comfortless enough, whatever she tried to do, a stern and soulless tower in a stern and soulless landscape, with no human love or company to warm it. The king had thrown out another hint or two to Ninian that, now she was back in favour, she should marry again, but his mind was on more important things and he hadn't pressed it.

She had put all the smaller tapestries she had brought from France on the bedchamber walls, and there was glass in the windows as well as shutters for wild nights. There was a fireplace, too, laboriously excavated out of the thickness of the wall, but she regretted none of the trouble it had taken because of the very real pleasure of being warm at last. It was always cold indoors at Dess, even in August. On the floor was a big, thick rug, a patchwork made from furs that had once belonged to Harry's mother, while the hangings round the bed, also brought from Villeneuve, were of pretty blue velvet embroidered with a design incorporating the fleur-de-lys – so very French, and so extravagant, that she had never dared even to unpack them when Harry was alive.

By the window stood her easel, with tightly covered pots of colours on the chest beside it, and the dried, pressed plants and leaves she was copying with such care. After the artificiality of Pol Limbourg, and the deadly counterpoint of the *dance macabre*, she had begun to teach herself, with care and infinite labour, how to draw and paint the reality of everyday things. Not until she had mastered every tiny detail of an individual rowan leaf in all its stages – bursting from enclosed bud into a clutch of silver fingers, opening out into a fronded green palm, and then drying into a fan of paper flames, did she even consider trying to paint the whole tree.

Some day, she knew now, when eyes and hand and feelings were at last attuned, she would be able to look at some thing, some person, some place she loved – and paint it as she would want to paint it.

Suddenly, she wondered whether by any extraordinary chance Gavin might have brought back, from Florence or somewhere, some properly ground pigments and fine vellums for the cathedral scriptorium. She must ask him. What was the point in being a bishop's mistress if one couldn't make a profit out of it! She danced a graceful *carole* around the room, laughing, hugging her happiness to her.

She was facing the door when it opened and Adam stood there, with a flask and two drinking cups in his hand, already very drunk, and stripped to white shirt and scarlet breech-hose.

The fabric of the breech-hose was swollen and strained across his loins.

Snapped back to reality, Ninian called instantly for her women, but Adam slammed the heavy door before they could hear her.

444

Reprovingly, he said, 'No, no, *p'tite*. We have no need for company. What is wrong? Are you shy of me after all this time? When all I have done is bring you something to warm you?' He giggled.

'I don't require any wine, thank you. Nor do I think you are in need of any more. Please send my women to me if you should see them on the way to your chamber, because I wish to retire. Good night to you, Adam. No doubt you will be more like yourself after a few hours' sleep.'

It was as if he hadn't noticed the ice in her voice, because he giggled again and said, 'I want to retire, too, and I have brought more than wine to warm you. Look, *p'tite*. Look at me!'

He was like some obscene small boy, as he took her chin in his hand and forced her to look down. The smell of wine was thick on his breath.

She shuddered and jerked away instinctively, and it was a mistake, because her revulsion penetrated the haze that enveloped him and the old, familiar glitter of anger reappeared in his eyes. His loose mouth tightening, he dropped the flask and cups, and lunged.

He had lost none of the speed of old, and as the cushioned bench caught her behind the knees and she fell backwards on to the seat, he was on top of her, the full weight of him, and his hips were on hers, grinding and twisting, and his face was only an inch away and he was alternately kissing her and mumbling words she couldn't understand.

She gasped and began to struggle, grimly and determinedly, against his solid six feet of muscle and fat, but she could make no impression. Kicking was impossible, because her legs and knees were pinned to the edge of the bench, and her elbows were pinned, too, so that when she reached for his face with her nails all he did was drop his forearm over hers and it was enough to immobilize her. But she went on fighting, every muscle in play, while she tried furiously to think whether there was any weapon within reach. The poker was too far away and too obvious, but on the chest at the foot of the bed was her sewing and, buried under its folds somewhere, the scissors.

His babbling had resolved itself into words now, a slurred, repetitive stream of them, a sickening claim of undying passion. She had haunted his mind and body for five whole years. Why was she fighting? Why had she changed? She loved him still, really. He liked her for fighting. He liked women who were strong and positive, when he could lie with them and take them. Take them! *Take them!*

His hips thudding hard and relentlessly against hers, he had contrived to snap her belt clasp free. And then his hands were at the neck of her gown, gripping it, trying to tear it open. But the strong country cloth wouldn't tear and, moaning now with rage and need, he jerked himself upright and, planting the brutal weight of his knee on her waist to hold her, bent and took the hems of both gown and shift between his hands.

And this time they yielded. Triumphantly, laughing as if it were all a splendid game, he began to rip them upwards, exposing the whole lower part of her body to his eyes.

He stopped, fists spread, when he had torn as far as the waist and could go no further because his own knee was in the way. His mouth was open and his breath coming in great gulps as he looked, and looked, and then, driven by a terrible excitement, moved his knee so that he could tear further and have her naked before him at last, after all the years of wanting.

But all she had been waiting for was that one brief respite. As his knee moved and she was momentarily free of the weight of him, she gathered together her nerves and muscles and flung herself sideways, out from under him, his fists still clinging to the two halves of her gown and an expression of ludicrous bewilderment and frustration on his face. She had only one aim in mind, to lay hands on the scissors, and stumbling desperately, half dragging him behind her, she had almost reached them when he gave a great roar of fury and, dropping the cloth, clamped his hands round her waist in an iron grip.

They fell together to the rug, Ninian underneath, and she opened her mouth and with all the breath left in her screamed, and screamed again until his palm came up to silence her. As she tried to sink her teeth in it, he panted, 'Stop it! Stop it, wildcat that you are! If you fight too much I will have to hurt you. Why are you fighting? Because you love me, you always have. Admit it!' With his free hand he began to drag the half-torn gown aside, out of his way. 'You love me! No, don't scream. There's no one to answer.'

But, miraculously, there was.

With a crash of inches-thick wood against stone, the door was flung back against the wall and Robert Graham hurtled in.

As an entrance, it was spectacular, although Ninian didn't appreciate it at the time.

With two hasty steps Sir Robert was beside them, and Adam was being plucked from the floor by the collar of his shirt and the crotch of his trunk-hose as if he were an overgrown puppy. He squalled like one, too, because the hose fitted like a second skin and the pain must have been as sudden and shocking as the first slash of the castrator's knife.

Tidily, the sinewy, red-haired man set his victim upright and then felled him again with a blow to the jaw so cruel that Ninian thought she heard the bone crack.

She struggled to her feet, finding her belt and tying the folds of her gown modestly around her as Adam also tried to rise, too out of condition to do it easily. And when he was up, Sir Robert hit him again, and then twice more.

Adam – Ninian's once-beautiful, invincible Adam – lay there on the floor groaning and snivelling, the blood running from nose and mouth over the creased white shirt while Sir Robert kicked him with all the force of his booted feet, again, and again, and again, utterly deaf to Ninian's cries of, 'Stop, Robert. That's enough. Stop, stop!'

By the time he had finished, Adam was grovelling. A drunkard, running to fat, insecurely propped on hands and knees, weeping, whining, begging, pleading now with Ninian and now with Graham. 'You love me. I love you. It's not fair. Why do you let him!' And, 'She loves me. She wants me. You need me.'

A world of contempt on the cruciform face, Sir Robert said, 'If you weren't needed, I would kill you.'

And then there was a kind of suspended stillness in the room, and Ninian, overcome by the sudden release from tension, blinked and began to feel hot and cold and sick, all at the same time, as if she were about to faint.

She staggered slightly.

A hand came to rest on her shoulder, holding her steady, and even as she felt gratitude for it she became aware of Robert Graham's lips, full and unexpectedly soft in the gaunt face, descending on hers. One of the sleeve seams of her gown had given under the strain, and she felt his long, hard fingers slip through the gap, fumbling for her breast and then taking it in a cradling, enveloping grip.

For a moment, it was altogether too much. She stood there while he kissed her, his lips dry and hot, murmuring between kisses, 'You don't know . . . even since before Harry died . . . And now, soon, I will be able to ask you . . .'

She didn't faint after all, and neither did she panic nor struggle.

Instead, without making too much fuss about it, she freed her mouth from his and, repressing an almost overpowering desire to giggle, said

447

in tones of genteel gratification, 'Gracious me. How delightful it is to be so popular.'

It took a few seconds for it to penetrate, but when it did it acted on Sir Robert like an ice-cold douche. Both mouth and hands were suddenly stilled, and she was able to slip, eel-like, out of his grasp.

She reached the door and had it open before she realized that there was neither sound nor movement behind her except for Adam's whimpering. So she took the risk, and stopped, and turned. Two men, both drunk. One a wreck and the other rigid as an offended statue. She was pleased to see that Adam was bleeding only over himself, not the rug.

She said coolly, 'Perhaps you can help each other to bed. And please be gone by the morning.'

3

NINIAN reached Perth four days later, during the afternoon. Her servants weren't accustomed to the pace she set, but she herself had scarcely noticed. All the way, there had been three thoughts running feverishly round in her head, thoughts of Gavin, and Columba, and of Robert Graham saying, 'If you weren't needed, I would kill you.' Why, why, why should Adam be needed? Could he be so very important in another Highland uprising? And would it be more than the Highlands, this time?

While she settled in to her lodgings, she sent two of the men off to find out what she wanted to know. When the first of the men returned, it was four o'clock and almost dark, because although the city was free from snow, it was a dull day and there was one of Perth's heavy mists on the river.

The Bishop of Glasgow, it seemed, had not yet arrived but was expected hourly.

And then Carniss came back, too. He was a sensible fellow, and having found out where Archdeacon Crozier was lodged, he had asked whether the archdeacon was at home and, if not, where he might be found. The archdeacon's servant had given him, confidentially, another address.

Ninian, brimming with impatience, said, 'Have something to eat, and be quick. I want you to come with me, and I have no idea how long

I will be.' She didn't know why she had been overcome by this sudden sense of urgency, but it was possible that Columba might know what was afoot.

She had wondered whether the second address might be where Adam was hidden, but it wasn't, because when she walked in, there was Sévèrine.

Some of the trouble lifted from Ninian's heart as they embraced, because Sévèrine had always been able to control Adam, and surely she could do so still. But then, as they stood back to survey each other after ten years of separation, she saw that although Sévèrine's sardonic manner was the same, she looked very much older, and her eyes were weary, as if she expected to see nothing but tragedy. Why was she here?

Sévèrine shrugged. 'I have never seen this cold, wet country of which Columba has spoken so much, and which he says he will not visit again after this time. And because very soon I will be fifty – *mon Dieu*! – I have told myself that I must see now, or never, whether he speaks the truth about the place. *Hélas*, he does. I should have believed him, and remained in comfort where I belong.' And then the brittle smile softened, and she added, 'But I was anxious to see you, *ma chère*. Columba says you have become strong and wise and perceptive – and thin! Some of this I might have doubted, but now I see that it is so.'

Despite herself, Ninian laughed. 'Oh, Sévèrine, if you had been here before, so many things might have been different. Because any strength or wisdom I may have learned are still no more than the palest reflections of yours!'

Then she and Columba had to embrace, and as he hugged her he let out a little puff of laughter. 'My dearest child, don't you know how like Sévèrine you have become? Not in looks, but in so many other ways.' He cast a humorous, surprisingly youthful glance at the woman he had loved and been faithful to – emotionally, if not always physically – for more than thirty years, and added, 'Although perhaps you are gentler and softer-hearted. You are not a Frenchwoman, after all!'

But as they sat down companionably before the fire, Ninian reflected that, even if Sévèrine had not been there, she could not have brought herself to tell Columba more than a hint of what had so recently happened at Dess. Strange how, all her life, she had been so anxious that he should not be hurt.

So she said only, 'Have you news of Adam?'

'Yes, he is coming to visit us within the hour.'

He said it very calmly, as if there was nothing wrong at all, and Ninian spoke before she could stop herself. 'But he is in terrible danger from the law. Does the thought not trouble you? And why has he come back to Scotland, in any case? Do you know?'

'He is a man, Ninian. More than thirty years old. He knows what he is about, and perhaps he will tell us tonight.'

Sévèrine said nothing.

It meant that Ninian would have to wait and see Adam again, after all. Thinking that perhaps Columba knew more than he was aware of, she began delicately to question him, and because the possibility of a threat to Gavin mattered more to her than anything else in the world, she began there.

She could still smile, inside, at Columba's capacity for self-delusion. It was as if the years of open war between himself and Gavin Cameron had been none of his making. He spoke, as an adviser to the papal legate should speak, with consideration and a bland magnanimity. He could afford it now, of course, when it seemed that at last his position was unassailable.

'Cameron, you know, has lost much of the royal confidence of late, which I begin to think a pity. It is always the fate of those who counsel caution to men of headstrong disposition, and from what I hear, Cameron has honestly tried to keep James under control. The apostolic legate, however, will succeed where he has failed.

'No, although I believed for so long that Cameron was determined to destroy me, time is beginning to moderate my view. Strange though it may sound after all that has happened between us, I believe Bishop Gavin and I are beginning to understand each other at last. There has been an unhappy and unnecessary war between church and state, and we have been on opposing sides. It is time that a truce was called.'

'Does Adam know how you feel?'

'Why?' Sévèrine asked unexpectedly.

Ninian hesitated. 'He hasn't the gift of forgiveness. His feelings don't mellow with time; they seem to become more intense. He has been to Dess – you know that? – and it seems to me that he has forgotten nothing of what he felt five years ago. I think he hates Gavin Cameron, and the king, more even than he did then.'

Columba exclaimed, 'Nonsense, my child. Did he tell you so? Of course not. Have you ever known Adam harbour a grudge?'

Ninian caught Sévèrine's eye; wilful blindness, it seemed to say.

Ninian wished very much that she could ask Sévèrine's advice about herself and Gavin. There was nothing Sévèrine did not know about loving a priest and bearing his children. But Sévèrine and Columba had always had Pierre de Verne to hide behind. Ninian remembered what Gavin had said, and knew that he was right; however sensible, however realistic, such a situation could never be for her. 'Oh, Gavin!' she thought suddenly. 'What will happen to us? Am I wrong in thinking that we can be together, after all?'

Wistfully, she said, 'I don't know. But Adam has changed a great deal, I think, or perhaps only hardened, since those days in Villeneuve when we were all so happy. Do you remember how we thought then that for you to lose your benefices was the worst thing that could possibly happen? And from that, what terrible things have come.'

Columba, staring down at his soft, unsullied hands, said nothing, and Ninian knew that he didn't even recognize how much of the responsibility was his. It wasn't personal selfishness that had set all the events of the last ten years in train, but the passion he felt for those who loved and depended on him. What he had done, he had done for them, and because they, in turn, loved him so much, they had believed that what they were doing, they were doing for him. Adam, Blane, Sévèrine, and herself. A whole little universe revolving round Columba. A vicious circle.

And Blane was dead now, and Ninian herself had withdrawn. There was only Adam, the most dedicated of them, who worshipped his father – and admired all of his attributes that were least worthy of praise.

Sévèrine knew. And Sévèrine had cut herself off, too. It was as if she had decided to leave the men to their own madness. And that was something else in which Ninian could not emulate her.

4

THERE was a nasty bruise on Adam's jaw and a seething tension in his manner, but he was cheerful enough, standing with his back to the fire, blocking the heat, as he tried to restore sensation to a part of his anatomy that had been numbed, he said, by too much time in the saddle.

He greeted Ninian with an extravagant display of his old charm, as if nothing whatever had happened between them, and it suddenly occurred to her that he had an ability to delude himself that matched Columba's own. It was as if he wasn't ignoring, but had genuinely forgotten the degrading scene of a few nights ago. Mentally, she shook her head. She had been distressed at the time, but it all seemed very unimportant now.

'It is not convenient for me to stay long,' he announced briskly. 'I have an appointment of importance elsewhere. But because I will be much occupied during these next weeks, I wished not to postpone this visit.'

Without warning, Séverine said, 'Adam! What are you doing? What dreadful thing have you planned?'

While Columba stared at her in surprise and reproval, Ninian sat and prayed that Adam might give his mother the answer he had withheld from her.

'Dreadful, *madame mère*? Not that. Certainly not that. You would like me to be restored to respectability, no? Well, after tonight, I will be an outlaw no longer. I will have the titles and land and wealth that I am owed. Tell me, is that dreadful?'

He turned to Columba. 'And you, *mon père*, will have satisfaction. For I have a promise that your enemy, Cameron, will be sent at last where he deserves. To the stake.'

It was fortunate that, for the moment, Columba and Séverine had all Adam's attention, and he theirs. None of them even heard Ninian's gasp, nor saw the horror on her face.

There was a silence except for the settling of coal on the hearth and the distant cries of the night.

Then Columba, defeat in every line of him, repeated Séverine's words. 'What dreadful thing have you planned? And who can have given you such a promise?'

Adam wagged a finger at him. 'No, no. You must not ask me to give away secrets. You must wait and see.'

Séverine's heavy-lidded eyes were wide, and her hand was on the crucifix at her throat.

Columba repeated sternly, 'My son, *what have you planned?*'

'Don't look at me like that, papa!' Adam's voice was childish and aggrieved. 'You will like it when you know. Truthfully! You must. You began it, after all. And everything I have done has been for you.'

Then, abruptly, he swung round, and his voice changed. 'Though what I do now, is for myself as well as you. For myself and for my Lady Fair.'

Ninian, her mind racing, wasn't even paying attention, so that it was with a gasp of astonishment that she found herself gripped by the arm and swung unceremoniously up to Adam's side.

'After tonight, I will have more to offer than it will be possible for you to refuse,' he said, smiling down into her eyes. 'We can be together always, *p'tite!* Think of it!'

She was beginning to be very tired of Adam. Snappishly, she said, 'I would rather not. I am flattered, of course. But, once and for all, Adam, *I am not interested.*'

'Don't be foolish, *p'tite!* You want to marry me, you know you do!'

It was only as she pulled away from him that she became aware of the quality of the silence in the room.

Columba, his face grey, was slumped in his chair like an old man, and Séverine had her crucifix to her lips. Praying? Ninian thought. For what, for whom?

Adam was reaching out to drag her back to him when Columba's voice said, 'My son, my son! Let Ninian go, I beg of you. Let her go, or may God strike you down.'

Ninian was just about to say, with more than a touch of acerbity, that she was perfectly capable of handling Adam and that there were more important things for Columba to worry about, when she glanced up at Adam and saw the smile on his face.

He held her eyes even while he addressed himself to his father. 'What? Because she is my sister, you mean? Nonsense, papa. *That* doesn't matter, does it, *p'tite?*'

5

AFTER an interminable, frozen interval, Ninian went to kneel before Columba's chair.

She didn't speak, and at last he took her hand and held it in both of his, then, avoiding her eyes, said, 'Yes, you are the child of my flesh, as you have always been of my heart.'

It didn't come as any real shock – irrationally, far less of a shock than the discovery that Adam was her brother. She turned her gaze towards Séverine.

'No,' Columba said. 'I fathered you, against all the laws of God, on my brother's wife. Your mother was, indeed, your mother. Don't judge her too harshly. Or me.' His hands squeezed hers convulsively. 'My penance has been long.'

She might have believed that, once, before she had learned to see him clearly. It probably troubled his conscience, now and again, she thought, but increasingly seldom as the years went by. Wearily, she said, 'And what sins have you laid on me, to be the child of such a union? Was there even – love – in it?'

The familiar tears were trickling down the clefts that bracketed his nose and mouth, the clefts that marked her face, too. If it had not been for her eyes and colouring, the resemblance might have been there for all to see.

'Love?' he repeated. 'No. Weakness, and loneliness. It was my fault, and at my urging.'

'Not predestined?' she asked drily. 'Your penance has been long, you say. I wonder whether everything that has happened to *me* in these last years has been part of the same penance? Do you think it has been paid, now, or will ever be paid? Do you think it matters?'

And then she turned away from him to Sévèrine, and said, 'How could you bear it?'

Sévèrine had stopped praying, and her eyes were calm. She shrugged. 'I love him, and I understand him. When that is so, one can forgive almost anything without being too much hurt, except perhaps in one's vanity. But I love you not only because you are part of him; I love you for yourself, and for – feeling like *my* daughter also.'

Ninian thought, 'Oh, Sévèrine, Sévèrine. So worldly, so saintly, so foolish!' Suddenly, there were tears in her own eyes.

Half smiling, Sévèrine said, 'Columba, my dear, perhaps it is fortunate that Ninian is not our child, for we have not been very successful.'

And then she turned to Adam, who had been watching them with a bored and rather vacuous grin on his face. Studying him, as if he were some foreign species, she said at last, 'No, Adam, you cannot have Ninian. And by wanting her, when you knew the truth, you have cut yourself off from all of us, forever.'

His mouth opened like a disappointed child's, and it occurred to Ninian for the first time that he had never really grown up. It would explain so many things – all the things that were lacking in his make-up. Things like a sense of responsibility, that came only with maturity.

'No, *maman*!' he exclaimed. 'Don't say that!' He looked as if he were about to run to her, and throw himself at her feet, but only for an instant. Then he had straightened up again, and there was a sense of purpose about him and an authority that would have been striking if it had not, at the same time, been almost slovenly.

His tone changed, too. 'We will talk again, some other time. Now, it is necessary that I leave, for it will soon be curfew. Tomorrow, *maman*, you will discover that your son has had a major part to play in affairs of the very greatest consequence. You will speak differently to me then. And now, *au r'voir*.'

6

THEY sat, stunned, listening to the sound of his feet moving away down the stone-flagged corridor.

Tomorrow!

Not an uprising, Ninian thought, her brain working faster than it had ever done before. Not unless it was to be in Perth itself. Or Edinburgh. Either was possible, and more than possible – dreadfully probable. But what in God's name did it all have to do with the promise that Gavin would go to the stake? Because that would involve Laurence of Lindores. She could have wept with frustration.

And while she sat here thinking, time was wasting.

The urgency of it brought her to her feet, and she took Columba by the shoulders and shook him violently. 'What is he up to? Columba, *you must have some idea*! What can we do? Oh, God, *I must warn Gavin somehow*!'

He noted the unwitting revelation, and couldn't believe it, but at this moment it scarcely seemed important in relation to everything else. He said heavily, 'You are right. He might have some idea what to do. I didn't even know he was back in Scotland. How can we find him?'

'He is due at any moment. He will go to the Bishop's Lodging first. I'll catch him there. I think the threat to him is only part of the plot, and he may know, or suspect, where the other danger lies.'

'*We* will catch him there. You cannot go alone.' His mind was working again. 'If we can warn him, it may still be possible to stop whatever is afoot.' He stopped, and there was a deep despair in his voice. 'But that we should have to go to him, of all men, to save my son . . .'

Ninian, wrapping herself in her cloak, exclaimed, 'More, many more, than your son, Columba!'

'Yes.' And then he said pleadingly, 'But we might save him, too, if we can prevent people from talking. We must not take any servants.'

She nodded, and kissed Séverine, and they left her sitting there, still and silent, as they went to the door.

There was a man outside.

He looked dirty, and smelled foul, but the longsword in his hand was clean and beautifully honed.

'I've orders ye're no' tae leave,' he said benignly. 'Ye might get intae trouble oot o' the hoose on a nasty, dark night like this.'

'Let me pass!'

'Och, no. Jist be a guid wee lassie and awa' back in. Huv a nice sitdoon by the fire.' The slack voice and easy tone didn't match either the sword or the quick, dark, beady eyes.

Columba raised a majestic hand to push the sword aside, but the man backed away hurriedly, and there was no mistaking his mood.

'Carefu', Your Grace, or whitever ye are. I'll no' hesitate tae use this!'

Columba, honestly shocked, exclaimed, 'On an adviser to the apostolic legate? You would never dare.'

'Would I no'? There's naebody gaun tae bother aboot a wee bit o' priest's blood, when the king's 'll soon be running a' ower the place! Back up, Your Grace!'

The silence reverberated along the corridor, and down the staircase, and up to the roof, and returned again to them, breathless.

When they had retreated into the placid, firelit chamber, they stared at each other.

'The king,' Ninian breathed. 'They're going to murder the king!'

Columba fell on his knees and began to pray.

CHAPTER THREE

I

THE man with the longsword was still laughing when Ninian felled him from behind. He had been so busy thinking that the priest was a fool to expect him to be taken in by the tale of some French lady, ill and needing a glass of water from the ewery, that he hadn't noticed the other one sidling round with the heavy pewter pot in her hand.

She looked down at him, her eyes wide, and gingerly set the dented pot on the floor beside him. Then she smiled a little nervously at Columba and turned away.

Someone had to warn the king, and secretly, because there was no telling who might be involved in the plot. And the someone had to be Ninian, who could move quickly and unobtrusively through the familiar streets of Perth, and knew the Blackfriars like the back of her hand. Columba was to go to the Bishop's Lodging and wait for Gavin.

Carniss was in the close below, and she took him part of the way with her, because the streets were dark and treacherous and, after curfew, any sound of human movement was a magnet for the vagrants and cut-purses who lurked in the shadowed wynds of the city. But they were cowards, most of them, and even one stalwart, well-armed man was protection enough. If they moved lightly, she thought, they might attract no attention at all.

When they emerged at last onto the water meadows, she whispered to him that she would go on alone. He, with no idea what was afoot except that it was something unpleasant and almost certainly dangerous, muttered, 'Ye'll not, my lady! I'm coming with ye!'

'No. Two people are twice as easily seen. I can't take the risk. Stay here and watch.' She gave a little catch of laughter. 'If you see anything happen before I reach the gates, you can rush to my rescue. But thank you, Carniss.'

It took the strongest effort of will to carry her across the meadows, slipping from one patch of illusory shelter to the next. There was a moon somewhere behind the mist, shedding an eerie glow on the far side of the river, turning the trees to ghostly halo-ed skeletons except where they bordered the water and cast their own dark reflections on it. It was impossible to tell where the trees ended and the water began.

The damp ground sucked at her feet as she struggled onwards, the nervous sweat cold on her back, towards the black bulk of the priory. There was no light to be seen, because only the main halls faced the river and, besides, the Dominicans retired early to their dim cells. Nor was there even a hint of a breeze, so that at every rustling night sound of bird or beast her furiously beating heart was jerked into her throat. Although she was in haste, the terrible breathlessness that gripped her had no physical origin.

It was an eternity before she reached the gates, silent, unlocked, unguarded. Idiotically, she couldn't remember whether there should be a porter there or not.

But it *was* silent, and it *was* dark. With a great, tearing sigh of relief, she realized that she was in time.

2

THROWING off his riding cloak, Gavin strode into his private chamber with no other thoughts in his mind than food and sleep, and was brought up short by the sight of the man who awaited him.

His steward's voice murmured reproachfully in his ear, 'I was trying to tell your lordship . . .'

'Yes. Very well. No doubt the archdeacon will join me in some supper.' The steward bowed and softly departed.

Crozier rose from the stool on which he had been huddled before the fire, and took a slow step forward so that the candlelight fell on his high-nosed Roman face, emphasizing the fleshy folds of it and turning the eye sockets into pits of darkness under the short, thick brushes of his brows.

This was a man Gavin had never seen before, although he had thought he knew every expression on that mobile, unreliable face. His heart turned over. Trouble. Honest trouble, desperate trouble that affected Crozier himself – and Gavin, too, or the man would not be here. For a sickening moment, he thought it might have to do with Ninian.

And then Crozier, without preliminary, said, 'There is a plot to murder the king. Tonight, we think.'

The grey Nordic eyes had no more emotion in them than the grey Nordic seas, and not a muscle moved in the strongly-boned face. 'How do you know?' Gavin said. 'Who are the people involved, and how many? Has the king been warned?'

Inside himself he was wondering whether there was still some trace in him of Highland vision, because the sense of doom had been with him for three months now. It had driven him back to Scotland against every argument his brain could muster.

He had known. Was he to be just in time – or just too late?

Without waiting for Columba to answer he went to the door, shouting for his servants to rouse every man in the Lodging and see that everyone was armed. 'Get the horses saddled again. And I want all four of my trumpet men, and every torch and flare that can be found. In the courtyard five minutes from now, no more!'

Then he turned back to Columba, his brows raised, and Columba said, 'We know because my son has told us. But as to how many . . .' He shook his head. 'Too many, perhaps. Robert Graham certainly, and Ninian thinks Rob Stewart, too.'

'*Ninian* thinks? How is she involved in this?'

'She has gone to warn James.'

'She has . . . *And you allowed it?*'

'There was no other way. Adam will see that she is not harmed.'

Gavin's eyes were like ice. 'Do you think he can protect her, when there is a throne at stake! With James dead, Atholl will be regent.'

He was thinking aloud, and it was as much as Columba could do to keep up with him. 'He will have the child killed later – children die all the time. Then Atholl will be king, and Rob Stewart after him, and they will give your son and Graham everything they ask, for having helped to make it possible. Or have them quietly murdered. But how do they think they can get away with it?'

Columba said, 'James has alienated everyone from the highest to the lowest. I have been thinking, this last hour. I believe they expect the country to be grateful to them, even the church.'

Gavin was busy strapping on his mail. 'Frightened of what the legate will find out?'

'No, the barratry laws. Ogily, Methven, Winchester and the others – they swore to His Holiness last March that the barratry statutes would be repealed within the year. And it is February now, and they haven't been.'

Gavin stopped short. It fitted. Dear God, it all fitted. 'Whereas with James dead, the statutes would cease to be valid.' Royal statutes lived only as long as the king who made them. He raised his voice to a bellow. 'Damn you, Geddes! Is everyone not ready yet?'

And then, without a backward glance, he hurried out, leaving behind him a silent middle-aged man, who knew himself too old to be of use.

3

INSIDE the Blackfriars, the last act had already begun.

Ninian, slipping quietly along the upper gallery, became aware of other presences.

She neither saw nor heard them at first. And then there was a clank of armour, almost inaudible, and a whispering.

Some way ahead of her, a cheerful door opened, and there was light for a moment, and the king's voice saying, 'The decent wine, Wat, my lad, the stuff from Châteauneuf-du-Pape; something warm for a chill night!' And Wat Stratton, the chamber page, emerged with a flagon in his hand.

The door closed again. Ninian listened, all her senses alert, as the boy's light footsteps descended the stairs. He was whistling quietly to himself. They wouldn't touch him, surely? There was no need, because although their eyes would be adjusted to the darkness by now, his would not, so he probably wouldn't see them unless they wanted to be seen. And he was only twelve years old.

The whistling stopped. There was a high-pitched exclamation, instantly cut off. And afterwards, a faint gurgling sound that could have only one meaning. Ninian had to grip her lips between her teeth, and for the first time fully realized the risk she herself was running.

Then, as if this easy victory had given them confidence, the men below became less careful, and Ninian for the first time had an impression of numbers. How many? A dozen? Two dozen? Far more than just Adam, and Robert Graham, and Rob Stewart. Far more than the king, alone, could hope to fight off – and he must be alone now, except for the queen, because it was customary for the household to retire at curfew.

Until that moment, Ninian had been so obsessed by the need to get a warning to the king that only her intelligence had been involved, but now she felt a wave of horror and nausea sweep through her at the thought of the queen, whom she had served and, in a way, loved for almost ten years, seeing the husband she worshipped struck down like a dog. And James himself, whatever his faults, didn't deserve to die so. No man did.

As she hurried along the last few yards to the door of the royal bedchamber, holding the folds of her gown and cloak in a vice-like grip so that there should be no sound of skirts to give her away, she prayed, 'Gavin! Oh, Gavin, come soon!' Because some of the household should have heard the sounds the assassins were making by now, and should have emerged to investigate. The fact that they hadn't told its own story.

Reaching the door, she hesitated. Light would spill out again when she opened it, but that was a risk that had to be run and the conspirators might not see it from below. Her heart pounding furiously, she lifted the latch and slipped inside.

4

THE king had laid aside his armour and was half undressed, standing before the fire, at his ease, talking to the queen who was already in her night robe.

They turned and stared, both of them, at the breathless, dishevelled vision before them, and James's mouth opened to snap a reprimand. And then it closed again within the silky thicket of grey-streaked

461

mahogany beard, as if he knew what she had come for. It was the queen, refusing to believe, who said, 'What is it?'

She hadn't thought how to break the news, and the words came blundering out of their own accord, crude and terrible. 'Assassins, Your Majesty. In the corridor below. They've murdered young Wat.'

James was on the move before she had finished, reaching for his armour, searching for his sword. 'How many of them? Who? Bolt the door, woman!'

'A dozen, perhaps. Sir Robert Graham, Rob Stewart . . .' She couldn't bring herself to mention Adam.

Even as she spoke, she was turning to push the big, thick wooden bolt home. Thick enough to hold the door for a while at least – for long enough, perhaps, for Gavin to arrive – even against a determined assault.

But there was no bolt there, only the empty sockets.

Wildly she looked round. 'The bolt!' she exclaimed. 'Where is it?'

The queen turned as white as a sheet, and all the high colour drained away from the king's face. There was a moment while all three of them stood and stared around them almost vacantly.

Then James said, his voice bleak and concise, 'Rob Stewart, my household chamberlain. Whom I trusted. It seems he must have taken my sword, too, because I can't find it.'

He had been trying, with the queen's help, to buckle on his breastplate, and making sad work of it. Now, he ripped it off and threw it with a clatter to the floor. 'Useless,' he said. 'It will only hamper me. Is there something else that will serve as a bolt?'

But both Ninian and the queen knew that he saw his death upon him.

Ninian leaned her full weight against the door, listening for any sound from outside, while the queen frantically tested and discarded the iron stave resting on the fire dogs – too thick – and the poker – too thin – the weighting pole from one of the tapestries – too thick again . . .

Ninian gasped, 'There must be *some*thing, anything that will last even for a few minutes. Bishop Gavin should be on his way by now with men he can trust. We need only hold out until then.'

James, who had been clumsily trying to manhandle his clothing chest towards the door to act as a barricade, looked up with a sudden light in his eyes. 'Bishop Gavin?' And then, typically, 'What is he doing back here against my express orders?'

It was at that moment, without any warning at all, that Ninian heard the sounds she had been waiting for, and they were right outside the door.

Despairingly, she began to thrust her own arm through the sockets of the bolt.

5

HER scream of pain as the door burst open was lost in the furore as two dozen men surged in, a sword or dagger in every hand – even in the hands of the two men who wore the robes of parish priests.

They stopped, jostling, for a moment, those in front scanning the room, those behind pushing. James had taken refuge behind the huge bulk of the bed, one hand grasping the queen's arm, but she tore herself from his grip and threw herself in front of the conspirators – whether to beg for her husband's life, or to protect him with her own body no one took time to discover. One of the swords slashed up, and then down, and she fell bleeding and unconscious to the floor. And then Rob Stewart kicked her aside.

Ninian, her arm broken and useless, her head swimming, staggered forward from her place of concealment behind the door. She had no idea what she meant to do, but even as Adam and three of the courtiers leapt on to the bed itself, even as James, with a mighty tug, brought the whole tester down on top of them, she felt a pair of iron-hard arms enfold her from behind. She didn't need to hear the fast-breathing voice say, 'Hold still, you can do nothing,' to know that it was Robert Graham.

She stood there trapped, struggling hopelessly, forced to watch as the king fought for his life – and then for his death. Because as arm after arm went up, and then down, as dagger followed sword, and sword dagger, still no man struck the killing blow.

And the king lay, the blood pouring from his wounds in a terrible torrent, and stabbed feebly at the air with the dagger that was all the weapon he had.

He knew most of the men, and had liked some of them and given them his favour. Ninian, sobbing in a grief that was not only for him, but for all of them, prayed that his eyes were blinded so that he could not see the pleasure on their faces as the blows went home – Rob

Stewart's fair and comely features transfigured into those of an angel of the Annunciation; Adam's laughter the laughter of ecstasy; and on Jamie Hall's stout burgess's face the satisfaction of a man who had concluded an excellent deal. One of the priests was praying.

Robert Graham's breath was hot against Ninian's neck as, avidly, he watched every blow that was struck, his own body twitching as the king's did. She knew that he was scarcely aware of her, but, 'Make an end, make an end,' she choked at last, her own eyes almost unseeing.

It was then that he flung her into Adam's grasp and himself stepped forward; then that, coolly and ceremoniously, he and Rob Stewart together plunged their daggers into the king's heart; then that, with one voice, they said loudly, 'Equal responsibility! We *all* take equal credit for seeing justice done!'

Everyone cheered.

Adam loosed his hold on Ninian and she began to struggle dully across the room to where the queen lay. It was like being at an over-crowded reception.

The guests seemed reluctant to leave, as if they were sorry the entertainment was over, and they straggled out in twos and threes, pocketing anything that took their fancy on the way. One of the Barclay brothers tucked the queen's gold hand mirror into his purse. Christopher Chambers helped himself to a silver-gilt ewer. Rob Stewart tore the big ruby from the king's finger, the setting as bloodily red as the stone itself.

And then, far too late, a solitary member of the royal household appeared. It was Davie Dunbar, who had taken time to put on every last piece of armour he possessed. Adam, laughing, severed the man's sword hand with a single blow.

It was just then that, in the distance, they heard the solid thud of a body of horse approaching at full gallop, and the sound of trumpets.

Adam cried merrily, 'It is time to go, my friends! *Au r'voir*, little one. Tell *maman* she will see me again soon!'

6

SÉVÈRINE saw her son again, once, on the scaffold.

She went alone, because Columba was in church, praying, and she would not allow Ninian, who had been through too much already, to bear her company.

It had been Ninian who had gone before the justiciar and sworn to the identity of all those who had helped to strike the king down on that February night at the Blackfriars of Perth. Ninian's voice that had condemned Adam, and Robert Graham, and Rob Stewart, and all the others, to the death, barbarous and obscene, that was everywhere the penalty for regicide. The queen had lived, and had confirmed some of the names, and Sir Davie Dunbar several others, including Adam's, but the burden had been Ninian's, and Sévèrine knew that it would stay with her for the rest of her life.

Most of the conspirators had vanished before Gavin Cameron reached the Blackfriars, but they had been caught easily enough once it was known who they were. On that, as on everything else, Gavin Cameron had moved with the speed of a man possessed. If he had not been there, and had not acted, no one else would have dared to – or not, at least, until much too late.

But even as he and his men had raced to try and save the king, another party had been on its way to arrest Atholl, supping wine innocently in his lodgings.

It transpired that Atholl's intention had been to wait only until he knew that the conspiracy had succeeded before having all the bells of Perth rung, to wake the town to hear his declaration that six-year-old Prince James, Duke of Rothesay, was now King James II, and that Atholl himself would act as regent and guardian during his minority. Atholl hadn't expected the queen to survive.

All the conspirators had thought, it seemed, that the country would greet what they had done with acclamation, but it had not been so, even though Sir Robert Graham, the prime mover, had declared during his trial, 'The day and the time will come when all of you will pray for my soul, out of gratitude for the great good I have done this realm of Scotland, in slaying and delivering you from so cruel a tyrant.'

But there were to be no prayers for him, and neither confession nor extreme unction, when he went to his execution, for the queen had decreed that the assassins should suffer the fullest rigour of the law. They were to die the day after the new little king had been crowned.

They were scourged naked through the streets, Atholl with an iron coronet instead of a toorie on his wild white head, his sagging, grey-pale winter flesh marked with the filth of the dungeon even before the shouting, cursing, weeping crowd began pelting the terrible little procession with anything and everything they could lay their hands on.

Some of the conspirators stumbled along in their ankle-chains, cringing, half blinded by the light after six weeks of darkness, trying with bound hands to ward off the missiles that flew at them from all directions. But others held their heads high. There was contempt on Atholl's pouched face; on Robert Graham's the same absence of expression as always; on Rob Stewart's an artificial, smiling pride belied by the dreadful quivering of his lips.

Adam was near the end of the procession.

Adam de Verne, who was in truth Adam Crozier, Sévèrine's once beautiful son, whose body had gone to seed and whose darting eyes betrayed the panic that was in him.

Sévèrine watched, and prayed for him, dry-eyed, the child she had borne with such love and reared with understanding; the vivid boy whose very presence had been enough to light up her heart; the dazzling young man whose charm she had seen beginning to go awry.

She had always known that she would have to suffer and perhaps share his death some day, and had not feared it. What she had feared was the manner of his dying.

He was one of the last to mount the scaffold, and by then the executioners had become expert at inflicting all the impossible pains, all the disgusting degradations that the human body was capable of bearing while life and consciousness endured. So he lived and was aware throughout the hanging, and the castration, and the dis-embowelling, until at last he shrieked, 'Oh, *Jésus! Jésus!*' as the executioner opened his chest and cut out his heart.

CHAPTER FOUR

I

GAVIN, his arm round Ninian's shoulders and her left hand in his, said quietly, 'It will all be over soon, and then I will take you to Kinveil.'

Her eyes smiled at him, intensely blue, and he felt again, as he had felt so many times in these last weeks, the fierce tide of gratitude swelling in his heart.

There had been blood everywhere when he had reached the royal bedchamber, and a stillness and silence that were absolute. The smell of death had been so thick, so cloying, so all-pervading, that it hadn't seemed possible that Ninian, collapsed over the senseless body of the queen, could still be alive. He had felt a depth of despair so complete that, for a moment, it had blinded him.

But as he kneeled over her, she had moaned, and moved, and opened her eyes on his, and he had known then that nothing else mattered to him, either in the world, or out of it.

He had told her, this evening, of his meeting with Séverine at Villeneuve – of which Séverine herself had said nothing – and of how it had shaken his resolve.

'She spoke only of happiness. I think, perhaps, that, knowing nothing of the kind of love and warmth that must have surrounded you in your growing up, I had been undervaluing it. And then, when I saw you and thought you were dead, every last doubt was swept away.

I believe now that the laws of the church are wrong, and that we have nothing to fear from God. Will you take your chance with me?'

It was all – almost all – she had ever prayed for. Her voice unsteady, she had said, 'Yes, I will take it, but not from choice. I have had no choice at all since the day I first saw you.'

There were obstacles still, but, the decision reached, they knew that none was insurmountable.

Now, she settled herself more comfortably in his arms and said, as if she couldn't quite believe it, '*Will* it all be over? Really?'

'Yes. We are seeing the end of one story, and the beginning of another. I can't tell whether it will be a happier one, but it will certainly be less eventful, for the time being, at least. The Earl of Douglas is to be named regent, and he is a careful man. Little worthwhile, if anything, will be done during the king's minority.'

She gave a little chuckle. 'No more reforms? *Poor* Gavin!'

He chuckled back at her. 'How dare you tease me, woman, when I have you at my mercy!' He dropped a kiss on her mouth, and ran a gentle hand over the soft, silken skin of her thighs so that her body stirred luxuriously, achingly, as it always did and always would do when he touched her.

Moving her bandaged right arm a little, she said, 'Ohhh! How it hurts still,' and then, with another chuckle, 'Do you realize that this is the third – the *third* – time in our lives that we have made love, and only once have we both been whole and uninjured!'

He remembered the time at Dess, after he had fought with Adam de Verne. 'I couldn't bend, last time – but we managed.' And now . . . Not since the assassination had he been able to see her other than publicly, and by day. Not until tonight.

Lightly, he swung himself over her. 'And we have managed twice tonight already. Do you know . . .' He paused for a moment and then, as their bodies joined and the faint, sweet sound of her sigh echoed in his ears, went on, 'Do you know, I wonder, how very much I love you? Far more than you can possibly love me.'

Her eyes opened wide on his, and her mouth opened, too, in mock outrage, but before she could speak he began to move inside her and she was able to find other ways than words to deny it.

THE Earl of Douglas said, 'How very helpful of you, my dear Gavin. I had, myself, been intending to suggest a brief hiatus in your reforming mission. What is needed, I believe, is a few months of unalloyed quietness and calm, so that we can all recover our breaths.'

It was true, Gavin knew. After the years of James's crusading rule, with which he himself had been so closely associated, the country needed a rest.

And so did he. He felt rudderless for the first time in his life, uncertain of what should be done next. He wanted Ninian. He wanted time to think. And he wanted peace – peace at Kinveil, the rough stone watchtower on the fringes of the western sea.

So he had gone to the regent, whose secretary he had once been, and had said that, if Douglas didn't need him for the moment, he would like to pay an extended visit to Kinveil, where there was much that needed to be done.

Douglas said expansively, 'Take a year, dear boy.'

And then his tone changed, and he said, 'Don't think I haven't been aware of how much you did during the late king's rule. I have been proud of my former secretary. More than that, I have admired him. I know you must need time to yourself, and you deserve it. No man can function without resting occasionally.

'But our poor, new, puny little king needs you, the queen relies on you, and when everything returns to normal again I, too, will feel more at ease with you at my side.'

And then, with equal suddenness, his tone changed back again, and once more it was the noble earl speaking, the man whose cynicism had been bred into him over almost three centuries of family involvement in affairs of state. 'Accept what is offered, dear boy, for you should know as well as anyone that it is the only payment your ungrateful country is likely to grant you.'

FROM Douglas, Gavin went on to see the papal legate, Anthony Altani, Bishop of Urbino, who had been a tower of strength after the assassination. The legate, with astonishing restraint, had uttered not one word of criticism over Gavin's forbidden presence in the country – or not until now, when Gavin said he would be grateful for official permission to have a year free from his episcopal duties. He had no real need to ask – there were bishops enough who never saw their cathedrals from one decade's end to another – but it seemed right to him that he should.

The legate removed the magnifying glass lentils from the bridge of his nose, leaving two bright red marks where the scissor-hinge had gripped it, and blinked at him.

'*Madonna santissima!*' he said. 'When you have been absolutely forbidden to show your face in Scotland without the express licence of His Holiness, and of myself also, you ask whether it is permitted for you to abandon one part of it in favour of another?'

Gavin grinned suddenly. 'I do!'

The legate put his spectacles down. 'Let us be quite clear on this matter. It was not your country that His Holiness was anxious you should stay away from, but its centres of power. This place you wish to go to – this Kinveil – is it a place where parliaments, or councils-general, or councils of the church, often meet?'

It was too much. Gavin sat down, regardless of protocol, and began to laugh as if he would never stop.

When he recovered himself, he saw that there was a twinkle in the Bishop of Urbino's elderly eye.

Planting the glass lentils firmly back on his nose again, the legate said, 'Go with God, my son,' and turned his eyes back to his psalter.

4

SÉVÈRINE sailed back to France from Dumbarton, on a brisk, bright, breezy day, and Ninian, Columba, and Gavin were there to see her go.

Columba had to speak to Ninian several times before she was brought back to the present. She was remembering the day when little Princess Margaret had sailed to marry the Dauphin; the day when Moragh had told her so many sad and hurtful things, and claimed that Gavin was hers, and would always be hers. In that, as in so many things, Moragh had been wrong.

She was thinking, too, that never in her wildest dreams could she have envisaged Columba and Gavin standing talking together, in harmony, here or anywhere.

It had been Columba who had made the first overtures. He had said, 'I have used, I know, ruthless means to attain desirable ends – for the sake of the church. You have done the same – for the sake of the realm. It is time that they, and we, came together.'

Ninian, knowing Columba, knew that he was accepting the inevitable. He had lost both his sons, and feared that he might lose his daughter, too, in a different way, if he could not accept her love for Gavin Cameron. What a pragmatist he was, she thought in everything except faith.

Sévèrine's control had never faltered in all these long weeks, but it had been as if she had needed Ninian's strength to sustain her own. They had always been close, but now there was a bond between them that nothing could break.

The night before she sailed, she had said to Ninian, 'I am going back to Villeneuve, now, because I need it desperately. It is possible to go into retreat without entering a convent. But when I have made peace with my soul, I think I will come back for a time, to this Kinveil of yours, perhaps. From what your lover tells me, it seems as if, there, one might also make one's peace with God.'

Ninian had hugged her convulsively, and wept with joy and sadness for her.

They stood for a whole, long hour as the little ship sailed away, until it was out of sight, until well after they could see Sévèrine herself standing quietly on deck, out of the bustle. The tears poured down Columba's cheeks without ceasing until Ninian took his hand in hers, and kissed him, and said, 'It is not an ending. The end has already been, and is past now, and the pain with it. Sévèrine will never have to face such tragedy again. But Columba – promise me this. That you will never, ever again, do anything to hurt her. That you will never again disregard what she asks of you. For she has more wisdom than all of us put together.'

He was old, suddenly, and he knew what he had done. He, whom she had once shocked very deeply by describing the whole disaster of Lochaber as 'my fault', now said heavily, 'Yes. It has all been my fault, and I do not know what my penance will be.'

Gavin, who had learned humanity, said suddenly, 'You have lost two sons. God cannot ask more of you, except self-knowledge.'

Columba stared at him for a moment. 'But that is the hardest penance of all,' he said.

5

THERE was only one more thing to be done.

Ninian, in full court mourning, went to the queen, whose wounded shoulder was healing slowly and whose heart had healed not at all.

She had expected the interview to be difficult, because the queen had always been reluctant to give her ladies leave of absence from court, and was more reluctant now than ever.

Wanting only to disappear, Ninian had thought of saying she intended to go back to France, but in the end had found she couldn't lie, even though so much depended on it.

So she went on her knees, and told Her Majesty the truth.

'Bishop Gavin has enemies, madame, who are envious and always have been. If they knew that he and I were lovers, he could be deprived of his see. He could not, then, hold office, or serve you and the king when you have need of him. For that reason, if for no other, I beg that you will allow me to go with him to Kinveil, where we will be safe from such dangers.'

The perfect semi-circles of the queen's brows rose, and she said, 'You would be safer still if I forbade you to be lovers.'

Ninian was silent.

'Do you love him truly, and deeply?'

Risking everything, Ninian said, 'I love him, I think, as truly and deeply as you yourself loved your husband.'

'And still love him.' The queen's voice was suspended for a moment, and then she sighed, and said, 'I have not, I believe, told you of the gratitude I feel towards you, and towards Bishop Gavin. And I, above all women, know how much love matters. I will not be responsible for stealing it from anyone. Go with him, my dear, with my blessing. I ask

472

only that, some day, perhaps, you will come back and tell me how things are with you.'

Ninian, tears standing in her eyes, kissed the queen's hand, and was dismissed.

And so one life was over, and the new one could begin.

EPILOGUE

I

IT was a perfect June evening when they breasted the hill and Ninian saw Kinveil for the first time, set in blue water among hills as rough and lucent and palely purple as amethysts broken from the shell. There was the faintest glow of rose beginning to tinge the sky.

She stared at it all, robbed of breath, and then turned accusingly to the man who rode beside her, the man who had been casting off a life-time's disciplines one by one, like unwanted garments, ever since they had come within sight of the mountains and the western sea.

'Gavin Cameron,' she exclaimed. 'How dare you? You're wicked. It's all been deliberate, hasn't it? *This* is why we rode so slowly yesterday when it rained! *This* is why we have been ambling along at a snail's pace today! So that you could show me Kinveil for the first time as you want me to see it. It's immoral, when you know it can't possibly always look like this.'

He laughed, and it was such a carefree, such an exhilarating and exhilarated sound, that her own heart turned over with love for him.

'Of course! But it can be more beautiful even than this. We do the finest range of sunsets you have ever seen – just wait! By the time we reach the shores of the loch, you will discover what a sunset can be.'

And it was true.

In the months that followed, she came to know many other moods of the landscape and of the sea, observing them all through a glow of happiness. The sea was something new to her, and she found she could stare at it in fascination for hours, at the slow satin ripples, and the short, white, predatory wave crests, and the thundering turbulence when the winds came raging in from the Atlantic – a strange, companionable feeling, a living presence. She saw the mountains change, too, under the changing seasons and the changing sky – purple or indigo, peat-brown or amber, soft olive or furious green.

One day, she and Gavin were on the hill when the hustling black clouds broke to leave a ragged gap that allowed a finger of sunlight to stab through, casting a sharp clear ring of brilliance on Kinveil, while the rest of the landscape stayed dark and obscure.

It was like the finger of God.

Gavin said, 'Are you happy?'

He knew the answer, so she put into words something she had been meaning to say for a long time, when the occasion presented itself.

'I have been wondering, for so long, why I – and you, for that matter – have worried so much about what is destiny, and what is not.

'I thought, at one stage, that you were right about free will, and then Jehane died and I knew it couldn't be the only answer. Jehane died, because she gave someone a loving kiss, and that only made sense if her death was a punishment for something I myself had done. But then I thought that a merciful God couldn't be so callous as to use an innocent child as a *weapon*, so it must have been Satan at work. And if that was so, why did God permit it?

'It seems to me, now, that there are no answers, and that perhaps Columba is right when he says the human mind isn't capable of encompassing the workings of the divine. Whether our love for each other is predestined, or something that stems from our own free will, I'm not sure that it matters.

'Because I think that real, deep human love is only another aspect of divine love. By loving you, I think – I *know* – that I am able to love God more.'

2

THEIR first son was born, easily and beautifully, on a crisp, pure, snowbright day in February, with all the world sparkling under the pale blue arch of the sky, and the sea shining like silver satin.

478

They had two months after that, and then, when the first buds were beginning to swell on the trees and the first birds were returning from their winter migration, Gavin had to leave.

It was a man transformed – a happier, and much wiser man – who went back to do what he could to save the youthful James II from the mistakes, and the fate, of his father. And because now there was no urgent driving force at the heart of things, he was able to come to Ninian at Kinveil, not often, but not so rarely that they starved.

They had two more sons, and Gavin, still a lawyer at heart, drew up an intricate document transferring everything he possessed to Ninian, on their behalf. She laughed at him for it, at first, but that was because she had forgotten that, when a bishop died, everything he owned except stones and mortar was forfeit to the crown. It was logical enough; men dedicated to God were not supposed to acquire worldly goods.

It was a strange reminder that life, elsewhere, went on as it had always done, because she couldn't now think of the man she loved as once she had thought of him. Looking back, in maturity, she knew that she had first loved him for what he was as much as for himself. But she had learned the worth of power, and now she knew that it was the warmth and the loving, the heart and the mind, the spirit and the humour, that tied her to him with chains as fine as gossamer, as strong and flexible as steel. Their relationship was richer, deeper, more idyllically happy than either of them could ever have imagined.

Sitting by the loch side at Kinveil, her sons busy in the rock pools under the benign gaze of Master Lindsay, seals flippering lazily in the water, martins swooping overhead, the soft, distant sounds of Gaelic voices – and other voices, too, from Dess – murmuring in the salt-sweet air, she smiled, often, as she sketched, in her own newly free and individual style, the wild Highland landscape that had captivated her, and that she was learning to make her own. Among the many things Gavin had taught her was that to reproduce the beauties of the created world with care, and love, and all her talents, was itself a form of worship and of gratitude.

She smiled, too, when she remembered that night at Villeneuve so long ago, when it had seemed that she could never have the two things in the world she most desired – a talent with brush and paint, and the love of Gavin John Cameron.

It had taken tragedy and heartbreak, but now, in the end, she had won through, and there was only joy for her and an abiding serenity.